THE LIVERPOOL UND
Crime in the City, 1750–1900

THE LIVERPOOL UNDERWORLD

Crime in the City, 1750–1900

Michael Macilwee

LIVERPOOL UNIVERSITY PRESS

First published 2011 by
Liverpool University Press
4 Cambridge Street
Liverpool
L69 7ZU

British Library Cataloguing-in-Publication data
A British Library CIP record is available

ISBN 978-1-84631-699-9 cased
ISBN 978-1-84631-700-2 limp

Typeset in Albertina by
Koinonia, Manchester
Printed and bound by
CPI Group (UK) Ltd, Croydon, CRO 4YY

To Jimmy, Sue, Gary and Aimee
and
Steven, Jackie, Stephanie and Alex

Contents

List of Tables

List of Abbreviations

BDP	*Birmingham Daily Post*
DP	*Daily Post*
LC	*Liverpool Courier*
LM	*Liverpool Mercury*
LR	*Liverpool Review*
LVRO	Liverpool Record Office
LWM	*Liverpool Weekly Mercury*
MC	*Morning Chronicle*
NAPSS	National Association for the Promotion of Social Sciences
TNA	The National Archives

Acknowledgements

Thanks to the following: David Carroll and Sue Mullin for proofreading the text; John Archer for offering valuable comments; Bobbie Rhys-Chadwick, Pam Dowsett, Lee Russell and my brother Steven for computer-related queries; Debbie Evans (belatedly); the staff of the Document Supply Office at Liverpool John Moores University, Liverpool University and the Liverpool Record Office for obtaining material. Thanks to Alison Welsby of Liverpool University Press for her help in getting the book published.

I am grateful to the following publishers, journals and institutions for permission to quote passages:

David Taylor, *Crime, Policing and Punishment in England, 1750–1914* and Helen Bosanquet (ed.), *Social Conditions in Provincial Towns*, reproduced with permission of Palgrave Macmillan.

John Saville, *1848: The British State and the Chartist Movement*, reproduced with permission of Cambridge University Press.

Lionel Rose, *Massacre of the Innocents: Infanticide in Britain, 1800–1939*, reproduced with permission of Routledge.

J. Matthew Gallman, *Receiving Erin's Children: Philadelphia, Liverpool, and the Irish Famine, 1845–1855*. Copyright © 2000 by the University of North Carolina Press. Used by permission of the publisher.

History Today Ltd for permission to quote from *History Today*.

R. M. Jones, 'The Liverpool Bread Riots, 1855', *Bulletin of the North West Labour History Society*, reproduced with permission of North West Labour History Society.

Letter from Thomas Reilly to Kelly, 19 June 1848, National Library of Ireland, reproduced with the permission of The Board of The National Library of Ireland.

W. H. N. Harding collection, Quarto Street Ballads, no. 2000, *Allegro* archive, Harkness, in the W. H. N. Harding collection, B 20, p. 198 and *Allegro* archive, Firth collection, c.19, p. 56, reproduced with permission of The Bodleian Library, Oxford.

MDHB/MISC/12, 'Minutes of Evidence Taken by a Sub-Committee of the Dock Committee, as to the Expediency of Uniting the Dock Police with the Town Police', 21 November 1836 and MDHB/MISC/12, Customs Officer to the Dock Committee, 18 July 1814, reproduced with permission of Maritime Archives & Library, National Museums Liverpool.

Adm 1/1618 (Smith Child), 27 October, 16 November 1793, Adm 1/1787 (John Fortescue), 6 September 1761, Adm 1/1788 (John Fortescue), 19 February 1762, Adm 1/1788 (John Fortescue), 18 April 1762, PRO CO904.7.77-92, statement of John Kelly, 6 December 1839, reproduced with permission of The National Archives.

Special thanks to Roger Hull from Liverpool City Libraries for supplying the photographs. Thanks also to Proquest for permission to reproduce the illustration of tattoos (from PP 1841 (339) V, p. 147) and the Trustees of the National Library of Scotland for permission to use the cartoon of the High Ripper. The poaching image is from *Illustrated Sporting and Dramatic News*, 1885.

Preface

For a number of years Liverpool has suffered a bad press.[1] The city was once a byword for political militancy and renowned for its strike-prone workforce. The Toxteth riots of 1981 became a crisis point in relations between young black people and the police. For the first time on the UK mainland CS gas was deployed against rioters. Liverpool's Chief Constable spoke of the 'aggressive nature' and historically 'turbulent character' of the 'true Liverpudlian', 'proportionally tougher, more violent and more pugnacious' than others.[2] The Hillsborough football stadium disaster of 1989 provoked libellous slurs about drunken and rowdy Liverpool FC supporters. The appalling child killings of James Bulger and Rhys Jones focused national media attention on violence within the city. The reputation of thieving Scousers is staple comic fare throughout the country. Suspicions of widespread fraud lie behind the city's current status as 'compensation capital' of Britain, a hotbed for legal claims against the council for damages following trips on the pavement and other mishaps.[3] Liverpool remains a major player in the international drugs trade. Other cities have been home to outrageous crimes and criminals and yet it is Liverpool that retains a special status for criminality and belligerence.

This is nothing new. 'What makes it our wickedest city?' asked the *Daily Herald* in 1950.[4] A few years earlier, a journalist from the *Daily Mirror* visited the city's south end only to find 1,000 juvenile gangsters on the loose.[5] After the transport strike of 1911 the city was denounced as '[a] nightmare of civilisation [...] The most criminal, the most drunken, the most lawless city in the United Kingdom.'[6] In the nineteenth century the situation was not much better. The *Liverpool Mercury* gave a damning verdict on Liverpool: 'in wickedness and misery it is unmatched by any city in the empire'.[7] In the biased view of one Birmingham town councillor, 'Liverpool was a sort of outlet sewer for all the vagabonds in the land'.[8] For *The Times*, Liverpool was particularly vile: 'the offscourings of humanity congregate in its docks, and crowd its foul courts and suffocating alleys'. Although the newspaper admitted that violent crime was not unique to Liverpool, what singled out the town was that such violence seemed to be 'approved by the brutalised population' and was not condemned strongly enough by the respectable inhabitants.[9]

Canon Abraham Hume, the vicar of the deprived parish of Vauxhall in the 1840s, also criticized the local acceptance of criminality. The idea that law-breaking was condoned by Liverpudlians was reflected, he felt, in the very language that people used to describe wrongdoers. A convict returning from transportation was 'a young man that has been abroad, God help him'; a captured burglar was a poor boy that had 'got into trouble'; a prostitute was an 'unfortunate girl'; a 'man-catcher' who had swindled emigrants out of their belongings 'needn't care, he'll never see them again'; women willing to skin a sailor of his money and clothes were 'clever girls, and served him just right'; juvenile criminals who managed to beat the judicial system were 'heroes'; retired boxers were a 'model of manliness'. Finally, an imprisoned thief was being held 'through hard swearing'.[10] Liverpool was a world where vice and virtue seemed to have changed positions, where morality had been turned upside down. In a letter to Lord Stanley, John Clay, the chaplain of Preston Gaol, observed that 'Liverpool has much to answer for in its long-continued indifference to the crime within it. In fact, crime in that town has far outgrown the means of adequately dealing with it.'[11]

Why has Liverpool gained this notoriety for crime and violence? A perceptive article in a local newspaper got straight to the point. 'Savage Liverpool' was the damning headline in 1886, a time when the north end of the city was being terrorized by gangs of knife-wielding ruffians known as the High Rip: 'The highest type of civilisation and the lowest type of savagery are to be found in Liverpool, existing side by side; and in no city in the world can a more startling contrast of the two races of mankind – the civilised and the uncivilised – be found.'[12] The sentiments echoed those of historian W. C. Taylor who, in 1840, claimed that 'no one can visit the streets in the vicinity of the docks without feeling that he has seen something very like savage life in close contact with Civilisation'.[13]

It was not so much the gap between rich and poor as the shocking intimacy between them that lay at the heart of Liverpool's social problems. Hume believed that the close relationship between the town's wealth and its poverty was 'a fruitful source of demoralization to both sexes'.[14] For the poor, the temptations must have been overwhelming. Richard Acland Armstrong wrote of his first impression of Liverpool when he arrived in 1884 to take up a post as minister to the Unitarian congregation in Hope Street. In addition to the brilliant shops and 'refined and elegant ladies' in their fine carriages, 'the hordes of the ragged and the wretched surged up from their native quarters and covered the noblest streets like a flood'. His conclusion: 'I had seen wealth. I had seen poverty. But never before had I seen the two so jammed together. Never before had I seen streets, loaded with all that wealth can buy, lined with the haunts of hopeless penury.'[5] Liverpool was a place of violent contradictions, a town characterized by vast mercantile riches accompanied by appalling poverty.

In the popular imagination, it was from the ranks of the impoverished lower classes that the hardened members of the criminal underworld were recruited. As late as 1892 distinctions were still being drawn between those who had fallen on hard times through no fault of their own and the 'vicious, the incurably lazy, the habitual beggar, the thoroughly degraded'.[6] Such people were believed to have rejected moral codes of sobriety, thrift and hard work to embrace instead a culture of crime, vice, gambling and black market survival. Whether a separate, easily distinguishable body of law-breakers actually existed is debatable. Certainly by the 1860s an immoral, feckless, dishonest and parasitic sub-group of the urban poor had emerged, at least in the disapproving eyes of the press and the ruling authorities. 'Criminal classes' and 'criminal types' became common labels for those inhabitants of the slums who had seemingly abandoned society's values. Members were said to boast their own lingo and culture. Lacking education and proper occupations, they were seemingly addicted to both crime and the pleasures of the beershop. In fact, many of these people were not full-time criminals but simply poor and destitute individuals, forced to supplement low and irregular wages with opportunistic petty pilfering. Even these people were given a label: they were known as 'half-and-half men'.[7]

Any discussion of the criminal underworld leads to problems of definition. When, for example, does an offender become a serious 'criminal'? Some of the poor people who appeared before the Victorian magistrates were certainly repeat offenders, continually arrested and punished while trying to eke out a living on the streets. Yet they were hardly organized and professional criminals, permanently engaged in crime. They begged, stole and prostituted themselves when needs demanded or opportunities arose. Rarely did they make comfortable livings for themselves out of their crimes. Some other offenders, such as receivers of stolen goods, brothel madams and skilled burglars, might have done quite well for themselves; but in the eyes of the press and other commentators all lower-class offenders were lumped together as being part of a 'criminal class', morally and socially separate from the rest of decent society. Wealthy people also committed crimes, of course, largely more lucrative and arguably less prone to attract the attentions of the authorities. Although corrupt bankers and light-fingered clerks were very much a reality in Victorian Britain, it was the poor who made up most of the clientele of the police, courts and prisons.[18] It is upon the activities of these lower-class criminals that this book is focused.

The question of what to do with the 'criminal classes' became the subject of much debate among churchmen, politicians, philanthropists and journalists. At this point, a word must be said about the sources used in the research of the book. Details of the crimes have largely been gleaned from contemporary newspaper and journal reports. Although a great deal of information comes from the reformist and liberal *Liverpool Mercury*, there were other Victorian Liverpool newspapers, including the Orange-supporting *Liverpool Herald*. The *Daily Post* and *Daily Courier* were both quality dailies while the *Evening Express* and *Liverpool Echo* were aimed at a more popular readership. In addition to a range of newspapers there were also many local journals, including the establishment-supporting *Liverpool Review*. *Porcupine* was a prickly satirical journal of current events while *Plain Talk* was a religious periodical offering a Christian viewpoint. Suffice it to say that these publications do not all agree with each other in their reporting of events. One has to be wary of the political bias and party affiliations of certain editors. Some had an obvious axe to grind against the town council or the Watch Committee, for example. Also, London-based newspapers often viewed northerners as less civilized than southerners. As for the members of the public who wrote to the newspapers, it is clear from some of the letters that the authors included ratepayers who were in regular employment, were literate and able to afford a daily paper. Their comments express the values and prejudices of their social standing.

Much was written about criminals but hardly anything by the criminals themselves, many of whom could neither read nor write. From 1846, at the Kirkdale House of Correction, the 'silent system' was rigorously enforced. This meant that the prisoners were not allowed to communicate with each other. The governor, however, on his daily round of the cells, encouraged the convicts to bare their souls. After hours of tedious silence they were only too delighted to speak to somebody. 'I have encouraged several of them to commit to paper some account of themselves, and the more remarkable passages of their past lives, more particularly with reference to the crimes for which they have been sent to prison; and I have now before me quite a pile of really very interesting autobiographies, which I have read with much painful pleasure.'[19]

What became of this library of Victorian 'gangster' autobiographies is not clear but it would have provided social historians and criminologists with a wealth of information. In the absence of this lost bibliographical treasure, the following pages aim to map out the lives and working practices of some of Liverpool's long-forgotten underworld characters. Using prison reports, government papers and contemporary newspaper and journal articles, the book looks at how these men, women and children tried to make a living on the streets of Liverpool between 1750 and 1900. Some begged, stole, gambled, rioted, poached from the surrounding countryside or invented clever scams to fleece gullible victims. Some women sank to prostitution while others took to fortune-telling, money-lending and performing back-street abortions. We will look at how these people fought among themselves, entertained themselves and looked after each other in their impoverished yet tight-knit communities. In search of an answer to the question, 'What makes it our wickedest city?' the book journeys through the streets, courts and back alleys of Liverpool's dockside rookeries via thieves' lodging-houses, beershops, music halls, brothels, pawnshops, magistrates' courts, workhouses and prisons.

Note on Sources

Unless otherwise stated, details of all crimes discussed in this book have been taken from the *Liverpool Mercury*. The newspaper is included in the British Library online newspaper database, which is widely available through libraries and easily searched using names, dates and keywords.

'Ghastly Statistics' – a Word of Warning

In 1850 Thomas Carter, the Anglican chaplain of the Liverpool Borough Gaol, admitted that 'Our town has been acknowledged to be one of the most unhealthy towns in the kingdom. It is certainly notorious for being (so far as the criminal statistics show it) the most immoral.'[1] Yet in the same year the *Liverpool Mercury* warned, 'There is nothing more dangerous, in our estimate of the causes of social evil, than an implicit reliance on statistical information.'[2]

Crime statistics have always been a problematic guide to both the amount and the type of criminal activity.[3] For a start, a great deal of crime goes unreported and hence unrecorded, the so-called 'dark figure'. In a lecture on 'Liverpool Slum Life', delivered in 1894, local JP and temperance campaigner Dr Whitford revealed the uselessness of crime statistics. On the one hand, the Head Constable's report could boast that there had been no significant increase in crime during the year. At the same time the *Liverpool Mercury* was informing its readers 'that the Liverpool slum dwellers are at present more degraded, more drunken, and more lawless than at any time during the past 15 years'. Whitfield helped explain the discrepancy by pointing out several cases of violent robbery that were never reported to the police. In the slums, intimidation and terror were so common that most people were afraid to complain. He concluded that 'most of the crime in the Liverpool slums never appears in any police return'.[4]

Comparisons between different periods are also complicated not only by population growth but by the enactment of new laws and the removal of old ones from the statute book. The result is that definitions of criminal behaviour change over time. Before 1856 crime statistics need to be treated with extra caution as the development of the constabulary after the Municipal Corporations Act of 1835 was irregular, and so the recording of crime is often patchy. Police priorities and policies also change over time. A clampdown on prostitution might be followed by one on drunkenness or street gambling, thereby temporarily inflating those particular figures.

Interpretation of offences will also affect the statistics. For example, a sub-committee of Manchester City Council revealed that in 1866 Liverpool recorded 56 cases of 'highway robbery' against 217 in Manchester. The huge difference had nothing to do with the thieving habits of Manchester's criminals. In Manchester every violent robbery taking place in the street 'or elsewhere' was classified as 'highway robbery'. In Liverpool and other places only those violent robberies taking place in the streets and highways were classified as such in the returns.[5]

A distinction must be made between indictable crimes, which are serious offences tried at the Quarter Sessions or Assizes, and summary offences, the more minor crimes tried daily in the magistrate's court. Some serious crimes which in other places would normally be punished with long terms of imprisonment were, in Liverpool, tried summarily because witnesses and victims were often sailors or travellers about to depart. Indeed, some crimes were probably not even reported because victims could not hang around long enough to prosecute.[6] Nevertheless, the increasing professionalization of policing improved summary justice procedures and helped boost the statistics. Up to the mid-nineteenth century, many people lacked the means and confidence to take out private prosecutions. As the police strengthened their role in the prosecution process, victims felt increasingly more willing to report crimes. It can be argued that the more police there are per head of population, the higher the crime statistics. As well as preventing some crime, a heavy police presence leads to more crimes being detected and prosecuted.[7]

Inter-town comparisons of figures for summary offences are often meaningless because of variations in local statutes and by-laws which create unique offences. According to the judicial statistics, the number of offences determined summarily for the year ending 29 September 1860 reveals that a whopping 37,214 persons in Liverpool were proceeded against. The Manchester figure is 8,508. The massive Liverpool figure includes the following classes (Manchester figure in brackets): offences relating to drunkenness, 10,693 (2,329); offences against local acts and borough by-laws, 14,459 (120); offences punishable as misdemeanours, 1,337 (nil); larceny under the value of 5s, 1,419 (137).[8] There are quite clearly different policies and practices involved here. In 1892 Liverpool's Head Constable replied to criticisms of massively increasing crime over the previous thirty years by pointing out the amount of extra legislation that had been passed creating new summary offences. In 1890 there were 11,279 cases under the Education and Health Acts alone.[9]

In an unflattering article, published in 1877, *The Times* used Liverpool's crime statistics to suggest that one in ten Liverpudlians was a criminal.[10] As the Mayor of Liverpool pointed out, a large proportion of the 45,000 cases referred to involved charges arising out of the Passenger Acts and other by-laws, hardly serious criminal cases.[11] A Liverpool magistrate further replied that Liverpool's statistics were the result of stricter policing and the policy of arresting prostitutes and drunks.[12] In the second half of the nineteenth century arrests for drunkenness generated the largest class of crime in Liverpool. In 1852 the ratio of arrests for drunkenness to the population was 1 in 96 in Liverpool against 1 in 600 in Manchester. Yet it is doubtful whether there was six times more drunkenness in Liverpool than in Manchester.[13] Major Greig, Liverpool's Head Constable, explained that when a man was arrested for drunkenness and taken to the bridewell he was never released before seeing the magistrate.[14] Yet in some other towns drunks were discharged from the cells without appearing before the magistrate, therefore leaving no official record of their drunkenness.

With regard to the policing of prostitution, in 1889 Head Constable Nott-Bower reported:

> It is impossible to compare Liverpool (as has been attempted) with other towns by quoting statistics. To state, on such evidence, that Liverpool has 443 brothels, whilst Manchester has only 5, and Glasgow has only 14, is simply fantastic. Such figures only profess to show the number of houses 'known to the police,' and all they can prove is the very superior 'knowledge' of the Police of Liverpool to that of the other towns quoted.[15]

After dissecting the Head Constable's annual report (and glossing over an actual reduction in recorded crime) *The Times* asked, 'what more can be done to stem this terrible tide of vice and crime?' The *Liverpool Mercury* responded with the question, 'What can be done to prevent leading journals being misled by "ghastly statistics?"'[16] With this thought in mind the figures included in this book should be read as only a rough index to some complex social problems and related criminal activities.

ONE

The Black Spot on the Mersey

A stone's throw from Liverpool's magnificent civic architecture and bustling promenades lay the filthy, cramped courts and grimy cellars, a 'nether world' teeming with desperate individuals fighting for economic survival. Social investigator and sanitary reformer Edwin Chadwick was appalled at the distribution of wealth in a town that could spend tens of thousands of pounds on civic monuments such as St George's Hall, while the streets were full of sewage, open latrines and overflowing cesspools.[1] Liverpool was the capital of squalor. In few places in the country was the population more overcrowded, poverty more pressing, housing more wretched, drunkenness so widespread and prostitution so shameless.[2]

To appreciate the brutality, boisterousness and vulgarity of Liverpool's early inhabitants, it is important to understand how the town once made its money. In the eighteenth century Liverpool's maritime industry was split between Greenland whaling ventures, slavery and privateering. None of these enterprises was for the faint-hearted. Any town teeming with 'fierce privateersmen, inhuman slavers, reckless merchantmen, and violent men-of-war's men' was bound to produce a tough, ruthless and bloodthirsty populace. Even children were brought up in a culture of grasping violence. This was the view of James Stonehouse who was born around 1770 and published a history of the town at the ripe age of 93. Recalling his childhood, he explained: 'it was a cruel time, and the effects of the slave-trade and privateering were visible in the conduct of the lower classes and of society generally'.[3] The barbarity is best reflected in the amusements of the time: prize-fighting, bull-baiting, cock-fighting and dog-fighting. Sir James Picton, Liverpool historian and architect, also regretted the damage to the Liverpool psyche caused by privateering: 'The practice of privateering could not but blunt the feelings of humanity of those engaged in it, combining as it did the greed of the gambler with the ferocity of the pirate.'[4]

Until the abolition of the slave trade in 1807, Liverpool had a vital and shameful role to play in human trafficking. In 1800 five-sixths of Britain's slave trade was based in the town. Since Liverpool derived its prosperity from such barbarous trades, it attracted a motley collection of visitors of the lowest character. Infamous captain Hugh Crow spoke unfavourably of slave-ship crews as

> the very dregs of the community. Some of them had escaped from jails: others were undiscovered offenders, who sought to withdraw themselves from their country, lest they should fall into the hands of the officers of justice. These wretched beings used to flock to Liverpool when the ships were fitting out, and, after acquiring a few sea phrases from some crimp or other, they were shipped as ordinary seamen, though they had never been at sea in their lives.[5]

The privateersmen were not much better. A contemporary witness described a typical crew: 'what a reckless, dreadnought, dare-devil collection of human beings, half-disciplined, but yet ready to obey every order, the more desperate the better. Your true privateersman was a sort of half-horse, half-alligator, with a streak of lightning in his composition.'[6]

Liverpudlians had a zeal for privateering. During the almost endless series of naval battles that characterized the eighteenth century, Liverpool privateer ships led the way in seizing enemy vessels. What distinguished a privateer ship from a pirate ship was a Letter of Marque. This was a licence, issued at the local post office, allowing merchant vessels to profit from the sale of the seized cargo and even the ship itself as prize money. In this way great riches flowed back into the town, seeping eventually into the dockside taverns and back-alley brothels. Stonehouse claimed that 'there was scarcely a man, woman, or child in Liverpool, of any standing, that did not hold a share in one of these ships'.[7] During the Seven Years' War (1756–63), which involved hostilities between England and France, Liverpool sailors gained a reputation for being the boldest privateers in England.[8] The economic downturn during the American War of Independence (1775–83) also encouraged many merchants to switch their boats and financial investments to the more rewarding profession of privateering. From August 1778 to April 1779 120 privateeer ships were fitted out in Liverpool.[9] In 1778 renewed animosity between the British and French was intensified following the Franco-American 'Treaty of Amity'. While the treaty signalled a new era of Franco-American trade, Liverpool merchants and sailors were quick to spot their own commercial opportunities. Fortunes were to be made through privateering and it wasn't long before valuable cargoes of tobacco, sugar, coffee and cotton were making their way back to Liverpool. In October 1778 the Liverpool ship *Mentor* captured the

French East Indiaman *Carnatic*, with a box of diamonds on board that would now be worth about £12m.

Liverpool wallowed as much in its wealth as in its filth. Its geographical location gave it an ideal trading position with the Atlantic economies that provided the raw materials needed to help kick-start the Industrial Revolution. In the late eighteenth century canals connected Liverpool with nearly all the major industrial areas of England, greatly expanding the market for produce. The promise of great riches seduced people from Ireland, Wales and Scotland as well as the surrounding rural areas. The Napoleonic Wars were over by 1815. Over the next twenty years eight new docks were built, along with new roads and warehouses. Such extensive building works made Liverpool a magnet for workmen. Between 1801 and 1831 the population more than doubled, while from 1831 to 1841 there was a further increase of 80,000.[10]

The town also attracted vagrants. The Vagrancy Act of 1824 specified that merely being of no fixed abode was a criminal offence, punishable by a short prison sentence. Nevertheless, professional trampers continued to pass through Liverpool, sometimes accompanied by young orphans. With no regular income, they survived by petty theft and begging. Henry Simpson, the relieving officer at Liverpool, stated that 'many young persons belonging to Liverpool are treated by us as tramps; they come around at intervals of two to three months, some of them go away all the summer and come back here to winter. I think they are encouraged by the system of relieving tramps, to make tramping their profession.'[11]

As the economy expanded, many poor people were left behind. Over the years these people were given many labels, including 'the lower orders', 'the bruitish masses', 'the great unwashed', 'the residuum' and 'the submerged tenth'. The increasing number of paupers became an urgent social problem. In the days before the welfare state, those without employment had a number of choices. They could divest themselves of their possessions through the pawnshop or steal from the street barrows. They could beg, seek private charity, request help from friends or apply to the parish for relief. Before 1834 relief for the destitute was provided by means of the Poor Law, which was regulated by place of birth. The parish in which a person was born was responsible for his or her upkeep. The system was funded by property owners in the parish, who were understandably unhappy at any increases in the poor rate. When people fell on hard times, help was offered either as outdoor relief in their own homes or indoor relief in the workhouse. Liverpool's destitute were sent to the Old Poor House, originally situated in Pool Lane, South Castle Street. The building proved too small for the growing population and in 1732 a new workhouse was built in College Lane, next to the Blue Coat Hospital. However, even this was unable to cope with the increasing number of paupers. In 1770 the corporation was forced to build a new workhouse at Brownlow Hill, on the site that now boasts the Metropolitan Cathedral. Throughout the country, outdoor relief became increasingly difficult to administer, particularly as more and more people began flocking to the new industrial towns in search of work. Improvements in transportation also meant that people no longer stayed in the same place for their entire lives. With the loss of close personal contact between the administrators of relief and the poor, the system became difficult to monitor and supervise.

A major development was the New Poor Law of 1834. This introduced indoor relief in the workhouse as the sole means of support. No longer could the poor apply for charity in their own homes. Those who couldn't (or wouldn't) support themselves were put in the workhouse. The resulting increase in the number of inmates meant that the institution at Brownlow Hill had to be rebuilt in 1842. Originally designed to house 1,800, by the 1860s there were over 3,500 inmates. The number eventually grew to 5,000, making it the biggest workhouse in Britain, 'a small town within a great city'.[12] Workhouses acted as schools, hospitals, asylums and old people's homes. Huge wards housed alcoholics, the senile and the incurably sick. There were lying-in wards and separate rooms for the insane. The workhouse system was designed to prevent the abuses that the previous system of outdoor relief sometimes encouraged, whereby paupers obtained relief simultaneously from different sources. To persuade people to find work outside, life in the institution had to be less attractive than that of the lowest-paid worker. To qualify for help, the poor had to give up all independence. Inmates were segregated by sex and families were split up. The conditions were spartan, with compulsory chapel, silent periods and spells of grinding toil. The diet was minimal, with just enough food to sustain life.

Liverpool was not alone in having to find solutions to the social problems created by the swift transition from rural to urban living. By 1851 just over half the population of England was urbanized. To meet the needs of the increasing number of town dwellers, nineteenth-century reformers not only built workhouses to look after the most desperate (or at least motivate them to look after themselves elsewhere), but they also laid the foundations of the public health system and devised mass education. They also developed the modern police force to keep order on the streets. Yet despite these efforts, the situation in Liverpool took a turn for the worse. Britain's second city, inferior only to London in size and commerce, was to experience a social upheaval that would overwhelm parts of the town. If Liverpool's prosperity was founded on its fortunate geographical position, its location also played a great part in its social ruin.

For as well as being an exit port for America, Liverpool was also an entry port from Ireland. Between 1845 and 1849 the repeated failures of the Irish potato crop created an explosion of Irish migration. Although many went on to begin new lives in America, thousands remained in Liverpool. The growth of the Irish community was rapid, leading to social tensions and outbreaks of sectarian violence between Catholics and supporters of the Orange Lodge. The 1841 Census shows almost 50,000 Irish-born people in Liverpool. Ten years later the numbers had increased to 80,000. Add to this figure the thousands of Liverpool-born children of Irish parentage and Liverpool simply could not cope. Mr Rushton, the stipendiary magistrate, feared that the sheer numbers of Irish poor would signal an end to the Vagrancy Act. He remarked that if he was to send to gaol all the beggars in Liverpool, the building would have to be big enough to hold 10,000 inmates.[13] The old institutions for health, housing, social welfare and law buckled under the pressure, resulting in slum housing, overcrowding, high mortality rates and epidemics of smallpox, cholera and typhus.

Dr Duncan, Liverpool's Public Health Officer, claimed that Liverpool was 'the most unhealthy town in England'.[14] *The Times* went further: 'Liverpool is notoriously the most unhealthy, the worst drained, and most miasmatic city of the empire.'[15] According to Sir Arnold Knight MD, feeble Liverpudlians 'were unfit to be shot at', since about 75 per cent of recruits for the army in the 1840s were rejected for service.[16] In the 1840s, owing to the high infant mortality rate, the average life expectancy was a mere seventeen years, less than anywhere else in the United Kingdom.[17] The Irish poor, who lived in the most insanitary dwellings in the most overcrowded areas, were hit hardest by each epidemic. Typhus, which was originally called 'gaol fever', became known as 'Irish fever' or 'famine fever'. Dr Duncan's annual report for 1847 shows that seven-eighths of Liverpool's typhus victims in that year were Irish.[18] The Registrar General described the town as 'the hospital and cemetery of Ireland'.[19]

The ever-present threat of disease and death led to a culture of binge and bust, not helped by a system of casual labour that kept workers in a state of nagging insecurity, rich one day and broke the next. With only a small manufacturing base, the Liverpool economy was largely built on trade and commerce. Jobs included shipping and related industries such as shipbuilding and the transportation of goods between ship, warehouse and railway. Such work came in urgent rushes and needed to be completed at high speed to save interest on costly ship, dock and warehouse space. Casual labour, by which men were intermittently hired for short spells, was a major condition of such employment. Construction industry workers, including bricklayers, painters and plasterers, were also subject to seasonal demands of work.

Working at sea or sporadically at the docks, Liverpool men were never subject to the time-work discipline of the industrial factories and therefore never developed a sense of subservience to figures of authority such as overseers, foremen or bosses. Liverpudlians' time was their own. The only clock that mattered was the one that signalled the opening and closing times of the public houses. Liverpool's maritime community was not ruled not by any human authority but by the vagaries of nature, particularly gales and fog. In a sense, everybody was their own boss, even though most remained at the bottom of the social pile. A fierce sense of individualism, pride and self-assertion had to exist uncomfortably alongside the poverty, squalor and uncertainties of life lived beside a fickle sea and unpredictable winds. The public houses must have represented a timeless certainty of life in the slums.

Of course, casual labour was not unique to Liverpool. It was the absence of other forms of labour such as factory work that made the town unique. People lived for the day because there was little hope of advancement or promotion. Knowing where the next meal or glass of beer was coming from was the extent of most Liverpudlians' horizons. In a world where immediate physical enjoyment was more important than planning for the future, the poor became addicted to instantaneous pleasures such as alcohol, by which they could quickly escape the pressures of poverty or numb the pain of back-breaking toil. Alcohol became the city's curse. 'Drink in Liverpool is one of the results of casual labour', claimed Thomas Burke, Nationalist councillor for the Vauxhall ward.[20] The casual labour system meant that some men were paid in particular public houses at the end of the week. Indeed, the failure to frequent a particular beershop reduced the chances of further employment. The large pool of surplus unskilled workers became a major social problem. The culture of unemployed men hanging about outside street-corner public houses led to a phenomenon known as Cornermen, raising public fears about the idle and unruly lower classes.

The employment situation for women was even worse. Not only were there few careers open for women but the available jobs were exploitative and unrewarding. Besides domestic service and bar work, women were forced onto the streets to sell their wares. Liverpool's street sellers or basket-girls offered a wide variety of produce, including flowers, fish, pigs' feet, watercress, cockles and firewood, but had to fight for their position on the streets. Using the powers of the by-laws, constables constantly harassed street traders for obstruction. If they loitered to rest themselves, or to try to sell their stock, the police would move them on. If they gave 'cheek' they were arrested. If convicted and unable to pay the fine they were sent to prison, swelling further the record numbers of female prisoners in Liverpool gaols. From their constant confrontations with authority, hawkers became hardened and extremely verbal.

Women also worked in the 'sweated' trades as shirtmakers, dressmakers and tailoresses.[21] For those toiling under this system, conditions and wages were poor and job security non-existent. Large stores and clothing outlets cut costs by delegating the work to 'sweaters', or middlemen, who in turn employed piece or 'slop' workers on a casual basis, forcing them to complete each order as quickly and cheaply as possible before laying them off. Cotton picking was another job for women. Bales of cotton from the ships were picked clean and then dried over hot kilns in dockside warehouses. It was thirsty work and the women were known for their drinking and rough habits. Like the street traders, cotton pickers were largely Irish and described as 'brawny' characters who didn't mince their words.[22] There was said to be more drunkenness among the cotton pickers than in almost any other trade in Liverpool. Father James Nugent, Roman Catholic chaplain of Walton Gaol and social reformer, described cotton pickers, who kept late hours and frequented the most disreputable public houses in Marybone, as 'very little removed from the girls of the streets'.[23] Yet for all their roughness, they were said to be decent women forced to live in squalid surroundings.[24] In the male-dominated world of the port, cotton pickers and street hawkers had to sacrifice their femininity to compete with the men for the right to earn their own livelihood.[25]

Another of Liverpool's problems was the large number of children on the streets. An 1867 census of Liverpool's streets revealed 48,782 youngsters, aged between 5 and 13, without schooling, 25,000 of them living on the streets with no natural protectors.[26] Without a comfortable home life, with no work and no schools to attend, young people spent their waking hours on the streets and were consequently blamed for widespread petty crime. *Porcupine* spoke of 'the army of "street arabs" who infest the thoroughfares, fill our gaols, increase our taxes, spread disease, and drive policemen and philanthropists to despair'.[27]

In the first half of the nineteenth century the city's status as a hotbed of squalor, crime and violence led to its being labelled 'the black spot on the Mersey', later amended to the 'bloody spot'.[28] Of course there were other rough towns with appalling reputations for poverty, crime and vice. Rapidly growing new industrial towns such as Middlesbrough, with its abundance of young male workers and seamen, also suffered from atrocious slums, disease and disorder, yet failed to match the scale of Liverpool's dockland problems.[29] Another industrial boom town, Merthyr Tydfil in Wales, housed problem districts equal in immorality and degradation to parts of Liverpool but again the scale was much smaller. One notorious district of Merthyr, inexplicably known as 'China', had its prostitutes, gang warfare, Irish faction fights and chronic drunkenness, but the town's population was a fraction of Liverpool's. In 1851 it held only 43,378 residents to Liverpool's 375,955.[30] London, the centre of the global economy and heart of the world's shipping, was a magnet for thieves, but it lacked Liverpool's intense sectarian divide since its numerically larger population of Irish migrants was dispersed over a greater area.

Manchester had its social problems and its fair share of Irish, yet it also had regular industry so that its inhabitants were not solely at the mercy of casual labour. Women and children could at least earn wages, although conditions in the factories were horrific. Liverpool's women and children, on the other hand, were often reduced to prostitution and theft. Although Manchester boasted England's first County Grand Lodge, together with anti-Catholic riots as early as 1807, the town's sectarian rivalries were never as bitter or ferocious as Liverpool's.[31] What Liverpool had that Manchester lacked was a bustling port filled with sailors with money in their pockets and an insatiable desire for entertainment. Prostitution was inevitable, along with an epidemic of dockside petty pilfering by hordes of streetwise juveniles. Liverpool's criminal landscape was distinctive. According to Alfred Aspland, a member of the New York Prison Association who examined the state of crime in Manchester in 1868, Liverpool had more than double the prostitutes and more than twice the number of brothels. Unlike Liverpool, Manchester had a more settled

Table 1: Proportion of crimes per 100,000 of the population, 1899

	Crimes known to the police	Crimes against the person	Crimes against property	Prosecutions for drunkenness
Liverpool	552.50	21.76	512.29	641.58
Birmingham	391.68	12.04	366.83	723.95
London	276.94	13.72	251.96	846.86
Leeds	224.82	11.09	204.77	402.94
England & Wales	239.34	11.55	220.12	674.64

Source: adapted from PP 1901 LXXXIX, *Judicial Statistics, England and Wales, 1899. Part I*, p. 70.

population 'and its police have not to contend with an ever-shifting, lawless class of ruffians congregated from all quarters of the globe'. Liverpool also had miles of dockyards to guard and needed an additional 300 policemen.[32]

In 1849 John Clay highlighted Liverpool's unique reputation for crime within Lancashire. Although Manchester, Salford, Bolton and Preston had a combined population one-fifth larger than Liverpool's, Liverpool's summary convictions for theft were 17 times greater than those of these four towns. In answer to those who blamed the manufacturing towns for producing crime, he pointed out, 'It is the *great seaport* of the southern division [i.e. Liverpool] which throws its dark aspect over the moral reputation of the entire county.'[33] As late as 1891 Liverpool constituted only 13.26 per cent of the population of Lancashire yet provided 31.15 per cent of the committals and 31.87 per cent of the summary prosecutions.[34]

For the *Birmingham Daily Post*, a glance at the comparative crime statistics of five major towns (Liverpool, Manchester, Birmingham, Leeds and Sheffield) showed that

the evil reputation possessed by Liverpool as a criminal centre is abundantly justified [...] in almost every description of crime Liverpool holds a like pre-eminence, and the total number of indictable offences committed in that city during the year [1889] was almost five times as great as that for Birmingham.[35]

With regard to charges of drunkenness, the Liverpool figure was six times higher than that for Birmingham. In fact Liverpool had a reputation for

Table 2: Average number of indictable offences per 1,000 of the Liverpool population

Year	Offences
1839	25.90
1849	19.90
1859	13.82
Five years ending 1869	14.40
Five years ending 1879	10.74
Five years ending 1889	11.61
Five years ending 1899	6.02

Source: adapted from PP 1901 LXXXIX, *Judicial Statistics, England and Wales, 1899. Part I*, p. 74.

having a higher level of drunkenness than any other town in England. It certainly appeared to be the worst seaport. It was pointed out that 'putting all the "commercial ports" together, Liverpool had two-fifths of the population and nearly four-fifths of the drunken cases'.[36] Liberal MP Samuel Smith, referring to Liverpool in the 1870s, declared that 'no city in the kingdom suffered so much from drunkenness and squalid vice'.[37] French visitor Hippolyte Taine agreed: 'I know no place where drunkenness is so flaunted, so impudent, not only in the crooked side streets and mean courtyards where one expects to find it, but everywhere.'[38]

Although at the end of the century Liverpool had lost its shameful crown for drunkenness, it retained league superiority in other areas (see Table 1). It is only fair to add that recorded cases of indictable crime in Liverpool had gradually decreased over the course of the century, as Table 2 shows. Indictable crime decreased in proportion to the population by at least four-fifths between 1840 and 1900.[39] By 1899 the marked reduction in lawlessness and disorder enabled the Head Constable to reduce the number of police by 100, saving £6,000.[40] Nevertheless, Liverpool's crime statistics were still high compared to those of other places and its reputation remained. At the end of the century, Revd Charles Garrett claimed that the 'black spot on the Mersey' had become the 'dark spot', a slight improvement.[41]

It is the combination of several factors that makes Liverpool unique, factors that will become recurrent themes in this book: the swift population growth that threatened to overwhelm the existing social institutions; the transitory habits of a large section of the population; the heavy presence of the migrant Irish, closely bound up with sectarian and factional animosities; the emphasis on casual labour with its economic and psychological uncertainties; the craving for alcohol; the unruliness of the dockland landscape with its enormous and (to some) irresistible opportunities for theft and vice; the high level of female offending; and the very density of poverty and squalor in the slum districts, generating endless friction and outbursts of hostility among neighbours.

It is not surprising that after London, Liverpool became the first major town to organize a modern, efficient and professional police force.

TWO

Policing

Rough Justice

On 5 February 1777 a woman called Mary Clarke was set upon, beaten and thrown into the Mersey. The community was so shocked at this heartless act that Mayor Crosbie set up an appeal for money to help the victim, who could no longer earn a living.[1] Since it was clear that the existing system of policing was not working, a new police committee was formed to sit daily. A curfew was also imposed, with all respectable people being advised that if they wished to avoid arrest they should not leave the house at night. These were worrying times. In 1779 detachments of the Yorkshire Militia were stationed at the town's garrison to keep order on the streets.[2]

Despite such local scares, it was not until the nineteenth century that crime became the national issue it is today. In the eighteenth century there was little sense of media or government concern about the causes of delinquency, no link between social conditions and criminal behaviour. Robbery and violence affected individuals but there was no great public debate about crime. Even into the early nineteenth century, law-breaking was simply put down to a moral weakness in people. When a woman, just released from the Borough Gaol, immediately committed another crime, the *Liverpool Mercury* enquired whether she was without employment. If so, it was suggested that she might have been driven to commit the offence through 'absolute want, as well as depravity'.[3] Even sociological explanations such as hunger could not erase a moralistic understanding of crime as a sinful lapse into temptation or wicked-ness. In this view criminals were responsible for their own actions and were to be punished accordingly.

In the eighteenth century the solution to crime was not social change but moral reformation, aided by the heavy hand of the military and harsher punishments for even the most trivial offences. Nor were women spared brutal chastisement. In 1776 Ellen Berry and Ann Melling were flogged, one for stealing some hand towels and the other a guinea.[4] The ultimate sanction was hanging. In the absence of proper policing, the only recourse that Parliament had was to increase the number of capital statutes in the hope that criminals would be deterred. This set of brutal laws, known as the 'Bloody Code', was reduced from the early nineteenth century onwards. Nevertheless, between 1814 and 1834 68 people in England were hanged for sheep-stealing. Burglary with violence was also a hanging offence. From the 1840s execution was reserved for murderers only, although it was not until the Offences Against the Person Act of 1861 that the death penalty was finally abolished for all crimes except high treason and murder.

Even during the years of the Bloody Code, judges often used their discretion and the justice system was more merciful than it seemed. Although most crimes of theft were capital offences, more than 90 per cent of death sentences were replaced by transportation for life. In 1834 the *Liverpool Mercury* pointed out that in the previous year, of the 118 people in England and Wales sentenced to death for burglary, only one was hanged. Similarly, of the 228 prisoners condemned to death for robbery only four had been executed. This ratio of 1 in 55 was said to have created a 'lottery of justice'. It was felt that 'the uncertainty of punishment encourages future offenders', leaving criminals underrating the actual penalty of their crimes.[5] Indeed, the harshness of the capital sentence deterred people from bringing prosecutions and discouraged juries from arriving at guilty verdicts.

Throughout the eighteenth century England remained a largely rural and agricultural society in which the vast majority of people scraped a subsistence living off the land. By the nineteenth century thousands were flocking to the new industrial towns in search of work, resulting in overcrowding in insanitary dwellings, disease and cyclical unemployment for those left surplus to requirements. Industrialization and accompanying urbanization led to massive social upheaval and threatened a breakdown in morality and social order. There was increased anxiety about the insurrectionary urban poor, what became known as the 'dangerous classes', demonized in the figure of the mob.

The extremes of wealth and poverty in the early nineteenth century were thought to have contributed to increased criminality, particularly among the poor and destitute. Put crudely, as some people's fortunes increased there was more for others to steal. Theft became more enticing as commercial expansion and financial growth generated masses of mobile wealth, particularly in terms of personal valuables, transportable goods and the transfer of money around the country. Larger populations also meant a greater pool of potential victims. Bigger towns meant that there were more opportunities to plan and commit crime. Thieves could operate under the cloak of anonymity, in a way that was difficult in small village communities where strangers were easily identified.

In rural England, farm workers were servants of their masters, the landowners, with whom they had a personal relationship. Liverpool MP and municipal reformer William Rathbone (1787–1868) was able to recall a society in which his father had been on intimate terms with each of his workers, who lived nearby in his cottages. Rathbone felt that the growth of wealth and population had created a 'wall of moral separation' between rich and poor.[6] In many large towns the impersonal factory system helped sweep away customary rights, duties and deference to paternal figures such as Rathbone.

By the 1850s the urban rich and poor had become increasingly segregated into distinct communities. In Liverpool, upwardly mobile merchants had all but abandoned the town centre for leafy suburbs such as Mossley Hill and Allerton, leaving the dockside slums to the poor. It could be argued that this social upheaval, which was not unique to Liverpool, left the working classes bereft of moral influence and therefore needing authority figures such as the police to step in to fill the void. For the Irish community in particular, the parish priest already filled a similar role, acting as policeman, doctor, relieving officer, Nuisances and School Board Inspector as well as spiritual father.[7] As a magistrate said of the imposing figure of Father Roche, of the Holy Cross Catholic Chapel, he was worth 'twenty constables in the district'.[8]

'Charlies'

In the eighteenth and early nineteenth centuries there was still no proper policing during the day; at night Liverpool's streets were looked after by a band of watchmen called 'Charlies'. In 1787 the town was subdivided into four districts controlled by a head constable and two assistant constables for each area. Nevertheless, policing still relied heavily on public cooperation: 'the inhabitants were earnestly called upon by the magistrates, to give information of whatever came to their knowledge respecting swindlers, receivers of stolen goods, persons not having a visible means of getting an honest livelihood, irregular publicans and nuisances'.[9]

Liverpool was a tough town to police. Drawing on the recollections of his father, who lived through the late eighteenth century, Richard Brooke noted that the 'amusements and habits of the lower classes in Liverpool were rude and coarse. Drunkenness was a common vice, and was indulged in without concealment.' Fuelled by an abundance of cheap smuggled rum, the dockside district provided countless scenes of depravity: 'abandoned women paraded themselves in considerable numbers, indulging in disgusting language, noises, and riotous conduct, without any effectual interference from the police'. In any case, the watchmen were no match for drunken gangs. A group of upper-class men, returning from a ball, were caught up in an affray with some watchmen opposite a brothel in Rainford Gardens, off Stanley Street. A watchman was killed and the men appeared at Lancaster Assizes on a charge of manslaughter. Partly because they appeared penitent, but more likely because they were wealthy and able to give the man's widow some money, they got off with a lenient sentence.[10]

As well as an awareness of the importance of social class, there needs to be recognition of the existence of different cultural attitudes towards 'violence' in the eighteenth century. The beating of servants and children, even wives, was deemed socially acceptable. Generally speaking, the authorities were not overly concerned with punishing acts of interpersonal violence. Until the mid-eighteenth century cases of assault were largely settled privately.[11] It was only in the late eighteenth century that the increasing intolerance of brutality began to be reflected in a greater conviction rate and a desire to imprison rather than merely fine offenders.[12] Yet even at the beginning of the nineteenth century many lower-class victims of assaults had little recourse to reparation through the courts and therefore developed their own form of instant justice involving tit-for-tat violence. Retribution on the streets was swift and brutal. In July 1802 a gang of drunken sailors laid siege to a brothel in Bridge Street, near the docks. One of the residents shot two of the intruders, killing one of them. The angry crowd then dragged the culprit out of the house and beat him to death.

Police reorganization in 1811 saw the borough divided into seven districts, each with a head constable and two assistant constables. With 21 policemen responsible for controlling a population of 100,000, the streets were still far from safe.[13] It was not until 1829, with the passing of the Metropolitan Police Act, that the foundations were laid for Robert Peel's 'New Police' in London. Liverpool was soon to benefit from the reforms. Lieutenant Parlour was recruited from the Metropolitan Police in 1830 to act as Superintendent of Liverpool's Night Watch. By applying metropolitan practices he began to reorganize the chaotic elements of the town's policing.[14]

It was a tall order. Until 1836 Liverpool was policed by three independent constabulary forces. A Corporation Constabulary, under the control of the town council, patrolled the daytime streets and Pier Head but stayed outside the docks. The officers' role was simply to catch criminals rather than to prevent crime taking place. The inadequacy of Liverpool's policing was a regular theme of letters sent to newspapers. In one incident, in 1827, a man taking an evening stroll through New Haymarket was attacked by a gang who battered him about the head with a blunt instrument. The victim pointed out that there had been two further robberies in the area, one man having his watch and money ripped from him. 'Where were the watchmen and constables?' he asked.[15]

Crooked and idle constables were not averse to bribes and would often ignore street disturbances.[16] Officers patrolled only as far as the parish boundaries. The policing of outlying districts such as Everton and Kirkdale was lax, with gangs of ruffians and thieves thriving largely unchecked. While the more wealthy residents of the southern part of Toxteth Park paid a few guineas each year for their own security patrols, the crowded streets of the poorer north end of the district were left lawless. The area was described as 'the Alsatia of Liverpool, whither all the bad characters driven out of the town flocked to settle down'.[17] It seems that the interference of the Liverpool constables and watchmen forced many villains to flee into the Toxteth and Harrington districts where there were only four paid constables for a population of 25,000. The outlying districts were particularly vulnerable. Owing to the large number of robberies and assaults in Edge Hill and Wavertree throughout 1821 it was felt that a Night Watch was required in the winter months.[18]

At night the day constables were relieved by a Night or Town Watch, working under the authority of the Commissioners of Watch, Scavengers and Lamps. In 1817 the Liverpool watchmen were issued with instructions: 'You are to apprehend all night-walkers, rogues, vagabonds, and other disorderly persons, disturbing the public.'[19] By 1830 the Night Watch consisted of eight captains and 120 men. Their uniform consisted of a cape, leggings packed with hay to keep out the cold and a hat, likewise filled with straw for added protection from blows to the head. Armed with a lamp and rattle, they would cry out the hours of the night. The watchman's tools, however, merely warned criminals of his approach and indeed attracted rowdies who would steal the implements. Some watchmen also carried a thick stick, which was not so much a weapon as an aid to walking.[20] It was jokingly claimed that the watchmen were kept in employment mainly to prevent them from claiming benefits off the Parish.

In addition to drinking and fighting among themselves, some watchmen would doze off in their sentry boxes. If their critics are to be believed, popular pranks included overturning the boxes or else nailing the door shut with the watchman inside. 'Pummelling a Charlie' apparently became something of a sport in Liverpool. Another jape was to get a watchman drunk before tying him to a lamp post.[21] Edward Jones was discharged for keeping chickens in his sentry box and killing them with his truncheon.[22] Captain Morrow was described as a typical watchman, sometimes drinking for two or three days before reporting himself as ill.[23] A watchman was removed to another area because he was able get a drink from every public house on his original beat. Another was fined one shilling after kissing his thumb instead of the Bible when taking the oath in court.[24] A captain of the Watch was also fined for stealing flowers from a gentleman's garden while on duty.[25] One drunken watchman accidentally ended up in Ireland after boarding a steamboat while looking for a drink.[26] It was quipped that five of the watchmen were fined so often that they died of starvation.[27] In the last year of the Night Watch, 61 men were dismissed for being drunk, and one man for having 'improper connection with a female prisoner'.[28]

Although the early watchmen were often caricatured as feeble, unprofessional and incompetent, one contemporary observer admitted that they were later replaced by men 'who looked as if they would stand no nonsense, and could do a little fighting at a pinch'.[29] Indeed, many watchmen were courageous individuals who, as will be seen, were not afraid of confronting armed and aggressive groups, even when hopelessly outnumbered. Furthermore, the new police were equally guilty of lapses. An entry in the Watch Committee minutes for 1843 starkly reveals the fate of one constable: 'Found drunk in privy with prostitute. Dismissed!'

The dockland area had its own police, controlled by the Dock Committee. Formed in 1815, this autonomous force was considered the most capable and professional of the three bodies, most likely because it was responsible for the security of valuable goods rather than the safety of the public.[30] Nevertheless, there was a lack of communication and coordination between the three arms of the law. Poor supervision and training was only exacerbated by the mistrust and rivalry between the men. Officers from the different forces occasionally came to blows. The dock police would sometimes lock up constables, leaving parts of the town short of officers. It was therefore vital that these disparate organizations became unified and properly managed.

The New Police

The success of the New Police in London was recognized by Parliament and in September 1835 the Municipal Corporations Act was passed. Provincial towns began to set up watch committees to establish and organize their own police forces, paving the way for the creation of professional policing in Liverpool. In February 1836 the day police and the night watchmen were amalgamated to form the basis of the new Liverpool Police Force. In the summer of the following year the dock police also merged. The new force consisted of 290 constables, 24 inspectors and four superintendents, plus 40 fire-policeman and various bridewell keepers and indoor personnel.[31] A detective department was formed in 1844, followed by a detachment of river police in 1865.

Michael J. Whitty, the former Superintendent of the Town Watch, became Liverpool's first Head Constable. Influenced by the metropolitan model, Whitty split the borough into northern and southern districts by drawing a line from Water Street, through Dale Street and Shaw's Brow across to Low Hill. A superintendent headed each area, which was further divided into eight smaller districts, each controlled by an inspector. The districts were then carved up into manageable beats patrolled by constables. The police-man's role was tough. For poor wages, the officers worked a seven-day week, averaging twelve hours a day, not including extra duties as town firemen; they also had to live where they were told. The transition from old to new police was not altogether abrupt. Of the 360 policemen who made up the new force, about a third were members of one or other of the previous forces. Many Liverpool constables stayed loyal to the force. In 1868 the Liverpool constab-ulary boasted many veterans dating back thirty years. Half the entire force had more than five years' service. They therefore had an advantage over the Manchester force, which was composed of many rookies.[32]

As required by the Act, a Watch Committee, consisting of elected members of the council, was formed to oversee police affairs. A sub-committee was also assembled to look into the state of crime and policing in the town. Its report, published in March 1836, gave an alarming diagnosis of Liverpool's moral health, although the figures must be treated with caution. It was calculated that the annual amount of money generated by crime was about £700,000. The report estimated that there were 300 brothels containing a total of 1,200 prostitutes, plus another 3,000 prostitutes living in private lodgings. There were said to be 1,000 adult thieves in addition to 1,200 juvenile robbers operating on the streets.[33] When the damning report was presented to the town council, there was debate as to whether it should be published. Some felt that it would leave a 'stigma on Liverpool' while others thought it was a brave attempt to confront evil.[34]

Details of the report were quoted by the *Royal Commission on Establishing an Efficient Constabulary Force in Counties of England and Wales*, published in 1839.[35] Again, a word of caution must be attached to the evidence presented in this later document. William Augustus Miles, who travelled the country researching parts of the report, has been described as a 'moral entrepreneur', a man who made a career exploiting fears about crime and disorder. Working for (or hoping to work for) various government committees and commissions of inquiry in the 1830s and 1840s, these entrepreneurs were intent on finding the worst examples of vice and delinquency in order to offer their remedies for the country's social ills. Miles fleshed out the earlier Watch Committee report with some alarming details. There were 1,000 'fancy men' who lived upon the thefts and prostitution of women. There were gangs of 'magsmen' who operated near the docks duping innocent travellers with various scams. Around 1,700 people were said to live upon the theft of merchandise from the docks. In all, the report stated that there were nearly 2,800 male thieves in the town, including pickpockets working in conjunction with pawnbrokers. Marine store dealers acted as receivers of stolen goods as well as helping launder high-value currency for thieving prostitutes. It is possible that Miles overstated his evidence in order to promote his strongly held views on the threat of the urban 'criminal classes' and light-fingered vagrants prowling the countryside.[36]

Other surveys, however, also reflect badly on Liverpool. Captain Miller of Glasgow police compared statistics to reveal that in Liverpool in 1838 the number of people taken into custody or charged with offences in proportion to the population was 1 in 16 (with 442 inhabitants to each policeman). Figures for the following year showed Glasgow had 1 in 22 (with 784 inhabitants to each policeman). In London the figure was 1 in 24 (with 356 inhabitants to each policeman).[37]

The methodical and intrusive nature of these crime surveys reflects a growing surveillance and scrutiny of working-class communities. For Joshua Walmsley, chairman of the Liverpool Watch Committee, the report's findings were to have a bearing on the role of the new police force, which 'was trained to be preventive [and] to watch closely all that had a tendency to corrupt morals'.[38] It was becoming clear that the new form of policing was not just about apprehending villains in the street but about collecting information, reconnaissance and, to put it bluntly, spying upon the lower orders of the Liverpool public. Problem districts containing troublesome residents were being carefully mapped out for special attention.

Social Control and Resistance

Yet the new role had its critics. From the beginning, one newspaper slated the new police, accusing them of 'an increase of remorseless, invidious and unpardonable oppression' while achieving no real reduction in crime.[39] Related to this element of social control, the second half of the nineteenth century saw a large increase in the use of local magistrates' courts to prosecute unruly aspects of working-class culture. Many activities on the edge of criminality were brought under legislation. The police were therefore required to enforce licensing laws (e.g. the Beer Act of 1848 which regulated the sale of beer on Sunday), seek out illegal stills, inspect lodging-houses and monitor street traders. As the century progressed, the police were joined by a growing army of inspectors prying into everything from child cruelty to school truancy to sanitary arrangements and the running of the markets. These nationwide attempts to control lower-class work, domestic and leisure pursuits can be seen as a means of instilling middle-class values into the poor. At the same time, industrialization demanded the suppression of low-level criminality, if only to help mould the working classes to the discipline of the factories.

However, attempts to reform the lives of working-class people, particularly on Liverpool's streets, were met with violent resistance. At the heart of most conflicts was the working man's right to stand on a street corner. For those brought up in overcrowded courts and damp cellars, the streets formed a vast public arena. American novelist Nathaniel Hawthorne, United States Consul in Liverpool in the 1850s, observed: 'In a drama of low life, the street might fairly and truly be the one scene where everything should take place – courtship, quarrels, plot and counter-plot, and what not besides.'[40] Yet despite all this bustling activity the police were given powers to clear the streets of undesirable activities. Constables focused on drunkenness, vagrancy, disorderly behaviour and unruly street entertainment. The Liverpool Improvement Act of 1842 allowed officers to arrest all 'loose, idle, or disorderly persons' (section 276) and gave stop-and-search powers on the streets (section 278). The public had the right of passage but little else. They were discouraged from assembling, loitering on the corners, sitting on the pavements, gossiping, selling goods, gambling or playing games. Harassed individuals relocated to the back alleys where the police seldom patrolled. It has been said that nineteenth-century policing was more about changing the location of people's behaviour than about suppressing the behaviour itself.[41]

Police powers were fiercely questioned. In 1835 a group of Irishmen hanged an effigy of the head of the Night Watch on the gates of the main bridewell.

Twenty years later, in Old Swan, the dummy of an unpopular police inspector was paraded through the streets to the accompaniment of a trumpet fanfare before being set alight.[42] Some people resorted to violence. In February 1862 a constable tried to disperse a group of prostitutes loitering on a corner in Paradise Street. A man standing nearby shouted, 'What do you want to move them for?' He then threw a stone at the officer, cutting his ear. According to one social historian, assaults on the police were 'a Liverpool speciality'.[43] The assaults took many forms, including resisting arrest, obstructing officers in their duty and rescuing colleagues from arrest. Many assaults were committed while the assailant was drunk and have their own category in the Head Constable's statistics. Few were listed as serious assaults. Indeed, officers could use the charge of assault as a catch-all charge for anyone struggling against arrest.

While the middle and 'respectable' lower classes were generally supportive of the police, there were always pockets of resistance to police authority, particularly from the Irish 'roughs', many of whom originated from isolated villages where police harassment was unknown. According to one newspaper, the Irish dock labourer exhibited a 'natural hostility to anything in the shape of a policeman'.[44] In June 1837 five Irish labourers were arguing among themselves in Hill Street in the south docks area when a policeman asked them to move on. Instead, the men attacked the officer before running off and barricading themselves inside a house in nearby Wolfe Street. When back-up arrived, a constable managed to gain entry but was cracked on the head with a fender. The Irishmen positioned themselves at the top of the stairs, armed with bedposts and staves. Hugh Keenan shouted, 'You bloody bastards, if you come one step forwards I will have your life.' A brave officer decided to launch an attack but was thrown head-first down the stairs. Superintendent Hatch was also hit so hard on the head with an iron bar that his hat was crushed flat.

In June 1842 police tried to arrest a drunken Patrick Murphy, 'one of the most notorious vagabonds in Liverpool'. On the way to Brick Street bridewell, the officers were targets of bricks, stones, broken mugs and mud as the neighbourhood came out in support of the prisoner. In April 1845, in Toxteth Park, William Jones killed PC Richard Fairclough by cracking his skull with a poker. Speaking after another attack on the police in Warwick Street, stipendiary magistrate Edward Rushton lamented: 'it was almost impossible to arrest a person in that district unless at the risk of life'.[45] In the enclosed courts the police were particularly vulnerable as there was only a narrow thoroughfare by which to escape and residents would throw objects out of the windows.

It has been stated that recorded attacks on Liverpool policemen rose during the period 1844 to 1850, coinciding with a degeneration of force discipline.[46] The arrival of the Irish migrants might also have had something to do with it. Between 1841 and 1871, 33 per cent of those arrested for assaulting constables in Liverpool were Irishmen, despite their forming only 13 per cent of the population.[47] To put this in context, between 1862 and 1877, 20 per cent of recorded assaults on the Birmingham police were committed by the Irish, although it should be noted that by 1861 the Irish formed only 4 per cent of the population.[48] If the south end was dangerous for constables, the north end of Liverpool, where many migrants settled, was no less resistant to police authority. In his report to the Watch Committee in 1849, Head Constable Dowling revealed the scale of the problem: 'Several men of the force have been seriously wounded and others severely bruised and beaten by the Irish population of the North Division of the Town, where almost daily fights and broils occur, which but for the presence of the police, would be a scene of constant uproar and bloodshed.'[49]

Women rescuing their partners from police clutches provided another dangerous scenario for officers. In July 1860 James Forrester assaulted another man in Vauxhall Road and was promptly arrested. However, a mob of women then attempted to liberate the prisoner. When another constable intervened he was knocked to the floor and held down by his hair while one woman struck him in the face with a bunch of keys. In May 1894, as a constable wrestled with a prisoner in Richmond Row, Bridget Doyle ran up to the officer and stabbed him in the eye with a pair of stocking needles. Catherine Bennett kept up the attack from the sidelines by throwing bricks.

Youths had their own issues with the police. They attacked constables as a means of gaining peer group status and developing their 'hard man' reputations in the community. Resisting arrest was the duty of any young ruffian. Thomas Copeland was a violent youth who had already served three months for stabbing his own brother. He was also believed to be the ringleader of a mob that attacked a house in Everton. In November 1853 Copeland was angry because he couldn't get served in a public house in Scotland Road. After threatening the publican he was chased by the police and managed to reach his own home in Cavendish Street. He was arrested and dragged outside. During the struggle he managed to stab PC Sunderland in the thigh, severing his femoral artery. 'The Lord receive my soul' were the officer's dying words. Copeland was later found guilty of manslaughter and transported for life. It was revealed in court that his relatives had threatened to kill the mother of one of the witnesses if she gave evidence.

Anti-police feelings were at their height in the 1850s and 1860s. In 1855 there were 573 reported assaults; in 1857 the figure had risen to 973, and it peaked in 1865 with 1,484 drunken assaults and 13 more serious attacks.[50] Statistical evidence, however, does not provide the whole picture. Not all police assaults were recorded since many constables prided themselves on being able to take care of themselves in a fight. No doubt some officers physically punished assailants on the spot without arresting them and adding them to the figures. If a constable came off worse he might have preferred to keep it quiet and save face among his colleagues.

Public criticism of the police was sometimes taken a little too far. Patrolling his beat in Toxteth Park, in August 1888, an officer was approached by a man called Woods who said, 'You are the laziest fellow in the world; you never do any work. I could have been a policeman but I wouldn't.' He then punched the officer in the face before promising that he would 'lick him up' in two minutes. Excuses for assaulting the police were many and varied. In November 1892, upon being arrested for begging in Anfield, Edward Williams decided to smack the arresting constable, reasoning that he 'might as well be hung for a sheep as a lamb'. It seems, however, that the majority of the Liverpool public gradually became resigned to a police presence on the streets. The following case from September 1864 tells us something about the public's grudging respect towards constables. Thomas Benson was among a group making a disturbance in Byrom Street. During a violent struggle as he was being arrested, Benson warned PC Waddington that he would 'pull his — throat out if it was not for the colour of his clothes'.

In the latter half of the nineteenth century assaults on the police appear to have steadily declined throughout the country, although in Liverpool the figures remained alarmingly high. A comparison with other major towns for the year ending September 1890 (see Table 3) is revealing. In 1889, in Liverpool, a constable was assaulted on average every 13 arrests. In Manchester the

Table 3: Number of assaults on police dealt with summarily by the justices, 1890

Town and population	Number of assaults
Liverpool (517,951)	1,142
Birmingham (429,171)	433
Manchester (379,437, estimated)	238
Leeds (367,606)	168
Sheffield (325,243)	94

Source: BDP, 19 October 1891

figure was one assault in every 20 arrests.[51] At the end of the century, there was still concern about violence towards the police. In 1899, in addition to fines for other offences, city magistrates had begun adding sentences of a month's imprisonment for assaults on policemen, the month being imposed without the option of a financial penalty.[52]

Police Brutality

Assaults on the police tell only half the story. There was also a considerable amount of brutality aimed by the police at the public, both criminal and law-abiding. The police court records display a steady stream of accusations of police heavy-handedness when making arrests. During 1849 and 1850 there were numerous incidents in which members of the public were randomly and indiscriminately hit over the head with police batons. Upon the inauguration of Major Greig as Head Constable of Liverpool in 1852, the chairman of the Watch Committee addressed the 400 serving policemen with some severe words:

> I cannot conceal my annoyance at the number of complaints against officers for unnecessary violence in the discharge of their duty. Some of these cases have been of the most cowardly and unmanly character. Weak and almost defenceless women have been dragged in a most violent way to bridewell; and men have been attacked and beaten when there was not the slightest occasion.[53]

To his credit, Greig replaced the heavy bludgeon with a lighter stick which was eventually removed completely from daytime patrols in 1854.[54]

In 1858 the Head Constable was able to report that although assaults against his men had increased there were few complaints of violence by the officers.[55] Ten years later, commenting on an assault by a policeman on a member of the public, Greig boasted that such assaults had been very rare lately.[56] Most constables were conscious of the damage that could be done by truncheons, both to their victims and to their own careers. Defending one of his officers in a court case against a charge of excessive use of the stick, Super-intendent Martin stated, 'I know there is a general feeling on the part of the officers not to use it, because they know an enquiry will follow.'[57] Yet police violence continued. In 1871 stipendiary magistrate Mr Raffles still had cause to advise the police on their use of the truncheon on the heads of members of the public. A newspaper pointed out that in the 'rough' districts 'there are no doubt some thicknesses of skull able to stand almost any amount of battering', but nevertheless constables were to be careful lest they ended up committing manslaughter.[58]

Social historian John Archer has investigated 120 cases of alleged assault by police between 1850 and 1910. His research shows that up to the mid-1860s the press displayed little concern for accusations of police brutality, but from about 1869 it was reported that police violence in Liverpool amounted to 'terrorism'. Officers were increasingly criticized for their use of force and disproportionate violence. In some cases, the police were said to be drunk when making the assault. It is possible that the officers were preventing potential assaults against themselves by 'getting their retaliation in first'. In the cases that came before the courts, 54 per cent were unprovoked assaults on the public, 31 per cent arose out of the arresting process and 15 per cent occurred in police custody back at the bridewell. Forty per cent of the victims were women.[59]

Local newspapers are littered with reports of police assaults.[60] In June 1869 Elizabeth Sherlock was arrested by police responding to an altercation in Everton Road. Believing that the woman was violently drunk, three officers carried her spread-eagled and face down. While clutching a male prisoner, a rookie PC called Francis Doyle shouted, 'Kill the —', 'Choke the —', 'Split her skull with your baton.' As the woman passed him, he kicked her in the stomach. The prisoner was in fact having an epileptic fit and the incident was witnessed by some passing journalists. Doyle was subsequently dismissed from the force.

An appalling case of police heavy-handedness occurred during an incident of crowd chaos and confusion. In February 1852 Dr Cahill was delivering a lecture to a packed audience at Holy Cross Catholic Chapel. One of the building's rafters snapped, sending those on the gallery into a state of panic. As people rushed for the stairs and doors, somebody outside informed a passing policeman that some Orangemen had entered the chapel and started a fight. The officer informed Sergeant Tomlinson, who then gathered together some constables. Thinking that they were dealing with a sectarian attack, the officers waded into the congregation as they spilled onto the street. Men, women and children were cracked on the heads and shoulders. A blind man was knocked to the floor. Later that night Tomlinson wrote a report of the day's events which was highly critical of the actions of his fellow officers. The next day the report was copied into the North Division Police Book.

In the meantime some of the constables were reported for assault and were summoned to the Police Court. Tomlinson's report was an embarrassment to the police and the day before the constables were due in court the damning page was carefully torn from the volume. However, in the face of contrary evidence from witnesses the deception was discovered and the magistrate enquired as to who was responsible. It seems that Head Constable Dowling had ordered the removal of the page and instructed Tomlinson to write another more sanitized report omitting references to police brutality. In court, Tomlinson swore by his revised evidence. Two constables were subsequently suspended for the violence along with Tomlinson. Asked to account for his actions, Dowling explained that he was suffering from bronchitis and had recently changed his doctor, who had prescribed an opium-based medicine. The new medication was said to have influenced his judgement. He was nevertheless dismissed.

In 1885 police violence against children also came in for criticism. The *Liverpool Review* rebuked dock policemen who used their canes against 'wretched, half-starved and ragged children', particularly those touting for bag-carrying jobs among the passengers disembarking at the Princes landing stage. In one incident a constable used his stick to beat a lad over the head, neck and shoulders.[61] In spite of these incidents, police violence against the public seems to have declined by the 1890s as the force became more professional with a lower turnover of recruits.

Although some people complained about police heavy-handedness, perhaps the most common accusation levelled against officers was that it was difficult to find one when needed. The force was known as the 'Invisible Blues'.[62] The absence of a police presence, particularly in the hidden courts and back alleys, meant that a great deal of crime must have gone unrecorded, unsolved and unpunished. Yet the police were not solely responsible for tackling crime in the slum-infested areas of Liverpool. The courts and the prisons provided two more levels by which the underworld was to be subdued.

THREE

Prison and Punishment

Capital Punishment

The medieval justice system was nothing if not robust. In 1565 a Liverpool purse-thief called Thomas Johnson was nailed by the ear to a post and afterwards whipped out of town by boys carrying bunches of twigs.[1] Over the centuries, pain and public humiliation remained essential elements of criminal justice. In 1785 Joseph Timms, another thief, was put in the pillory and flogged.[2] Stocks were situated at High Cross in High Street and the punishment was still used in the nineteenth century. Walton-on-the-Hill, three miles from Liverpool, housed an iron stocks. As late as 1857 a prisoner was confined there by order of the local magistrate.[3] James Stonehouse recalled that children were particularly cruel to victims held in the stocks: 'I have seen stout and sturdy fellows faint under the sufferings they endured.' He also remembered the large pond in Marybone, called the Flashes, which once held a ducking stool for women.[4]

People had their own form of community justice, operating independently of the official authority of the police and the courts. 'Rough music', also called 'charivari', was a ceremonial shaming ritual involving loud, jarring noise and dramatic performance inflicted upon those who had failed to conform to communal standards of behaviour. In 1825 Liverpool ropemakers carried two strike-breakers around town in a cart with their coats turned inside out and placards around their necks accusing them of being 'black sheep' (black-legs).[5] Two years later, during a dispute among the shipwrights, a worker was surrounded by unemployed journeymen and greeted by cries of 'Baa! Black sheep.'[6] Rough music was used well into the nineteenth century. In November 1855 it was inflicted on an Irish woman called Mrs Blake who lived in Grafton Street, Toxteth. It was believed that she was having an affair with the landlord of the Erin Vaults in Scotland Road. On behalf of the wronged wife, a woman called Ellen Delaney (alias Kerrigan) mustered a posse of about two dozen female hawkers and marched on the culprit's home early one morning to confront her. The disturbance led to a riot involving 200 people.

It has already been mentioned that under the Bloody Code theft was a capital offence. For stealing the regalia from the Town Hall in 1794, Charles Coney was hanged after a trial at Lancaster.[7] Public hangings were meant to have a moral and educational purpose, instilling fear into the hearts of spectators, particularly young boys. They were certainly gruesome spectacles. In March 1788 John Silvester Dowling and Patrick Burne became the first prisoners in seventy-three years to be publicly executed in Liverpool. Four months earlier, the men had burgled the home of Mrs Graham in the Richmond district. A crowd of between 20,000 and 30,000 gathered at the temporary gallows erected outside the Borough Gaol in Great Howard Street. When the men dropped to their death, many in the crowd, both male and female, fainted at the sight.[8]

Reformers who wished to see the abolition of public executions were keen to stress the disorderly nature of the events, arguing that for some people hangings were more a form of popular entertainment than a deterrent to crime. Executions outside Kirkdale House of Correction often attracted 'scenes of ruffianism and disorder'.[9] Crowds with picnic baskets and beer would arrive early to gain the best views. Mothers holding babies, curious children and gangs of pickpockets were regular spectators. When poisoner Betty Rowland was hanged at Kirkdale in 1836, a mix-up over the time of execution meant that spectators who had arrived early at 5 a.m. had to wait until 3 p.m. for their amusement. Determined not to lose their first-class views, they relieved the boredom by pelting each other with missiles. Women in the crowd were attacked and robbed of their bonnets and shawls and had to take refuge in the prison.[10] When fellow poisoner Betty Eccles was hanged in 1843, the crowd 'indulged in coarse jests, cursing, swearing, laughing and shouting, and coaches loaded with the inmates of brothels drove to the spot, and Scotland Road bore much of the same appearance that it does during the races'.[11] The lower orders sometimes amused themselves by splashing and pushing one another into the numerous pools of water which pitted the adjoining brickfields.[12] A familiar sight at executions were two ballad singers. Fifteen minutes before proceedings had even started, by some amazing act of premonition, they would offer for sale the last dying speech and confession of the murderer. The fact the sheet was written and printed days earlier did not deter the crowd from snapping up copies.[13]

Leveson Street murderer John Gleeson Wilson (Maurice Gleeson) was hanged in September 1849 in front of about 60,000 spectators. When he was cut down from the gallows the crowd called for pieces of the rope as mementoes. So popular was the event that excursion trains were run, the forerunners of the 'football specials'. Railway companies advertised 'Reduced fares for this occasion only'. A quadruple execution in September 1863 drew a crowd of over 100,000, supplemented by late arrivals from Huddersfield, Bradford and Blackburn. The crowd included gentleman 'swells' carrying opera glasses for a better view. Similarly, Liverpudlians travelled to hangings in other towns. In June 1856 trains from Liverpool took morbid tourists to Stafford to see Dr Palmer, another poisoner, strung up.

In 1868 public hangings were abolished, no doubt to put a stop to such unruly gatherings. Whether hanging, performed in public or in private, ever provided a deterrent is an interesting point. One of the most publicized murder cases in Liverpool was the 'Tithebarn Street Outrage' which resulted in the execution of two youths, Michael Mullen and John McCrave. In September 1874, a month after this murder, a gang robbed a shop till in Great Crosshall Street. The young thieves ran away but then turned upon the pursuing shopkeeper, thrashing him with belts until he was 'like a piece of jelly' and hardly able to stand up. During the beating, one of the gang, Michael Queeney, shouted that he would 'hang for him along with Mullen'. The words were not an idle boast. If the shopkeeper had died from his injuries (and the gang had no idea whether he would survive) Queeney and his accomplices would almost certainly have been hanged, not long after Michael Mullen. Nor did the execution of McCrave and Mullen deter other members of their families from kicking a man to death three years later.[14] Some people were quite prepared to pay the ultimate price for their crimes.

Transportation

A less brutal means of ridding the country of its criminals was transportation, which can be traced back to the sixteenth century. Rather than being granted absolute freedom, those pardoned for capital offences were shipped to Virginia or the West Indies for fourteen years or sometimes life. After a lull in the late seventeenth century, the Transportation Act of 1718 offered new impetus to relieve the country of its undesirables. Prisoners were transported for even minor offences. Seven years' transportation was the typical sentence for women convicted of stealing small items such as handkerchiefs. In 1822 Mary Gleaves was banished for seven years for picking a man's pocket. On hearing her sentence she managed to throw a stone at the judge, reasoning, 'If I'm going to go, I may as well go for something decent.'[15]

The War of Independence halted the transportation of prisoners to America. In 1776, as a stopgap substitute, prison ships known as hulks were used. Berthed around the country, and even as far away as the West Indies, they continued in service into the 1850s. In 1838 the prison inspector witnessed convicts leaving the Borough Gaol to be taken to the hulks. Although they were dejected, they made attempts at bravado, cheering as they were driven through the streets. Their friends, waiting outside the prison gates, responded with their own cries and shouts.[16] The lists of convicts in national prisons show that in 1838 four Liverpudlians (under 21 years of age) were housed in various ships berthed off Bermuda. They were serving sentences ranging from seven to fourteen years for stealing items such as knives and candlesticks. Another 37 prisoners convicted at Liverpool were kept on the *Fortitude* at Chatham in Kent.[17] Prisoners sentenced to transportation languished in prison or the hulks for up to two years before beginning their lengthy voyage. They were therefore weakened before they even began their journey. Their health must have been further damaged by the cramped conditions and deteriorating quality of the food on board the ships. Unsurprisingly, countless passengers suffered dysentery and scurvy. It has been claimed that up to half of the prisoners transported from Kirkdale died during the passage.[18]

In 1787 transportation was resumed using the new colonies in Australia. Between 1787 and 1857, 160,000 prisoners, aged between 10 and 80, were exiled, the vast majority of them male.[19] In Liverpool, however, women sometimes bucked the national trend. During the period 1818 to 1822, of 177 prisoners sentenced to transportation, 128 were women (69 per cent).[20] Transportation not only banished criminals but also provided a workforce for the new colonies. In what became a massive open prison, convicts were put to work either for individuals, such as farmers, or for government institutions. By instilling a work ethic the system aimed to reform the convict's character. By the 1850s, if they behaved well and worked hard, prisoners could be granted a ticket of leave which enabled them to seek paid employment and become model colonial citizens. After completing their sentences, and if they could afford the fare, convicts could return home.

Since transportation offered some convicts a new world of opportunity, rather than punishment, its deterrent effect came under scrutiny, particularly since most convicts chose to remain in Australia after the end of their sentence. In 1837 Isabella Arnett (or Harnett) of Virgil Street was sent to Australia after being convicted with her brother of making fake coins. Two years later, she wrote to the solicitor of the Mint thanking him for the part he had played in her good fortune, for she had recently married a rich gentleman.[21] Australians also came to object to their country being used as a dumping ground for unsavoury characters.

The last convict ship set sail in 1867 but by then transportation had already declined, succeeded from the 1850s onwards by lengthy sentences of penal servitude with hard labour, to be served in special convict prisons rather than local gaols. With the accompanying decline in sentences of hanging and other physical chastisements such as flogging and the stocks, the deterrent theatre of public retribution shifted to the private sphere of the prison and more particularly the prisoner's mind. The age of protracted psychological punishment-cum-reform had begun.

Prison

Early prisons were not aimed at reforming or even punishing criminals. In the eighteenth and early nineteenth centuries gaols were merely holding bays used to detain debtors until they could pay their debts, for suspects awaiting trial and for convicted criminals awaiting execution, transportation or flogging. Between 1836 and 1842, in the 36 largest English county prisons, the average term of confinement was forty-six days. With transportation catering for long-term sentences, spells in prison rarely lasted more than two years.[22] When the death penalty was abolished except for murder, and transportation was eventually phased out, prisons became increasingly more important as centres of punishment, correction and reform.

In addition to various small bridewells, used for drunks and the short-term incarceration of prisoners until trial, Liverpool had five major centres of detention. The Tower at the bottom of Water Street became a gaol in 1740. Prisoners of all ages and sexes, felons and debtors, were confined together with no segregation, order or regulation. Inmates were housed in seven dank underground dungeons about six feet square, lit and ventilated by holes in the doors. With three prisoners to a cell, conditions were cramped. By 1803 a larger dungeon contained 12 men and women, although it could hold up to 40 prisoners at a pinch. There were two courtyards, one for felons and one for debtors. The courtyards were carpeted with chicken dung and mud. Rubbish was rarely cleared up and the lack of hygiene meant that illness, particularly low typhoid fever, was common. Debtors had the better deal and were housed in the tower where they had the luxury of a bed at the cost of one shilling a week. In an effort to gain charity, they would attach a glove or bag to a stick and dangle it from the tower window. Passers-by would donate money to help the 'poor debtors' although it was most likely spent on alcohol. Child pranksters would put stones in the bag and laugh at the hapless recipients. When James Stonehouse visited the Tower he found 'the strong prisoners used to tyrannise over the weak, and the most frightful cases of extortion and cruelty were practised among them'.[23] In 1770 a debtor called James Donavan set fire to a room housing 15 prisoners. Fortunately nobody was hurt.[24] In 1811 the prisoners were removed to the Borough Gaol.

Liverpool's House of Correction, situated next to the workhouse in Brownlow Hill, opened in 1776 'for the punishment and setting to work of vagabonds and idle disorderly persons'.[25] In addition to prostitutes and the work-shy, some regular offenders were also committed. In 1811 the inmates were also transferred to the Borough Gaol and the building converted to an asylum. Liverpool Borough Gaol in Great Howard Street opened in 1786. The street was named after prison reformer John Howard, who had a say in the building's construction. The chaos, filth and cruelty of the Tower were replaced by a more hygienic, ordered and structured environment. Whether the regime was more humane is debatable. Inspired by the work of Howard, and the utilitarian ideas of legal philosopher Jeremy Bentham, nineteenth-century prisons became places of strict control and routine. Regular prayers, work discipline, silence, isolation and constant surveillance were designed to break intractable spirits and reform criminal tendencies. Uniformity, both sartorial and architectural, was a key feature of the new prisons.

Described as having 'heavy walls, fifteen or twenty feet high, with a coping stuck full of broken glass bottles', the Borough Gaol comprised six T-shaped wings of several storeys.[26] A contemporary observer noted that the building 'covers more than twice the ground, and contains more than twice the number of cells and domitories [sic] than the prison of Newgate, and on fair calculation will hold more than half the inhabitants of Liverpool'.[27] Known as the French Prison, for the next twenty years the building was used for French prisoners of war. Local criminals could not use the gaol until 1811 and were forced to languish in the Tower.[28] In the early 1850s the gaol, which was originally intended for 400 prisoners, held 1,200. In 1855 the prisoners were removed to the newly built prison at Walton.

In 1818 the authorities decided to build a second house of correction at Kirkdale. While minor offenders continued to be sent to the Borough Gaol, more serious criminals appearing at the Assizes, and serving sentences of more than one month, were put in the Kirkdale House of Correction.[29] Completed in 1821, the prison was constructed as a mixture of cells and larger rooms for four or five prisoners, although women had their own cells. Despite having up to 384 cells, the prison was sometimes home to more than 600 prisoners, including children.[30] In February 1892 the last two prisoners left for Liverpool Prison in Walton. Walton Gaol, as it is now known, opened in 1855 to replace the Borough Gaol. Also called 'the Model', it was the most modern penal establishment in Europe, offering single-cell accommodation. Located two miles from Kirkdale, it was designed to house up to 1,000 inmates from all over Lancashire. A growing prison population, however, meant that 300 hammocks had to be added.

Although these new prisons were an improvement on earlier makeshift places of incarceration, such as the Tower, conditions were still grim. A turnkey in the overcrowded reception ward at the old Borough Gaol complained: 'the smell in the morning is dreadful, I have sometimes hardly been able to draw my breath in getting up'.[31] Another witness found the stench 'unbearable, especially in the morning. To keep the putrid fevers – indeed to render the corridors at all passable – it is found necessary to burn chloride of lime in them incessantly, as well as in the day-rooms and eating rooms.' At Kirkdale, the use of chamber pots at night made the cells intolerable. It was not unknown for warders, coming from the fresh air to inspect a cell, to be violently sick.[32] Hygiene was basic. Prisoners at the Borough Gaol would file out of their cells with uncovered slop buckets and water-cans, to empty one and fill the other in the yard outside. According to one inmate, prisoners had to 'carry out the nuisance tins – wash them in a large stone trough [...] Next, we were to undergo ablutions ourselves, in the same stone trough [...] After breakfast, recourse was had again to the trough, to cleanse our *dishes*.'[33]

Prison food could be a punishment in itself. Breakfast at the Borough Gaol consisted of oatmeal gruel and a half-pound loaf of 'brown tommy' (black barley and pea bread). Dinner consisted of a 'half-pound of bread, and a pint of "scouse, made of cows heads", boiled to a jelly with lips and gullet yet covered with the provender the beast had last eaten'.[34] Years earlier, one of the French prisoners at the Borough Gaol earned for himself legendary status for his eating abilities. If the incredible testimony of a contemporary doctor can be believed, Charles Domery, a Pole by birth, developed a curious medical condition as a teenager, a quirk shared with his father and eight brothers. Domery would apparently eat anything. At six foot three inches, the glutton could munch up to 5lbs of grass in a day. Preferring raw meat, in one year he was said to have devoured 174 cats, in addition to dogs and rats, some of the animals apparently still alive when devoured. When his frigate was captured off the coast of Ireland, the famished man was caught tearing at the mangled limb of one of his comrades. He normally had to be supplied with the rations of ten men. In prison, the doctor decided to conduct a scientific experiment to test the man's extraordinary gastronomic powers. Domery was set the task of eating 14lbs of raw meat and 2lbs of candles washed down with five bottles of porter. After completing his snack, the Pole claimed that he would have eaten more only for the restrictions of the experiment.[35]

To compensate for the loathsome food, other prisoners relied on illicit rations. Prison inspector Captain Williams saw some Kirkdale prisoners in one of the dayrooms brewing coffee that 'had come over the wall'. Thefts of flour from the mill were common. Prisoners working at the 'cook-house' evidently used it to bake cakes for themselves. Some prisoners worked outside the prison and it was suspected that they smuggled forbidden articles back inside.[36] In 1839 a turnkey was sacked for bringing in tobacco and letters for the prisoners.[37] At Kirkdale, the keeper's journal, dated 25 August 1837, revealed the problem of goods being thrown over the wall: 'On Tuesday three men were observed to get out of a coach at the west corner near the gate near the court house; they walked to the north-west corner near the treadmill, and threw over some tobacco and bacon.' The gatekeeper was informed of the incident but before he could reach the items the prisoners had taken them.[38] At the Borough Gaol, the prison inspector thought that it would be better if the small space around the inside walls was discontinued as a garden and gravel laid instead. This was to make it easier to spot the articles thrown over the wall.[39]

The prison experience corrupted rather than reformed some prisoners. An 18-year-old thief who had spent thirty weeks at Kirkdale said that he 'spent the day in Idleness […] There was very bad Talk; the longer a Man stops in such a Place the worse he is.'[40] Lax discipline and poor management made prison less of a deterrent. In 1837 Williams was critical of the running of Kirkdale. Punishments were not enforced and prisoners regularly communicated with each other. Bribery was a reality; one of the gaolers admitted that 'there is an idea among the prisoners that they can obtain offices in the prison such as that of cook, for money'.[41] For those without cushy jobs, it was not impossible to skive. In 1843 Williams found two prisoners reading in the privies; one had gone for some peace and quiet and the other for warmth.[42] It was felt that the governor and matron had grown too old and frail to carry out their duties. It was not until 1845 that Williams noted improvements with the replacement of the pair. Punishments at Kirkdale were also irregular. There were 17 whippings in 1825 but then hardly any until 1841. A rise in floggings between 1844 and 1845 coincided with the harsher regime of the new governor.[43]

The Borough Gaol had a more repressive regime. An inmate from Salford felt that there was 'not near so much liberty in Borough Gaol as Kirkdale'.[44] The entries in the punishment book for one week in May 1843 reveal the severity of discipline. Punishable misdemeanours included talking, insolence, using insubordinate language, neglecting to keep a proper distance when exercising, stealing gruel and giving it to another prisoner, swearing, singing, missing one's number at roll call, attempting to take bread from other boys, throwing wool in the workroom, getting up from a seat and looking out of the window, repeatedly looking around and laughing in the chapel. Punishments included loss of supper and spells in solitary confinement.[45]

Yet if the regime at Kirkdale was less severe than the Borough Gaol, it distinguished itself in other ways. The gaol had a high death rate. Between 1823 and 1832, for example, 110 inmates died while serving their sentences. During the same period, 82 prisoners died at Lancaster prison and only 13 at Preston.[46] Tuberculosis was the primary cause of death at Kirkdale, although venereal disease, scurvy and typhus were also common. Before 1847 prisoners who complained of feeling unwell were put on reduced rations, the so-called 'sick diet'.[47] This was designed to discourage bogus requests to see the doctor. Simulated diseases were common. Men would feign rheumatic fever by tying their hands tightly or by leaning their arm over the edge of the bedstead until it swelled. Some endured violent purging and vomiting. One man made himself ill by stuffing tobacco up his rectum.[48]

A spell in the hospital quarters must have provided welcome relief from the drudgery of prison life. One inmate found that the regime in the Kirkdale hospital quite relaxed.

> The hospital warder always closed our door at six o'clock in the evening, and we then had no fear of again being disturbed until six o'clock the next morning. After we had finished our tea, the tea leaves were collected and put upon the hob to dry. We then made cigarettes and smoked them instead of tobacco. Disgusting and obscene language was predominant, tales of crime were unblushingly told, and acquaintances were formed which would soon add considerably to future records of crime.[49]

A visit to chapel likewise gave brief respite. Some disgraceful scenes took place at Kirkdale chapel. One man witnessed a fight between women, which caused 'much amusement among the male prisoners'.[50] Some old hands had ulterior reasons for taking Holy Communion. The same witness heard one man tell another 'that his only motive [...] was to taste the wine'.[51] Indeed, the chaplains were forced to keep a tight grip on the goblets when offering Communion. The chaplain was also not convinced that the prisoners were taking their faith seriously. One woman, immediately after partaking of the sacrament, persuaded another in her class to commit a robbery.[52] A batch of Bibles brought in by the chaplain was 'destroyed or smoked' by the prisoners, probably to keep warm.[53]

Suicide

For some, suicide became the only means of escaping the horror of incarceration. In 1847 the keeper of Rose Hill bridewell warned that the hinges inside the cell doors were being used by prisoners trying to hang themselves. When a woman was thus caught hanging, the turnkeys had great difficulty opening the door to save her.[54] Hugh Shimmin, campaigning journalist and owner/editor of a journal called *Porcupine*, visited the bridewell ten years later. The keeper informed him that 'it was frequently necessary to fasten both hands of a person to one of the rings in the wall, as they often tried to commit suicide, the women especially […] by putting the strings of their dresses around their throats'.[55]

A feature of all modern prisons is the wire netting suspended between the upper galleries. Its origin lies in an incident that happened at Walton. A young Irishman with repeated convictions for drunkenness plunged 33 feet, hitting the stone floor head first. Amazingly, he survived with a fractured skull. After three weeks, and against medical advice, he demanded his release. The incident resulted in all the 60 prisons in England and Wales attaching wire netting from landing to landing.[56] Suicide attempts eventually forced other changes in prison design, including the removal of gaslights from inside the cells: 'In the prison at Liverpool […] the gaslights, instead of being outside the cells, were placed inside, so that the naked flame consumed the oxygen, besides providing the intending suicide with an opportunity for inhaling the coal-gas or hanging himself to the gas-bracket.'[57]

The Borough Gaol was the scene of many suicide attempts. In June 1845 Ann S____ used her handkerchief to make a noose and placed it at the corner of her cell door. Despite the efforts of the matron and governor, she died. In July a prisoner used a razor he had hidden to cut his arms and slash at his throat. It was thought that he was trying to avoid the whipping he was due to be given. A couple of weeks later a prisoner used a length of rope, made of the oakum that he was unpicking, to feign a suicide attempt. He was found on the floor after the feeble cord snapped, and was thought merely to have been seeking sympathy. The following day another prisoner used a strip of blanket in a similar failed attempt. At the end of the month a man used material torn from his shirt in yet another botched attempt. All these rehearsals for the afterlife were seen as a means of avoiding the sentence of transportation.[58] In 1875 William 'Cock' Hardy, aged 24, was sentenced to ten years for assaulting and biting two policemen in Conway Street. He was described as 'one of the greatest ruffians in Liverpool' and 'a candidate for a muzzle'. Since the age of

13 he had been incarcerated 31 times, including a five-year spell in a reformatory. On his first evening at Walton he took off his shirt and tied it to a bar in his cell, reserving his greatest act of violence for himself.[59]

New Approaches

Despite the ordeals of prison life, the same old faces were frequently convicted and sent back to what must have seemed a second home. A resident of a rough Bootle neighbourhood was pessimistic about the local street loafers: 'All the police and gaols in the world will never make them decent, or tame them in the least. They brag about gaol, and care as little about being boxed up there as in their own hovels.'[60] Politicians and social commentators had long been looking for alternative means of punishing and reforming criminals. Speaking at a conference in 1860, Liverpool banker George Melly outlined his own novel means of reparation. If a professional burglar, for example, was caught in the act he would be sentenced to maintain himself in prison until he had done work to the value of £62. If he worked a twelve-hour day his imprisonment would last four years; if he chose to work a ten-hour day his sentence would last eight years; if he worked only eight hours he would stay in prison indefinitely; if he chose to work less than eight hours a day he would also debar himself from certain prison comforts and privileges, calculated on a sliding scale. A five-hour day would result in a bread and water diet. Below five hours would mean the loss of his bed. A two-hour day would mean he would lose the shelter of his roof. If the prisoner refused to co-operate and was completely idle he would pass each night in the prison courtyard without food, warmth or shelter.[61]

The idea of toughening up the prison regime was nothing new. Two innovations, first introduced in the 1830s, had by the 1850s already helped bring order to Britain's gaols. The separate system involved solitary confinement and was aimed at transforming the character of prisoners. Their only contact was with the chaplain to discuss religious matters. For the rest of the time the convict was meant to brood over his evil ways, if he didn't go mad first. The second innovation was called the silent system. This allowed prisoners to mix but not to talk, therefore preventing them from corrupting each other and bullying weaker inmates. At Walton, the silent system was so effective that it was said you could hear the tower clock ticking.[62]

Forcing prisoners to embrace the discipline of work was another important element of imprisonment. Kirkdale's tread-wheel, or treadmill, was the largest in the country. It could accommodate up to 130 prisoners at one time and was used to grind flour. A revolution of the wheel would be completed every 24 steps. Thirty revolutions would take about 15 minutes at which interval a bell would sound to signal a rest period. Prisoners were required to complete 15 spells on the wheel, a total of four hours' soul-destroying labour. Yet some were not to be defeated by the prison system. Experienced old hands would avoid the work by not stepping on the steps but waiting for them to descend to their proper level and slipping their feet in. On a visit to Kirkdale, Captain Williams found tread-wheel prisoners unsupervised and talking loudly to each other. It was not uncommon to see prisoners smoking while on the wheel.[63]

The Walton treadmill was used to pump water. When Basil Thomson, deputy governor from 1896, visited the tread-wheel shed he found 'a row of men with their faces to the wall [...] These were they who would rather undergo dietary punishment than climb another step up the endless stair-case.'[64] The tread-wheel was eventually abolished and dismantled. The governor remarked that the prisoners had never used so much energy as they did when breaking it up.[65]

Both prisons also used crank labour to pump water. The crank, a handle with a resistance of up to 6lbs, required at least 1,800 revolutions per hour and had to be turned for between five and eight hours, up to a total of 14,400 turns. At Kirkdale, shot-drill was also used. Cannon balls had to be carried from one side of the yard to the other, from a stack of 91 balls. When the task was completed it was repeated, this time back to the original side of the yard. Oakum picking involved untwisting old pieces of rope into separate strands, to be used for caulking ships. Work discipline was supplemented by harsh punishments. In addition to flogging, punishments included shack-ling with balls and chains. Solitary confinement on bread and water was also used although turnkeys reported that the punishment was useless. Work-shy thieves opted for it because they preferred sitting in a cell to climbing the tread-wheel.[66]

The prison system took on many roles and expectations. A key feature of the sentence of penal servitude was that it involved a substantial sentence that prevented the prisoner committing more crimes in the community. Through the enforcement of work discipline, the convict was to be moulded into a reformed member of society. Yet the punishing regime was also retributory and aimed to provide a strong deterrent to other potential offenders. The roles sometimes clashed. A big question was whether prison was a place to reform or simply punish offenders. For most of the century attitudes swung like a pendulum, from liberal to severe regimes, from developing work skills and trades to inflicting pointless repetitive labour such as the crank. The problem was in creating regimes humane enough to promote and instil civilized values without making prisons a more attractive alternative to life outside and thereby destroying any deterrent effect.

Victorian prison conditions were tough but they have to be judged in the context of equally harsh social conditions on the outside. For some destitute people, prison was less a punishment than a better alternative to living on the streets. Convicts at least had a bed and regular meals. Following the famine invasion of Irish, stipendiary magistrate Edward Rushton pointed out that 'English gaols are excellent winter quarters for starving Irish paupers', offering them better food, shelter, clothing and more cleanliness than they could get elsewhere.[67] The governor of the Borough Gaol agreed: 'It is well known that, in some instances, the Irish have committed offences with the express object of getting into prison.'[68] While the quality of prison food might have been objectionable, the quantity raised some questions. A newspaper correspondent complained that the weekly cost of food and clothing per man in Kirkdale prison was 5s while in the Liverpool workhouse it was just over 2s, 'a proof that poverty is punished more than crime'.[69] The head warder made a similar point: 'I was long in the army, and I am sure that the food is better and more abundant that what any soldier gets.'[70]

Rather than being a place of terror, for some prison was quite attractive. At Kirkdale the chaplain stated 'that a female prisoner [...] appeared greatly distressed at coming in, but upon [...] seeing the garden her grief vanished, and she exclaimed with astonishment, "Dear me, what a pretty place!"'[71] Indeed, the hospital at Walton Gaol had such excellent facilities that pregnant women on the outside would arrange to break a window to come in for their confinement. Such scams were not exclusive to the poor. Liverpool's workhouse infirmary also had such a good reputation that thrifty respectable people were known to wangle their way into it for free surgery.[72] With regards to prison comforts, a writer in the *Edinburgh Review* complained: 'there will be more danger of a conspiracy to break into, than break out of gaol'.[73]

From 1865, however, there was a further tightening of prison discipline. In 1863 a House of Lords committee recommended that the prison system should aim to deter, based on a system of 'hard labour, hard fare and a hard bed'.[74] It was not until 1895 that the Gladstone Committee reversed government policy after concluding that oppressive prison systems did not work. The discipline neither deterred nor reformed prisoners. Instead, they became embittered and brutalized by their experience. After 1895 the emphasis on severe sentences of penal servitude gradually shifted to more liberal remedies, including probation and aftercare. The Prison Act of 1898 abolished the treadmill and crank and reduced physical punishments for breaking prison rules. The founding of specialist detention centres for alcoholics and the feeble-minded saw the beginning of attempts to replace punishment with medical treatment.

Meanwhile, by the mid-century prison overcrowding had become a problem for administrators. By the 1830s committals in Lancashire already exceeded 10,000 per annum. In 1858 they exceeded 40,000.[75] Non-custodial alternatives, such as the ticket-of-leave system, became increasingly necessary.

Ticket of Leave

The real test of prison's effectiveness was how well convicts did upon their release. When petty criminals were no longer being hanged or transported, the challenge became how to manage them once they had stepped out of the prison gates. The chaplain at Kirkdale thought that the reform of criminals in prison was futile as long as the state of society remained what it was outside.[76] Poverty and lack of regular employment almost guaranteed that many would return to theft and a further spell in prison. The temptation to re-offend was enormous. At Kirkdale, prisoners were released with earnings in their pockets. Their associates knew when they would be released and would crowd around the prison gates waiting for them. It was said that the men were drunk before they left Kirkdale village.[77]

Yet it was back on the streets that offenders had to prove whether they could stay out of trouble or else stray back into their old ways. It was recognized by the authorities that prisoners needed the opportunity to show that they had reformed. In the 1850s sentences of penal servitude were therefore divided into three parts. A nine-month spell of solitary confinement was followed by a stint of hard labour. If the prisoner's behaviour was good he was awarded a ticket of leave, an early form of probation introduced by the Penal Servitude Act of 1853. On early release, prisoners were given tickets granting them licence to free movement within certain limits. For example, they might be restricted to certain districts or barred from associating with other offenders. In 1864 the police were made responsible for supervising prisoners.

The system had its critics. The conditions were not strictly enforced and were often practically useless. Ticket-of-leavers ripped up their licences (which they were never made to keep) and were suspected of committing further crimes rather than seeking work. If arrested for a new offence they simply denied their previous convictions. It was difficult to prove otherwise.[78] Head Constable Greig complained that vagrants and ticket-of-leave men constantly shuttled back and forth between Liverpool and Manchester and if questioned as to their home address would always reply with the opposite place from where they were.[79] Addressing the grand jury at Liverpool Assizes in 1856, Baron Alderson made a link between a spate of garrotting robberies and the demise of transportation which left a number of ticket-of-leavers lurking the streets: 'you have the result in a great number of crimes committed by these people who are not really reformed, but pretend to be so for the purpose of escaping punishment'.[80] By the 1860s violent crimes committed by such men were a cause of concern for both press and politicians. The newspapers regularly printed accounts of crimes committed by newly released prisoners. James Jeffers, for example, was a returned convict living in Ben Jonson Street, near Scotland Road. He had previously been transported for seven years but allowed home after three years on a ticket of leave. He then stabbed another man in the stomach, 'letting his bowels out'. He was given six months for manslaughter and made to complete the remainder of his sentence. After his release, in February 1860, he was accused of stabbing another man in the face.

Incidents such as these forced people to rethink the role of prison and punishment. Of greater consequence was another well-publicized spate of violent robberies in London in 1862 in which victims were beaten into submission. Some victims were garrotted or strangled, giving the newspapers plenty of opportunity for shock-horror headlines. Ticket-of-leavers were again believed to be responsible. The so-called garrotting panic led to a media frenzy that in turn forced changes to the law.[81] The Garrotter's Act was passed as a direct result of newspaper pressure for the government to do something. Flogging, which had been abolished in 1861, was reintroduced in 1863 for robbery with violence.

Flogging

Flogging was done with the 'cat o' nine tails', nine strings of hard whipcord, each string having nine knots to multiply the punishment. Eventually, the weapon was modernized with softer strings without knots, leaving one warder at Walton to complain, 'I cannot even warm them up with it.'[82] Whether the beatings did anything to deter violent crime is debatable. The Liverpool press occasionally printed bloodthirsty accounts of the prison floggings of violent robbers.[83] After receiving his twentieth lash in Kirkdale Gaol, sailor James Wilson turned to the warder who had just beaten him and commented, 'If you think that has done me any good, you are mistaken.' In a separate flogging, however, William Woodward, on receiving his twentieth-fourth lash, turned to his colleagues, watching from the landing, and shouted, 'Let this be a warning to you, chaps.' The warning, however, was often ignored. Reverend Morris, chaplain at Walton Gaol, revealed that the official flogger had once admitted to him that whipping was useless. In the man's thirty years' experience, he had inflicted the lash in hundreds of cases 'and the same people had come back to the gaol'.[84] How far the punishment deterred others from committing crime will never be known. Fear of the whip certainly did not deter a hard core of violent offenders. When the High Rip Gang burst on the scene in the mid-1880s they met a formidable foe in a fearsome judge called Justice Day, better known as 'Judgement Day'. Using the powers of the Garrotter's Act, Day punished violent robbery with short spells of imprisonment, combined with multiple doses of the lash. Far from deterring the ruffians, however, there is evidence to show that cases of robbery with violence had actually increased in Liverpool by the end of Day's brutal regime in 1893.[85]

While the *Daily Telegraph*, commenting on the prevalence of northern brutality, could confidently assert that 'fear is the only scourge with which these ignorant savages can be governed', the *Liverpool Mercury* felt that 'the utmost terrors of the law are of only very partial effect in curbing the proneness to violence'.[86] The situation was not helped by inconsistencies in sentencing between judges. Prisoners preferred to appear before Justice Day's soft-hearted colleague, Mr Hopwood QC, who rarely ordered floggings.[87] It was pot luck, however, as to which judge heard a particular case.

Ideas about uniformity of sentencing and the certainty of punishment became part of a debate about the fairness of criminal justice. Victorian sentencing was characterized by extremes, randomly lenient and draconian. The punishments for property crime were often more severe than those for violent offences. Working-class men were often subject to stiffer penalties than middle-class offenders. The debate posed some serious questions. Should the punishment fit the crime or fit the criminal? Should all people be considered equal before the law or should punishments be tailored to the needs and motivations of individual criminals to provide the maximum deterrent? Fining a rich merchant 5s is clearly not the same as fining a destitute pauper 5s. Should a hungry person who has stolen a loaf of bread out of sheer desperation be given the same sentence as a professional shoplifter who makes a good living out of crime? Is it fair that a first-time offender is given the same sentence as a repeat offender?

The idea that some people are biologically predisposed towards crime also had some bearing on the debate. Cesare Lombroso was an Italian criminologist who, in the 1870s, developed a theory that criminals are a special human

type with certain recognizable physiological and psychological characteristics.[88] His ideas, along with theories of eugenics, influenced arguments
that the punishment should fit the criminal rather than the crime. Others,
however, believed that criminals are ultimately responsible for their actions
and should therefore be punished proportionately. It was issues such as these
that lay behind the move to formally identify and deal with a hard core of
criminals.

Identifying Persistent Offenders

Recidivism was a problem aggravated, in the age of railways, by the ease by
which criminals could move around the country and from gaol to gaol, giving
false names to retain their anonymity. In the days when no central records
or photographs were kept this caused problems. In the 1830s Liverpool's
Head Constable, M. J. Whitty, suggested a novel means of identifying career
criminals. He proposed that those convicted of felony should be tattooed
on the sole of the foot or some other intimate place not publicly visible. If
a prisoner was found to have three such marks it was to be concluded that
he was an incorrigible rogue and therefore to be transported.[89] Tattoos were
a boon for recognition. During an inspection of the Borough Bridewell in
1841 the prison inspector praised the register of thieves which included hand-
drawn copies of the prisoners' tattoos. One returned convict had tried to
efface the marks of an anchor on the back of his hand by vigorously rubbing
nitric acid into his skin.[90]

Towards the end of the 1860s social policies and policing practices combined
to formally categorize and deal with a class of repeat offenders. Incorrigible
rogues could now find themselves being given harsh sentences even for minor
crimes simply because they were persistent offenders. Previous convictions
were now a millstone around the necks of prisoners.[91] The Habitual Criminals Act of 1869 and Prevention of Crime Act of 1871 required prisoners to
register with the police after their release. When Michael Kelly assaulted
Bernard McGovern in Sparling Street his previous two convictions were taken
into account and he was sentenced to seven years' imprisonment followed
by seven years' police surveillance. The judge stated, 'to persons of criminal
lives there could be no greater punishment than to have the eyes of the police
constantly upon them'.[92]

This intense supervision meant that known offenders were constantly
targeted. A special detective patrol scoured the main streets from afternoon
until midnight looking out for 'suspected characters, reputed thieves and

their associates', arresting them if they stepped out of line.[93] However, the Act had an unforeseen effect in Liverpool. Superintendent Kehoe reported that although thieves had been deterred from loitering at night, they had instead taken to committing burglaries in the early afternoon.[94]

The increased concern with the criminal, rather than the crime, was reflected in the greater use of apparatus for identifying, recording, measuring and classifying offenders. A national database was created of all those imprisoned for serious offences, listing known aliases, distinguishing marks such as tattoos etc. Anthropometry, or body measurement, was also implemented by the prison service. By giving a false name, one Liverpool prisoner at Walton persuaded the court that he was a first-time offender and therefore received a lenient sentence. The warder suspected that he knew the man and decided to take measurements of his head, which established beyond doubt that he was a certain repeat offender. The prisoner, who had a keen sense of his human rights, was disgusted: 'This measuring of a bloke's head is what gets me. Let a warder come honest and straightforward to my cell and look me over and say, "Bill, I knew you when you was Jack Taylor." That's what I call recognition, but this new business with the callipers is not right.'[95] 'Kirkdale Gaol', a ballad popular with prisoners in the middle of the century, describes the intrusive reception process for new arrivals:

> Now when we got to the end of the route
> The turnkey turned my pockets out,
> To see if I had got such stuff
> As blunt [money] or grub, tobacco, snuff.
> They took me then to try my size,
> Colour of hair, colour of eyes,
> The length of my nose from root to tip,
> Or if I'd more than one top lip.[96]

The system didn't work successfully until the introduction of a fingerprint index at the start of the twentieth century. This was the ultimate tool in identification. A prisoner at Walton admitted to the name of a man with one previous conviction on his record. However, his fingerprints proved him to be somebody else. When asked why he had lied, he replied that he had in fact 17 previous convictions and was better off under his false name.[97]

FOUR

Children and Women in the Justice System

In the Dale Street Police Court the children were as numerous as the adults: 'Small mites, some of them little more than babies whose heads do not reach the top of the dock, woful [*sic*] little specimens of humanity encrusted with filth and barely covered with rags, are brought charged with begging and burglary.'[1] Although it now seems cruel that young children were sent to prison for committing petty thefts, Victorian magistrates were faced with a dilemma. In the 1860s a girl aged six stood in the dock accused of begging on the streets. She was so small that officers had to raise her up so that the magistrate could see her. A policeman traced her mother to an overcrowded lodging-house where 51 people were huddled together. The mother had five other children that she couldn't support. The siblings were also beggars, frequently punished if they did not bring home enough money. The magistrate had either to send the girl back to an inadequate mother or commit her to gaol for twenty-one days. He sent her to gaol.[2]

Prison at least removed children from atrocious home environments. On the other hand, prisons were hardly safe places for youngsters. Bullying by older prisoners was rife. At Kirkdale the boys shared cells with the wardsmen, adults in charge of each section. One child was made to get up three times a night to use the tinderbox to light his cellmate's pipe. The wardsmen carried leather straps to beat their young charges. A 13-year-old criticized the regime at Kirkdale. He claimed that boys robbed each other of their food: '_____ often took my dinner from me; he used to take the beef out of my scowse'.[3] The 1839 prison report records an 'abominable crime' committed by two young men the previous February. The youths were subsequently brought before the magistrate and charged with robbing younger boys of their food and kicking and beating them. Further charges stated that they were guilty of a 'crime formerly capital' (no doubt a homosexual act) and that one of them had made an attempt on another boy who had reported it to a turnkey and refused to share the same cell any longer. The charges were dismissed because they rested solely on the testimony of 'criminals'. Shortly after, however, both prisoners were placed in separate night cells.[4]

In 1850 there were 15,000 young prisoners sharing cells with adult felons.[5] The campaign to separate children from adults had been fought since 1817 with the foundation of the Society for the Improvement of Prison Discipline and the Reformation of Juvenile Offenders. However, it was not until 1838 that the idea bore fruit in the provision of separate sections for boys in Parkhurst Prison on the Isle of White. This led to a similar separation in other prisons. There were other attempts at preventing children being contaminated by older prisoners. The 1847 Juvenile Offenders Act forced the legal system to deal with young criminals more quickly. Magistrates were given powers to deal promptly with simple cases and to sentence convicted children to no more than three months' imprisonment.

If conditions in Victorian prisons were tough for adults, for children they must have seemed like hell on earth. Social reformer Mary Carpenter visited the Borough Gaol in 1850. In the punishment cells she saw two young boys, aged 8 and 9, 'crying bitterly in the dark cells'. One boy was said to be very unruly and hardened, although this was his first imprisonment. The other boy was being punished 'for beating poor little T.H as they went up stairs!'[6]

Suicide became a way out for some children. In 1840 a boy, days from release, tried to hang himself at the Borough Gaol. Apparently he was disappointed at failing to find a position at sea. Three days later another boy was found hanging. It seems that he was demonstrating to a friend how the first youth was found. Fortunately, he was saved.[7] Others were not so lucky. In 1855 Joseph Davies, aged 12, committed suicide at Walton Gaol. He was three weeks into an eight-week sentence. Two years later another 12-year-old called William Scarry hanged himself in the same prison, the morning after his admittance on remand for seven days for assaulting his mother.[8]

Prison's Failure to Reform

Yet despite such tough judicial responses to juvenile crime, youngsters continued to break the law. Punishment rarely changed their offending behaviour. As early as 1826, when more than 70 prisoners in the Calendar were less than 20 years of age, the Recorder of Liverpool regretted that prison discipline was failing to reform young criminals.[9] There were a number of reasons why prison was unsuccessful at keeping youngsters from crime. On Carpenter's visit to the Borough Gaol, the matron of the girls' section told her that for some inmates the prison was their only true home. She believed that the reason girls returned to the gaol so soon after release was that they had no helping hand and that 'tempters often lie in wait for them as they leave the prison. They know their character is already lost so they yield and are shortly again committed.'[10] Boys who knew each other from the prison yard would meet again on the outside and form new criminal partnerships. A return to the cells was inevitable, as the chaplain of the Borough Gaol confirmed: 'Some of the boys tell us they will come back, and even name the day.'[11] The tough regime in prison merely hardened some youngsters. 'Before the boys come in they dread prison,' revealed a Kirkdale warder, 'but afterwards I have frequently heard them say they do not care about it.'[12] For some, prison might even have been a luxury: 'I am a good deal better fed in prison than out,' admitted one 14-year-old.[13]

The chaplain expressed despair at the younger prisoners. They seemed irredeemable: 'They are, unquestionably, the most troublesome and, I fear, the most hopeless of any that are to be found.'[14] For Head Constable Whitty, 'Young boys are more hardened in crime, more daring in exploit, more reckless of punishment, and far more troublesome in prison than adults.' He felt that 'a jail is a thief's college' and dismissed those who felt that by crowding together a whole load of rogues, a villain could be transformed into a saint. Gaols were seen as an expensive means of educating young criminals in crime. Most prisoners admitted that, however bad they might have been when imprisoned, they learned more inside than they ever dreamed outside.[15]

Juvenile imprisonment was not only a social but also an economic failure. In 1846 Edward Rushton presented a petition to both Houses of Parliament setting forth the expense of juvenile justice. After offering figures of expenditure for 14 young prisoners, 'fairly selected' from the mass of boys and girls locked up in the Borough Gaol in 1842, the report traced their subsequent careers. It was noted that none of them could write and only one could read imperfectly. Of the 14, four were under sentence of transportation; one had died in prison; three had been imprisoned again before being transported; one had been imprisoned twice before being transported; two had been locked up a further six times before being transported; after a further 16 spells of imprisonment one was in custody awaiting trial; one had been imprisoned on seven occasions but was now working as a prostitute; one had not been heard of since in Liverpool. The cost of apprehension, detention and imprisonment of each prisoner was estimated to be about 100 guineas, not including the subsequent cost of transportation. The report contrasted the results and expenditure with the fate of juveniles sent to a reformatory institution in Warwick. From 1833 to 1841 77 boys, aged between 14 and 16, were admitted.

It was claimed that 44 had been reformed. The cost of reformation, including clothing and maintenance, was said to be about £25 per head.[16]

Reformatories and Industrial Schools

The economic argument was sound. Yet there were other reasons for the shift towards reformatories. The late 1840s were a time of great social unrest and revolution throughout Europe. There were genuine middle-class concerns about the lower classes rising up. The sight of thousands of hungry and desperate children roaming the streets did not bode well for future social harmony. Such fears led social reformers and philanthropists to consider new and experimental ways of treating young miscreants.[17] For Mary Carpenter, badly behaved boys were at risk of becoming adult criminals while lewd girls were heading for lives as prostitutes. Carpenter identified two classes among the immoral poor, the destitute and the delinquent, and called for the State to intervene. The former, including boys at risk of offending, could be offered training in industrial schools while the latter needed to be reformed. Carpenter's ideas bore fruit in the Youthful Offenders Act of 1854 and the Industrial Schools Act of 1857. The latter Act provided institutions for vagrant children aged between 7 and 14. To gain admission, children had to be issued with a magistrate's order confirming that they were 'unruly'. This covered children found begging or wandering the streets without any home to return to or lacking visible means of support. Children found in the company of thieves or those classed as beyond parental control were also eligible.

While convicted delinquents were put in reformatories, potential young criminals were sent to industrial schools. Liverpool already had a system of industrial education, although some felt that the training at the Kirkdale Industrial Schools, founded in 1843, was failing children. As part of their schooling, boys were given apprenticeships and girls put into service. Some were returned for laziness and theft from their employers. One lad spent ten of his twenty days out of the school in prison. A 12-year-old was returned after two days for having 'offensive breath'![18] A stipendiary magistrate remarked that 'from time to time the young female prisoners in the dock say that they have been brought up in the Kirkdale Schools. This must be a very unsuccessful institution, else so many of its scholars would not be brought before me.' Father Henry Gibson declared that boys from the Kirkdale school were rapidly transformed into thieves.[19] It was ironic that the school was situated close to the gaol.

The 1854 Act stated that boys could be sent to a reformatory after first spending fourteen days in prison. The minimum stay in the reformatory was two years, the maximum five. The Liverpool Reformatory Association, formed in 1855, founded various establishments. Troublesome girls did laundry work at Mount Vernon Green in Edge Hill or were sent to the Toxteth Park Girls' Reformatory. Here, in 1860, a number of disruptive girls tested the school's strict regime. The toughest matron in the Association had to be drafted in to restore order.[20] By 1860 4,000 young offenders were held in 48 reformatories throughout the country; by 1900 over 30,000 youngsters were lodged in over 200 state reformatories or industrial schools.[21] Many Catholic lads from the north-west were sent to the Mount St Bernard Reformatory in Whitwick, Leicestershire. In 1863 some were involved in a violent mutiny. During the subsequent riot, John Glennon beat a constable over the head with an iron bar.[22]

Yet reformation did not simply replace punishment. Flogging children was still a common cure for bad behaviour. Speaking to parents whose children had just been released from the Borough Gaol, the Anglican chaplain, Revd Carter, was often told that the parents had done their best for their offspring. When asked exactly what they had done, in nine out of ten cases the reply was that they had given their sons 'a good beating'. Boys were often sent to gaol for a couple of days, flogged and then discharged. Carter explained why they were not simply whipped at the police court and then released. The court was originally situated near the Exchange where merchants and businessmen congregated: 'it is so small that if a boy is flogged there his screams raise the whole neighbourhood'. Instead, the boys were beaten in the gaol 'which has a deterring effect only as long as boys keep out it'. In the 1850s the chaplain witnessed a 'little fellow' being whipped. The moment the beating was over the child pulled up his trousers and threatened the six-foot officer with vengeance on the outside.[23] Despite opposition from some campaigners, for almost 100 years, until its abolition in 1948, the birch continued to be seen as the solution to youth crime.

The movement to reform children rather than simply beat and imprison them was a slow process. Magistrates still had the option of sending youngsters to prison for more than fourteen days. It was not until the 1908 Children Act that imprisonment was finally abolished for children below the age of 14. However, the Crime Prevention Act of the same year also saw the foundation of youth detention centres as an alternative to prison. The first of these was in Borstal in Kent and the name was adopted by other centres throughout the country.

Youths in Liverpool prisons often reported that they had attempted to stow away on ships, either to escape the dismal streets for better climes or to become sailors. Many stowaways were discovered out at sea and sent back on the pilot boats. In 1845 the prison inspector asked a class of 31 juveniles in the Borough Prison if they wanted to go to sea. Twenty-seven said yes. The same question was asked at a prison in Manchester. Only one boy said yes.[24] This Liverpool obsession with the sea led to the use of training ships, or floating reformatories, as an alternative to prison. Young criminals could be isolated from their former associates while being closely monitored in the confined space of the ship. Detention on the vessel was not in itself a punishment but an attempt to introduce habits of discipline and provide useful training in seamanship. The *Akbar*, acquired in 1855, was a 50-gun frigate formerly used as a quarantine hulk off the Sloyne at Rock Ferry. It housed up to 200 boys, aged 12 to 16. Due to its dilapidated condition the ship was broken up in 1862 and replaced by another vessel. Discipline was strict but often breached. There were numerous attempts to set the ship ablaze. One attempt, in 1877, resulted in the arsonist receiving eighteen months' hard labour. Ten years later, a mutiny gave 17 boys the chance to escape by boat, although they were recaptured a few days later.[25] In 1907 the floating reformatory was finished. The ship was towed away and the boys sent to the Nautical Training School at Heswall.

In 1864 the Liverpool Catholic Reformatory Association decided to acquire its own training ship offering Catholic boys seamanship, carpentry and shoemaking. Through the efforts of Father Nugent an old warship called the *Clarence* was loaned from the Admiralty and berthed not far from the *Akbar*. Again, not all boys were appreciative of their training. In 1884 six arsonists managed to destroy the ship. Another vessel was acquired but two years later there was a serious mutiny led by a boy called Patrick Scully. Scully armed himself with a knife while his colleagues grabbed belaying pins and broken oars. The schoolmaster almost died after being stabbed. Other boys who tried to intervene were badly beaten. When help arrived in boats, the boys threw lifeboats overboard to capsize them. Only the arrival of the captain with a pistol quelled the mutiny. The boys were unaware that the weapon had no ammunition. Scully received five years' gaol while the other boys were handed twelve months' imprisonment.[26] In 1899 the ship was again destroyed by arson and the boys transferred to St David's College, Mold.

If they weren't trying to destroy the vessels, some lads were desperate to get back on shore, no doubt to resume their old ways. Escapees had a 20s bounty placed on their heads and parents were prosecuted for harbouring absconders. Some lads drowned during the third-of-a-mile swim to freedom. After countless escape attempts, one *Akbar* lad became such an expert swimmer that he won a medal in a swimming competition against lads from other reformatories. Some successful escapees found life on the Liverpool streets much worse than the ship and returned voluntarily despite the harsh conditions. Masturbation, for example, was frowned upon. The Captain reported: 'Smith who is nearly blind through bad habits is being kept in the sick bay for security and put in a straight jacket.' Not all boys were physically or mentally tough enough for life at sea. One lad called Saville suffered psychological problems. After he failed to drown himself he decided to hide away in the bowels of the ship in the hope that he would die of starvation.[27] For those not suitable for careers as sailors, an alternative form of training was given at the Liverpool Farm School, opened in Newton le Willows in 1858. The Birkdale Farm School, established in 1872, was the Catholic version.

Emigration

Liverpool's tearaways faced spells in prisons, reformatories, industrial schools, not to mention a good flogging, and yet a sizeable portion continued offending. Some social commentators held the view that while children remained in Liverpool they would continue to lead dissolute lives. The prison inspector commented that neither punishment nor public shame would change the behaviour of many of Liverpool's juvenile criminals. Only by removing them from their environment via transportation would they be prevented from offending.[28] Some children were sent to Australia but even after transportation was abolished in 1868 the idea of removing at-risk children from Liverpool remained. In 1870, in a pioneer emigration scheme, Father Nugent took a group of youngsters to Canada.[29] In 1881 the Catholic Children's Protection Society continued the scheme while Mrs Birt's Homes in Myrtle Street similarly catered for Protestant children. Emigration schemes had mixed results. Some children thrived in their new environment while others were simply used by families as a source of cheap labour. One magistrate even contributed financially towards sending a girl to America where her only relatives lived. Unfortunately, she arrived back in Liverpool on the same boat, having been seduced by the mate who promptly deserted her on landing.[30]

Women in Prison

It has been remarked that men have been the main subject of the criminal justice system for over two centuries.[31] Women, however, have played a major role in the Liverpool judicial system. In his charge to the grand jury in 1847 the Recorder commented on the large number of women appearing in court. In 1805, in England and Wales, the proportion of offenders was one female to four males. In Liverpool, in 1847, nearly 50 per cent of offenders appearing in court were women. The Recorder thought that the statistic was 'unparalleled' in any previous calendar.[32] The number of female committals to Walton Gaol in 1861 exceeded that of males (4,440 females to 4,419 males). The gap widened. Of 12,420 committals to the gaol in 1873, 6,673 were women.[33] Elsewhere in the country, the ratio of female to male prisoners did not normally exceed one-third.[34] The problem was particularly acute among a hard core of Irish Catholic women. In 1865 female Catholic committals to the gaol amounted to 2,253, 131 more than the total for male Catholics. Father Nugent declared that in no other prison in the world did the female convicts outnumber the men.[35] Common crimes committed by women were largely drink-related, for example fighting, smashing windows, swearing and assaulting policemen as they were being arrested. Flower-seller Bridget McMullen once held the national record for convictions. In 1897 she had been prosecuted 356 times for drunkenness, assaults, criminal damage and begging.[36] Women were also punished for illegal attempts at earning a living, for example unlawful pawning, being unable to account for property in their possession (particularly cotton), breaches of street trading regulations and prostitution.[37] By the end of the century the situation hadn't improved. In 1899 Liverpool women made up 46.96 per cent of the total number convicted of offences tried summarily. In London the figure was 26.90 per cent and for England and Wales, 23.89 per cent.[38]

In the early nineteenth century female vagrants and prostitutes were sent to the house of correction in Mount Pleasant. A contemporary observer recalls that 'in 1790 it was a vile hole of iniquity'.[39] Inmates could expect a rough time. Prison reformer John Howard noted that 'in the men's court is a pump, to which the women are tied every week and receive discipline'.[40] Until 1779, and perhaps even as late as 1805, women, dressed only in a flannel shift, were put on a ducking stool and immersed in a large bath in the courtyard.[41] This seems to have been performed for the men's entertainment, an early version of a wet T-shirt competition. Conditions in the Borough Gaol in Great Howard Street were also atrocious. In 1837 Captain Williams described the women as 'creeping alive' with vermin in their hair.[42] Ten years later their lot had not improved: 'Sometimes three, four or five women are placed in cells together, lying like pigs, doing nothing.'[43] The reformative value of such prisons was nil. When Mary Ann _____ was being searched on discharge, she was found to have hidden two prison petticoats. She ended up back in court.[44]

Brownlow Hill Workhouse

Unlike the Borough Gaol, the Brownlow Hill workhouse had plenty of work for the women to do. On the ground floor there was a bridewell for females, consisting of large cellars called 'oakum sheds'. Some of the inmates were prostitutes and others simply destitute, driven from the streets by the winter cold or illness. Several had been sentenced to a short spell for drunken brawling. In return for unpicking tarred rope, the women were served the barest minimum of food, usually a slice of bread and water. It was a particularly unpleasant task, which would rip their finger-nails apart. A few women were obviously ill and needed healthcare rather than punishment. Frederick Lowndes, the Liverpool police surgeon and chief physician of the Lock hospital, witnessed one prostitute crouched in the corner begging to be taken to the workhouse hospital.[45] He describes the physical condition of patients in the venereal ward: 'enormous condylomata and warts, buboes of some weeks standing in each groin, immense rupial crusts all over the body'.[46] Once discharged from the oakum sheds, many prostitutes were tempted back into the brothels.

Owing to the number of dissolute and desperate characters they attracted, workhouses were sometimes the scenes of crime, riot and disorderly behaviour. Due to a lack of proper segregation, respectable women who had fallen on hard times had to mix with out-and-out ruffians. Edward Rushton criticized the lack of discipline and supervision that allowed women to mutiny and run amok. He resented having to send unruly inmates to prison when the gaols were already overcrowded. He also criticized the placing of notorious women such as Ellen Roach in the open quadrangle where she was able to corrupt other inmates with her violent and rowdy behaviour. Roach was no stranger to the Police Court and seemed to divide her time between the prison and the workhouse.

Maintaining segregation between the sexes was another problem. The authorities could not suppress people's sexual needs, no matter how hard they tried. There was a wall topped with broken bottles separating the men from the women. However, the bottles had been knocked off and only smooth sandstone separated the sexes. Men would climb over to meet with the women. Indeed, women, wearing only their shifts, would use ladders to get at the men. Mary Smith and Charlotte Bright were caught using pokers to smash a hole through the wall.[47] In 1849 the workhouse sheds, which had been built to provide poor people with a night's lodgings, were said to have been taken over by a gang of 50 to 100 disorderly prostitutes who not only stole from other inmates but smashed the beds to pieces.[48]

Women's campaigner Josephine Butler was a regular visitor to the workhouse. She had moved to Liverpool in 1866, looking for a fresh start after the death of her daughter two years earlier. When Butler visited the oakum sheds she shocked the 200 inmates by sitting on the cold, damp floor and joining them in their soul-destroying work. The depressing experience inspired her to provide a 'House of Rest' for the incurable and later an industrial home to train destitute girls in more useful laundry work and envelope-making. Butler campaigned tirelessly to improve the lot of these unfortunate women, even caring for them in her home.

Butler's empathy with these women is remarkable, for they were not all likeable. Many were uneducated, foul-mouthed and brutalized. Around this time, a dozen of the workhouse's most 'violent, strong amazons' were in custody awaiting trial for beating to death one of the matrons.[49] In another incident, four inmates beat up and nearly killed a female member of staff because she threatened to inform the matron of their refusal to work. Later, in court, the 'vicious-looking' Eliza Jones shouted to her victim: 'It's a pity you were not murdered. I will kick the guts out of you the next time I see you.'[50] The charismatic Butler once quelled a potential riot in the workhouse punishment wing involving 100 women.[51]

Prison Discipline

Rough Liverpool women did not submit easily to prison discipline. In 1842, at Kirkdale, a woman placed in solitary confinement smashed up her bed, barricaded the door and threw a length of wood at the chaplain as he walked past her window. Some of the women were wild. According to one prison report: 'They are constantly going on the roof, and in fact all is confusion, insubordination, and misconduct of every description.'[52] The governor of Walton Gaol declared that the only group to give him trouble was 'the incorrigible class of females'.[53] Until 1933 Walton was a mixed prison. Basil Thomson, the deputy governor, revealed that 'as a rule, the men were easy to manage, but when it came to the women, the mere male prison official had to take his chance'. Liverpool lasses were said to be rougher than the native women he had met in his previous job in the South Seas. After he became the new chairman of the Prison Commission in 1895, Sir Evelyn Ruggles-Brise made a tour of the gaol. Thomson commented, 'I remember taking a wicked delight in showing him the Liverpool women as a sample of the material for which he had to legislate. I thought that I detected a faint blanching of his cheek as he emerged from the female wing.'

Thomson recalls the routine as the women were discharged at the end of their sentences. At seven in the morning the governor would enter the female section to be greeted by 30 to 40 women standing in their own clothes ready for release. The women would sing, not in unison, but any song that came to mind. The result was a tuneless racket, mixed with rude comments about the governor's appearance. Although he was usually a stickler for discipline, the governor would choose to ignore the women. He explained to Thomson that any attempt to punish them would make them worse and the news would go round the streets of Liverpool with the possibility 'you would be set upon in the streets'. Undeterred by such intimidation, his deputy thought that he would like to impose some order. The next morning he declared that until the noise stopped nobody would be discharged. He was surprised when the ploy worked and he could hear a pin drop.[54]

Present-day problems with drugs and contraband in prison are nothing new. At Kirkdale, the smoking habit was rife among women. They would climb up on the roof of their day house to trade their food allowance for tobacco from the men working in the garden. In 1837 one turnkey reported: 'We have had a number of prisoners addicted to the taking of opium, and the depriving them of it was like taking a child from the breast […] some of the women used to be wild for it. They tell me that out of prison their custom is to buy two pennyworth at a time, make it into pills, and swallow them.'[55]

Reformation

Re-offending rates among women were a cause of concern. Father Nugent pointed out that the yearly total of 5,000 female committals in 1877 represented only 700 individuals.[56] His Anglican counterpart, Revd Carter, was critical of the failure to reform inmates: 'Nearly the whole of these women […] have been returned to Liverpool to mix again with our population, and to spread *the leaven of their pernicious influence*.'[57] Most of the women were prolific offenders, particularly the prostitutes and drunks who almost served life sentences by instalments. It was felt that the fleeting nature of imprisonment was part of the problem. Father Nugent believed that 'female criminals are manufactured in Liverpool to a large extent by repeated short sentences. If young girls in the early stages of crime, drink and prostitution, instead of receiving again and again seven or fourteen days, received longer and more deterrent sentences this jail would not be crowded all the year round by young women who have been here 30, 40, and many of them over 70 times.'[58] For Nugent, longer sentences at least allowed time for reformation of the prisoner's character.

Another problem was that there was inadequate supervision once the women were released early from their sentences. Following the Habitual Criminals Act of 1869, a strict condition of a released prisoner's licence was that he or she was forbidden to associate with bad characters or lead a dissolute life. If the ex-prisoners had no visible means of earning an honest livelihood it could be assumed that they would relapse into crime and were liable to be recalled to prison. Ironically, for some, a spell in prison promised a better life. The chaplain at Kirkdale recounted the story of Sarah H., a prostitute who was persuaded by a friend to commit a petty theft in order to be sent to prison, 'for she had heard that a good situation would be given to a girl having conducted herself well in that place after the term of imprisonment had ended'. In her case she was disappointed and continued to lead 'a wretched and miserable life'.[59] In 1867 a Discharged Prisoners' Aid Society was formed, offering help either through emigration or in finding employment.[60]

The large number of socially inadequate female repeat offenders in the prison system proved that simply locking them up for short spells did not work. It was believed that many of these women were impossible to reform as they were too disruptive and generally unable to cope with harsh prison regimes. Since some of these women needed medical help rather than punishment, a supplement or alternative to prison was needed. By the late nineteenth century prison administrators and those in charge of penal policy increasingly pathologized female offenders by channelling 'feeble-minded' and drunken women into semi-penal institutions such as refuges, asylums, reformatories and rescue homes. In 1891, for example, two women charged with murdering their babies were considered to be insane and ordered to be detained in a lunatic asylum.[61] The Inebriates Act of 1898 removed alcoholics from the prison system. Inmates were mostly women although there were also institutions for men. One beneficiary of the new system was Margaret Sweeney. Between 1897 and 1905 she had amassed 49 convictions for drunkenness and wilful damage. After smashing the windows of a public house in Christian Street, Islington, she was charged not only with criminal damage but also with being an habitual drunkard. Sweeney was imprisoned for ten days followed by three years at the Lancashire Inebriates Reformatory at Whalley.[62] The institutions, however, proved a failure and by the 1920s they had largely closed down and the women were sent back to prison.[63]

Churches and philanthropists had a long tradition of providing prostitutes and unmarried mothers with education, work discipline and a large helping of religion. Yet attempts to help these women were hampered by the same sectarian divide that resulted in two separate floating youth reformatories on the River Mersey. Rather than embrace all-comers, the refuges asked women their religion on admittance. Some despondent and diseased specimens would be turned away. 'What a pitiful satire on nineteenth century Christianity,' commented the *Liverpool Review*.[64] The Willows annexe of Mount Vernon Green Reformatory would admit only Church of England girls. The Good Shepherd Sisters founded an asylum for penitent prostitutes newly released from prison. Opened in Netherfield Road, the Catholic home suffered vandalism. The nuns also met Orange hostility for being based in a Protestant neighbourhood.[65] Other institutes for the reformation and rehabilitation of prostitutes included the Liverpool Female Penitentiary, opened in Edge Hill in 1811, and the Benevolent Society for Reclaiming Unfortunate Females, established in Mill Street, Toxteth in 1838.[66] Admittance to these institutions depended upon penitence and the recognition that the individual had done wrong and was eager to repent and beg forgiveness.

Yet even a spell in a refuge did not guarantee reformation. Prison officials often referred women to the Penitentiary after completion of their sentences. Although their stay was voluntary, for some women the harsh regime must have seemed like an extension of their sentences. The annual reports of the institution often declare mixed results. While some women completed the recommended two-year stay and graduated to employment in service, others could not accept the strict discipline. The 1856 report shows that 43 of the 64 inmates left before completing their term.[67] Some women went back to prostitution while others were thrown out for bad behaviour, although not before many warnings. In March 1860 Eliza Rimmer and Elizabeth Whittle absconded and then pawned their shawls, which belonged to the Penitentiary. They were sent to gaol for three months.

Towards the end of the century, when reformatories were being considered as an alternative to prison, there was criticism that some women were treating the places as an easy option. If a prostitute was sentenced to a month's imprisonment she would plead with the magistrate that she wished to mend her ways in order to be sent to a refuge instead. After being made clean and given a good meal, she would find some excuse to sign herself out and then carry on as normal. This left no time for reformation.[68] Even some of those desperate to be reformed were liable to relapse after being treated with prejudice upon release. One young woman graduated from the Alwin Home for reclaimed prostitutes in Upper Stanhope Street and went into domestic service. After a tiff with her mistress the maid was reminded of her former station in life and that but for charity she would still be on the streets. She was so insulted that she walked out and did indeed go back to prostitution.[69] The reformation of prostitutes was clearly no easy task. Women faced so many obstacles, not least socio-economic and psychological, particularly crippling dependency on alcohol. Speaking of the futility of institutions such as the Liverpool Rescue Society, founded in Falkner Street in 1890, the *Liverpool Review* concluded: 'For every woman reclaimed there is another to take her place.'[70]

Such pessimism is understandable given the level of recidivism and the chronic nature of the underlying social problems. On the streets of Liverpool the police were daily faced with the problem of re-offending. Since it was not unusual to see some men and women imprisoned for the fiftieth or sixtieth time for some petty offence, it was clear to some people that prison and punishment did not work. Such a state of affairs also pointed towards the existence of a hard core of repeat offenders, in other words a 'criminal class'. For the press and various social commentators, Liverpool's criminal class had long been synonymous with the lower orders of Irish migrants and their descendants.

FIVE

'The Scum of Ireland'

For centuries the rural Irish have migrated, either to work, trade, beg or set up permanent home in Britain. For those wishing to travel to America, Liverpool was the gateway to the west. For as little as one shilling, travellers, known as 'deckers', would endure a rough crossing on the deck of the ship. By 1822 steam power allowed people to travel swiftly and regularly across the Irish Sea. Some would come over in spring for hay harvesting, remain for the corn harvest and return home in the autumn with money in their pockets. Besides these seasonal migrants, known as 'harvest men', pedlars and tramping artisans such as shoemakers would pass through Liverpool in search of work. The town also played host to paupers and convicted vagrants being deported back to their parishes in Ireland under the Settlement and Removal laws. In 1790 the Irish community in Liverpool numbered about 1,000. After the Irish uprising of 1798, and partly owing to growing rural poverty, migration continued to increase. In 1800 the number of Irish had reached almost 5,000, out of a Liverpool population of 77,653. By 1841 there were almost 50,000 Irish-born residents in a town of 286,656.[1]

Navvies

In addition to harvesting, Irish labour was required for construction work, particularly for the building of new houses for the growing population. Industrialization also saw widespread improvements in transportation. This called for a strong manual workforce to lay railways and roads, cut canals and expand the docks. Such men were known as 'canal bankers' or 'navvies', short for navigators.[2] The navvies worked sixty to seventy hours a week. A seven-day week was not uncommon. The work was hazardous with almost no consideration for safety. Indeed, workers would routinely drink alcohol on site. On 6 February 1827, at Edge Hill, an anonymous navvy became the first recorded fatality of the railway age: 'the poor fellow was in the act of undermining a heavy head of clay, fourteen or fifteen feet high, when the mass fell upon him, and literally crushed his bowels out of his body'.[3] From August 1844 to June 1846, 118 men were seriously injured excavating the docks. Eleven were killed on the spot and another 18 died in hospital shortly after. Other deaths were not recorded.[4]

Such heavy and dangerous work attracted big, rough, fearless men. To relieve the stress they swore, brawled and went on wild drinking sprees. The presence of distinctively dressed navvies in their moleskin trousers, canvas shirts and hobnailed boots provoked some terror on the streets. Not all labourers were Irish but it was the Irish who had the worst reputation. Head Constable Matthew Dowling described the Irish labourers working on the docks as 'the most reckless, violent set of people that can be imagined'.[5] The Irish workforce was a challenge to keep in order. In the mid-1840s the northern parts of Liverpool had a heavy concentration of Irish, some lodging in cellars and small houses they had broken into. According to Dowling, 'They assist each other and attack the authorities, whoever they may be; they keep the neighbourhood where they reside [...] in a constant state of uproar and confusion on Saturday nights, Sundays and Monday, and generally a portion of Tuesday.' The navvies lived by their own rules and routinely defied the authority of the watchmen and later the police constables. 'Some of my men on several occasions have been nearly killed by them; they make most violent assaults,' stated Dowling. Navvies were particularly dangerous, since they took home their sharp-edged spades, which doubled as deadly weapons. In December 1827 watchmen tried to disperse a group of Irishmen assembled in Harrison Street. One of the men warned the watchmen to keep out of it and added, 'Go it, boys, and remember that spades is trumps.' In the subsequent rumpus, one watchman had his head split open with a spade, one was stabbed with a pitchfork, one hit with a banister and a colleague cracked with a mallet.

The navvies specialized in particular unlawful activities, such as the illicit distilling of whiskey. The distinctly Irish district sandwiched between Vauxhall Road and Scotland Road was a hotbed of poteen production. From 1845 to 1848 over a dozen properties were raided by excise officers. Equipment was seized in Marybone, Maguire Street, Arley Street, Banastre Street and Ford Street. Patrick and James Traynor were regular offenders.[6] Head Constable Whitty complained that he would sometimes discover a still when raiding a house in pursuit of a thief but before he could get an Excise officer to come it had disappeared. 'The quantity of illicit distillation in this town', added Whitty, 'is very great indeed, and the smuggling too.'[7] Whiskey, which had been matured in the stills of rural Ireland, was shipped to Liverpool. If it could be successfully smuggled past the Customs and Excise inspectors it would then be distributed throughout the northern towns by Irish hawkers or agents.[8] In the Vauxhall district, the Irish would smuggle spirits to sell among their friends.[9]

Dowling also accused the navvies of issuing fake shillings and sixpences, particularly in the intervals between jobs. When times were hard the fake coins were a necessity. The navvies, however, did not make the coins. Dowling traced the money to an Irish family who came over with the men when they began work on the docks. Bringing bogus money into the country was big business. In March 1840 a search of a Dublin steamer berthed at the docks revealed three boxes of fake pennies. In August Bernard Hickey was stopped at the Clarence Dock with a huge box of dummy coins weighing seven stones. He had brought them over on the *Hibernia* steamer. In his pocket was a letter addressed to somebody called Thomas, warning him 'not to let his business be known to any person trading backwards and forwards, lest their profits should be injured by other persons entering the trade'. The public was warned of a quantity of copper coin of Irish manufacture circulating in the town.[10]

There was an uneasy relationship between the local workforce and the Irish. The Irish navvies were seen as bitter rivals for jobs. Because they were poor, unskilled and willing to work for little money, they flooded the market for day labourers and forced down wages. Over three-quarters of the entire dock workforce was Irish.[11] At Ellesmere Port, on the Wirral, a young navvy was bluntly told 'that I ought to consider myself a fortunate kind of Irish animal because I was not driven from the place with sticks or stones, as many of my countrymen had been before my coming, for no other reason than being Irish'.[12] These feelings of resentment were to increase dramatically in the mid-1840s. For it was during the Great Famine in Ireland that Liverpool experienced a dramatic invasion of poverty-stricken Irish. Between 1846 and 1853 roughly one-and-a-half million Irish people disembarked at Liverpool.[13]

The Famine Invasion

Although many went on to begin new lives in America, or moved to London and other towns, about 60,000 Irish people remained in Liverpool, making up the country's largest concentration of Irish-born people. Whereas other towns benefited from the skills and economic drive of the new arrivals, it was felt by some that the migrants who remained in Liverpool lacked ambition, energy or talents. They were the 'failures', wrote Head Constable William Nott-Bower in his autobiography published in 1926.[14] For *Porcupine*, the town was said to act as something of a sieve 'retaining the dregs and impurities of the ever-changing population and letting the clear grit pass through to havens beyond'.[15] It was as if Liverpool was being burdened with the very worst cases of humanity, the ones most likely to turn to crime to survive.

The numbers of Irish declined in the 1860s, but by then there were many Liverpool-born children of the Irish brought up in the expatriate enclaves around the Vauxhall, Exchange and Scotland wards. It is worth noting the distinction between the Irish-born citizens of Liverpool and the Liverpool Irish. The latter term refers both to the native Irish and to the English-born children of Irish parents. The offspring of Irish parents, raised in an Irish culture in distinctively Irish districts such as Scotland Road, would eventually exceed the number of Irish-born.[16] To their critics in the media, however, there was no great distinction as regards place of birth; they were all 'Irish'. By 1871 the population of the borough of Liverpool was 493,405. The number of Irish-born was 76,761, which amounts to 15.6 per cent of the population. Since relatively few Irish Protestants settled in Liverpool, most of the Irish were Roman Catholics. As there were few English Catholics in Liverpool, the terms Roman Catholic and (Liverpool) Irish were almost interchangeable.[17] Father Nugent, in 1870, estimated the Catholic (Irish) population of Liverpool to be at least 150,000.[18]

The town's nascent social services were simply unable to cope with the deluge of migrants. The Liverpool Domestic Mission Society concluded: 'Every tide floated in a new importation of Irish misery, and the snow was loosened from our doors by hordes of bare-footed beggars.'[19] It was felt that Ireland was simply unloading its problems onto England. Indeed, some migrants were sent over from the Irish workhouse after being given one shilling.[20] The flood raised three main concerns. There was the financial expense of supporting the migrants, the social cost of their lawless behaviour and finally political fears of Irish revolution. The year 1848 was the year of revolutions, a period of brooding social unrest in Europe.

Many Irish arrived in Liverpool with nothing but the clothes they stood in. Unlike the physically strong 'harvest men' of previous years, many Famine migrants were weak and sickly and unable to cope with strenuous work. Besides, the surplus of workers meant that even those seeking employment were left destitute. A report on vagrancy, addressed to the Poor Law Board, highlighted the laziness of some of the migrants. While acknowledging that the Liverpool Irish were less of a social burden than those who settled in Wales, the report's author noted: 'I fear they yield too readily to their disposition to idleness.' The worry was that the Irish would end up relying on casual relief, in other words charity.[21] In a letter from the Poor Law Commissioners, the folly of doling out relief indiscriminately was criticized: 'It cannot be supposed that Irish paupers will seek employment so long as they can live upon the alms so liberally bestowed by the inhabitants of Liverpool.' It was felt that giving donations not only discouraged the Irish from seeking work but also actively encouraged even more beggars to cross the Channel. The danger was that the level of charity would financially ruin the town.[22]

Before leaving the gangway of the ship the Irish were desperate to know the directions to the parish office where they could receive relief. Even as they were being medically examined at the docks they were begging for alms.[23] Stipendiary magistrate Edward Rushton claimed that within twelve hours of their arrival in Liverpool the Irish could 'be found among one of three classes, viz. paupers, vagrants or thieves'.[24] Some migrants refused parochial help in case they were sent back to Ireland, as poor-relief regulations allowed. This meant that they were likely to turn to begging and crime as an alternative source of income. Some Irish viewed with suspicion the free vouchers for soup in case they were tickets for a return journey.[25] They felt that they would rather die in Liverpool than be sent back to Ireland.

Some did just that. In December 1846 Sarah Burns, an Irish mother of seven from Thomas Street, died an appalling death. Between the Sunday and her death on Tuesday all she had eaten was a piece of bread. She had lived day to day by begging. The following month Mary Meganey, from Vauxhall Road, starved to death after having only a cup of tea in three days.[26] In May 1847, 8-year-old Luke Brothers died without 'the least particle of food in the stomach'. Since their arrival from Ireland, the Brothers family had lived in a 'wretched hole' in Banastre Street. The parents and their four or five children were allowed three shillings a week from the parish but it was doubtful whether they ever received that amount in full. A neighbour brought them the money and it was suspected that on one occasion at least she handed over only one shilling, presumably pocketing the rest herself. Whenever the sickly and starving children were well enough to crawl out of their room they begged from door to door. When they became weaker the opportunities for such relief became more remote. In the same room as the dead boy were five others lying on a mud floor suffering from typhus. There were also four other cases of fever in the same house.[27]

While some slipped through the net, others clearly exploited the system as soon as they arrived in Liverpool. The famished migrants immediately made for a shed in Fenwick Street where they were given bread and soup. Relief was doled out to families depending on the number of children they had. The claims were difficult for the officials to verify and scams were inevitable. In the Vauxhall district the Irish borrowed children. When a policeman visited the home of Mary Grimes (also known as Duff) in Gascoyne Street, he found on the floor of her coal vault, lying next to a large dog and some fowl, a skeletal 3-year-old child. A neighbour claimed that the mother hired out the emaciated youngster to professional beggars.[28] Indeed, some would hire a dingy cellar so that they could be visited there to receive relief.[29] In February 1847 an Irish beggar was found in Great George Street, apparently at death's door. When searched at the bridewell, he was found to have eight pence and four soup tickets. He was already in receipt of weekly parish relief. The following month an Irishwoman applying for relief was found to have seven soup tickets in her pockets. In January 1848 'a poor half-starved-looking man' called John Spencer was caught selling the soup tickets that he had obtained from the Parish Office. The magistrate dismissed the case since the tickets were the man's property.

The local population was understandably unhappy that the poor rates were being increased as more migrants arrived. At a meeting of ratepayers, one canny speaker suggested that the Irish be met off the boats, given bread, soup and a railway ticket to London.[30] One newspaper correspondent viewed the Irish poor as 'beggars by profession, people who would not work were it offered to them'.[31] The public was asked to refrain from offering charity so as to force the Irish to move on, find work or better still apply for official relief. That way, they could, theoretically, be identified and sent back to Ireland. The newspaper warned: 'To give a single […] penny to an Irish beggar […] is actually to pay him for stopping in Liverpool.'[32]

Yet Liverpudlians carried on giving. When the American landscape designer Frederick Olmsted toured Liverpool in 1850 he saw placards in the streets: 'The SELECT VESTRY inform their fellow-citizens, that in consequence of the extremely low price of passage from Ireland – 4d – great numbers are coming apparently with no other object than to beg.' The placard warned people against giving to the Irish. The following example was given: 'An Irish woman pretending to be a widow, was taken up, who had obtained 3s 2d in an hour and a half of her arrival. Her husband was already in custody.'[33]

The link between the Irish and begging scams had been made years earlier. George Forwood, assistant overseer of the parish of Liverpool, explained that the 'harvest men' sent their families begging while they were at work. When the employment season was over they would give their earnings to one of their party to take back to Ireland. They would then apply for relief as paupers. In the winter of 1830 some 63 per cent of paupers relieved by the Liverpool

District Provident Society were unemployed Irish. The following year, the figure was 71 per cent. In 1836 James Shaw, an agent of the Society, insisted that 'the Irish are more addicted to begging than the English and there are more imposters among the Irish than the people of any other country'.[34]

The Backlash

As the migrants continued to arrive, the press turned upon the 'Scum of Ireland':

> The people that come here from the sister island are not labourers [...] They are beggars and paupers. They never were labourers. They never did an honest day's work in their lives. They lived by begging [...] Thousands of cases could be proved, in which Irish beggars and paupers have come from Waterford and Dublin to obtain medical treatment in the cellars of Liverpool.

The answer was simple: 'Keep out the shoals of Irish and Liverpool, in three months, will cease being one of the unhealthiest towns in the kingdom.'[35] The Irish were also called 'semi-savages'.[36] Newspapers made capital out of the number of Irish appearing in court. The *Liverpool Mail* took pains to point out that of 145 prisoners brought up before the magistrate one Monday morning, 40 beggars and 30 thieves were from Ireland. The prisoners refused to return home despite the offer of a free passage and some warm clothes. One elderly man was said to making five shillings a day by begging.[37]

Evidence of the unsustainable flood of migrants was seen not only in the crammed police courts but also the overflowing hospitals and overcrowded prisons. Of the 90 patients in the Fever Hospital in 1847, 73 were Irish.[38] In May of that year a policeman found two people dying of the fever in Newhall Street. Since both the workhouse and the infirmary were full, he had to lock them in the bridewell with prisoners. Around the same time, somebody laid a small coffin outside the door of a Mr Hughes and refused to remove it until he had donated some charity, presumably the cost of burial. It was thought that the casket contained a dead child who had just landed from Drogheda.[39]

It was believed that the fever-ridden Irish threatened not only the health but also the moral welfare of the Liverpool population. In 1849 John Clay argued that the reason for high crime in Liverpool was the presence of the Irish: 'It is her peculiar misfortune that her harbour is too easily gained by a race of persons who, whatever may have been their habits at home, no sooner reach Liverpool, than such of them as are in a destitute state, either give way to the temptation to plunder round the docks, or become an oppressive and demoralizing burden to the town.' He further pointed out that although the Irish made up one-quarter of Liverpool's population, they provided more than half of its criminals.[40]

Others made similar points about the over-representation of the Irish in the criminal justice system. Giving evidence to a Lords' Committee in 1847, Edward Rushton stated that there had been no serious cases of crime or violence resulting from the influx of Irish.[41] Yet this was early days. Two years later, in a letter to the Secretary of State, Rushton revealed how greatly the Irish misery had increased crime in Liverpool. In 1846, 18,171 prisoners were brought before the police court; the following year the number had risen to 19,719; in 1848 there were 22,036. The Irish were blamed. The governor of the Borough Gaol spoke of the increased cost to the Liverpool ratepayer of policing, prosecuting and gaoling the significant number of Irish criminals. By this means, 'Ireland is still thrusting much of her pauperism on England'.[42]

The percentage of Irish-born offenders in Liverpool gradually decreased from 37 per cent in 1863 to 34 per cent in 1871, 24 per cent in 1881 and 16 per cent in 1891.[43] Whether the Irish, in percentage terms, committed a disproportionate amount of crime is a question that has exercised social historians.[44] The Victorians certainly viewed the Irish as more prone to criminality and not simply for obvious sociological reasons such as dire poverty driving the Famine migrants to steal or become prostitutes to survive. It was as if the Irish were biologically unequipped to deal with the complexities of modern city life. For one Edwardian writer, Liverpool's Irish population presented a 'serious problem':

> Gay, irresponsible, idle and quarrelsome, they seem by nature unfitted for the controlled life of a large town, which tends only to accentuate their feelings. It seems impossible for them to adopt the restraints, the responsibilities, and the sense of corporate citizenship which should be essential characteristics of the town dweller. They contribute abnormally to the work of the police court and fill the workhouse and charitable institutions. They are the despair of the social reformer while they win his heart with their frolicsome humour.[45]

The Irish are portrayed almost as unruly children. It is true that they were largely unskilled and uneducated. Some spoke only Gaelic. Many had rural traditions and had difficulty adapting to an urban society. It was a view long held. In 1835 a Liverpool man gave his own verdict: 'The Irish give infinitely more trouble, and are infinitely more riotous and disorderly in the streets, than any other class of persons, or than all others put together; they make a great deal of noise, they are in fact more accustomed to a country than a town life.'[46]

Drink was the undoing of the Irish. Captain Nott-Bower, Head Constable from 1881 to 1902, spoke of their 'reckless, violent disposition' and their 'unfortunate taste of preferring whisky, which makes them dangerous, to beer, which would make them sleepy'.[47] Dr Duncan was under the impression 'that spirits produce a greater effect on the Irish than on others. It makes them, in fact, insane when under its influence, and they are then so violent as to be regardless of the consequences of their acts.'[48] Indeed the behaviour of some Irish became more outrageous in their new country. Reverend Murphy, of St Patrick's Chapel, felt that the Irish 'become more drunken and greater thieves in general' than they had been in Ireland. These were 'the scum of the country', who had already 'forfeited their character' before they had even left their homeland.[49]

It must be said that much of the crime committed by the Irish was petty, opportunistic and driven by poverty or exacerbated by drink. Although there were a few who made a comfortable living out of crime, such as receivers of stolen goods, there was no major network of organized crime, no Irish mafia. In an 1836 report into the Irish poor in Liverpool, Head Constable Whitty observed: 'as to crimes against property, few robbers or regular thieves are Irish'. The Irish were probably more amateur in their approach, stealing only when the opportunity arose. Superintendent William Parlour revealed that one-third of people taken into custody in Liverpool were Irish, despite the Irish comprising only 25 per cent of the town's population.[50] It has been argued that as a proportion of the working classes in Liverpool, the percentage of Irish was nearer one-third. It was from the ranks of these poorer members of society that the prison population was largely drawn.[51]

What tended to land the Irish in court was alcohol-related violence. For Parlour, 'assaults are extremely frequent among the lower class of Irish, and in almost every case arise from drunkenness. There are perhaps from four to six cases of manslaughter among the Irish in a year, deliberate murders are very rare among them.'[52] The migrants mostly fought among themselves, 'Irish rows' being infamous. Through boisterous celebrations of weddings, wakes and St Patrick's Day, the Irish were also a visible and audible presence in the town and this often brought them into conflict with the police, who had the unenviable job of keeping order on the streets. The Irish would violently resist any attempts at arrest.

After the Famine influx, the situation worsened. The sheer numbers of Irish crammed into a limited space around the docks, together with the intensified levels of poverty, were bound to have social repercussions. In 1850 the prison inspector pointed out the presence of a large number of Irish in the Liverpool prison system. Not all were incarcerated for begging and trifling thefts. More than half were guilty of more serious offences. Indeed, the previous three criminals hanged in Liverpool (over a period of five years) had all been Irish. These included the notorious John Gleeson Wilson, guilty of slaughtering four people in Leveson Street.[53]

Five years later an Orange-supporting newspaper claimed that three-quarters of crime now committed in the town was by Irish papists: 'they are the very dregs of society steeped to the very lips in all manner of vice, from murder to pocket picking'.[54] Media accounts of crimes committed by the Irish only served to increase anti-Irish feeling.[55] Distrust and discrimination were rife among the middle classes. William Dillon, a local linen and woollen draper, felt that 'the Irish do a great deal more harm than good in Liverpool'.[56] 'No Irish need apply' was often put at the end of vacancies for domestic servants and errand boys. Between 1847 and 1885 the Liverpool Mercury regularly published such stipulations in its advertisements.[57] Victorian employers were indeed rather picky. One job advertisement promised good wages to a boy, although 'corner loafers need not apply'.[58] The advert echoes those stating, 'Windsor men need not apply', intended to deter unsuitable 'roughs' from the south-end district.[59]

In 1892 prominent Liverpool-Irishman John Denvir was still able to conclude: 'You seldom hear of Irishmen in connection with more serious crime.'[60] Yet in the aftermath of the Famine, the Irish were handy scape-goats for the social ills of the time. Although there were thousands of decent migrants struggling to bring up their families, newspaper representations of the Irish gave native Liverpudlians plenty of reasons to dislike them. To sum up: if the Irish worked, they undercut local labour in competition for jobs; if they didn't work, they were parasites, feeding off the industry of others and inflating the poor rates. They were seen as subhuman and uncivilized, addicted to drinking and brawling. They were dirty, diseased and depraved. They even looked like villains. Phrenologists believed that criminals could be identified by the unusual shape of their heads. John Clay admitted that he was no expert in the pseudo-science, but it was well known that criminals had small, ill-shaped skulls, with (and among the Irish particularly) 'foreheads villainous low'.[61]

Finally, there were, as one newspaper put it, hordes of lazy Irish in Liver-pool who became energetic only when there was booty to be obtained or a riot to be fought.[62] The Irish were indeed experts in rioting. Yet to be fair the tradition of riotous behaviour and direct action in Liverpool pre-dated the Irish invasion. From the eighteenth century people had been taking to the streets to air their grievances and make their voices known.

SIX

Protest, Riot and Disorder

The Victorians feared lower-class crowds, particularly when people banded together at political demonstrations, fairs and public executions. When such crowds met, public disorder was always a distinct possibility. Social reformer Mary Carpenter noted that the existence of the underclass was largely unknown to the middle and upper classes, 'but they may be seen in large numbers when a great exciting cause arises, whether a mob, or a trial of some of their associates, or an execution [...] when their wild yells and heartless demeanour reveal the worse than heathen barbarism which is in our midst'.[1] Yet, as historian R. M. Jones has written, 'The crowd may well have been one of the most important characters in the history of Liverpool.'[2]

A great deal of disorder in the eighteenth century involved the activities of the press-gang. The Impress Service, as it was properly known, provided recruits for Royal Navy warships. The tyrannical discipline of life aboard a man-of-war, compared to the relatively less strict conditions on merchant vessels, discouraged sailors from enlisting, hence the need for a little encouragement. To put it bluntly, the navy sanctioned the press-gang to impress (in other words, enslave) seamen. A thriving port, Liverpool was a prime target for their activities. In the eighteenth century about a quarter of Liverpool's adult male population was at risk of impressment.[3]

The press-gang was particularly busy during times of crisis. The resulting recruitment drives were known as 'hot presses'. During the American War of Independence the town council was prompted to encourage men to volunteer for bounties. In 1779 the incentive was increased to ten guineas for able seamen and five guineas for ordinary. During the hot press of 1794 sailings from Liverpool were embargoed as the Royal Navy prepared for the French War. The following year Liverpool was ordered to provide over 1,700 sailors for the navy. No ships were permitted to leave port until the quota was made up.

A crucial element in the press-gang operation was the 'rendezvous', usually an inn with a secure room used to hold new recruits before they were transferred to the press tenders, small vessels that would then take the men to the receiving ship. The inns in Pool Lane and Old Strand Street were used as bases.[4] The Liverpool press-gang consisted of 18 men, led by seven officers and supported by a flotilla of three tenders, each under the command of a lieutenant.[5] The leader of the Old Strand Street rendezvous was described as a rakish, dissipated, but determined-looking officer, in a very seedy uniform and shabby hat. His followers were 'fierce, savage, stern, villainous-looking fellows […] as ready to cut a throat as eat a breakfast'.[6] Sailors, or 'blue jackets', lived in constant fear of the press-gang. Some were seized while at sea. A navy warship encountering a merchant vessel would steal from the ship her best tars, leaving her with just enough crew to navigate home. In June 1755 the man-of-war *Winchelsea* attempted to capture the crew of the Maryland ship *Upton* as she entered the Mersey. Shots were exchanged, killing seamen on both sides. An officer of the *Winchelsea* was blasted in the cheek, the bullet passing clean through his mouth. Fifteen of the *Upton*'s crew were captured but two managed to swim ashore. Two others drowned in the attempt.[7]

In July 1759, in the Mersey estuary, four boats belonging to a navy warship called the *Vengeance* pursued the *Golden Lion*, a whaling ship returning from Greenland. Once the men boarded the whaler, the lieutenant in command threatened to conscript all crew except the officers if they did not volunteer. The 60-strong crew immediately reached for their harpoons and knives, vowing retribution. The terrified intruders jumped back into their boats, leaving their lieutenant aboard the *Golden Lion*, where he ordered the *Vengeance* to start firing at the whaler. The crew kept the lieutenant on deck so that he ran the risk of being hit by his own men. In the fierce battle that followed, several 9lb shots were fired in the direction of the town, one destroying a boat in a builder's yard but fortunately missing nearby spectators. Although the whaler's rigging and sails were damaged in the fray, she managed to reach the dock safely.

The crew of the whaler then rushed to the Custom House to renew their protections from impressment. However, the press-gang cornered them and fired several shots inside the building. The whaling men jumped out of windows and over walls and rooftops to escape. Even so, the captain and five crewmen were caught and impressed. The captives were taken back to the ship, followed by hundreds of angry men, women and children booing and hissing. The crowd then began to throw missiles, forcing the press-gang to fire shots over their heads to disperse them. In what appears to have been an accident, one woman was shot through the legs. Some determined women carried on the pursuit until they were up to their knees in the water.[8]

When the press-gang went on recruiting drives there would be confusion and panic in the maze of narrow dockside streets around Bridge Street, Wapping and Little Bird Street.[9] Not only did the gang invade brothels to kidnap sailors, men were also torn from their own homes without warning. Stonehouse recalls a man being seized in Pool Lane. He was not heard of for four years. When he returned, his wife was about to be married for the third time.[10] William Roscoe, Liverpool's MP and antiquarian, once lodged with a ship's captain who lived in nightly fear of the press-gang. The poor man drank himself to death.[11]

Yet the press-gang did not have it all their own way. Privateersmen made it their duty to rescue impressed men from the rendezvous. Indeed, sailors, riggers and ships' carpenters would also band together to forcibly liberate unfortunate colleagues who had been seized. The graving dock bells were used to signal sightings of the press-gang. Thousands would rally to the call.[12] Attached to the Old Strand Street gang was a 'piratical-looking scoundrel' called 'Jack the Nabber'. A contemporary witness recalls this fiendish individual being chased through the dockside streets by a baying mob. Trapped at the edge of the dock, Jack dived into the Mersey and swam to a nearby hulk. The crowd retired, satisfied that their sport could be renewed on another occasion.[13] Another infamous press-gang leader was 'Irish John' who led a 'motley crew of desperadoes'.[14] He was involved in many scrapes on the streets of Liverpool. On two occasions he was nearly torn to pieces and had his rendezvous gutted and furniture set ablaze in the street.

For the Liverpool public there was an understandable tradition of non-cooperation and hostility towards the gangs. If pressmen were spotted on the streets, the cry would go up, 'hawks abroad'. Mobs would jostle the officers and shield men from the gangs. In court, witnesses would refuse to testify against ringleaders accused of assaulting the pressmen. The community would also keep silent as to the whereabouts of seamen. Liverpudlians who informed on sailors to the press-gang risked a serious beating. In January 1777 an aggrieved woman who 'grassed' on her partner was dragged from her house in Frederick Street by a mob, stripped and ducked a number of times in the dock.[15] The sailor had recently married the woman in the north and brought her back to Liverpool. She had then discovered that he had been married before. Because he would not give her two shillings to return home, she decided to gain her revenge.

The headquarters of the press-gang were occasionally gutted and levelled to the ground. In 1762 the rendezvous at the Talbot Inn, in Water Street, was attacked by a mob of 200 men in an act of revenge for 25 sailors being impressed. Troops sent to protect the building were injured. One man lost an eye, another his thumb and a soldier was stabbed in the leg. The inn was then set ablaze and its contents destroyed.[16] Fourteen years later, the press-gang tried to seize a sailor called Boulton from his house. The man immediately grabbed his blunderbuss and shot dead a lieutenant.[17]

The press-gang could be just as ruthless. In 1780 they paid an evening visit to the home of James Richards in Hackins Hey following reports that there were several sailors taking refuge inside. Richards refused to open the door and in the ensuing half-hour siege, during which shots were fired at the house, he was blasted in the face. Robert Higginbottom, a member of the Yorkshire Militia who was visiting the premises, was also shot in the stomach and died the next day.[18] In 1793, in Redcross Street, an attempt was made to abduct Captain Felix McIlroy, master of the sloop *Ann*. During a scuffle, one of the gang shot him dead. The next evening, in an act of revenge, a group of sailors attacked the rendezvous in Strand Street before gutting another in New Quay.[19]

Navy recruiting officer Captain Fortescue wrote: 'There is not a seaport in England where a man fights so much uphill to carry on the impress service as Liverpool.' Two of his terrified officers could not face a night's duty 'without keeping [to] their room a month afterwards'. Indeed, one of his men, Lieutenant Skryme, almost went mad with stress. In August 1762, as Lieutenant Rogers walked about the town, a large mob armed with firearms and cutlasses fired two pistols at him. He saved himself from being butchered by escaping over the roof of a house. Captain Smith Child also lived in constant terror of mobs rescuing impressed men from his tender. Turbulent crowds had already ransacked and pulled down two rendezvous.[20]

It was this ongoing tension between the press-gang and the town's seafaring community that helped forge Liverpool's spirit of rebelliousness and defiance. Indeed, Liverpool's fierce resistance to impressment gave it a reputation as one of the most brutal ports in the country. From 1739 to 1805 there were 66 violent incidents directed against the press-gang and its allies.[21]

The Sailors' Strike

Violent opposition to the press-gang was not the only form of disorder on the streets of Georgian Liverpool. During the American War of Independence, Liverpool shipping received a setback, resulting in severe unemployment among mariners, particularly those employed in the Africa trades. On 25 August 1775 the town's seamen were devastated by the news that their wages would be slashed from 30s a month to 20s.[22] With over 2,000 unemployed sailors in the town, the men had little bargaining power. However, they were not going to take the matter lying down. To the cheers of crowds of dockside spectators, angry seamen began slicing the rigging of the *Derby*. A group of constables, armed with pistols and cutlasses, dashed to the scene to restore order. Nine of the crew were arrested and taken to the town hall to face instant justice. The prisoners, along with a female supporter, were locked up in the dungeons of the Tower prison.

However, the trouble was only just beginning. Many more seamen began clambering up the rigging of ships about to sail to hack at the ropes. Meanwhile an armed mob, 2,000 to 3,000 strong, marched to the Tower to set free the prisoners. The authorities, fearing anarchy on the streets, wisely decided to release the captives. Yet despite this action, sporadic eruptions of vandalism and riotous behaviour continued, until the drunken festivities fizzled out at midnight.

The following day the seamen paraded through the streets in protest. The next day, being Sunday, allowed a period of peaceful respite. However, on the Monday about 150 strikers scoured the docks urging support for their cause and beating up those who dared carry on working. The atmosphere in the town turned menacing as sailors tramped around in gangs, knocking at the doors of wealthy merchants asking for money. On Tuesday, after negotiations between their leaders and some merchants, the seamen mistakenly thought that a settlement had been reached. However, when they realized that their wages were not going to be restored, the mood of optimism turned sour.

The magistrates had already hired a body of special constables to quell the anticipated disorder. These were public volunteers (usually middle class) sworn in for emergencies to help maintain public order during disturbances and riots. By nine o'clock in the evening, hundreds of disgruntled sailors surrounded the Town Hall in High Street, known as the Exchange. Inside the building were 120 armed constables as well as magistrates and merchants seeking sanctuary. The Riot Act was read from the balcony, as the protestors laid siege to the building, bombarding it with missiles. Suddenly, a volley of shots fired from within the building killed three protestors and wounded 15 others. The mob fled.

The next day the men sought revenge by visiting the homes of merchants they thought were responsible for their plight. Houses were ransacked and an arms warehouse and gun shop looted. Armed with muskets, swords, blunderbusses, knives, cutlasses, clubs and bricks, the men combed the streets demanding money from rich businessmen. The protesters hauled three cannons from a ship berthed in the South Dock and dragged them to strategic points outside the Exchange. At one o'clock the mob blitzed the building as those inside returned fire with their own muskets. Since the solid walls of the building offered the better protection, the rioters came off worse, with four fatalities.

Later in the afternoon a message was sent to the Royal Regiment of Dragoons in Manchester seeking urgent help. A hundred cavalrymen and six officers rode through the night, taking rest at Prescot. On being informed that an attack awaited them at their destination, they continued their journey with loaded weapons, arriving in Liverpool at four in the afternoon. The disturbances were soon quelled and suspected ringleaders rounded up and imprisoned. Throughout the following month the troops remained in the town to keep order. Fourteen men were later taken to Lancaster Gaol to await trial. At the Lent Assizes in 1776 eight were found guilty, although all 14 of those accused received the very same punishment. They were discharged on condition that they joined His Majesty's Navy.

By the 1850s Liverpool was a disorderly town where outbursts of collective violence were common and almost inevitable. Whether it was in defence of sectarian borders or cultural traditions or whether arising from legitimate political demonstrations or accompanying outbreaks of looting, riot became a typical form of Liverpool protest.

Sectarian Disorder

In a strange town, the Irish typically banded together, particularly when faced with threats from the authorities. In June 1819 a man called Murphy was arrested for being in possession of rope at the docks. He called to bystanders for aid, appealing to them as 'fellow Irishmen'. This resulted in an affray between the dock police and a crowd of Irish. In a separate incident on the same day, as watchmen attempted to arrest two women, a crowd of onlookers made attempts to rescue the prisoners. Despite cries of 'Let them go – rescue them,' the watchmen managed to escort the women to the bridewell. The situation escalated with the arrival of a troop of Irish mercenaries ready to sail for South America. A crowd, 8,000 to 10,000 strong, gathered outside the bridewell demanding the women's release. The troops ripped up the pavement and smashed their way into the building. Two constables were dragged from Hanover Street and thrown into the Mersey. Fortunately, the officers managed to grab hold of a ship to avoid drowning. The mob gave three cheers and went off in search of more constables. By chance, English soldiers had just disembarked from Ireland and were able to quell the trouble.[23]

In the spring of 1839 there were violent disturbances between the Irish and the carpenters at the south docks. Along the docks, the work of the shipwrights and carpenters was a Protestant closed shop. The Orange celebration of 12 July was also known as 'Carpenter's Day'.[24] Animosity between the carpenters and the Catholics went back a long way. As early as April 1746 a mob of carpenters set fire to a Catholic chapel in Edmond Street. The following month they also torched a lady's house in which there was a private Catholic chapel.[25] The latest trouble originated in false rumours circulated by both sides. The carpenters had heard that 3,000 men were on their way from Dublin to attack them. The Irish believed that the Protestant carpenters were going to pull down St Patrick's Chapel. In Park Lane, the police dispersed 400 Irishmen armed with staves, pikes and bludgeons. Public houses around New Bird Street were trashed as sporadic skirmishes erupted in various parts of the town. Reinforcements from the north end joined the Irish ranks until a 500-strong mob took on the police. However, the newly disciplined force was more than a match for the rioters, despite stones being stockpiled in anticipation of further trouble.

The authorities were to face a great deal more trouble from the Irish as increasing numbers of migrants attempted to settle into the existing social, religious, cultural and political landscape. Politics and religion were inseparable in Liverpool where sectarian animosities were related to party affiliation. The Anglicans were Conservatives and the Catholics Radicals. In early nineteenth century Liverpool municipal election campaigns were rowdy affairs fuelled by drink and marred by bribery. Antagonisms would be inflamed by the parading of effigies of unpopular rivals. Insults would lead to fights and candidates would be pelted with stones. Large noisy gangs would march through the town, sometimes smashing windows displaying rival party emblems.[26]

Working-class Toryism became closely linked to Orangeism as the century progressed. The Liverpool Lodge was formed in 1807 and by 1830 the town could claim 13 Lodges.[27] Although the Irish had a tradition of St Patrick's Day parades, which in theory were open to all Irishmen, the occasion was viewed as a Catholic celebration and this might have motivated Orangemen to hold their own parades. While Orangemen believed that it was their right to roam the King's highway, Catholics viewed the demonstrations as a reminder of the 'Protestant Ascendency', a mark of their subservience and lack of political power. Resentment and hostility from Liverpool's large Catholic population meant that Orange marches were regularly accompanied by outbreaks of violence.

On the Catholic side, a new form of communal society called Ribbonism also developed. Ribbon societies, with their identifying ribbons, secret oaths and passwords, existed on many levels, political, social and cultural. In one sense, Ribbonism was an underground nationalist movement formed in support of an independent Ireland to be achieved by armed insurrection. Ribbon societies were the Catholic equivalent of the Lodges and provided a force of opposition to Orangeism. Ribbon societies also acted as trade unions by offering members workplace solidarity, although there was also a hint of a protection racket. Many dock labourers were 'ribbon men'. With Irish migration, Ribbon societies developed in centres of Irish settlement, particularly in the public houses, which acted as welfare and information centres for those newly arrived from Ireland. Members of organizations such as the Ancient Order of Hibernians would offer hospitality and support to compatriots. Although Ribbon societies did not advocate terrorism, they were not averse to violence. In County Down, a group of Ribbonmen, known as 'Thrashers', identified themselves with greetings attuned to the season and the hour of the day or night:

'It's a dark night.'
Brother Thrasher: 'And so are our enemies.'[28]

Members, some of whom went on to migrate to the north of England, were given secret passwords to be used when a fight threatened. One such password was, 'Provoke me not, Sir.' The reply, 'I hope you will not give me reason,' identified an associate.[29] In December 1851 Patrick M'Tagg smashed the windows of a public house in Addison Street before assaulting the publican, Francis Heany. In court, M'Tagg stated that the premises were used by a Ribbon society and that he was being pressured to join. He also claimed that Heany was 'commander of 1000 men'. This was not seen as a good enough reason for vandalism and M'Tagg was fined.

On 12 July 1819 Liverpool's first Catholic–Orange riot erupted after 90 Orangemen attended St Peter's Church for a service marking the Battle of the Boyne. Accompanied by a band, a procession carrying Orange insignia toured the town via Lord Street and Castle Street. Waiting for them at the bottom of Dale Street were 2,000 Catholics. One Irishman shouted, 'Now, my boys, it is time to begin.' The words were the signal for a volley of missiles which left many Orangemen bruised and injured. Poles holding Orange banners were broken into cudgels and used to smash heads. Eleven ringleaders were arrested and received three months' imprisonment.

Another riot took place the following year. Sensing a violent pattern emerging, in 1822 the authorities banned Orange marches in Liverpool. The ban remained until 1842. Instead, Orangeman took to celebrating in the public houses. Predictably, Catholics went looking for them. On 12 July 1824 groups of Irish labourers congregated in the neighbourhood of Preston Street, Whitechapel and Williamson Square to insult Orangemen as they attended their clubs. Sectarian trouble was difficult to subdue. Orange funerals accompanied by elaborate processions became a substitute for full-blown parades and attracted the same sort of attention from Catholics. After the marches were banned in the town, the processions were replaced by outings to the nearby countryside, a welcome escape from the squalid slums. Catholics would be waiting for the Orangemen when they returned.

In the mid-1830s Orangeism became a formidable political force in Liverpool. The reform of local government in 1835 opened up a wider electorate battling for power over the corporation. The Liberals took control. In response, the Tories began to exploit anti-Catholic feeling. The 'No Popery' campaign began in 1835 with the decision to make the town's two schools non-denominational. Such attempts to promote religious harmony only divided the parties and inflamed sectarian tensions. The Irish rioted again on 12 July 1835, after rumours spread of an Orange procession. The disturbance, however, was more a battle between Catholics and the police than between Catholics and Orangemen. A crowd of Irishmen, many of them drunk, gathered around Tithebarn Street, Vauxhall Road and Marybone but caused no trouble. At 10 p.m., however, a row erupted in Ben Jonson Street and the night watchmen arrested one of the ringleaders. The crowd then turned on the watchmen and rescued the prisoner. Another disturbance took place simultaneously in Great Crosshall Street. Watchmen from surrounding areas were drafted in to help out. Outnumbered, the watchmen were driven up Great Crosshall Street towards Tithebarn Street, eventually taking refuge in Vauxhall Road bridewell, which was surrounded by 2,000 Irishmen armed with bludgeons. The attackers used axes to break down the door, forcing the terrified watchmen to retreat to a loft. Safely barricaded, they rang the bell to summon help. M. J. Whitty, Superintendent of the Night Watch and Fire Police, based in nearby Hatton Garden, heard the alarm. He raced to the scene and was fortunate to gain access to the building. He called for assistance from all over the town. Reinforcements arrived and drove back the Irish and arrested three ringleaders. The Irish regrouped and resumed their attack on the police. Meanwhile, help continued to arrive from all quarters. William Parlour, head of the daytime police, came with some of his men. Mathew Dowling, Superintendent of the Dock Police, arrived with 100 men and Alderman Sir Thomas Brancker brought 200 troops from the 80th Regiment. An extra 400 special constables were also sworn in as a precaution. In all there were fire police, night watchmen, day police, dock police, 500 special constables and 200 troops, the greatest show of strength that the corporation had ever called upon.

The disturbance was quelled but as the prisoners attended court on the following Monday, crowds of Irish gathered in Park Lane in the south end, still waiting for the Orange parade. There were cries of 'ten pounds for the head of an Orangeman'.[30] William Parlour arrived to assure them that there would be no parade. He was not believed and the mob, some armed with staves, drove away the police. The 80th Regiment was recalled to regain control. The crowd threatened to attack the bridewell if the prisoners were not released. They then marched to Vauxhall Road to meet up with the north-end Irishmen. However, despite the tense atmosphere, there was no further trouble. Between 60 and 70 people eventually appeared in court.

Two years later, during the 1837 election campaign, relations between the police and Catholics further deteriorated. Early in the morning of 25 July Irishmen carrying bludgeons met in the Vauxhall ward. In nearby Tithebarn Street, rioters confronted the police with cries of 'Come on, let us kill them.' Whitty led the police in dispersing the crowd before arresting the ringleaders. After more trouble, reinforcements were requested. At the same time, 1,000 Irish gathered in Park Lane. The police were beaten and retreated. There was more trouble in Great George ward. In the north end, Whitty became trapped by a mob of Irishmen but managed to fight his way out of the melee. He returned with more police who fiercely attacked the rioters. In the south end the Protestant ships' carpenters went on the rampage and attacked Irishmen and Liberals. The disturbances took place all day. In Greenland Street in the south end, Irishmen shouted, 'Murder the bloody Protestant,' as they beat an old Irish woman. Several police were injured trying to maintain order.

The Burking Riots

Sectarian hostility was not the only source of mayhem involving Irishmen. During the cholera epidemic of 1832 a fear of 'burking' led to several cases of public disorder in Liverpool. 'Burking' was the practice of illegally selling dead bodies to anatomists for medical research, a crime synonymous with the case of Burke and Hare in Scotland. Before the 1832 Anatomy Act, dissection of corpses was illegal, despite the need for medical students to study the workings of the human form. In 1827 William Burke and William Hare began a lucrative business suffocating tramps and prostitutes to sell the unmarked bodies to surgeons. Burke was hanged after confessing to 16 murders.[31] From then on people who killed in order to sell the body for dissection were called 'Burkers'. 'Resurrectionists', on the other hand, exhumed and sold cadavers. They were also known as 'bodysnatchers', 'fishermen' and 'sack-'em-up-men'. It was not unknown for gangs to sell a body to one surgeon, then steal it back and sell it to another. Another scam involved delivering a comatose drunk in a sack, and pocketing the money before quickly disappearing.

Yet the practice of selling bodies was flourishing in Liverpool years earlier. Corpses would be smuggled into the dissecting rooms in Pomona Street and Seel Street.[32] In 1823 a newspaper correspondent complained about the stench that had been wafting for about a week from a cellar in Great George Street. Such was the sense of unease at the time regarding dissection that he wondered whether it contained body parts, particularly since a putrescent head wrapped in a parcel had been found in a Pomona Street cellar a week earlier.[33] Three years later three casks, labelled 'bitter salts', were sent to George's Dock bound for Leith in Scotland. After dockers noticed a foul smell, the casks were removed to the Old City Deadhouse in Chapel Street. Here, 11 bodies, salted and pickled, were found. When questioned, the carter who had transported the containers revealed that he had taken them from Hope Street. Here, police found a further 20 cadavers in a cellar. One cask, one-third full of brine, contained the bodies of babies. The corpses had been disinterred from the cemetery attached to the workhouse about a quarter of a mile away. Anatomical lectures were just beginning in the Scottish medical schools. Because of the regulations, anatomists would send to England for bodies, paying between £10 and £15 each. James Donaldson, the leader of the gang responsible, was convicted and sentenced to twelve months' imprisonment.

The incident was not an isolated one. Mary Harrison died in October 1827 and was buried at Walton churchyard. The next day her grave was empty. Enquiries led police to the Seel Street home of surgeon William Gill. A search of his rooms uncovered an infant's body preserved in spirits and the dissected body of a woman believed to be from Ireland. There was no sign of Mrs Harrison until somebody suggested that the officers search the property next door. Here they found the woman with the skin stripped from her face.[34] So common was the practice that a surgeon in Hunter Street was constantly disturbed at night by the noise of grave-digging in the neighbouring churchyard. One evening his wife was interrupted by a knock on the door. Two rough-looking men asked, 'Do you think the doctor wants a kid?'[35]

It was against a background of fear, ignorance and mistrust of doctors that the impoverished Irish resisted medical intervention. In an age when the authorities often failed to give the lower classes adequate protection or social justice, the poor found it difficult to believe that the medical profession could have any concern for their welfare.[36] Some believed that cholera was a mere invention of the doctors to fill their pockets and that hospital patients were victims of cruel experiments while living and subjects for the dissecting knife when dead.[37] The Irish, in particular, didn't want the bodies of their loved ones removed for it was their custom to hold boisterous wakes in their own homes.

The Irish were also reluctant to allow people to be taken to hospital for treatment. In May 1832 a desperately ill woman called Clarke, from a cellar in Perry Street, had to be taken to the hospital in Toxteth Park. In the evening a palanquin (a covered stretcher) arrived at her house to transport her. However, friends and relatives feared that she was going to be used for anatomical dissection. During the entire journey a mob of women and boys followed, hooting at the medical attendants. Shortly after, the woman's husband became ill and also had to be removed to the hospital. About 1,000 people surrounded the building shouting, 'Bring out the burkers!' and 'There go the murderers.' Three of the four ringleaders were Irishmen. Stones were thrown at the windows of the hospital, smashing one in the room where the dying woman lay. Anyone believed to be a doctor was physically attacked. Police were initially overwhelmed and reinforcements were required to quell the riot and disperse the mob. The woman died in the evening. In the ensuing frenzy, a woman leaving the Lime Street cholera hospital was attacked, presumably because she had allowed a relative to be admitted.

There were other incidents when crowds attempted to rescue patients. One sick woman was forcibly released from medical care and taken back to her infected hovel where she promptly died. A surgeon called to a patient in Vauxhall Road was attacked by a crowd who claimed 'the doctors merely wanted to get the poor into their clutches to Burke them'.[38] Throughout May and June there were similar disturbances across Liverpool. The riots stopped only after priests pleaded with parishioners to cooperate with medical efforts to control the spread of the disease.[39]

The Corn Law Riots of 1841

Other forms of protest were inevitably hijacked by sectarian animosities. On 9 June 1841, 20,000 people attended an Anti-Corn Law Association meeting in Great George Place. The Corn Laws (passed from 1815 to 1846) protected the interests of farmers and land-owning MPs by banning foreign corn imports and keeping the price of bread artificially high. The crowd included a few thousand Irish. Around this time wild rumours were circulating of the 'murder' of seven Protestant clergymen in Ireland. Thinking that the meeting was to do with religion, and being generally hostile to Catholics, some shipwrights' apprentices threatened disruption. They were soon dispersed by the police who had anticipated trouble by hiding in nearby St James' Market. The apprentices later regrouped at the top of Parliament Street, armed with bludgeons. They then threw stones at the police who made another charge. In the commotion some apprentices descended on St Patrick's Chapel in Toxteth Park where they smashed the windows, together with those of the adjacent school. Mrs Sullivan, the wife of a policeman, was saying prayers in the chapel and suffered such a fright that she took to her bed and died days later.[40]

There was another anti-Corn Law meeting the next day. Afterwards, large numbers of Irish sought revenge by smashing the windows of a school in Moorfields and several public houses frequented by the apprentices. The next morning the shipwrights heard rumours that the Irish had damaged their club in Bond Street. Up to 2,000 left their work at the docks and marched to the town centre to hand in a petition to the Mayor. In James Street they were stopped by Head Constable Whitty and his men. Further trouble was avoided after he gave promises of protection. It was a tense time. In Whitty's own words: 'My men were occupied without intermission, in pursuing the most desperate mobs, armed with every kind of weapon, and dispersing dense crowds of curious and idle people.'[41] The Corn Laws were repealed in 1846, although the legislation did not come into full operation until 1849.

In the absence of Orange processions, elections became focal points for sectarian disorder. In 1841 the three-day parliamentary election saw more trouble between carpenters and the Irish. Shortly after the anti-Corn Law protests took place, at the end of June, Whitty once again had to save the town from disturbances. Riots erupted in the south end as carpenters' boys paraded with their sticks and renewed old grudges with the Irish. Dale Street was also the scene of disorder. Two carpenters were badly beaten in nearby Tithebarn Street. In Vauxhall Road the 'lower orders' went on the rampage, smashing up the houses of the wealthy. In one house a feeble old woman was badly mistreated. Even young girls wearing Reform colours were chased down the streets, kicked, abused and the ribbons torn from their necks. Men wearing the wrong colours also had the clothes ripped from their backs. In Great Cross-hall Street a mob of 2,000 greeted the police with volleys of bricks. On 8 July, as the Legs of Man pub in Salthouse Dock came under attack, the landlord shot at the mob, injuring three people. In further disturbances both factions turned on the police who had arrived to quell the trouble. Around this time, Irishmen began to adopt a new tactic by climbing onto the roofs to throw slates at the people below.[42] A Protestant called George Myers (or Meyers) was killed, the first casualty of this new form of urban warfare.

After a gap of twenty years the first Orange Parade took place on 12 July 1842. Inevitably there was trouble despite the presence of mounted police armed with cutlasses. Protestants were mistaken for Orangemen, dragged out of their houses and attacked. Carpenters were badly beaten in Lime Street. In response, some Orangemen armed themselves with pistols. On 15 July, in the south end, Catherine Carney was called an 'Orange and an Irish bastard' before being kicked and beaten to death by two unknown men.

The Chartist Threat

If the authorities didn't have enough to contend with keeping the peace between rival sectarian factions, there remained a pervading threat of insurrection in relation to Chartism. Chartism was the first large-scale working-class movement in Britain, aimed at improving conditions for the poor and giving them their rightful share of political power. In support of the 'People's Charter', the Chartists held numerous demonstrations and protests in a bid to extend the vote to all men over the age of 21. They also sought to abolish the property qualifications that prevented working men standing for Parliament. They presented three mass petitions to Parliament in 1839, 1842 and 1848.

The rise of Chartism helped to further the threat of the rebellious poor. Yet once again in Liverpool working-class politics became bound up with Irish problems. Although many northern industrial towns saw Chartist activity, and despite Liverpool's strong history of political militancy, the place remained surprisingly quiet. There were a number of local Chartists but the movement had little following in Liverpool.[43] It was not until 1848, when Irish-Catholic protests and the aims of the Chartists briefly converged in a series of joint meetings, that the Liverpool authorities showed some alarm. These were revolutionary times. In addition to serious disorder in Paris, trouble was also brewing in Ireland as Repealers campaigned for an end to the Act of Union. In 1846 the Repeal movement had divided. Those who split from the main body became known as 'Young Ireland' and 'Confederates'. A number of secret Confederate clubs, with names such as 'the Sarsfield', 'the 82' and 'the Robert Emmett', sprang up in Liverpool. An estimated 30 to 40 clubs had the power to quickly muster between 2,000 and 4,000 armed men on the streets.[44] It was feared that these Liverpool Irish militants would use physical force to achieve their goals, perhaps even rising up in response to a successful rebellion in Ireland. In the words of social historian John Saville, 'There was no town with more violent potential in the whole of England.'[45]

Against this background of simmering social revolution, the massed ranks of the Liverpool poor, the unemployed and the Irish were viewed with trepidation. The tension was heightened in April when Dr Laurence Reynolds, a Young Irelander, told the audience of a joint Chartist–Confederate meeting in Liverpool that he intended opening both a foundry in Leeds Street and an ironmonger's shop to make and sell cheap weapons such as muskets, pikes and swords.[46] To make the arms accessible to the poor, an instalment plan was drawn up. Fourpence a week for twelve weeks could buy a pistol. The threat of an uprising was taken seriously. In the summer two men were arrested for carrying pikes. Reynolds' salesman, Joseph Cuddy, took some weapons to a metalsmith for sharpening. When asked what they would be used for he replied, 'To kill people with.'[47] In police raids, pikes and bullets were seized from known Confederates. Officers discovered a cache of 500 cutlasses and canisters of gunpowder hidden in a cellar. Police also searched a number of houses in Thomas Street. In rooms belonging to Richard King, used by Chartists for drilling, a musket was found. In the home of Charles James, described as 'a notorious Chartist', a blunderbuss and pike head were discovered.[48]

The Liverpool police anticipated trouble by practising with cutlasses. They also sought help from other forces and enrolled thousands of special constables. When word arrived of an attempted uprising in Tipperary, 500 Liverpool dockworkers were sacked for refusing to be sworn in as specials. A military encampment was formed at Everton and 2,000 troops stationed in the borough.[49] However, despite or perhaps because of these precautions, the Chartist threat turned out to be a damp squib. Nor did the uprising in Ireland take place.

After the Famine

Whereas Chartism was dominant in some northern towns, it was sectarian conflict that continued to define Liverpool. After the great Famine influx of 1847, anti-Irish feeling increased, fed by daily newspaper reports of begging, crime, filth and disease among the newcomers. Tensions were punctuated by bouts of senseless violence on both sides. After an Orange parade in July 1850 a mob gathered outside the Chadwick Street home of Henry Wright. Stones were thrown, smashing windows and a police guard had to be posted outside for protection. Eventually, Wright decided to fire two shots out of his window into the crowd, wounding four people. Nineteen-year-old John Sangster was hit in the knee and later died from his injuries.

In September 1850, after 265 years, the Pope restored the Catholic hierarchy in England and Wales and appointed a Roman Catholic Bishop of Liverpool. This only stirred up further anti-Catholic feeling. These were dangerous times for anyone showing allegiance to Catholicism. Two roughs from the 'Protestant underworld' attacked Father Ignatius Spencer as he was walking from St Patrick's Chapel. The priest, who was conspicuously clothed in the coarse black habit and sandals of the Passionist Order, was 'hustled and finally thrown into a cellar full of people'.[50] In response to the Pope's actions there was a revival of Orangeism and an escalation of violence. On 12 July 1851, at the start of their procession, Orangeman congregated around the monument in London Road. They were soon attacked by Irish navvies and lumpers from the docks armed with stones and staves. Sabre-welding Orangemen drove them away. In the melee, pistols were also discharged. Constable Jackson was almost beaten to death before colleagues arrived to restore order. Sporadic violence continued as the marchers were ambushed at various points during the procession. The Orangemen proceeded along Scotland Road where John Malley was shot in the thigh. He died two days later. A 14-year-old called Richard Brown was also shot in the shoulder while innocently sitting near his drawing room window.

The following year the magistrates introduced a ban on processions within the borough boundary. Despite the absence of the focal point of a parade, outbreaks of disorder continued. On a pleasant evening in April 1857 the Catholic and Orange factions in Chadwick Street decided to turn out for a fight. Bricks had already been stockpiled in each house ready for hostilities to begin. A selection of Kellys, Connollys and O'Haras made up the opposing teams. From midnight until two o'clock in the morning the battle raged before 12 officers managed to quell the riot. Anne O'Hara, the mother of one of the combatants, acted as weapons conveyor, passing bricks to her son. After a struggle, in which it took four policemen to arrest her, she was found to be carrying stones in her apron.[51] A plentiful supply of stones from Liverpool's streets provided handy weapons during sectarian conflicts. Cabinet-maker James Hopkinson pointed out that some Liverpool girls were very dangerous during times of riot. They would fill their baskets with brickbats and store them in the top rooms of houses in the courts. If any Orangeman was foolish enough to enter the court he would be lucky to come out alive.[52] Stone-throwing became a Liverpool sport. The Head Constable's report for 1874 revealed that 754 people were taken into custody and a further 542 summoned for stone-throwing in the city, a total of 1,296.[53]

The Bread Riots

It was not only sectarian warfare but also Irish petty crime and drunkenness that continued to occupy the police. The presence of a considerable number of destitute and disorderly Irish clogging up the bridewells, prisons, fever hospitals and workhouses became a major concern. In his report for 1851, the prison inspector commented on the increasing seriousness of Irish crime in Liverpool before warning that 'such facts as these show how great a calamity it is to a country advanced in wealth and civilization, to have near it another country in the low condition of Ireland, and how strong an interest it has in removing the causes of its neighbour's poverty and barbarism'.[54] The geographically close but politically uneasy relationship between England and Ireland, between Catholics and Protestants, between wealth and poverty, between 'civilization' and 'barbarism', was reproduced in microcosm on the very streets of Liverpool. This dangerous intimacy caused friction that would eventually ignite passions in Liverpool's own 'Little Ireland' districts.

During the economic depression of the mid-1850s the friction intensified. Sparks were soon to fly. With little money in their pockets and no voice through the ballot box, the disenfranchised resorted to looting the shops. The explosion itself was a series of bread riots that swept through Liverpool's north end for three days in February 1855. The trouble, once again, was over the cost of bread. A series of bad harvests inflated bread prices, which had already been high the previous summer. In the coldest winter in living memory, the River Mersey froze and an easterly wind continued until the end of February. This prevented inward-bound ships entering port and brought the docks to a standstill. Between 15,000 and 20,000 dockers, porters and casual labourers were laid off.

While the Crimean War raged in Russia, hundreds of desperate Liverpudlians queued at the Parish Relief Offices for coal and bread. On Monday 19 February a 1,000-strong mob desperate for relief gathered in St Paul's Square, off Scotland Road. At 10 a.m. the crowd went on the rampage, splitting into smaller gangs to loot the shops of bread and food. The disorder spread to Vauxhall Road, Brownlow Hill and Great Howard Street, even as far as Bootle. The south end was largely unaffected. People stormed the bread shop of Mr Huntington at the corner of Collingwood Street. Five or six shop workers threw loaves out of the window hoping to keep the crowd outside. However, marching in military order, the looters raised a loud cry, 'Make way for the Russians', before breaking in and ransacking the shop. Women turned up aprons and took three loaves while others turned up their dresses and filled them with flour. Caps were also used to carry off the booty. In the struggle for the handouts, three elderly women were crushed, leaving one of them lifeless on the floor.

The looting continued the next day. A baker at Copperas Hill confronted the rioters with a case of loaded pistols. He threatened to shoot the first person who entered his premises. In Kirkdale, shopkeepers and bakers, alerted to the approaching hordes, heated up pokers in readiness. One looter made a grab at a red-hot poker and stripped the skin off his palm. Some weren't after bread but cash from the tills. 'We don't want your crusts; we want your brass,' was the message from one man. Money was even snatched from the public houses. One Irishman was arrested for being in possession of two loaves but simply handed one loaf to a woman running behind him, as if passing on the baton in a relay race. Another man grabbed a number of loaves from a shop and cheekily begged the shopkeeper to let him out the back door to avoid being molested by the mob. A woman stole some peameal instead of flour. On discovering her mistake she coolly went back to the shop to demand a swap.[55] Later, in court, several rioters attempted to cover up their looting by claiming to have acted within the spirit of the relief effort. Thomas Gavan argued that he was given two loaves as he innocently walked past a shop. He naturally thought that official relief workers were donating the bread.

For three days the town was in turmoil. The Royal Lancashire Artillery Militia was kept on standby at Seel Street police station and special constables, armed with staves, patrolled with the regular police. When Head Constable Greig took to the streets to speak to the crowds, a woman threw a sickle at him, narrowly missing his head. In response to the riots several voluntary bodies and Church agencies handed out loaves and soup. A temporary relief fund using a ticket system was set up to distribute food and coal. However, widespread attacks on shops continued with half of Liverpool affected. Some felt that the distribution of tickets out of the Exchange Relief Fund was unfair. The main recipients were 'the disorderly mobs from the Irish districts'.[56] According to one newspaper, 'beggars and imposters from the moral plague spots in the neighbourhood of Marybone [...] were loudest in their exclamations of distress; and relief was extended to them to the exclusion of many deserving dock porters, for whom the fund was specifically designed'.[57] In the struggle for survival, the best fighters got the tickets. The middle-class distinction between 'deserving' and 'non-deserving poor' was obliterated. Indeed, the crowds redefined the very concept of charity by brazenly bypassing the relief system and heading directly to the source of the donations. These people didn't want to overthrow the government: they simply wanted something to eat. This was not the politics of smash and grab. Behind the aggression there were deeply held notions of fairness and justice at stake.

Indeed the behaviour of members of the crowd in defending their rights and customs formed part of a tradition stretching back to the time of the sailors' strike and the press-gang. Whether it was motivated by the soaring price of bread, malpractices by bakers and shopkeepers or simple hunger, direct action was seen as a legitimate means for those without a political voice to make their grievances known to their social superiors. In the words of historian E. P. Thompson, this was 'the moral economy' of the poor.[58] Although the disturbances took place in the middle of the nineteenth century, in a densely populated town, the Liverpool bread riots harked back to an earlier form of popular protest that was widespread in agricultural communities right up to end of the eighteenth century. If such collective action seemed out of place and time, it must be remembered that many men and women in the crowd hailed from pre-industrial communities across the Irish Sea.

'Who were the rioters?' asked the *Liverpool Weekly Albion*. In addition to local loafers and ruffians, there was a large percentage of '"low Irish," a reckless horde who never knew what it is to eat the bread of industry, but who are ever ready to seize the first opportunity to revel in riot and plunder'.[59] *The Times* felt that the ringleaders were 'ferocious looking fellows [...] chiefly natives of Ireland, and are known to the police to belong to the most disorderly and worthless classes in the town'.[60] Of those rioting, 99 out of 100 were Irish claimed the *Liverpool Courier*.[61] In court it was stated that most of those arrested belonged 'to the lowest and most vicious class of the Irish population of the town'.[62] The hostility of the press towards the rioters merely deflects from an uncomfortable truth, that starving people have a perfectly good reason to steal bread. Yet whatever the justifications and motivations for their actions, the authorities continued to view all lower-class rioters as a dangerous criminal element to be put down. Another economic depression in January 1867 saw thousands of Scotland Road 'roughs' and 'questionable characters' take to the streets on another menacing tour of the bread shops but potential disturbances were soon quelled by the police.[63]

The 'brutish' Irish, for their part, maintained their reputations for riot and disorder. In 1863, 45 per cent of those arrested for rioting and breach of the peace in Liverpool were Irish-born.[64] As the century progressed, Catholics continued to press for an independent Ireland using whatever means necessary and Orangemen sought to defend themselves and the nation against Irish rebels. After several Fenian scares in the 1860s, sectarian outrages and violent responses continued throughout the 1880s, particularly during the

1886 Home Rule election campaign.[65] Street clashes were by then part of the local culture, giving many an excuse to indulge in gratuitous violence. Francis Bishop, of the Liverpool Domestic Mission Society, pointed out the hypocrisy of those who used religion as an excuse to spread hatred and fear: 'men who neglect their duties as husbands and fathers, who spend their earnings in the public-houses, and allow their children to wander the streets, are ready on the slightest provocation, to fight in the name of religion, and to treat with the greatest ferocity all who are of the opposite party'. The violence was carried on from generation to generation. Small children armed with sticks played Catholics and Protestants, holding mock processions, which were then attacked. They would shout, 'Three groans for the Pope' or alternatively 'Three groans for the Jumpers [Protestants].' In the heat of battle, youngsters would drop to the floor and feign unconsciousness, as if hit by bricks.[66] Liverpool's streets continued to be blighted by seasonal sectarian battles at least until the inter-war slum clearance programme began to demolish the traditional geographical and cultural borders.[67]

It was these territorial boundaries that helped define the Irish community in Victorian Liverpool. Marked out by economic circumstances, by religion, race and politics, the Irish were also segregated spatially within the city in squalid north-end slums that became associated with crime and disorder.

SEVEN

The Lowest Circle of Hell

Mark Falvey, an Irish-born Liverpool merchant, claimed that the 'Irish herd together very much in this country. They live like a distinct colony, both parents and children.'[1] Since the area behind the docks was the first place the Irish encountered it was the obvious place to settle. The housing was near to the available jobs and cheaper to rent than more desirable properties in the suburbs. This was an important consideration in an age that lacked cheap public transport. The very idea of a home meant something different to the poor. The dwelling was merely a space for sleeping rather than for living in. A woman from the dockside slums justified the wretchedness of her home by pointing out that 'her husband never came home, scarcely except to sleep, and it didn't matter much how they lived for the matter of that. He was near his work and whatever sort of house she kept he would be very little in it.'[2]

If the poor wanted warmth and comfort they would find it in the brightly lit public houses. This is where they would meet with friends to listen to the latest gossip, keep informed about available work and seek financial and emotional support from fellow countrymen. The Irish poor were also tied to particular neighbourhoods by the need for credit from sympathetic shopkeepers and familiar landlords. Food was cheaper in the city-centre markets. Generation after generation would be brought up in the same areas. Although people would move constantly from street to street they never moved too far away from each other. Abraham Hume noted that 'a court will change the whole of its inhabitants in three or four weeks, and even whole streets will alter their character and population in an incredibly short period'.[3]

Working-class life was lived at close quarters in confined spaces, either domestically in overcrowded dwellings or out on the bustling streets. Liverpool was the most densely populated town in the country. In 1844 Dr Duncan pointed out that between Great Crosshall Street and Addison Street in the north end a population of 7,938 occupied 811 houses, a density of 657,963 people per square mile. This was double the most recent figure for the most crowded parts of London.[4] The situation didn't improve. Nearly forty years later Liverpool had the highest population density of any large town in England, with up to 1,210 people per acre in some of the most squalid areas, including the four-mile strip sandwiched between the River Mersey and Scotland Road, largely populated by the Irish poor.[5]

A lack of space on which to build new properties, combined with an insatiable desire to construct as many houses as possible, created a unique style of working-class architecture. Before 1840 builders built whatever they pleased wherever they wanted, with little consideration for sanitation, safety or housing standards. There was no provision for light or air. In the area close to the docks, the scarcity of land meant that warehouses and manufacturing industries devoured the available space, leaving only nooks and crannies for dwellings to spring up. Houses were built next to factories, forcing residents to share the noxious smells of industry. The practice of cramming as many poor tenants as possible into each property only added to the congestion, both demographic and nasal. Some houses were so shoddily built that in 1822 a violent wind blew many of them down.[6]

Although the Liverpool Building Act of 1842 was meant to restrain such jerry-building practices, builders, faced with the extra cost of constructing legally acceptable housing, quickly built as many cheap and insanitary dwellings as possible before the deadline took effect. Afterwards, builders no longer found it profitable to build inexpensive housing that complied with the standards, focusing instead on a better class of property that was no longer affordable to the poor. Although many of the insanitary properties began to be demolished from the 1860s, squalid dwellings were still quite common at the beginning of the twentieth century.

Hordes of wretched paupers were condemned to live in three of the unhealthiest and most degrading forms of housing, namely courts, cellars and lodging-houses. Courts were clusters of houses in claustrophobic cul-de-sacs. The visitor entered the court through a narrow unlit archway built into a row of terraced houses. Sanitary facilities were minimal. Up to 60 people would share a communal public tap and a couple of privies next to an ash pit. With hardly enough water for drinking and cooking, the washing of bodies and clothes and the cleaning of rooms was almost impossible. The overflow from the stinking privies seeped into the courts, which were already paved with decaying animal and vegetable refuse, creating a toxic stew. The enclosed nature of the courts, combined with the lack of ventilation in the back-to-back houses, meant that fresh air could not circulate. An Irishman living in Spencer Court, off North Street, complained of 'a smell bad enough to raise the roof off his skull'.[7] Dimly lit and largely bypassed by the beat constables, the courts were ideal locations for crime and vice. In the 1840s Liverpool had 2,400 courts housing 86,000 people.[8]

In addition to the dismal courts, the Irish poor could also be found in subterranean dwellings. At around this time there were 39,000 people crammed into 7,800 cellars.[9] Cellars were less than six feet high, continually damp and susceptible to flooding. Largely unpaved, the flooring was at best scattered straw and at worst mud. During the Famine invasion, when housing was in short supply, they provided a slightly better alternative to sleeping in the street. For the fortunate, bedding consisted of straw stuffed into a tattered sack. Cellars, sometimes housing up to 30 sleepers, provided barely enough oxygen to breathe.[10]

Under the conditions of the 1842 Liverpool Improvement Act, about 3,000 cellars were condemned as unfit for habitation. They were cleared, filled and a large number of families ejected. The programme eventually resulted in the eviction of 20,000 people, many of them Irish.[11] Cellar clearances, however well intentioned, only exacerbated the problem of homelessness. The dispossessed did not simply move to newly built houses but were pushed into already overcrowded tenements and lodging-houses. Some roamed the streets and smashed down the doors of the same cellars to illegally re-enter them. They also slept rough in warehouses and under bridges. An entire family moved into an old boiler found on some waste ground in the north end.[12]

For the really desperate there was the Liverpool Night Asylum for the Homeless Poor, which opened on Christmas Day 1830 to provide shelter 'for the most wretched and destitute outcasts'.[13] The building, in Freemason's Row, was a large double house converted into accommodation. There were initial objections that the facility would become so attractive that thousands of vagrants would flock to Liverpool, thereby encouraging beggary and attracting disease-ridden undesirables.[14] Critics opposed the night shelters on the grounds that they gave food and a bed indiscriminately without first setting a work task. In the workhouse, as the name suggests, people had to work for such luxuries. Some of these criticisms might have been valid. According to an official report, it seems that a different class of pauper began using the charity: 'A vast number of abandoned characters, known thieves and prostitutes, found nightly shelter there. Almost every destitute person, having any clothes worth stealing in his possession, would surely be robbed in the course of the night. The filthy state of the room, the vermin, and the obscene language, made it disgusting to every decent person.'[15] By 1848 the future of the refuge was being called into question as it was attracting undesirable characters.[16]

Between 1847 and 1850 the expansion of the railways around Victoria Street and Lime Street swallowed up much-needed housing and land, leading to further evictions. Between January 1857 and October 1859 nearly 5,000 houses were constructed in the borough. Yet in the same period the population increased by 30,000. Ironically, the authorities were forced to bring back into use thousands of cellars that had already been condemned. Families who could not afford to rent cellars were housed in penny-a-night doss-houses, described as 'the rank hot-beds of profligacy and vice'.[17] They were usually filthy and crammed with as many beds as space would allow. Lodging-houses for emigrants were often the worst. With little money for the most basic comforts, men and women were squeezed intimately together during their temporary stay in Liverpool. Sir George Stephen inspected the appalling sleeping arrangements in one house and spoke to man called Doyle who had spent several nights in a room with four females. Stephen asked the man whether he had slept in the same bed as the women or merely in the same room. A bashful Doyle admitted, 'I could not manage more than two of them, I was not man enough.' One of the women laughed and confirmed the case.[18] Businessman George Melly accompanied an inspector of lodging-houses on an evening tour of the town's north end. He visited a room packed with bodies lying in abject squalor. What shocked him most was the stench: 'when the doors were open a dense vapour, palpable to the touch, so heavy was it and so dank, came out upon me, almost turning me sick'.[19]

Although there were some clean, well-organized lodging-houses, many were known as 'dens of thieves' or 'flash houses'. These low lodging-houses catered for thieves, tramps, vagabonds and prostitutes.[20] Since lodgings were sometimes used for the receipt and sale of stolen goods, strangers were viewed with suspicion. A journalist explored one thieves' den: 'As we enter a number of men most villainous in appearance gather in a group before the fire […] they mutter to each other and regard us with fixed looks of hate and apprehension.'[21] Mr Pritchard, one of the lodging-house inspectors, cited the following case: 'There is one person who keeps a lodging house in _____ Street, that has three houses together, and in different partitions of the wall he has square holes made, over which there are slides, so that as soon as any person comes in, who has a bad character, he can raise the slide and jump through the hole, till perhaps there are 30 or 40 in the house together.' In this way, fleeing criminals could escape from the police.[22] Young prostitutes would use their earnings to move from the family home into lodging-houses, many run by women.[23] These dwellings were also a great contributor to juvenile crime. Children would leave home to rent a room, supporting themselves entirely by thieving.[24]

Domestic overcrowding was paralleled by congestion on the streets. Liverpool experienced phenomenal population growth during the mid-nineteenth century. As one modern historian has put it, somebody born in the town in 1821 entered a place with 138,000 inhabitants. He would celebrate his twentieth birthday in a town with 286,000 inhabitants. By the time he was 40 there would have been 444,000 inhabitants.[25] Yet it is contemporary visitors to Liverpool who have left us some of the most vivid accounts of the seething mass of bodies that jostled and collided with each other in the town. An acute observer of this choking intimacy was American writer Nathaniel Hawthorne who arrived in Liverpool in 1853 and stayed for four years. He was drawn to the low life of the poorer districts where he was struck by 'the multitudinousness and continual motion of all this kind of life. The people are as numerous as maggots in cheese; you behold them, disgusting, and all moving about, as when you raise a plank or log that has long lain on the ground, and find many vivacious bugs and insects beneath it.'[26] On a visit to Leeds Street in the 1860s, French writer Hippolyte Taine was alarmed by 'this swarming mass of human ugliness and misery'. He called the Irish quarter 'the nethermost circle of hell'.[27]

Little Irelands

Any district with a high concentration of Irish became known as 'Little Ireland'. Early migrants settled in the south end, in the Great George ward. Crosbie Street, for example, contained 80 per cent Roman Catholics.[28] With the Famine invasion, a more significant number began to populate the north end, particularly the Vauxhall, Exchange and Scotland wards. In the 1830s Head Constable Whitty reported, 'I have heard several places in Liverpool called Little Ireland, particularly Back Portland Street; they have all been the lowest and most disorderly places in town.'[29] Irish neighbourhoods were often associated with crime and disorder. Without identifying any particular district, a local linen draper called William Dillon explained that

> there is a place in Liverpool called *Little Ireland*, for the most part inhabited by Irish. It was a great place for making smuggled whisky, drinking it, and disposing of it; and for fighting, quarrelling and killing each other, or any person who happened to come there. It is filthily dirty, and covers a small space, in which a great many people live, perhaps as many as three families in a house. Few of them work; the rest live by smuggling and begging.[30]

The Scotland Road area was the most famous Little Ireland district. 'Seven-eighths of my parishioners are Irish,' noted the vicar of St Albans, in Limekiln Lane. Father Roche agreed: 'Every other person you meet in Scotland Road is a Catholic.'[31] According to Head Constable Nott-Bower, the Irish were

> all crowded together in the lowest quarter of the town, veritable slums. They lived mostly in the 'Scotland Division' [...] There were many absolute ruffians among them, brought up in poverty, without educa-tion or religious influence, wearied with the struggle of life, with a hatred of society, and none of the surroundings which might wean them from drink and vice and violence.[32]

Scotland Road's inhabitants were elsewhere described as 'the lowest type of squalid life. They are more uncivilised, more dangerous, more drunken than any to be found elsewhere.'[33]

At various times different areas were labelled the worst in Liverpool. They were usually Irish districts. Bootle was traditionally known as 'Brutal Bootle', where 'the police ran far greater danger than soldiers on active service'.[34] Slum-packed Dale Street was once described as 'the vilest part of the parish'.[35] Yet it was the Scotland Road district that became synonymous with crime and vice. The parallel yet interlinked thoroughfares of Scotland Road, Great Homer Street and Vauxhall Road were described as the 'Ratcliff Highways' of Liverpool, after a notorious London district: 'In the two-storied blind alleys, with cellars for living and sleeping rooms, dwell in their thousands the workless, the helpless immigrant, the vicious, and the destitute.'[36] The quarter housed a warren of streets competing for the title of most depraved. A policeman declared that 'no respectable person lived in Maguire Street, and that 30 or 40 housebreakers were generally captured every year in the neigh-bourhood'.[37] In 1866 Ben Jonson Street was seen as 'the haunt of thieves and prowlers from all parts of the country'. Nearly twenty years later it was still being labelled 'the worst street in the city'. Taking into account the numbers living in the adjoining courts, the street contained about 1,000 residents, yet it was claimed that only six men had proper jobs. With its 19 lodging-houses for beggars and eight brothels within 200 yards, it was normally allocated an extra three constables.[38] In the 1880s Luton Street, situated to the north-west of Scotland Road, was the headquarters of the High Rip Gang. Known locally as 'Sebastopol', after the scene of a notable battle in the Crimean War of 1854, the place became a byword for carnage and bloodshed.[39] In 1899, in the neighbourhood of Christian Street, there was a slum area called Baptist Street which, in the view of an investigative journalist from the *Liverpool*

Review, 'should not be permitted to exist for a day in any civilised city'.[40]

Parts of the south end could rival the tough north end. On the same tour of the slums the journalist discovered a south-end district of less than 500 square yards where there had occurred eight murders, countless robberies and indecent assaults and a case where a policeman was stripped and left naked in the street. In what may be an apocryphal story, another constable was allegedly dropped down a drain because he interfered in some criminal activity.[41] A court near Princes Road was known as the 'Murderer's Court': 'a man could be killed in this den, and a passer-by in the main street might be none the wiser'.[42] Myrtle Street was known as 'Little Hell'.[43] In the 1860s the brothel-packed parish of St Nathaniel's, Windsor (off Upper Parliament Street) was 'socially and morally, the lowest [district] in all the south-east portion of Liverpool'. It was 'sixteen acres of sin'.[44]

These atrocious environments were often seen as the refuges of the criminal classes rather than nurseries that helped breed the criminals in the first place. One of the first in Liverpool to explore the social pathology of a working-class impoverished area was Abraham Hume. In 1847, when Vauxhall became a new ecclesiastical district, Hume, together with volunteers from Birkenhead College, conducted an in-depth social investigation of the neighbourhood. The statistics paint a depressing picture. With 76 public houses, 51 beershops and various pawnshops, brothels and 'haunts of habitual thieves', the residents of the area were surrounded by vice and temptation: 'The usual results are seen everywhere, idleness, dishonesty, unchastity, brutality, misery.'[45]

In 1858 Hume published a moral map, entitled 'Liverpool Ecclesiastical and Social', in which he identified the pauper streets and the criminal areas. For Hume the two most poverty-stricken areas in Liverpool were the region between Netherfield Road and the northern docks and the southern district bounded by Park Lane, St James Street, Windsor Street, Northumberland Street and the docks. The map pinpointed the worst neighbourhoods: 'In five streets of St John's district there are one hundred houses [existing for evil purposes], and four hundred abandoned families; independent of houses which are understood to be receptacles for stolen goods, and of pugilists and bullies whose vocation it is to assist in robberies.' Under the heading 'Violent Deaths', Hume analysed 605 inquests. After deducting the deaths occurring at the river and docks and a few in Walton Gaol, he pointed out that out of the 16 wards of the borough, just under half the violent deaths occurred in two wards, Vauxhall and Scotland.[46]

In further reports Hume identified districts comprised of 'man-catchers' (rogues who preyed upon emigrants), bands of 'prigs' (juvenile thieves), poachers, begging letter impostors, professional smugglers, dog stealers, marine store dealers, 'keepers of miscellaneous lodging-houses &c.'[47] Around St Anne's Church, St Anne Street, where Catholics predominated, Hume concluded: 'It is the moral cesspool for half a million people. It is burdened on one side by a main artery of crime in the town: and it is the home of all gross sin and immorality – the den of convicted felons, conspirators against law and order, of drunkards and persons who have never known purity of morals.'[48]

One might add that they had also never known purity of water or cleanliness of home. The residents were more likely to be concerned about the very real cesspools stagnating outside their front doors. 'Is it not notorious,' a journalist asked, 'that the worst dens of the worst vices are found where the drainage is bad, and the supply of water limited?'[49] In the nineteenth century concerns about public health, poverty, squalor and poor sanitation were closely linked to fears about crime. For the Victorians, cleanliness was next to godliness. In the eyes of social reformers, dirt, poverty, bodily sickness and moral corruption were all part of the same social malaise. The sight and stench of the ragged urban poor therefore suggested immorality and depravity. For the middle classes, the problem intensified when the filth, both physical and moral, began seeping into respectable areas. A newspaper correspondent complained of the rough inhabitants of the back streets branching off Lime Street 'who may be seen issuing from their dens at all hours, in a state outraging public decency, and disgusting the eyes and ears of the passers by [...] polluting our great thoroughfares'.[50]

During a stroll along Scotland Road one Saturday evening in 1857, Hugh Shimmin saw 'a number of lazy fellows standing grouped at a street corner in the most dirty and besotted condition, obstructing the thoroughfare, if not insulting all decent passers-by'. Groups of young girls, licentious and 'utterly brutal in their appearance, demeanour and conversation', started talking to the boys who sported short pipes in their mouths.[51] Speaking of Scotland Road, a report stated that 'disorder is perpetual, and disease is never absent'.[52] For one newspaper: 'There are whole courts and streets in which vice and disorder reign supreme [...] Such places [...] are the nurseries of pauperism, disease and crime.'[53]

Nearby Lace Street was described as the 'filthiest, most densely peopled and worst-conditioned in the town'.[54] Situated off Fontenoy Street, it was the most Irish street in Liverpool, every head of household being Irish.[55] At only 160 yards long, overcrowding was acute with 1,434 people crammed into 109 properties. This allowed only four square yards of space for each inhabitant.[56] One cellar, measuring 14 feet by 10 feet, was sleeping quarters for 12 people.[57] Prison regulations would not permit such sardine-like conditions. Overcrowding was exacerbated by the abundance of cheap lodging-houses and the practice of sub-letting rooms. When fever arrived, it spread quickly and devastated the district. In 1847 a third of the street (472 residents) was wiped out.[58] The violence of disease was matched by the brutality of the residents. Lace Street, along with Marybone, was once judged 'the most disorderly part of the town'.[59] Following a mass brawl between Irish families in 1844, the stipendiary magistrate claimed that the Irish in the street were 'actuated by a spirit ungovernable and reckless as that of the wildest savages'.[60] A boy in the Borough Gaol admitted, 'I first became acquainted with bad company by my father going to live in Lace Street.'[61]

In January 1855 some boys entered a disused cellar in the street to play around with a barrel of gunpowder and a lit candle. The inevitable explosion killed a 10-year-old and almost demolished the house above. An Irishman was sitting discussing the Crimean War as the blast ripped through the room. 'Sure enough,' he shouted, 'the Russians have come.' Police investigations into the accident were hampered by the hostility of the neighbours. After inspecting the damage the building surveyor called it 'a horrible place, abounding in filth, and the resort of thieves, the cellars of the houses being the receptacles of stolen property'. Since the houses were in such a dilapidated state and not fit for human habitation, he felt that it would be better to knock down the entire street.[62]

The Pig and the Sty

It was usually the residents, rather than the architects, builders or landlords, who were blamed for the ramshackle state of the houses. While acknowledging that sometimes houses make the people and sometimes people make the houses, Revd Hugh Stowell Brown, a Liverpool Baptist minister, suggested that even if some residents were put into magnificent properties, within a short time the abodes would be wrecked and vandalized. Brown concluded with a proverb: 'Wash a dog, comb a dog, still a dog.'[63] As if to prove the point, in the 1880s many respectable dockworkers moved into new properties near the Bootle and Seaforth docks, leaving houses empty between Netherfield Road and Great Homer Street. Landlords tried to find new tenants by reducing the rents but they succeeded only in attracting unsuitable Irish residents, such as 'chip merchants, donkey owners, pigeon breeders and all kinds of ruffians of all shades. In some streets, doors, stairs, and floors, become the spoil of the chip merchants, lead piping and iron removed to marine store dealers.'[64]

On the other hand, Revd Charles Garrett, Superintendent of the Wesleyan Mission, had a more positive message: 'Give [people] the opportunity of better houses, and […] they would take advantage of it, turn over a new leaf, and endeavour to live honest and respectable lives.'[65]

Who or what was to blame for the dilapidation, disease and disorder of the slums was a question that exercised churchmen, journalists and social commentators throughout the Victorian period. Some critics of the Irish thought that social ills were simply the result of personal failings such as ignorance, laziness and bad character. Particularly from the time of the Famine invasion, the Irish were largely seen as responsible for the squalor of certain neighbourhoods. In Dr Duncan's view, 'It is they who inhabit the filthiest and worst ventilated courts and cellars, who congregate the most numerously in dirty lodging-houses, who are the least cleanly in their habits and the most apathetic about everything that befalls them.'[66] Duncan suggested that the Irish were partly to blame for the insanitary conditions in the filthy courts for even when there was plenty of water available they rarely used it.[67] A Domestic Mission Society report claimed that 'there are many, especially among the lower classes of Irish who seem to have no idea of a dwelling, except as a place of shelter from the weather. If it does this, they ask no more of it, and take little or no care to keep it in cleanliness or order.'[68] Such indifference to comfort and dirt was an obvious danger to health. Indeed, the link between the Irish and disease became a source of propaganda for those who believed that the migrants threatened the physical condition of the native working-class population. One Orange-supporting newspaper fumed: 'The lower order of Irish papists are the filthiest beings in the habitable globe, they abound in dirt and vermin and have no care for anything but self gratification that would degrade the brute creation.'[69]

'Is it the pig who makes the sty or the sty that makes the pig?'[70] The question had special resonance for the Irish, since some were pig-mongers who kept the animals at home. Despite the existence of by-laws penalizing those who kept 'swine sties fronting the street, and […] swine in the rooms or cellars of dwelling houses', the Irish pig-keepers continued with their rural custom.[71] In October 1840 the owners of 20 pigsties in Eldon Street, in the Vauxhall district, appeared in court accused of letting muck from the pigs run into the street. Some kept pigs in their cellars.[72] In April 1827 a baby left alone in a house had its ear chewed off by a pig. The child later died of complications from its injuries. Other animals were also kept indoors. Dr Duncan described a house in a court in Thomas Street where his patient lay on a heap of straw in one corner, while in the opposite corner stood a donkey.

mmediately under the window was the dunghill, for which the donkey was used as transport.[73]

Links Between Environment and Crime

While some people viewed the Irish poor as agents of disease, dirt and disorder, others felt that they were simply the victims of fever and squalor over which they had little control. In this more enlightened view, the riotous behaviour and criminality were mere symptoms of deeper environmental and historical maladies. Atrocious living conditions were bound to have an adverse impact on people's behaviour. Overcrowding meant that there was no escape from the vice and criminality. Abraham Hume writes of the numbing of 'moral sensitiveness' resulting from cramped slum conditions.[74] Samuel Smith admitted that decent individuals lived in Liverpool but that 'it would be almost a miracle for people to maintain their self-respect in many parts of our city, so foul are the language and habits of the people'.[75] Overcrowding, combined with a lack of domestic comfort, drove people into the public houses or onto the street corners where they came into direct conflict with the police who were trying to clear the streets of loiterers. Clashes were inevitable.

The link between bad housing conditions and crime was obvious to some. In 1875 *The Times* published a letter from a Kirkdale gentleman.[76] The author's message was clear: atrocious living conditions produced a brutalized population that was easily recruited into the ranks of the criminal classes. In his account of warrens of tightly packed back-to-back courts the writer described a nether world, self-enclosed, alienated from respectable middle-class society, cut off even from the beneficial forces of law and order. The inhabitants were neither controlled nor protected by the police and consequently only a few acts of violence were ever reported to the authorities.

By the 1880s the bestial condition of the lower classes was seen as a direct result of their being submerged in the squalor and filth of the slums. Environment and moral character became fused, creating a unique DNA to be passed on to future generations. A social investigation of the slums concluded:

> These people are what the conditions of the environment have made them [...] The wretches you see in Scotland-road inherit probably the proclivities of a dozen generations of degradation. Many of them come from Ireland, and bitterly has the sister country repaid us for centuries of wrong inflicted by our hands [...] But the blame is not theirs. They have been born to ugliness and destitution, and with predispositions to vice transmitted from many a savage, ignorant ancestor.[77]

Samuel Smith agreed: 'this human deposit of vice and poverty is hereditary'.[78] Historical misfortunes also played their part. In 1910 Thomas Burke traced the legacy of Irish delinquency to the social catastrophe of the famine and epidemics of fever in Liverpool:

> he who would pass judgement on Irish poverty or 'crime' of later years, let him read the story which every stone of the charnel house in Vauxhall, Exchange, Scotland, Great George and Pitt Street Wards, told and still tell. Here were sown the dragon's teeth, and they have sprung up, not in armed men, but workhouses, reformatories, and gaols.[79]

In the densely populated courts and crammed cellars, genetics, geography, history and social conditions combined to produce a peculiar kind of Liverpool low life. Describing a group of tenants and landlords from the Lace Street area accused of contravening cellar regulations, a newspaper remarked that 'there appeared in court a number of men and women, pale, yellow, ghastly, parchment-faced looking creatures, more like the offspring of a foreign land, than the natives of these kingdoms'.[80] These troglodytes were viewed as specimens of a primitive race or undiscovered tribe hidden deep in the heart of Britain's second city.

For much of the nineteenth century the world of the urban poor was concealed in impenetrable ghettoes, largely ignored by the upper classes. While doctors, priests and rent collectors were familiar faces in the slums, constables, bailiffs, public health inspectors and School Board officials remained unwelcome visitors. Samuel Smith stated that Liverpool districts were 'so depressing that none will visit these slums except on errands of religion or philanthropy'.[81] In the words of the *Daily Post*: 'the older and more densely-populated districts of the town are to a great majority of the people as much unknown and as little understood as the hut of the Esquimaux is to the African savage'.[82]

This geographical and cultural isolation was to change as the century progressed. As Christian Britain continued to colonize the rest of the world, it took upon itself the role of civilizing the natives of foreign countries. The expansion of the British Empire, particularly into Africa, inspired imperial racist debates about civilization and savagery. The irony was that the inner-city slums contained a breed of savages equally in need of cultivation.[83] Indeed, as early as 1753 the Welsh curate at Walton Church, Goronwy Owen, wrote to a friend, 'The people around here, so far as I can see, are but little better than Hottentots; immoral untamed creatures.'[84] The depiction of the lower classes in terms of primitiveness became a common media device as social anthropologists, moral reformers and intrepid journalists diverted their attention from the wild tribes of distant lands to the ungodly brutes loitering on the corners of their own slum-infested cities.[85] Members of the middle classes even took up 'slum tourism' to see for themselves the horrific conditions of the hidden poor. The result was a range of interventions, including charity, housing renewal programmes and religion, aimed at rescuing and reclaiming the destitute.

This concern was inspired as much by political unease as by altruism. The 1880s experienced renewed fears of the 'dangerous classes' as a threat to the moral and social order. The existence of a large casual labour force with little economic security and seemingly no moral foundations provided an ever-present threat of insurrection and mob violence on the streets. Against a backdrop of bubbling working-class political agitation, the middle classes feared that this ungovernable rabble was being drawn into the new socialist movement.[86] The concern also masked an anxiety about youth crime, particularly the growth of teenage street gangs such as Liverpool's High Rip and Manchester's Scuttlers. Not only in 'Savage Liverpool' but throughout the country readers were shocked by published revelations of the lower orders.

What these social explorers discovered alarmed Victorian Britain. With a lack of space to grow and develop, dense overcrowding and the crushing routine of the daily grind left inhabitants stunted both physically and morally. Although professing to be Roman Catholic, the illiterate Irish poor knew next to nothing about God or religion. In 1876 it was estimated that 200,000 Liverpudlians were living 'in the neglect of public worship', a factor seen as contributing to the large number of criminals. Although it was felt that the clergy 'form Liverpool's best guard against the encroachments of crime', there was clearly much work to be done, with less than 300 ministers and priests serving a population of 520,000.[87] Despite the best efforts of parish priests, the lower classes lacked moral example. At the Borough Gaol, the prison inspector revealed that one 10-year-old boy 'was never at Chapel; has never heard of God, a Saviour, or Commandments; never heard of one, "Thou shalt not steal".' The boy had more pressing concerns: 'he wanted food when his mother was drunk, and took the money he is now in for, having been without bread all day'.[88]

After noting the abundance of mission halls, churches and chapels in a rough Toxteth district, an investigator from the *Liverpool Review* asked:

Has this atmosphere of sacred dogma and religious autocracy ever been a finger's breadth assistance in softening the depravity of its breathers? –

Has it ever saved one woman from the cowardly fist and the brutal boot? Has it by so much as the fraction of a copper lessened the takings of the thousand beer-shops and public houses whose flaring lights 'illumine' the unwholesome haze on every side?[89]

The answer was a resounding NO! And the reason was drink.

EIGHT

The Demon Drink

Alcohol and Poverty

'You fat _____ if you don't give her a _____ good hiding I'll give you one! You _____!' Urged on by such stirring motivational speeches from her husband, a large drunken woman tore into her 'scraggy opponent' during a Saturday night catfight in a south-end court. Hours earlier the women had been happily drinking together but on the way home from the pub an argument turned violent: 'Her ragged bodice was torn from her back, and the thin blood streaks showed the marks of her enemy's fingers on her naked chest. The further the combatants approached to nudity the greater was the delight of the bystanders.'

While touring the slums, middle-class social commentators were confronted with similar shocking scenes of vice, crime and rowdiness. In subsequent pamphlets, sermons and newspaper editorials the depravity was blamed on a variety of social ills such as poverty, insanitary housing, overcrowding, squalor and disease. The Irish temperament was another contributory factor. Yet perhaps the most important reason cited for the social breakdown of lower-class neighbourhoods was alcohol. Beer and spirits were the fuel that drove the poor to delinquency, debauchery, destitution, depravity and destruction.

As casual workers staggered between poverty and drunken oblivion, social commentators were left to debate whether heavy drinking was a result of pauperism or the very cause of it. The main purpose of the *Liverpool Review* series on slum life was to demonstrate over and over again that the major cause of poverty in Liverpool was alcohol. Although other factors were involved, such as the death of the family breadwinner, the journal saw drink as the primary cause of people's downfall. Whereas H. Lee Jones, the director of the Liverpool Food and Betterment Association, thought that only about 20 per cent of poverty in the slums was caused by drink, the *Liverpool Review* put the figure at nearly 75 per cent. Its verdict was damning: 'The majority of the inhabitants of the slums are drunkards, debauchers, sots and sluts […] they are the dregs of the social system, and they get to the bottom of the social cup by reason of their own shortcomings and misdeeds.'[2] In this view, it was not simply poverty that caused crime: it was idleness and a love of vice, particularly gambling and drinking, that led to poverty. If the poor then committed crime it was their own fault for becoming poor in the first place.

Alcohol and Crime

Yet if excessive drinking resulted in poverty and poverty drove people to drink, wealth created an even greater market for alcohol. John Clay, the chaplain of Preston Gaol, used crime statistics to support his argument that there was a direct relationship between the crime rate and the business cycle. When people's economic situation improved, the crime rate rose because people had more money for alcohol, which fuelled disorder on the streets. When times were hard, people drank less.[3] For *The Times*, the root cause of social disorder was not unemployment but higher wages, which led to increased drinking which in turn resulted in escalating violence.[4] In opposition to those who believed that poverty caused crime, Father Nugent also argued that prosperity was a more likely cause. He believed that the prison population multiplied as employment opportunities increased. The underlying reason was that higher wages led to a surge in drinking and hence more crime and disorder on the streets.[5] Others blamed the increasing consumption of alcohol among the working classes on three factors; higher wages, shorter working hours and more outlets for buying alcohol, especially grocers' stores. The latter was seen as particularly harmful for women.[6] Indeed, it was believed that Liverpool ladies, 'muddled with drink', often became victims of kleptomania.[7] It is interesting that for the more respectable offenders, theft became an illness rather than a crime.

It could also be argued that when money was scarce, people committed more thefts to fund their drink habits. Nugent, elsewhere, estimated that 75 per cent of money gained through crime was spent on alcohol.[8] Periodic unemployment must also have had an effect on crime rates since some casual labourers survived only through recourse to pilfering and various scams. Petty crime provided an important source of income for people unable or unwilling to receive charity or reluctant to admit themselves into the workhouse.

A great many street robberies were also committed by people either under the influence of drink or desperate to get money for alcohol. Over the years numerous judges sitting at Liverpool Assizes remarked upon the regularity of alcohol-fuelled violence. Judge Weightman, in 1846, stated that 'in almost all the cases of personal violence and injury, the scene was a public house or a beershop'. In 1869 Justice Lush pointed out that 'the two prisoners [charged with wounding] were in a state of drunkenness, which, unhappily, seems to be the condition of the great proportion of the criminals mentioned in this calendar'.[9] Liberal Robert Gladstone felt that the building of the new Borough Gaol would not have been necessary 'if it were not for the existence of the licensed public-houses and beer-houses; I believe that they are the source of all the mischief'.[10] In 1851 the Kirkdale chaplain stated, 'I am not guilty of exaggeration when I state that about two thirds of those who come before me are in some way or other indebted to the public house or gin-shop for their appearance within these walls.'[11] The percentage worsened. 'Drunkenness,' claimed Mr Baron Martin at the 1866 Liverpool Assizes, 'seems to be the cause of nine-tenths of the crime which was committed.'[12] Judge Collins, in his speech to the grand jury at the 1895 Assizes, also remarked that two-thirds of the crimes committed in Liverpool were due to alcohol. In response, Dr McCann, a Liberal candidate, remarked that two-thirds of crime were due to the way that the poorer classes were housed and that the abuse of alcohol in the city was a result of the poor quality of the air that the slum dwellers were forced to breathe.[13] Yet the poor could not escape sub-standard housing if they spent all their money on drink.

The relationship between alcohol, crime, poverty and squalid living conditions is a complex issue. These factors were so closely linked that it was difficult to break free of any one of them. Drunkenness certainly aggravated pauperism and was the root cause of numerous other social problems, particularly for families. Heavy drinking brutalized parents and led to domestic violence. It also contributed to the high death rate, which produced orphans. Uncared-for children were pushed onto the streets to beg or steal. Many poor families got drunk on a Saturday evening and spent the weekend in a state of violent inebriation until there was no money left for drink. They would then starve themselves and their children through the rest of the week till the next wages.[14] Father Nugent spoke of a mother of seven children who had already sold everything she had for alcohol. She went into a public house where she met a barber and sold him locks of her hair for some beer. Hugh Shimmin recalls that another woman had sold every stitch of clothing except her chemise. Yet another case involved a woman in a rough pub who similarly stood drinking in only her chemise and when asked jokingly by the publican whether she would sell that also, took it off and finished her drink stark naked.[15]

At a social level, women enjoyed friendship and camaraderie in the pubs. While men usually got drunk after being paid on a Saturday, wives used the money left over to drink on a Monday.[16] After a hard stint hawking goods in the cold and rain, the pub became a welcome haven, although some women sought sanctuary before the day had barely begun. James Hopkinson, a cabinet-maker, noted that the ratio of customers at the spirit vault facing his shop in Mill Street was two women to every man. Just after nine in the morning, women would arrive, some with baskets, others with plates of liver or fish for their husband's dinner. They couldn't resist calling in for a few drinks before hurrying home to cook the meal just before their husbands arrived.[17] Dried salt fish was a particular favourite among the lower classes. The salt made people thirsty, much to the delight of publicans selling ale. According to the *Liverpool Review*: 'thirst production and destruction are the foremost amusements of the slums'.[18]

In an age when beer was often safer to drink than water, the public house was the vibrant hub and cultural centre of the community. Working-class recreation centred on drinking establishments. Social conventions such as weddings, funerals and births made it difficult to avoid 'having a drain'. The pubs were home to returning seamen celebrating their first night of freedom. For emigrants passing through Liverpool, the public house served as a sort of post office where letters could be collected. With no Irish consulate, the pub acted as a meeting place where countrymen could receive information.

Yet despite the benefits to the community of the public houses, excessive drinking led to physical and mental ruin and often a spell in gaol. For those unfortunate enough to be arrested after the weekend Bacchanalia, a Monday morning appearance at the Dale Street Police Court was a sobering experience. The overwhelming first impression of the court was the stench of unwashed and filthy ragged bodies. The *Liverpool Review* summed up the pattern of existence of the typical slum dweller: 'A life of sordid squalor and wretchedness, varied by frantic outbursts of drunkenness, and then the pawning or selling of every miserable rag and stick to pay the fine.' Imprisonment was almost part of working-class culture. 'To this class of people it would appear that a certain number of visits to the bridewell every year were among the necessary excitements of existence.'[19] Men and women aged between 16 and 60 would pack the waiting room awaiting a verdict on their orgies of drink and violence. The proceedings were not without humour. One 'brawny-looking son of the Emerald Isle' was brought before the magistrate charged with being drunk and disorderly. The man admitted, 'I took a little drop of drink yesterday for a novelty but it was not much.'[20] One woman vehemently denied ever having been drunk in her life, despite having been locked up for drunkenness over 20 times.[21] Magistrate Clarke Aspinall would sentence drunken women to eight days' imprisonment instead of the usual seven days. This was so that the prisoner would not be released by the following weekend when temptation to get drunk again was greatest. At reception in Walton Gaol on Monday morning there would be a more than usual number of inmates, some of them dangerous. Basil Thomson, the deputy governor, remarked: 'The "drunks" were often still in the reaction stage of intoxication and might do anything.'[22]

Father Nugent, as prison chaplain, saw the effects of drink on a daily basis, particularly among females. He believed that nine-tenths of women under his care were admitted because of excessive drinking.[23] For women at the bottom of the social pile, the personal and social cost of alcohol was enormous, 'changing wives and mothers into brutal savages [...] Not a week passes without some being brought to the prison whom drink had maddened and robbed of all female decency, whose language and actions are so horrible that they seem no longer rational beings, but fiends.'[24] Frenchman Hippolyte Taine was fascinated by Liverpool's female drunks: 'Livid, bearded old women came out of gin shops: their reeling gait, dismal eyes and fixed idiot grin are indescribable. They look as if their features had been slowly corroded by vitriol.'[25]

Legislation

In the 1820s and 1830s the immorality of drinking was chiefly related to spirits. Gin, known as 'mother's ruin', was cheaper than beer and therefore the pauper's tipple of choice. A poem in *Punch* magazine summed up the attraction:

> All is filthiness without me;
> All is ignorance within;
> I ache with cramps – I shake with damps –
> Oh, the warmth of glorious gin.[26]

Gin palaces thrived in the poorer districts. Nathaniel Hawthorne gives a vivid description of a Liverpool establishment:

Gin shops, or what the English call spirit-vaults, are numerous in the vicinity of these poor streets and are set off with the magnificence of gilded door-posts, tarnished by contact with the unclean customers who haunt there [...] Inconceivably sluttish women enter at noonday and stand at the counter among boon companions of both sexes, stirring up misery and jollity in a bumper together and quaffing off the mixture with relish.[27]

Compared to gin, beer was seen as harmless. In an effort to divert people's attention from spirits, the Beer House Act of 1830 was passed. This meant that on the payment of two guineas to the Excise Office, anybody with their name listed on the Rate Book could open their home as a beer house. By 1834 there were at least 700 beer houses in addition to 1,500 public houses.[28] With a little simple construction work, ordinary homes could be modified and a pub sign erected outside. Before the rise of commercial breweries, ale was brewed at home. However, the practice faded and by the 1840s there were ten breweries in the Vauxhall Road and Scotland Road districts.[29] There were no licensing laws in force and many pubs re-opened early in the morning. This meant that carters and dockers could fortify themselves with a nip before a gruelling shift. It was alleged that in one public house facing the docks, a publican would have 300 to 400 glasses of spirits lined up on the counter at 6 a.m. Crowds of dockers would stream in for a drink even as the bell was ringing for them to begin work.[30] In many of the poorer districts, drunkenness reigned supreme. In the early 1830s a publican in Brick Street decided to open all night. This early experiment in 24-hour opening left the entire neighbourhood in a state of uproar. Up to 30 people were arrested as watchmen were called in from other beats to help quell the riot.[31]

As a seaport with a huge clientele of sailors, Liverpool had an abundance of grogshops and whisky and penny ale cellars. It was estimated that if all the drinking establishments in the borough of Liverpool were put in a straight line they would stretch for 11½ miles.[32] The mind boggles at the potential pub crawl. The Victorians were great statisticians, excelling in particular in figures about drink and public houses. It was calculated that each year every public house in Liverpool made ten paupers, sent eight people to the police court and cost the public £160.[33] It wasn't just the number of drinking premises but also their density in particular areas. The Sailors' Home in Canning Place had 46 public houses within 150 yards.[34] The number of drinkers per establishment was also astounding. A public house survey conducted in 1873 revealed that one pub had 904 visitors in a space of four hours on a fine Sunday evening.[35]

Non-Liverpudlians were shocked by the abundance of the town's watering holes. James Hopkinson noted that there were no less than 25 spirit vaults near his home in Mill Street.[36] For temperance campaigner Revd Lundie, the public houses, 'like the fungus that flourishes upon the decaying tree, suck the living sap out of the district'.[37] Alcohol itself also sucked the life-blood out of the Liverpool poor. On his daily walks through the lower districts, where every ten steps revealed a spirit vault, Nathaniel Hawthorne discovered 'men haggard, drunken, careworn, hopeless, but with a kind of patience, as if all this were the rule of their life'.[38] Even hardy seamen were made impotent by the lure of alcohol. Speaking of the multitude of public houses in Liverpool, one sailor lamented, 'I am a man at sea, but ashore all my manhood is gone. How can I resist these snares and traps laid everywhere for me? Shut them up and I shall be as good a man as any one of you.'[39]

The distribution of public houses altered the criminal landscape. The explosion of beershops after the 1830 Act meant that many pubs sprang up in secluded places, hidden from the attentions of the police. These establishments sheltered gambling and illegal sports such as dog fights. The governor of the Borough Gaol felt that public houses, together with lodging-houses, were the meeting points where thieves 'concoct their wicked plans, and prepare themselves by drink to carry them out'.[40] Some publicans were known as 'thieves' bankers' for allowing their premises to be used for the reception of stolen goods.[41] Certain beershops attracted rough characters and acted as magnets of the underworld. On a Sunday evening walk in the north end, Hugh Shimmin encountered a public house whose regulars included 'women, without shoes and very few garments on [...] whilst brawny loafers skulked about, and vicious cripples stuttered blasphemy at the door'.[42]

The heavy concentration of low-life characters in one place caused endless problems for the police and only added to the reputation some areas had for being 'problem' districts. Inspector O'Brien reported that it took six constables to deal with drink-related disorder in Lime Street. The area was described as 'a disgrace to the town'.[43] Drunkenness took up a lot of police time. Head Constable Greig complained that every arrest for drunkenness withdrew a constable from his duties. If the drunk was violent it often took two officers to escort him or her to the bridewell. The next day the officer would be tied up for hours in the Police Court. In this way the streets were stripped of constables. He didn't wonder that the public complained of a lack of visible police.[44]

To tackle the disorderly behaviour associated with public houses, in 1854 the police gained the right to enter any premises where intoxicating liquor was sold. Yet in 1857 a magistrate (perhaps under pressure from the brewers) dismissed several cases against landlords on the grounds that the policemen had visited the pubs in plain clothes. This was seen as underhand. Between 1862 and 1865 the licensing laws were relaxed even further and the licensing bench started to grant licences freely to anyone with suitable premises. There was little consideration for the number of pubs already in existence. Indeed, it was hoped that good pubs would replace the worst pubs by the pressure of competition. The result, however, was simply more pubs.[45] Within four years a further 370 drinking establishments joined the already crowded market.[46] The trial was abandoned as drunkenness increased. In the House of Commons, Sir Wilfred Lawson claimed that Free Licensing had made Liverpool 'a place next to a hell upon earth'.[47] The Head Constable hoped that drunkenness had hit a peak in 1869 after the number of cases had reached 18,303. This was nearly double the total for 1861. However, in 1870 the figure went up yet again by nearly 3,000.[48] Indeed, the figures continued to rise. In 1874 there were 23,303 cases and yet only three publicans were convicted that year for permitting drunkenness. It was felt that the law was not being upheld in Liverpool.[49]

The social and personal devastation of alcohol was laid bare by Revd John Jones who published a series of pamphlets called *The Slain in Liverpool by Drink*, an annual catalogue of alcohol-related deaths.[50] The year 1864, for example, produced a tragic roll call of victims aged from 4 months to 74 years, casualties of suffocation, suicide, falls, fights, fires and drowning. Amid the destruction and death, Jones and other temperance campaigners called out for a change to Liverpool's binge-drinking culture.

It was not until 1872 and the passing of the Intoxicating Liquor Licensing Act that public houses became better managed. The law restricted the sale of alcohol in pubs to the hours between 7 a.m. and 11 p.m. on weekdays. Sunday drinking time was also reduced. Thus the town's streets became quieter at night. The Head Constable, however, revealed that weekend revellers were simply taking beer and spirits home to continue their festivities. Prostitutes would also move on to the night cafés, which were not included in the legislation. There was a growth in such establishments.[51] The Act was not without its opponents and met with protests up and down the country. On Sunday 3 November 1872 two demonstrations were held at St George's Hall, one in the afternoon and the other in the evening. Up to 20,000 people gathered to voice their objection to 9 p.m. closing on a Sunday. The authorities feared riots among the Scotland Road 'roughs' but the 400 policeman and 50 dock constables kept the trouble to a minimum.[52] The restrictions of the Act might even have encouraged bootleg activities. An illicit still was discovered in Great Howard Street as late as 1875, long after they were thought to have been banished.[53]

Of course, not all drinking took place in pubs. Buying ale to drink off the premises was cheaper. An incentive was the 'long pull', an extra measure of liquor given over and above the quantity paid for. In Liverpool, for example, in 1897 a gill of beer cost 1½d to drink at the counter while twice the amount, or even more, could be bought to take away for the same price. This was a big inducement to the poorest. Women would muster some coppers to buy ale in an old jug or bottle. They would then drink the beer on the very steps of the public house where they bought it.[54]

Children and Alcohol

Alcohol was also consumed in the home. Men liked to have a drink with their evening meal and often sent out for a jug of beer. 'Ragged children,' wrote Hawthorne, 'come thither with old shaving-mugs or broken-nosed teapots or any such makeshift receptacle to get a little poison or madness for their parents.'[55] There was great competition for outdoor custom. Since children were the main messengers, publicans would offer them sweets and fruit as a reward for bringing custom. Brewers provided public houses with toffees with the name of the pub stamped into the centre. Children were therefore exposed to alcohol advertising from an early age. By visiting these establishments, youngsters were also forced to witness blasphemies, foul language, violence and drunken behaviour.

Children carrying home beer were often tempted to have a sneaky swig before handing it over. 'Who has the first sip?' asked Father Nugent. A 5-year-old girl was observed taking two mouthfuls of a bottle of rum she was carrying. A 3-year-old was also seen being served in a public house.[56] Harriett M. Johnson, a campaigner against children being served alcohol, tells the following shocking story: 'A little girl of seven startled the matron of a Children's Home the night of her arrival by asking "if it wasn't time to have her gin."'[57] One 9-year-old girl admitted to the Children's Shelter was found to be suffering from delirium tremens after being plied with drink by her parents and made to sing in the public houses.[58]

Boys of 12 or 13 would buy beer and drink it in the back alleys. In 1876 some 352 convicted drunks were less than 12 years of age.[59] Furthermore, only a small proportion of drunken children ever got arrested. Living in the back streets and courts, where the constables rarely patrolled, they were largely hidden from the view of the authorities. In 1896 Liverpool became the first city to require publicans to promise not to serve alcohol to children under the age of 13.[60] This was long before Parliament was involved in the issue and indeed helped pave the way for the 1901 Act that banned children entirely from public houses. The change of policy in Liverpool didn't go down well with the business interests of the drink trade. The following year, a deputation of

unhappy brewers, spirit merchants and licensed victuallers presented Liverpool magistrates with a petition calling for the age to be lowered to 10.[61]

Children drinking alcohol was of great social concern. Many of the boys in
the Borough Gaol, some of them only 14 years old, explained that most of their
stolen money was spent on drink.[62] A young prisoner revealed that 'many of
the boys in Liverpool drink rum'.[63] The chaplain of Kirkdale Gaol lamented
that 'boys of the tenderest age are now often found among the victims of
intoxication'.[64] When 14-year-old Lillian Gregory appeared in court in March
1888, accused of being drunk and disorderly, she was on a downward spiral
and had already been expelled from school. A product of a difficult family, she
was sent to the Mount Vernon Home for treatment.

Another concern was the availability of alcohol to children at theatres and
concert halls. Reverend Bishop, of the Unitarian Liverpool Domestic Mission
Society, revealed that 'one great source of crime amongst the youth of our
town was the concert rooms, where persons were admitted gratuitously,
but with the understanding that they consumed a certain quantity of drink,
and supplied themselves with tobacco'.[65] In 1850 a journalist visited one of
the largest concert rooms in Liverpool. Along with men and women, the
audience consisted of a large number of unruly adolescents, aged between 14
and 16. Almost all of the boys clenched a pipe or cigar between their teeth.
The journalist was most disturbed by their behaviour: 'Their applause rang
loudest throughout the room – their commands to the waiters for drink were
more frequent, obstreperous, and rude, than those of other persons – and
their whole behaviour was unbecoming and offensive.'[66]

The Anglican chaplain of Liverpool Borough Gaol, Thomas Carter, thought
that public houses that provided entertainment also contributed to juvenile
crime: 'they are particularly the resort of juvenile thieves. I recognised many
of them when I was there; and I gathered from the police, that if a robbery
was committed by a juvenile, the first thing they did was look for him at these
places.'[67] The Head Constable agreed: 'Singing and dancing saloons and what
are called "Free and Easies" at Public Houses and Beer Houses, have a most
pernicious effect upon young persons of both sexes.'[68] 'Free and Easies' were
the Victorian version of the modern karaoke bars.

The clientele of some public houses consisted almost entirely of young
people. In the 1890s the Sportsman's Arms in Christian Street was frequented
nightly by up to 80 lads and young women up to the age of 20, 'many of them
being without hats or stockings', according to Johnson. It seems that teenagers
had taken over the pub after older drinkers moved elsewhere. 'Drinking,
disorder, confusion prevailed, while the piano gave out its own tune, and at

the same time numerous voices shouted songs that had no relation to the piano music.' Brawling at closing time was also a regular occurrence as the youths, including some girls under the age of 16, staggered home drunk. The pub, described as a 'seminary of vice', was eventually closed down.[69]

Alcohol and Vice

The two great social evils of the Victorian period were drink and prostitution and the two were inevitably linked. Speaking of the abundance of liquor shops around the Sailors' Home, temperance campaigner Nathaniel Smyth was certain that 'were it not for prostitution and the fleecing of sailors, many of the public houses would have to close'.[70] So bad was the area that it was suggested that the police do no more than three months' duty there since it was too easy for them to become corrupted and immune to crime. Until the 1890s Liverpool had earned a reputation for taking a lax and lenient approach to prostitution. Some, such as Samuel Smith, felt that the authorities tolerated vice.[71] For Unitarian minister and temperance activist Revd Richard Acland Armstrong, the flesh trade and the brewing industry worked hand in glove. The public houses were implicated for two reasons. After a night of debauchery prostitutes would retire to the pubs. Father Nugent estimated that 75 per cent of their ill-gotten gains were spent on drink.[72] The pubs also acted as meeting points for clients, particularly in Lime Street, Parker Street and Church Street. Armstrong, writing in 1890, witnessed the pubs emptying at closing time with couples leaving in search of places to have sex. There were cabstands that largely catered for this immoral traffic. Armstrong thought that Liverpool's vice was being sponsored by business interests: 'Prostitution […] is an essential element in building up the mighty fortunes which many of our public-house proprietors enjoy.' He spoke of a pyramid of vice. At the pinnacle were the brewers and owners of public house properties. The next level included the publicans themselves followed by the landlords of brothels who lived upon the rents of prostitutes. Below them were the brothel-keepers and their pimps or bullies. Finally, the bottom layer consisted of the mass of prostitutes.[73]

The issues around drink and prostitution had political implications. The ruling Tories, with their links to the brewing trade and drinks industry, were accused of having no interest in tackling prostitution since doing so would affect the custom of the public houses and therefore reduce their profits. The Liberals, however, sided with the temperance movement. Armstrong points out that the confidential legal adviser of the two largest public house owners in Liverpool, Alderman John Hughes, not only sat on the Licensing Bench but also occupied the chair of the Watch Committee. There was a glaring conflict of interest with no impartiality. Samuel Smith pointed out that 'even in streets where people were in rags and tatters the drinkshops at each end took thousands of pounds from their earnings, and huge fortunes were made by the publican interest, especially the great brewers, some of whom left millions'. He concluded that 'great grog', rather than the town council, ruled Liverpool.[74]

Alcohol ruled people's lives, much to the frustration of churchmen and social reformers. The moral passions aroused by excessive drinking were part of a wider attack on popular amusements that debased rather than uplifted the human spirit. There was plenty of middle-class anxiety about unruly working-class leisure activities, particularly the Victorian equivalent of today's nightclub scene, where the lower classes were free to let off steam, indulge their baser instincts and seemingly abandon themselves to riot and debauchery. For Lucas P. Stubbs of the Borough Magistrates Office, one of the major causes of crime and vice in Liverpool was the abundance of 'singing saloons, frequented by women of the lowest class, where indecent songs demoralised large audiences, and these places acted as cheap schools where minds already vile were educated for crime'.[75] Despite the best efforts of the authorities to civilize, elevate and enlighten the lower classes through 'rational recreation', people's entertainment remained unrestrained, licentious and bawdy. Through a mixture of drink, dance, coloured lights and lewd songs, a clientele of dockworkers, street hawkers, prostitutes and sailors found temporary release from their drudgery and poverty.

For his series of investigative reports, originally published in the *Liverpool Mercury* under the title 'Liverpool Life', Hugh Shimmin did a tour of the minor theatres, 'twopenny hops', casinos and singing saloons. He wasn't impressed. His judgement on a free concert room: 'it combines the degradation, depravity, filth, squalor, and misery of the gin palace with what is very inappropriately called the jollity, sociality, conviviality and harmonious merriment of the "free and easy"'. Lowbrow entertainment, full of crude innuendo and double entendres, seemed to be the staple diet of the lower classes. Musical entertainment consisted of men singing obscene songs such as 'The Lively Flea', accompanied by vile actions. At the Salle de Danse in Lime Street, Shimmin witnessed 'fathers and sons, husbands and brothers, merchants, captains, and clerks, bullies and pimps, stepping and hopping, whirling and twirling, entwined and entwisted in the arms of the vilest harlots that infest our town'. Concert audiences were also titillated by dramatic scenes of pseudo-nudity, featuring Adam and Eve in body stockings. Shimmin lamented the fact that apart from the drink-free Saturday evening concerts held in Lord Nelson Street there were hardly any morally improving entertainments on offer in Liverpool.[76]

Temperance

Moral reformers did try to offer alternative attractions. Father Nugent provided entertainment at his temperance meetings, including professional Irish jig dancing and negro-minstrelsy. He wouldn't allow even soda water to be drunk at the meetings in case a drunk got hold of the bottle and cracked somebody with it.[77] To counteract the social menace of the Cornermen, Revd Garrett proposed a chain of alcohol-free establishments along the line of docks where those casual workers surplus to requirements could better spend their time.[78] The first of these teetotal pubs opened in October 1875 and within two years there were 28 similar facilities serving tea, cocoa and coffee.[79]

For some social commentators the solution to poverty and other social ills was not political change but abstention from alcohol. Temperance campaigners focused on reforming the morals of the poor rather than trying to improve their social conditions, although it was also believed that social conditions would eventually improve once alcohol was given up. However simplistic the reasoning, the temperance movement claimed some success. A number of parishes, such as St Peter's in Seel Street, started their own temperance societies. The Liverpool Temperance Society was founded in 1830. The cause lapsed with the Roman Catholics until Father Nugent formed a local branch of the Total Abstinence League of the Cross in 1875. Around this time Samuel Smith also began temperance meetings at the Coliseum Theatre in Paradise Street. People were encouraged to attend by being given a loaf of bread. Smith believed that the crusade was a great success among the lower classes: 'From being brute beasts they have regained self control and decency of life.'[80]

If alcohol helped put people in gaol, the temperance movement could help keep them out of it. The Church of England Temperance Society, based at the Dale Street Police Court, offered support to drunkards. Officers of the Police Court and Prison Gate Mission, founded in 1879, would also stand outside Walton Gaol ready to greet the newly released prisoners. They would be taken to the mission room and offered breakfast and a spiritual pep talk before being urged to sign the pledge not to drink. In 1898, 7,949 meals were given and 1,074 pledges signed. The Society also ran a firewood factory in Bootle offering

Table 4: Average annual number of cases of drunkenness

Five year period ending	Number
1874	19,193
1879	17,717
1884	15,462
1889	14,868
1894	9,724
1899	4,768

Source: Liverpool Mercury, 6 February 1900

employment for released prisoners. Sir William Forwood, as chairman of the visiting justices of Walton Gaol, was familiar with the factory. He felt that 12 of the men had been there too long and should be sent away to find work elsewhere: 'The following week there was an outbreak of burglaries in Bootle, and the whole crowd were back again in gaol.'[81] There was also a Women's Shelter in Upper Parliament Street with accommodation for 20 destitute and intemperate women.[82]

There were wider social experiments in drink-free living. By the 1890s Toxteth Park, with a population of 50,000, had banned public houses and become 'the largest prohibition area in England'. However, it was not entirely a drink-free zone as residents merely crossed the border into Liverpool carrying bottles to fill with beer. Wine and spirit merchants' carts could also be seen daily dropping off supplies of alcohol and carrying away the empties.[83]

Nevertheless, after sustained campaigns from the 1870s onwards to regulate licensed premises, cases of drunkenness gradually decreased.[84] Yet there are problems with any statistics relating to drunkenness. The figures might be more reflective of the zealousness of police actions at any particular time than an indicator of the public's sobriety. Liverpool's Head Constable admitted that the fall did not necessarily mean a decrease in actual drunkenness, only illegal drunkenness. Due to stricter controls of the public houses, drunks who were refused alcohol probably went home to continue drinking. In this way they were off the streets and less likely to be arrested.[85] The reduction might also indicate that the police were becoming less efficient at arresting drunks. Dr Whitford pointed out that during the period from 1890 to 1895, assaults increased from 1,958 to 3,117 a year. The reason given was that the drunks who weren't being arrested were fighting on the streets and beating up members of the public![86]

Nevertheless, it is generally agreed that there was some improvement in sobriety towards the end of the century. Various reasons were cited. Tougher restrictions on licensing and stricter police scrutiny of public houses kept licensees on their toes. Housing renewal and slum clearance programmes gave people more comfortable homes which encouraged them to enjoy family life. They were no longer compelled to visit cosy public houses for warmth. Improved public transport facilities enabled workers to move away from the squalid dockside areas with their abundance of public houses. Men could travel to and from work without visiting the pub as they walked home. The growth in outdoor leisure activities gave people better things to do than drink themselves silly. Compulsory education also played its part, as did the role of benefit societies that disapproved of men who drank too much.[87]

Greater restrictions on drinking hours meant that the evening streets became less disorderly. Yet the drink problem never completely went away. In fact, the drunken catfight that began this chapter occurred in 1899 after so many social improvements had been made. The Head Constable noted that although drunkenness decreased towards the end of the century, the rate of decrease was slower among women than men. Also, habitual drunkards tended to be women.[88] Many lower-class women spent their lives trapped in the most deprived and dismal neighbourhoods, under the submission of husbands, trying to raise families while forced to earn their own pittance hawking goods on the streets. Alcohol might have been one of the causes of the destitution, degradation and despair of slum life but ironically it was also a means of escape from all these things.

NINE

Violence

'A Bit of Liverpool'

Strolling through the slums of Liverpool in 1883, a journalist made a startling observation. Although there were plenty of old women, there were few old men. It was as if males didn't survive long in such a dangerous environment. Indeed, many men had the 'bruised and baited look of a fighting bulldog'.[1] Hugh Shimmin described the typical Liverpool 'rough' in similar terms: 'men of short stature, with big heads, broad, flat faces, and thick necks [with] white trousers turned up at the bottom to show their high-laced, greasy boots'.[2] Physically, Liverpool men were built for fighting. Add to this a psychological propensity for violence and the police courts were destined to remain busy. Shimmin, again, makes a revealing comment about the volatile nature of the Liverpool temperament: 'The transition from a coarse word or a ribald jest to a kick, from a poker to a knife, is made with alarming rapidity.'[3] The hospitals, as much the police courts, were well aware of this. The north-end hospital, each Saturday night, required two extra nurses to prepare bandages.[4]

Liverpool had a notorious reputation for violence. In 1874, in Blackburn, a local ruffian armed with a knife severely kicked two policemen. Upon severing the finger of one of them, he vowed to 'give them a bit of Liverpool'.[5] The town's reputation owed much to its history of sectarian battles and ruffianism imported from the Emerald Isle. The Irish were viewed as particularly savage street fighters who kicked, bit and scratched.[6]

Faction Fights

The Irish were seen as the race 'who broke each others' heads as an amusement'.[7] Back in Ireland there was a tradition of hostility between men from rival villages, counties and provinces. The resulting brawls, sometimes involving hundreds of men on each side, were known as 'faction fights'. These skirmishes, using fists, sticks and stones, provided communal entertainment similar to football matches today. Some bloodthirsty people attended Irish fairs or markets in the hope of catching a good faction fight. The venues were pre-arranged and the clashes governed by a number of well-defined rules and rituals. Fights usually began with the ritual of 'wheeling', in which the sides would formally call each other out. The traditional wheel included the names of the person(s) issuing the challenge, followed by the intended opponent, for example: 'Here is Connors and Delahunty. Is there any Madden will come before us?'[8]

When the Irish migrated, their rural village rivalries were randomly transplanted into the crowded back alleys and courts of dockland Liverpool. In 1826 the district of Great Crosshall Street contained numerous small streets and entries inhabited by a fearless Irish mob called the Rosannah Gang. Whenever one of them needed help he would use a shrill whistle. The resulting horde of followers was more than a match for the watchmen on duty. At 11.30 p.m. one evening in November, the landlord of a public house in Scotland Place called the watchmen to help him clear his premises of Irishmen. After some difficulty the men were ejected but continued to loiter outside, defying the watchmen's orders to move on. Soon the Rosannah whistle was heard and 200 bodies swiftly answered the call. The eight watchmen realized that they were outnumbered and sought refuge in the pub, but not before some were attacked. One suffered two broken ribs and another had his shoulder bone broken in two. Only the arrival of soldiers managed to quell the disturbance.[9]

In the press, faction fights also became known as 'Irish rows', although the term later came to be used for any brawls, whether or not any Irish were involved. On a Sunday evening in March 1834 a battle between Ulster and Leinster men kicked off in the neighbourhood of Thomas Street and Atherton Street. A few arrests were made. The following morning, hostilities were transferred to Cheshire, presumably to avoid interference from the authorities. After three separate pitched battles, the men returned home later that day. On entering Atherton Street one of the parties started to assault people indiscriminately. Watchmen on duty were then attacked with crowbars, pokers and spades. At the end of the disturbance 19 prisoners had been taken into custody.[10]

Police Inspector William Ross was beaten to death as he tried to break up a faction fight at the tannery near Windsor on the evening of 28 May 1838. The fight was originally scheduled to take place at the Parliament Fields but was interrupted by police and had to change venue. Ross, along with other officers, found that a crowd had already formed a ring and that two men, stripped to the waist, had completed two or three rounds. As the officers took one of the combatants into custody about 30 men pulled long sticks out of their pockets and proceeded to beat the officers. To shouts of 'Go it, go it' and 'Kill them, murder them,' Inspector Ross was savagely bludgeoned. At one point, six or seven men were thrashing him as he lay helpless on the floor. He died a week later of his injuries.

A group of Irishmen, believed to have backed and promoted the fight, were arrested when reinforcements arrived. George McCarty, James Durning, Martin Murphy, James Macklin and Patrick Cumming, whose ages ranged from 18 to 26, were convicted of murder and transported for life. The bravery of Inspector Ross was commemorated in an elegiac sonnet written by a police constable:

> 'Tis true he has fall'n – our champion in danger –
> Brutality's victim! He sleeps with the dead;
> But he fell in his duty, and fear was a stranger
> Unknown to the bosom whose spirit is fled.[11]

A great many such rows and brawls went unrecorded, as police would often stop the battle without making any arrests. In June 1842 two men from New Bird Street went to Toxteth Park to fight for money. Word spread that it was a battle between ships' carpenters and the Irish. An inspector and 30 dock police, armed with cutlasses, reached the park only for the crowd to run away. In court, one Irishwoman made reference to two separate incidents involving up to 50 people that were not mentioned in the press.[12] Other incidents were stopped by the police before anybody was injured. Nothing could unite rival factions as effectively as the presence of the police. In 1851, 200 people, armed with sticks, pokers and cleavers, were engaged in a mass brawl in Addison Street. On the arrival of the police, both sides immediately ceased hostilities and proceeded to break up a wall to provide ammunition to throw at the officers.[13]

In July 1844, as he walked down Lace Street, Pat Condon was greeted with a shower of bricks thrown by Matthew (or Michael) Regan, the leader of a faction that ruled the district with fear. Regan then hit his victim over the head with a bludgeon and kicked him while he lay helpless on the floor. Police found neat heaps of bricks piled in different parts of the street ready for throwing. Neighbours were too terrified to give evidence against Regan, who had a reputation for cudgelling his enemies. A female witness of the Regan faction gave evidence in his favour. She claimed that Condon, while walking past Regan's house, had shouted, 'Matthew you prig, come out here, and I'll knock the hump on you.' Regan was then said to have flown out of the door with the cry, 'I'll have blood for my supper, blood!' Condon was said to have replied, 'Death or glory, hurrah!' However, the magistrate soon proved that the woman was making it all up and Regan was found guilty of assault.[14]

Minor feuds sometimes degenerated into free-for-alls. In June 1863, in Collingwood Street, a 'fair stand-up fight' between a man called McKenny and a member of the McHugh family got out of hand. The magistrate said that 'it was almost impossible to get to the bottom of these Irish rows'. In 1847 groups of Irishmen were having a Sunday drinking session in the upstairs room of an alehouse in Prescot, a few miles outside Liverpool. A feud between the Shannons and the Molloys broke out, during which the candle was extinguished, leaving the men in darkness. In the confusion, the fight spilled downstairs into the street. James Murray, of the Shannon faction, offered to fight any one of the Molloys. Armed with a poker, Murray approached Martin Molloy who was clutching a stick. Molloy was hit on the head and later died. Sentencing Murray to two years' imprisonment, the judge expressed the wish that the Irish could learn 'some of the phlegm and unexcitable habits of the English'.[15]

On a Friday night in May 1849 the residents of St Martin's Street began a fight between Sligo and Mayo factions. Police dispersed the combatants but the whole affair kicked off again the following night. Men, armed with bludgeons, threw stones at each other while the women took to the windows to rain missiles on the officers' heads. One constable received severe head injuries after a blow from a poker. Michael McCormick, James Kelly and Martin and Michael Callagan were among those arrested and fined for the disorder. During a disturbance in Addison Street, Marybone, in 1852, a big, rough-looking Irishman called MacToyd began throwing stones at a rival faction. Several women with their aprons full of bricks waited on him, handing him missiles. When a constable arrived MacToyd threatened to 'rip him up'.[16] Four months later, in nearby Hodson Street, between 400 and 500 Irish engaged in a Sunday night mass brawl before both sides turned on the police. One woman threw a stone weighing 4lbs.[17]

Irish rows were endemic in the neighbourhood of Fontenoy Street. Injuries were commonplace. In 1854 a lame cobbler called Duffy told the court that on a Sunday night a mob of Irish neighbours, including a contingent of Sweeneys, Cusacks and Barretts, gave him a good hiding. He claimed to have been jumped upon, kicked, stabbed three times and struck with a cosh, called a 'neddy'. Although Duffy appeared in court swathed in bloodstained bandages, the surgeon felt that his injuries were not severe and the case was dismissed.[18] It was not unusual for families to amalgamate for particular fights. On a Sunday evening in May 1853 the Kellys, Fitzpatricks and Murphys banded together to take on the Molly Maguires in Marybone. A crowd of about 200 people laid into each other, with some combatants diverting their energies to throw bricks at policemen making arrests. The crowd made repeated attempts to rescue any prisoners.

The Molly Maguires derived from an organization of peasants who wore women's dress and other disguises to attack rent collectors in rural Ireland. The group also had origins in the anthracite coal region of Northern Pennsylvania where they had a reputation for violent industrial action.[19] The mysterious organization was first mentioned in Liverpool in 1853.[20] They had their headquarters in an alehouse in Sawney Pope Street kept by Pat Flynn, the secretary of the 'Molly Maguire Clubs'. Members swore an oath to give mutual help, 'an insult or injury to one being taken as an insult to all, for which all sought satisfaction'. They therefore benefited if prosecuted for assaulting policemen or getting into rows, the fines imposed by the court being paid out of a communal fund. In 1858 Flynn was charged with beating up Pat Nolan but when the court case drew near Flynn gave Nolan £2 15s not to turn up. Nolan took the money but then decided to press on with the case. Flynn understandably assaulted him again.[21] Around this time Anthony Fay assaulted Catherine Finnegan, after he accused her of attacking his daughter. In court the victim explained, 'He is in "Molly's Club" and his wife told me that he could beat anyone he liked, and that any fine would be paid for him.' The arrangement proved useless as he was sent to prison for two months instead.[22] Fights between the Irish became part and parcel of everyday Liverpool life. In 1864 a magistrate declared, 'The other day when I sat here there were 45 cases of assault, 43 of which were connected with Irish squabbles or Irish "faction fights."'[23]

Yet Liverpool could draw on a number of traditions of violence. In addition to Irish savagery there was customary Lancastrian brutality. In 1847 the *Liverpool Mercury* offered some tongue-in-cheek monthly predictions: 'Two murders, attended with horrible atrocities, will be committed at Ballinaruffian, and the people will make no effort to discover, or, rather, to give up the perpetrators. There will be a brutal up-and-down fight at Wigan, Bolton or Oldham, when one of the cannibals will bite off the end of the other's nose.'[24]

Lancashire was famous for a type of fighting called 'purring' or 'up and down fighting', which involved kicking opponents even when they were on the floor. Kicking was largely associated with northern men who wore clogs and iron-tipped boots. Brutal northerners were seen to lack the proper pugilistic skills of civilized Englishmen who, allegedly, used only their fists in a stand-up boxing style. In 1874 there were 17 cases of purring in Lancashire, two or three of them fatal. It was pointed out that 'the common tendency to substitute the clog for the fist in Lancashire has no parallel in any other county in the kingdom'.[25] After a kicking fatality in Bolton in 1832, a Manchester newspaper described a typical contest: 'They seize their victims with a deadly gripe [*sic*], and then assail them with teeth, hand, and foot, until the wretched beings lie prostrate on the ground, mutilated and bleeding, and too often in the last stage of life.' Such fighters were likened to 'New Zealand savages, or Hottentot spearmen'.[26]

Knives

Add to this explosive mix the 'foreign' use of the knife and we are left with a deadly combination. Along with biting and kicking, knife crime was judged most un-English. At the Lancashire Summer Assizes in 1852, Chief Justice Lord Campbell pointed out an increase in the use of the knife: 'It used to be unknown in England, and the English nation were famous that they never made use of deadly weapons [...] But I am sorry to say the use of the stiletto or knife has become very general, and it is most essential that this un-English practice should be repressed by punishment.'[27] The following year, the grand jury at the Assizes heard of 'an alarming increase of violence, accompanied by the barbarous use of the knife'. Watch committee statistics also revealed that during the previous three years there had been no fewer than 233 knife attacks.[28] By the end of 1853 magistrates had dealt with 179 cases of knife crime, including the stabbing to death of PC Sunderland by Thomas Copeland. The coroner lamented the prevalence of knives on Liverpool's streets, stating that he preferred to see a stand-up fight rather than the use of a weapon 'peculiar to barbarous nations'. When the Copeland case was tried, the judge sadly revealed that stabbing somebody to death was 'no longer an un-English crime'.[29] Hugh Shimmin reports that a local sparring match was advertised thus: 'Now is the time or never for all Englishmen to join heart and hand to prevent their truly national sport from being put down and utterly extinguished – the foreigner's *stiletto* substituted for the English *fist*!'[30]

Yet even fair stand-up fights sometimes degenerated into bloodbaths when weapons were unexpectedly produced. In 1896, after a number of previous quarrels, 21-year-old John Donnelly stabbed Robert Devine to death in Sumner Street. The victim challenged Donnelly: 'If you want to fight me, come now and fight fair.' Donnelly approached, only for Devine to pull a short stick out of his pocket. His attempt to whack his opponent was thwarted when Donnelly produced a knife and stabbed him a couple of times in the back, penetrating his lung.[31]

The dagger was the traditional weapon of the docklands, capable of transforming petty arguments into murder inquiries. Liverpool sailors routinely carried sheath-knives or clasp-knives while some foreign seamen favoured stilettos. Most smokers also carried penknives to cut up tobacco. However, foreigners, particularly Mediterranean and South American sailors, were said to have a different cultural attitude towards knife fights. In 1858 a stipendiary magistrate stated 'that the use of the knife by coloured men in Liverpool was intolerable'.[32] Two years later, a judge remarked that 'great numbers of American seaman come to this port, and they must be taught that they could not use the knife with impunity in this country'.[33] The following year, in Hood Street, a Spanish seaman stabbed to death a countryman after a row over a Liverpool woman.[34] By 1863 knifings were so common that the stipendiary magistrate, Mr Raffles, produced notices in seven languages warning sailors against carrying knives and weapons.[35] The notices were issued to captains, foreign crew and boarding-house keepers and were believed to have had a good effect, despite one black seaman admitting to stabbing a countryman *after* reading the warning.[36] The success, however, was tempered by an unforeseen development. At the Borough sessions in 1862 the Recorder observed that although knife crime had decreased among sailors 'it seems to have increased amongst the disorderly residents in the town'.[37]

Knives were not the only worry in Liverpool. Victorian court reports are littered with assaults with unidentified 'sharp instruments', sometimes belaying pins or work tools. Available weapons depended on the occupation of the attacker. Navvies favoured spades while dockworkers were handy with the cotton hook. All men wore leather belts and these could be swung through the air to deadly effect. The slash from a brass buckle was similar to a knife wound. Firearms were legal until 1920 and pistols were easily bought from pawn shops. In 1877, after sentencing Matthew McCullough in a double shooting case, the judge warned that 'the use of firearms was becoming so common among young men'.[38] Upper-class gentlemen had long used pistols to settle disputes. Duels were an acceptable means of defending one's honour. In 1804, in Dingle, Lieutenant William Sparling shot Edward Grayson in the thigh. He died the following week. The dispute was over Grayson's niece to whom Sparling was engaged. Sparling was acquitted of murder.[39] Liverpool's last duel took place in a field near Pembroke Place and Low Hill in December 1805. After a row over salary, following which some public comments were made, John Bolton shot Major Edward Brooks in the eye, killing him. Although the inquest jury returned a verdict of wilful murder, there was no prosecution.

Street Fights

Duelling was outlawed after 1838 but the spirit of such contests survived in the countless street brawls in the lower-class neighbourhoods. In a humorous attempt to link the two styles of combat, Hugh Shimmin published an account of a scrap between two residents of Ben Jonson Street. Fighting over the attentions of Bridget Malone, a basket-girl from Milton Street, the men arranged to settle their differences at Parliament Fields. The choice of weapon, between cosh and knuckle dusters, had already been decided when a detective stopped the proceedings.[40] An earlier row saw two lumpers called Tom Megraw and Paddy Clarke heading to Toxteth Park to battle over the charms of Mary Matthews. A journalist noted that 'nature in a sportive mood had blessed Tom with a long, spare body, and by way of a finish to his proportions, had given him a short left leg and a long right one'. At a dramatic point in the fight, Clarke connected with an almighty blow to Megraw's stomach. Perhaps unfamiliar with the protocols of boxing, the winded man spluttered, 'Blood and 'ouns! What did you do that for?' After fifteen minutes and 16 rounds, Clarke decided to run off, with Megraw limping after him.[41]

The lenient verdicts on the duellists suggest that those living in the early nineteenth century displayed a greater tolerance towards acts of interpersonal violence compared to the present day.[42] As the century progressed the authorities increasingly frowned upon duelling and other forms of violence. In the poorer districts, however, physical brutality remained a valid means of expression. In rough neighbourhoods, fisticuffs provided an opportunity to gain a reputation. Indeed, street-fighting became a form of sport used to display toughness and status in the neighbourhood. Street brawlers emulated some of the ceremonies of the professional prize-fight, coming up to scratch and so on. Today such a fight would be called a 'straightener', that is a pre-arranged one-to-one scrap by mutual agreement, with no weapons. In 1825, after officers broke up a prize-fight in Toxteth Park, the complaint was made that similar scenes involving both men and boys were 'becoming a nightly nuisance, collecting mobs, and inducing idleness and riot'.[43] The North Shore in Bootle, a site now occupied by the Clarence Dock, was another favourite venue.[44] The fights were exciting but disorderly affairs. To relieve the suffocating crush of the crowds, the 'beaters' would use their belts to lash the spectators into order. Such events were rarely single-fight bills. The rival factions of the headlining fight would sometimes kick off and attack each other. In 1849, after a Saturday night argument in a public house in Pownall Square, two men agreed to settle their differences with a fight the following

Sunday. Heatley Campbell beat Robert Owens to death and was convicted of manslaughter.[45]

Such fights were the spectator sport of the slums. One pitched battle took place by appointment. In May 1859 a barrel of beer was set up for refreshments in Parliament Fields at the top of Parliament Street. Between 300 and 400 'roughs' from the Harding Street and Windsor district joined in 'what Americans call a free fight'. At one point up to 14 men were brawling at the same time. 'The two "armies" were enjoying themselves heartily in their own fashion' when the police arrived to make arrests. Yet police were nowhere to be seen five years later, when the same location hosted a bout between two drunken youths. One lad, armed with a belt, kept the ring while friends of the contestants acted as seconds. When the fight ended, the large crowd began to disperse only for an impromptu fight to break out between two older spectators. The event lasted 45 minutes.[46]

Nevertheless, police intervention remained a risk. Fighters sometimes had to travel to evade patrolling constables. In July 1876 constabulary officers saw a large group of 'roughs' from the Scotland Road area congregated in Balliol Road, Bootle. It seems that a pre-arranged fight had just taken place between two men. The police dispersed the crowd but they reassembled at Miller's Bridge and the fight resumed, this time with weapons and sticks being used. Police intervention forced the men to cross back over the borough boundary into Sandhills where the police once again found them fighting. Patrick Derry, from Athol Street, later admitted himself into the Bootle Hospital with stab wounds to his stomach. He refused to give any details as to how he received his injuries but it was thought to be related to the earlier altercation.

A lack of space in the slums was at the root of some violence. Overcrowded lodging-houses offered little physical escape from assaults and 'murderous quarrels often sprang up between lodgers'.[47] In tightly packed public houses, rows could develop out of seemingly trivial incidents such as bumping into somebody and spilling their beer. In a dockside public house on Christmas Day 1863, Joseph McGrath drunkenly stepped backwards and accidentally knocked into a seaman from Manila who was making his way outside. Words passed between the two and the seaman declared, 'I will have revenge.' As McGrath left the pub shortly afterwards he was stabbed to death. Insults, real or perceived, had to be avenged, making violence a completely acceptable response for some, a form of instant justice bypassing the cumbersome processes of the police court. This was particularly important when the task of prosecuting somebody was difficult, time-consuming and costly. Indeed, other than violence, there were few legitimate means of resolving neighbourhood disputes. People needed to stand their ground in the struggle for survival in the un-policed back alleys and enclosed courts where there was little chance of walking away or summoning help.

The crowded streets were the arena for more serious bloodshed. Random acts of gratuitous violence were not unknown. In May 1850, in Great Crosshall Street, a 'ferocious-looking fellow' called Patrick McGinnis knocked Robert Hughes unconscious using a ball of lead tied to a piece of a rope. The victim was merely standing outside the shop where he worked. In November 1865 Michael Ryan was also minding his own business when a stranger called Stephen Knight came up to him and stabbed him in the head. When Ryan asked him why he did it, Knight replied, 'I'll stab any _____.'

Racial Violence

Racial violence was a feature of Liverpool life. A busy port, the town entertained seamen of many nationalities. Relations between white men and darker skinned foreigners were sometimes marked by prejudice, discrimination and violent hostility, despite the view of American mariner-turned-novelist Herman Melville in the late 1830s: 'In Liverpool indeed the negro steps with a prouder pace, and lifts his head like a man [...] owing to the friendly reception extended to them, and the unwonted immunities they enjoy in Liverpool, the black cooks and stewards of American ships are very much attached to the place and like to make voyages to it.'[48] The reality was somewhat different, although not all racial discrimination came from native Liverpudlians. In August 1846 a Hindu, who made his living selling tracts from door to door, approached two American sailors who proceeded to destroy his stock before beating him. The same two sailors also spat in the face of a passing black man before assaulting him. A white woman holding a mixed-race child in her arms was also hit in the face and the child knocked down. The magistrate criticized the appalling racial prejudice of the sailors which fortunately was not reflective of the majority of Americans staying in Liverpool. Yet feelings of white American superiority over blacks continued. In 1850 a black man, who made his living exhibiting waxworks at the Haymarket, was having a quiet drink in a public house in Roe Street when he was spotted by a group of American seamen. One said, 'Come out of this; we'll have no Negroes here.' The black man was then forcibly ejected before a riot broke out in which glasses and jugs were thrown. Police were called and after one of the attackers was fined, a group of about 15 sailors returned to the pub to have words with the publican whom they accused of lying about the incident. After buying drinks, each sailor took it in turns to throw beer over him. The group ended up in court where the magistrate remarked that the sailors seemed to think they were back in the southern states where skin colour mattered.[49]

Unfortunately, even in Liverpool colour sometimes did matter. A member of the public, walking by the docks in 1853, saw a black child on his knees surrounded by a group of English and Irish sailors. They asked, 'Is your mother white?' 'Was your father a chimney sweep?' and 'Where did you get your curly wig from?' The child pleaded, 'I want something to eat.' Their reply was 'Get up you young nigger.'[50] In September 1857, under the headline 'White v. Black at the Sailors' Home', the *Liverpool Mercury* reported a couple of racial incidents that had occurred on the same day. It was alleged that children were also schooled in racism. In May 1858 a drunken black man savagely kicked a small boy in Dale Street. In court, the man accused the boy of being part of a group of children who had followed him calling him 'Black Jack' and other names. This was denied and the man was fined. Andrew Robertson was a black unemployed seaman who had walked from Middlesbrough to Liverpool in search of work. He complained that people in the streets were calling him 'Blackman' and 'Snowball', probably a reference to 'Professor Snowball', a member of the Negro Nomads, a popular minstrel troupe. With quiet dignity, the man stated that he 'looked upon himself as flesh and blood like other people'.[51] In April 1876 a black seaman was hit on the head with a bottle for singing 'a nigger song' in a public house in Price Street.

Relations between black men and white women were often a source of conflict. In October 1866 a black seaman called Alexander Montgomery was talking to a white female brothel-keeper in Old Hall Street when William Morgan came up and asked the woman why she was talking to a '_____ nigger'. When Montgomery later approached Morgan, a fight broke out and Montgomery was fatally stabbed in the stomach. Morgan was sentenced to ten years for manslaughter.

White men saw black people as an easy target for cadging money and drinks. In August 1855 a black boarding-house keeper from Titchfield Street was walking past a street-corner gang when they asked him for a 'treat'. He refused and was subjected to a volley of abuse before being knocked unconscious. In December 1862 James Williams entered a public house in Frederick Street. John McKay asked him to pay for a drink. Because he refused, the black man was dragged outside and kicked senseless. In July 1867 two men stopped a black man called Robert Brown in Chisenhale Street and asked him to buy them drinks. His refusal led to him being beaten insensible. In April 1875, in Leeds Street, John Dickinson and James Wilson demanded money from

James Lorand, a black sailor. After thrashing him for refusing, they followed him back to his lodgings where they also attacked his black lodging-house keeper.

Children and Violence

If foreigners did not appreciate the sanctity of life, neither did children. In a tough seafaring town like Liverpool it is not surprising that youngsters were influenced by the violence around them. In 1832 a member of the public warned of the number of boys found fighting in the streets. He had lately witnessed two youngsters brawling in Ranelagh Street, one of them using a piece of slate to cut his opponent. 'I think something might be done to stop this long-continued evil,' the man concluded.[52] Being able to fight was a valuable skill in the slums. Children were required to stand up for themselves against attack from other youngsters. In May 1864 14-year-old Richard Gray stabbed 13-year-old Maurice Fitzgibbon after the younger boy had slapped him first. Children also engaged in gang fights. In 1834 there were numerous stone-throwing battles between small boys from rival schools in Hope Street and Hardman Street. In November a crowd of boys armed with missiles congregated outside the school in Hardman Street, waiting to 'lead the assault'. The headmaster managed to take one of the gang into custody. In court, the Mayor revealed that he had witnessed similar scenes of juvenile civil war and on one occasion had attempted to remonstrate with the boys only to be pelted with missiles. He had to take refuge at the house of a nearby doctor.[53] The following year, the stone-throwing between rival schoolboys was still taking place in Duke Street. In February a stray missile struck a lady walking in the nearby cemetery. Women were consequently afraid to take walks in the neighbourhood.[54] In 1847 70 panes of glass were broken in the neighbourhood of St Martin's School during a fight between boys from rival schools.[55]

Some children collaborated in fatal violence. In July 1855 a gang of boys were playing on the brickfields near the Leeds–Liverpool canal. During a game of leapfrog an argument broke out between James Fleeson, aged 7, and Alfred Fitz, aged 9. Fitz threw a brick at the younger boy's head, felling him. While on the floor, the groaning youngster was hit with another brick. Fitz calmly turned to his friend John Breen and suggested throwing the boy into the canal 40 yards away. Fleeson floated momentarily before sinking. The body was not found until Thursday when it was fished out of the Stanley Dock. The boys were convicted of manslaughter and sentenced to 12 months' imprisonment. The judge hoped that they would gain an education while incarcerated.

Thirty-six years later, friends Samuel Crawford, aged 9, and Robert Shearer (alias O'Brien), aged 8, were both charged with murdering 8-year-old David Dawson Eccles. All three boys were regular truants from school. Crawford and Shearer were also fond of staying away from home for days at a time. In September 1891 Shearer had been grounded. His mother put him to bed and confiscated his clothes in an effort to keep him indoors. Undeterred, the boy dressed himself in an old sack and sneaked out to play with Crawford. On a building site at the corner of Stanley Street and Victoria Street, a large pool had formed in the foundations. Known as 'the rafts', the murky pit was a popular attraction for children. On their way, the two children met Eccles, whom they didn't know, and invited him for a swim. Shearer had other motives. When Eccles was naked they pushed him into the water and left him to drown. Shearer threw the victim's boots, stockings and cap into the pool and then changed his sack for the trousers and shirt. Crawford took the coat. In December the boys were found guilty of murder. Considered to be too young to be responsible for their actions, they were placed in a refuge under the care of Father Nugent. Crawford, however, remained attracted to the streets and absconded four times. In March 1892 he was again found living rough on the streets and remanded. Cases such as these illustrate the uncomfortable ambiguity that characterized Victorian representations of lower-class children. They were viewed either as pathetic and neglected waifs or violent savages. It was perhaps difficult to accept that they could sometimes be both.

Women and Violence

Violence was not confined to men and boys. Reported assaults by Liverpool lasses were twice the national average. Between 1850 and 1914 Liverpool women accounted for about a third of common assault prosecutions in the city.[56] Nathaniel Hawthorne described the behaviour of local women: 'where a sharp tongue will not serve the purpose, they trust to the sharpness of their finger-nails, or incarnate a whole vocabulary of vituperative words in a resounding slap, or the downright blow of a doubled fist'.[57] In Tithebarn Street, Hawthorne 'saw a woman suddenly assault a man, clutch at his hair, and cuff him about the ears. The man, who was of decent aspect enough, immediately took to his heels, full speed, and the woman after him; and as far as I could discern the pair, the chase continued.'[58] Speaking of women, M. J. Whitty, at the time the Superintendent of the Night Watch, declared that aggravated assaults are frequent among them, arising from sudden provocation and drink. These are the results of the drunken rows in which women and men are indiscriminately engaged. I never knew an Irish row in which women were not concerned; on these occasions they use any thing that comes to their hand; if there is nothing they fight with their fists; they never fight with fists if they can get a weapon'.[59]

One ferocious Liverpool woman, armed with a rasp, 'knocked down seven men with her own hand'.[60]

Samuel Smith recalled that 'the women engaged in hand to hand fights, and the police court each Monday morning exhibited a mass of blackened eyes and broken heads, showing how the Sunday had been spent'.[61] Liverpool had its fair share of hard women. Elizabeth Kelly and her daughters were described as 'terrors of Midgehall Street'.[62] When drunk, they fought with anyone. The slums were the scenes of much female violence, most but not all of it directed against other women. Ann Baylan and Bridget Cowley, who lived at the same address in Leeds Street, kept a New Year's drinking session going till 8 a.m. After numerous quarrels, Baylan struck Cowley on the head with a poker, causing a serious scalp injury. She also smashed her in the face with a cup, knocking out a tooth and leaving her upper lip hanging by a shred of skin. Children were also occasional victims of female violence. Two young women called Mary Mullen and Mary Costello ambushed 10-year-old Mary Foy and dragged her by the hair before striking her head against the pavement. There was no apparent motive. Some female assaults were triggered by trivial disputes. Elizabeth Driscoll, of Raglan Street, stabbed Ann Howard in the head after a row about the loan of a pocket handkerchief. Sarah Regan knocked at Sarah Welsh's house in Maguire Street to ask for the return of a book that she had loaned her. After a quarrel, Welsh hit Regan on the head with a poker. The book was called *Life of Peace*. Pokers were a handy household weapon. Bridget Heneghan cracked her brother-in-law over the head with a poker after warning him, 'I will split you open.'[63]

If they couldn't grab a poker, housewives used the nearest jug. Hannah Mellon met Eliza Bell in Pitt Street and, after calling her a prostitute, smacked her on the head with a jug. Boiling water was also used to good effect. Margaret Wilson, a resident of a brothel in Hotham Street, threw a pot of scalding water over the servant of the house for no apparent reason. After an argument, Bridget McConchie poured boiling water over Mary Ann Henry. Susannah Kelly had a quarrel with Catherine Fitzgerald in a court off Ben Jonson Street. A crack on the head with a hatchet proving inadequate punishment, Kelly finished off her rival with hot water.[64]

A more lethal fluid was vitriol, a sulphuric acid easily bought in bottles at chemists for cleaning purposes. This was occasionally used by women to throw in the faces of opponents, particularly unfaithful or drunken husbands, seducers and ex-lovers. Gabriel Webster of Hotham Street was lying on his bed at the end of a six-week drinking spree when his wife Ann finally snapped and threw vitriol at him: 'the whole of the skin was off the poor fellow's face', leaving him badly disfigured. Margaret Maloney threw vitriol at the postman after he denied fathering her child. A 17-year-old tried to blind her older seducer who had left her holding the baby, a transgression that prompted a letter to the newspaper siding with the young woman. A rarer crime was for women to throw the fluid in the face of another woman, as Mary Lovell was alleged to have done to a fellow prostitute after a row.[65]

In the absence of weapons, women resorted to their teeth. In 1863 the Recorder of the Borough Sessions reported that biting offences were 'becoming very common'.[66] The newspapers occasionally reported cases of 'female cannibalism'. MaryAnn Douglas bit a four-inch long strip of flesh from the arm of an old woman called Isabella McCann, leaving the muscles and tendons exposed. Near Vauxhall Road, Rose Ann Burns bit a two-inch chunk out of Catherine O'Brien's ear. This followed a drinking spree to celebrate Burns' release from prison. Mary Ann McNab, holding a baby in her arms, walked past a group of fish sellers in Northumberland Street when Barbara Searry yelled, 'There's one of the Orange _____ from Henderson Street.' One of the other women shouted, 'Pitch into her.' Searry then knocked the child from McNab's arms, grabbed her by the hair and pulled her to the floor where she bit the 'whole of the left side of the cartilage' of her nose, leaving her permanently disfigured. Catherine Larkin bit the end of Susan Fagan's finger in an unprovoked street attack. In a brothel in Pellow Street, drunken Caroline Rogers bit off and chewed the ear of fellow prostitute Lucy Saunders, after threatening to 'eat' anybody who came near her.[67]

The Rise or Fall in Violence

Despite the brutality of the previous cases, there is a variety of evidence to show that violence decreased over the course of the nineteenth century.[68] Of course, a whole host of legal and social factors, including changes in the laws and rapid population growth in the industrial towns, make any statistical comparisons problematic. Nevertheless, most historians agree that there was a fall in all crimes of interpersonal violence, particularly between 1850 and 1914.[69] It is generally accepted that this slump was part of a long-term decline in criminal activity in the second half of the nineteenth century.[70] In addition to external curbs, such as improved policing, an increased conviction rate and stiffer penalties from the courts, there were also strong internal impulses towards more harmonious interpersonal relations. The growing working-class desire for respectability helped foster new ideals of manhood, particularly through the promotion of self-discipline and self-restraint. There were also cultural constraints upon violence. Brutality came to be associated with foreign barbarism, something alien to the English character.

How far this general trend is relevant to specific crime 'hot spots', such as dockland slums and seaports with their ever-changing populations, is debatable. Liverpool remained a volatile place, a situation reflected in the rollercoaster nature of the annual crime statistics. The level of recorded violence fluctuated, often sharply, from year to year. In 1855 there were 61 cases of using the knife: in the first nine months of 1856 there were 165 cases.[71] In 1860 the Head Constable's annual report records three cases of murder. In 1863, however, there were seven murders with five people convicted and executed. In 1864 only one man was committed for trial for murder, although there were also seven cases of infanticide. In his report for 1886 the Head Constable states that although there had been only two murder cases (including one infanticide), wounding and stabbing cases had risen from 145 the previous year to 207. In his report for 1888, however, he announces that 'the total number of crimes of violence shows a considerable decrease'. Yet for the year ending September 1890 indictable crimes of violence were said to have increased from 323 the previous year to 347.[72]

The *Birmingham Daily Post* had its own slant on the Liverpool figures. By comparing the Liverpool Head Constable's 1890 report with those of other towns, the newspaper revealed 251 serious assaults of shooting and wounding in Liverpool against 28 in Birmingham and 10 in Manchester. It acknowledged that Liverpool was a seaport, but even so the combined total for murderous assaults in Cardiff, Hull, Southampton, Bristol and Grimsby, during the same period, was only 47.[73] Yet in his report for 1891 the Head Constable was able to congratulate the Watch Committee. Never, since the first returns of 1857, had the statistics disclosed 'so small an amount of crime or so large a success in making criminals amenable to justice'. Serious indictable crimes of violence had dropped from 347 the previous year to 201. As regards summary offences, minor crimes of violence had dropped from 1,952 to 1,546. Nevertheless, whereas in 1890 there were only two murders, in 1891 there were six. Also, the following year saw cases of wounding and other serious indictable crimes of violence rise once again, this time to 229.[74] By then, the *Birmingham Daily Post* felt obliged to comment that shooting and wounding were 'a class of crime for which Liverpool enjoys an unenviable notoriety'.[75] Nevertheless, recorded violence did begin to decline towards the end of the century. For the five years ending in 1889, coinciding with the reign of the High Rip Gang, there were 1,515 violent offences: for the five years ending in 1899 the figure had nearly halved to 790 offences.[76]

Yet a great deal of violent crime must also have gone unrecorded, the so-called 'dark figure'. It has been estimated that an annual total of 9,000 cases of assault went unreported in the north end of Liverpool alone.[77] Although at the end of the nineteenth century people were able to look back and conclude that there had been a decrease in interpersonal violence, the fact remains that many private brawls and violent incidents went unrecorded. The walking wounded attended one of the three local dispensaries where for a penny they could have their lacerations dressed by a doctor. The more serious cases were transferred to hospital. In the 1880s the dispensaries treated up to 60,000 patients a year.[78]

On the Saturday night of 13 July 1891 a journalist spent a two-hour vigil at the East Dispensary.[79] Unfortunately his visit coincided with the aftermath of the annual Orange celebrations, which must have made the place exceptionally busy. Still, he noted that most patients were victims of street brawls and that few would bother reporting the assault to the police. A number of attacks took place in back alleys and courts, out of sight of the patrolling beat constables, and were therefore never brought to the attention of the authorities. In the rough districts many victims were reluctant to press charges. In place of a court case, they either resorted to acts of physical retaliation or merely accepted their beating. The working-class code of honour discouraged 'grassing up' somebody to the police. Over a number of weeks in 1848 John Fitzgibbon and Patrick Donald waged a war of terror against Bartholomew Monogan for giving evidence in court. Monogan had stones thrown at him while out walking and even had his life threatened.

Along with a fear of revenge, the bureaucratic complexities of taking out a private prosecution also deterred victims. The dispensaries and the police used to operate a scheme by which patients were given a note confirming the nature of their injuries. This could be handed to the police who would then take action against the accused. However, the note system was changed and notes were handed out only in the most serious cases. Since the police refused to prosecute without a note, this meant that victims were responsible for taking out their own private summonses, which many could ill afford. In this way, many assaults went unreported. The *Saturday Review* pointed out that 'scores of men and women are struck down with some dangerous weapon; struck down bleeding and insensible in the streets of Liverpool every Saturday night – and the public never never hear word about it all'.[80]

Modern historians are therefore divided as to whether violent crime rose, fell or remained static during the nineteenth century. The judicial statistics, for example, reveal a national average of 150 murders a year between 1880 and 1966. Using these statistics as his starting point, Howard Taylor argues that the data regarding murder are useless and suggests that simple economics had more influence on the figures than any number of murders.[81] The stopping of the Treasury Grant in 1887 meant that prosecution costs fell increasingly on the police and local authorities, resulting in the rationing of the number of expensive murder trials to an average of around 150 per year. Government monitoring of police efficiency in the second half of the nineteenth century also created obvious pressures. This might have led some officers to downgrade certain suspicious deaths to save prosecution costs, while also improving clear-up rates. There is therefore the possibility that violence and murder actually increased even though the figures say otherwise.

It is now being recognized that a host of factors might have helped skew the figures, leaving open the possibility of a shocking amount of unreported murders. Social historian John Archer has analysed a range of deaths in Victorian Liverpool and suggests ways in which some cases could have been wiped from the statistical records. For example, a number of suspicious deaths, particularly of infants, were returned as open verdicts in the coroner's court. Open verdicts were also returned on adults who had died under questionable circumstances, for example those recovered from the River Mersey with marks of violence upon their bodies. These cases could well have involved murder. The lack of forensic knowledge at the time meant that the authorities only prosecuted when presented with irrefutable evidence. In July 1850 21-year-old Ann Dodds was found on the beach. Her corpse had 'discoloration about her eyes'. She was last seen alive with a group of drunken sailors. Since there were no witnesses, the jury returned an open verdict. In May 1854 Elizabeth Graham was found dead in a barrel of water in Green Street while in November John Murray was found suffocated to death at Waterloo Dock. Again, open verdicts were recorded. Between January and May 1854 the coroner's court was unable to decide the cause of five deaths in which the bodies were found with marks of injury. The cases include 18-year-old Thomas Regan who died in the North Hospital and an unknown man found in the River Mersey.[82]

Washed-up bodies created their own macabre industry. The Church of St Nicholas contained the 'Dead House', where the corpses of the drowned were kept until claimed by their friends or buried at public expense. Herman Melville describes crowds gazing through the iron grating of the door to see if they recognized a corpse. One dead sailor had his own name and date of birth tattooed on his arm, as if to help in such an eventuality. Standing rewards were offered for the recovery of people who had fallen into the dock. So much was given if the person was restored to life and less if found drowned. However, a dead body also offered the chance of a bonus, in the removal of any money, jewellery or watches. According to Melville, 'lured by this, several horrid old men and women are constantly prying about the docks, searching after bodies'.[83] These corpse-hunters went out early in the morning along with the rubbish-pickers and rag-rakers. It was all in a day's work.

It was living people, however, particularly sailors and travellers, who provided the greatest source of plunder at the docks.

1 The Borough Gaol, Great Howard Street (LVRO)

2 The cat-o'-nine-tails as the solution to High Rip violence
(*Judy*, 1 June 1887; Trustees of the National Library of Scotland)

3. *Register of prisoners' tattoos in Liverpool Bridewell, 1841. (Proquest)*

3 Register of prisoners' tattoos in Liverpool Bridewell, 1841 (Proquest)

4 The *Clarence* reformatory ship on fire, 1884 (LVRO)

5 Narrow entrance to Smithfield Street court, 1899 (LVRO)

6 Lace Street, 1899, once the 'filthiest, most densely peopled and worst-conditioned in the town' (LVRO)

7 Secondhand clothes market – a good place to fence stolen goods (LVRO)

8 Poaching wars (*Illustrated Sporting and Dramatic News*, 1885)

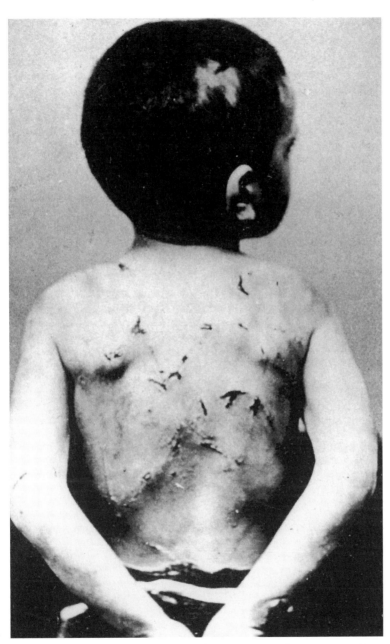

9 Young victim of domestic violence (Liverpool SPCC, LVRO)

10 Blandford Street (now Kempston Street), 1926, a notorious centre of prostitution in the 1880s (LVRO)

TEN

Maritime Crime

Dockland Theft

Dockland districts throughout the world have always had a reputation for wickedness and depravity. Teeming with sex-starved sailors and gullible travellers loaded with money, such areas are magnets for thieves and prostitutes. Nevertheless, Liverpool was singled out as being exceptionally bad. The worst quarter was Gibraltar Row, running from Great Howard Street to the Princes Dock. In the 1830s, Herman Melville described the area as 'putrid with vice and crime to which perhaps the round globe does not furnish a parallel [...] These are the haunts in which cursing, gambling, pick-pocketing and common iniquities are virtues too lofty for the infected gorgons and hydras to practise.'[1] Nearby Waterloo Road, with its 16 public houses, was also infested with 'desperate and abandoned characters'.[2]

Maritime crime was a lucrative business. In 1836 Head Constable Whitty claimed that 1,700 people lived upon merchandise plundered from the docks, although the figure seems somewhat excessive.[3] Liverpool docks were one of the wonders of the Western world, yet the dearth of secure warehousing facilities was cited as a major reason for so much crime.[4] In the 1840s only the Albert Dock was completely enclosed and protected. The northern docks were sheltered by walls but had no warehouses within the enclosures. The southern docks were unprotected by walls and were open to the public. Valuable goods such as sugar, coffee and spices were stored on the quays for long periods, awaiting removal to the warehouses. In the meantime, thieves would pilfer what they could. One customs officer, in 1814, revealed that a great deal of dockside robbery was carried out by gangs of females, up to 50-strong, hanging around the coffee ships. It was the women's sole occupation which they carried out without fear of arrest.[5] In the 1830s a former dockyard officer revealed the various scams for illegally removing goods from the docks. Thieves, known as 'carriers', not only wore specially made jackets with 'false wings' to conceal sugar but also tied their 'drawers' around their ankles and filled them with coffee. Some carriers earned two guineas a week by stashing contraband under their hats. Tobacco smuggling also seemed to be thriving 'since a large number of people appear to dress well who have no known means of subsistence'.[6]

At the south graving docks, where ships were re-coppered, the corporation paid a contractor to clear the docks every time the tide went out. The mud would then be laid up in a heap at the side of the docks. Desperate people soon realized that the mud hid treasure in the form of copper nails and bits of copper sheathing. After every tide hundreds of street urchins and starving men and women would descend with baskets and other containers to carry away the mud for sifting. In 1845 an 11-year-old was sentenced to a month in prison for stealing 16lbs of copper nails from the dock. He didn't think that it was theft since the nails were scattered about the floor. The authorities soon got wise to the scam and employed a man to collect the mud before drying and riddling it to extract the copper fragments. In one year, the recycling netted the corporation £1,600.

Unguarded ships were also plundered. At the opening of the Quarter Sessions in 1854 the Recorder remarked, 'I know that a very large class of thieves in the town regularly live by stealing from the ships and the docks, entering the ships, stealing ropes, the clothes of the sailors, and everything they can lay their hands upon.'[7] It was claimed that a large number of petty thefts on ships were carried out 'chiefly by men of colour', although the crimes were 'seldom registered'.[8] 'Watermen' also stole rum and sacks of wheat from the ships. The 'dumpers' would pass the goods through the scuttles and portholes.

Goods were stolen not only from the warehouses and ships but also as they moved in transit through the streets from ship to warehouse. Children would swarm around the carts carrying cotton bales, deftly grabbing handfuls and concealing them under their ragged clothing.[9] They would then transfer the loot to their parents who would be waiting in dark alleys or in the shade of the huge warehouses. Women would sometimes stuff stolen cotton into their bosoms and under their clothes, giving them the appearance of obesity. Dresses were adapted with large inside pockets to hold illicit goods. The women often worked in gangs, passing the cotton from one to the other to evade capture. Before a bale of cotton reached the railway station in Great Howard Street it could lose between 3lbs and 4lbs. Gangs also swarmed around the station, waiting for the cotton to be loaded for transportation to Manchester. During one shipment in October 1849 an entire bale was lost through pilfering. Carters were also blamed for stopping off at public houses, leaving their loaded wagons at the mercy of child thieves.[10]

Although cotton was the main source of plunder, sacks of beans, rice and coffee were also targeted. Women would follow the carts transporting loads of Indian corn. Using a knife they would pierce the bags and catch the contents in their aprons as they walked. When their aprons were full, they would squat down under the cart just before it reached the dock gate on its way out. Creeping under the feet of the horses, they would attempt to slip away unnoticed. Old rope and ship-store items would also be stolen and sold back to one of the 437 marine store dealers that occupied the dockside streets and back alleys. A great deal of the loot taken from the docks was fenced through these dealers. Many premises had back entrances to provide a quick escape for dodgy customers. There was a band of crooked marine store dealers known as the 'Forty Thieves', the 'most noted receivers of stolen goods in the town'. During 1848 and 1849, 68 dealers were deprived of their licences and/or imprisoned. One of the most infamous marine store dealers in the 1860s was Bernard Connelly of Birkenhead. At six feet five inches, he was a 'terror to the police' and public. When 'Long Barney', as he was known, walked into a public house the terrified landlady would draw him beer for nothing. The man's misdemeanours were numerous. His portfolio included assaulting seamen, passing dodgy coins, receiving stolen money, swindling visitors to the town, stealing from ships and attending sectarian riots looking 'for a bit of fun'.[11]

After two dealers were convicted of receiving stolen cotton, Head Constable Dowling placed two policemen undercover in a marine store to find out who was passing on the contraband. Women and children were the main culprits along with porters and labourers. Larger portions of cotton were pulled from bales and trodden in the dirt to make them look like damaged stock. 'Samples' were also taken from offices and warehouses. The blame for much of the robbery was placed on the 'starving Irish' migrants who faced great temptation as they disembarked at the docks. The theft of cotton reached new heights in 1848, coinciding with the Famine influx. Irish lumpers were also blamed. These were labourers who worked at the docks and on ships, unloading the cargo. They worked on a casual basis for a 'lump' sum and were said to be employed more for their strength than their honesty. Working in league with the carters who transported the goods, they would steal whole bales of cotton to sell on to otherwise respectable tradesmen.[12]

The network of canals connecting Liverpool to the manufacturing districts provided ideal opportunities for thieves. In the 1839 Constabulary report, Matthew Dowling gave evidence about a spate of canal robberies. Since the canals were not protected by the police, boats were often plundered and bales of cotton and wool ransacked in transit on isolated stretches of the waterway. Before being transported the goods were tightly packed in bales by means of a hydraulic press. However, using a tackle fixed to the boat's mast, thieves would draw cotton from the centre of the bale, leaving the bundle looking secure from the outside. To avoid suspicion, seals would also be broken from packages and substituted with fake but authentic-looking replacements. The theft of finished goods while in transit from Manchester to Liverpool docks for export was often not discovered until the merchandise had reached its destination abroad. It was six to eight months before news of the loss reached the original supplier. Dowling was convinced that the boatmen were implicated in the thefts and that along the line of the canal there were houses for the reception of stolen goods, particularly bales of cotton, canvas, cambric and calico.[13]

Smuggling

Smuggling was another rewarding maritime crime. Higher taxes on imports led to a demand for cheaper supplies of luxury items such as coffee and spirits. Around Britain's coastal areas smugglers supplied the demand. Wirral became notorious for this illicit industry. During the building of the New Brighton Palace a cave was discovered, thought to be used by smugglers concealing goods. In the sandstone rocks known as the Red Noses, in Wallasey, there was a series of smugglers' caves, including one called the Wormhole. Boats would also run contraband at night right up to the front door of Mother Redcap's Inn, on the promenade halfway between Egremont and New Brighton, to be dropped straight into the cellar. Redcap's real name was Poll Jones but she was known for her distinctive headgear. A well-known figure among sailors, she would take care of their wages and any prize money. Wirral smugglers were up to all kinds of tricks. In one incident a ship laden with tobacco was grounded. The preventive officers, or customs men, on guard saw two men leave the stranded ship carrying bales. The officers chased them along the shore but after catching them and opening the bales found them to contain only cabbage leaves and ferns. In the meantime, the regulars from Mother Redcap's cottage made off with the tobacco.[14]

Less dramatically, homecoming sailors and passengers would smuggle contraband through Liverpool docks. Ships' firemen would bring back bladders of whisky secreted about their body.[15] When Bridget Loftus was stopped after disembarking with seven bladders of whisky (totalling six-and-a-half gallons) concealed under her clothes, she claimed that a woman from

Dublin had paid her to transport the goods and that she was unaware of their content.[16] In May 1845 a ship's carpenter was found with tobacco cleverly concealed in a hollow plank of wood, which turned out to be two separate pieces carefully nailed together. Five years later, after a spate of arrests for tobacco smuggling, the magistrate remarked that if such cases continued to increase, a prison would be required exclusively for smugglers.[17] The high duties on tobacco were blamed. A *Liverpool Mercury* reader urged a curb on duty to deter smuggling.[18] In 1868 tobacco smuggling was said to be on the rise throughout the country. In Liverpool 1,100lbs of cigars were found concealed in a consignment of glue which came on a warrant for free goods.[19]

Runners

Liverpool criminals saw lucrative opportunities not only in the goods brought into the country but also the people seeking to leave. Duping travellers and emigrants was a Liverpool speciality.[20] By 1850 the former capital of the slave trade had become the major player in the British emigrant trade. Migrants would enter Liverpool temporarily before re-embarking for North America and Australia. Between 1819 and 1859 about five million emigrants sailed to the United States and about half a million to Canada. Two-thirds of them sailed from Liverpool's Waterloo Dock. One Irish migrant on his way to America was warned, 'Liverpool is full of Imposters if they can trick any person they can lay hold of [...] you will require to be very cautious & clever & no way shy without getting your rights.'[21] It was good advice, for a whole industry of fraud and deception had sprung up around the docks involving shipping touts, crimps, lodging-house keepers, currency converters, ticket brokers and various dockland chancers, all working to the same end, to systematically fleece the traveller of lodging money, sea fare and supplies.

The fraud took many forms. Liverpool crooks would convince the emigrants that their money was not legitimate in America and would offer to change it. As if by some reverse alchemy, 40 English gold sovereigns would be turned into 40 'Californian pieces' each worth the eighth part of a farthing.[22] Some emigrants were cheated in the retail shops attached to ship brokers' offices, the headquarters of the emigration agents; others suffered through broken contracts, doctored tickets and delays arising from the practices of pre-paying passages or booking them through sub-agents of the ship brokers.[23] Brokers did not own the ships, but merely sold space in the packet-boats in return for a commission on each berth sold. Sometimes a broker would charter the whole ship by buying the entire space in it for a one-off voyage. He would then

pack it with as many bodies as he could, legally or otherwise. Sub-agents of
the brokers would sell tickets when there was no space available. Although
figures are difficult to estimate, perhaps up to 10 per cent of those arriving in
Liverpool for outward-bound vessels were victims of ticket fraud.[24] Contracts
between emigrant and broker were virtually worthless since there was difficulty proving that the rogue agent in fact worked legitimately for the broker.
Besides, emigrants hardly had time or money to sue anybody.

Emigrants arriving without pre-paid tickets were often defrauded. Despite
repeated warnings to book their trips in advance, many Irish emigrants arrived
in Liverpool without tickets.[25] This left them prey to the shipping touts, better
known as runners. A journalist called Sylvester Redmond spoke of two types
of 'runner', the reputable and the more ruthless 'man-catchers'.[26] The latter
were likened to 'pirates', although working on land rather than sea. The 400
Liverpool runners were organized into syndicates resembling trade unions,
the most notorious and powerful being 'The Forty Thieves' or 'Forties', not
to be confused with the cartel of marine store dealers similarly referred to
by the press.[27] Indeed, everyone tried to get in on the act, from ships' mates
smuggling a few extra bodies on board to (it was rumoured) Roman Catholic
priests who received commissions for the consignment of emigrants.[28]

Various factors worked in the runners' favour. Disembarkations were scenes
of pandemonium. According to an eyewitness, the emigrants were 'actually
driven from the ship with sticks into the hands of [the runners]'. Those who
would not submit were 'almost torn to pieces'.[29] The travellers would then be
met by an 'unscrupulous set of scoundrels' posing as porters. Many of them
were, in fact, lodging-house keepers. The porters would seize the passenger's
luggage and refuse to release it until paid an exorbitant fee. The emigrant and
his bags would be dragged away to book the next stage of their passage or
taken to the particular lodging-house for which the porter worked.[30] One
lodging-house keeper called Farrington refused to let his guests have their
luggage until they had paid 12s for two nights' storage. The Irish emigrants
had already paid 4d for their beds and were unaware that luggage storage was
an extra service. The magistrate warned Farrington: 'The moment poor men
like these set foot in Liverpool, a gang of you get about them with no object
but that of plundering them.'[31]

A rule forbidding fire or lights on ships meant that emigrants had to spend
two nights or more in Liverpool lodgings before setting sail for their final
destination. Conveniently, there were numerous dockside boarding-houses
around Denison Street, Regent Street and Great Howard Street. In these sordid
dwellings, families were crammed in and forced to sleep on straw scattered

on cold, damp floors. One lodging-house, licensed for 19 people, housed 92 lodgers.[32] Many emigrants were from the rural backwaters, illiterate, naive, bewildered and exhausted after their journey. They had no experience of migration or of handling large sums of money and were unfamiliar with passage tickets, calendars and travel schedules.[33] Not surprisingly, they could offer little resistance.

The more devious runners had associates in different parts of Ireland who researched where the migrants came from and where they were heading. They would then pass on the information to their colleagues in Liverpool. Sometimes a member of the man-catching community, suitably disguised as a 'raw Irishman', would travel on the cross-channel steamer to Liverpool. He would strike up conversation with the passengers, finding out their home districts, their parish priests and any local gossip. He would also cheekily warn them of the dangers of Liverpool rogues. The confidence trickster would be first off the boat to pass on this information to a member of the gang who would likewise befriend the emigrants by pretending to come from their home town. The unwary traveller disembarks and 'one of these fellows goes up and says, "How are you Jack Dimpsey?" Jack Dimpsey is very much surprised at hearing the voice of his countryman and finding he knows all about him, reposes confidence in him, and commits himself entirely to his disposal afterwards.'[34] The poor man little suspects that his new 'friend' is out to fleece him.

The more sophisticated fraudsters were the runners or agents of the passenger brokers who traded in commissions on the passage money. They would get whatever sum they could from the emigrants as passage money (as much as £6) and then pay as little as possible to the passenger broker (often as little as £3). They also demanded a commission of 7½ per cent from the broker. In 1846, 150 passengers arrived from Cork with tickets for which they had already paid a deposit of £1. They were to give the balance to Messrs. Shaw, the firm with which the contract had been made. Upon disembarkation, however, they were seized by a runner under the pay of Keenan's, another agent, who led them to Keenan's office under the pretence that it was Shaw's. There they paid the remaining £4 and were therefore left unable to sail, losing their money into the bargain.[35] Some runners claimed to represent passengers that they hadn't even approached for business. They would simply stand outside the passenger broker's door and wait until the traveller had negotiated his passage before claiming him. Non-existent voyages to America were also sold.

Sometimes the emigrants were their own worst enemy. They played into the runners' hands by trying to improve the terms of their passage. Irishmen were not averse to their own scams. Although many of them arrived in

Liverpool looking poor and miserable, they would have sovereigns stitched into their tattered garments. They would tell tales of destitution in an attempt to get passages at a cheaper rate. Runners, however, were 'principally Irishmen themselves, and knew both the strength and weakness of the Irish character'.

The deception would continue as the runners persuaded the emigrants that they needed certain items for their long voyage. Indeed, they claimed that some articles were compulsory. In this way they tricked them into purchasing merchandise both useful and useless, such as alcohol, telescopes, knives or anything else the shop had to trade. The goods were invariably of inferior quality and sold at inflated prices. Again, the runners were in league with the provision dealers and clothes shops who allowed them up to 10 per cent commission. On sailing day the boatmen would then charge exorbitant prices to ferry out the passengers to boats lying out in the river. Embarkations were rushed and often chaotic affairs. Passengers were not allowed to board their ship until it was almost ready to sail. The confusion and panic distracted the emigrants. Sylvester Redmond revealed, 'I have seen people who have lost their passage in boats half way across to Birkenhead, where the boatman would not go for under half a sovereign [...] I have known cases where they absolutely rob them, keeping them to the very instant the tug boat is ready to take them to the ship, or the ship leaving the dock gate.'[36]

The deception did not stop when the emigrants left Liverpool. Runners would also have tipped off their colleagues in New York with the names and personal details of the new arrivals. American man-catchers, posing as friends of the family, would similarly meet the travellers as they disembarked, ready to milk them of any money their Liverpool counterparts had generously left them. The New York gang would continue fleecing them, in some cases even selling them non-existent plots of land. Emigrants were also plundered by 'blackballers', crooks who would make chance voyages across the Atlantic to steal from passengers' luggage. Some returned with £45 worth of clothing and other items. The crime rarely figured in any statistics or reports since the victims were in America before the loss was discovered.[37]

The authorities waged their own war against this fraudulent industry. Five Liverpool brokers lost their licences in 1849. The government agent for immigration at Liverpool tried to put a stop to crooked practices. Before the renewal of their licences in February 1850, he made sure that the passenger brokers signed a declaration to the effect that they would not give any fee, commission or reward, directly or indirectly, to any person for procuring passengers in Liverpool for ships sailing to America. Nevertheless, it was feared that the system would continue in some other form.

To counter the actions of the runners, a German called Frederick Sabel opened an emigrants' home in Moorfields with encouragement from the Dock Committee. More than 4,000 travellers stayed there during 1850. However, runners fought back by entering the building and seizing the emigrants. Sabel felt that it would require at least 1,000 men to control the runners in Liverpool: 'indeed, no force could keep them in order; there would be a continuous fight'.[38] Another respectable hostel keeper, Frederick Marshall, also spoke of the fierce resistance of the runners who assaulted and 'dragged away' the emigrants, seized their luggage and loudly demonstrated and cursed in front of the house.[39] Even the Passenger Act of 1855 failed to stamp out the abuses. Fifteen months later the situation in Liverpool was still causing concern. In 1858 a police detective called Sam Povey was appointed as 'special emigration officer' with responsibility for the runners.[40]

Crimps

It wasn't only naive emigrants who were snared and plucked by scheming rogues. In dockside towns throughout the world sailors were seen as easy targets for every type of scam: 'It is chiefly on land that the sailor suffers his worst shipwreck. It is the worst fate of the seaman that when he comes to land it is always at the worst and weakest spots which civilisation and commerce have called into existence.'[41] Yet with regard to duping sailors, Liverpool was in a league of its own. According to the *Liverpool Mercury*, 'Crimps, dock runners, and sharpers, dishonest lodging-house keepers, and pilfering hucksters, are a numerous class in every seaport. In no place do these rapacious individuals abound to a more alarming extent than in Liverpool.'[42] An American captain claimed that 'Liverpool is notorious for the depravity of the population, male and female, that make it their business to prey upon the sailor'.[43] As a young sailor Herman Melville experienced all this at first hand: 'of all the sea-ports in the world, Liverpool, perhaps, most abounds in all the variety of land-shark, land-rats, and other vermin, which make the hapless mariner their prey. In the shape of landlords, barkeepers, clothiers, crimps and boardinghouse loungers, the land sharks devour him, limb by limb: while the land-rats and mice constantly nibble at his purse.'[44]

Crimps were lodging-house touts or pimps, the commercial equivalent of the press-gang. Their job was to persuade a sailor to stay in a particular establishment and buy clothes from a certain tailor for whom they worked. It was a highly competitive business. Infamous characters around Paradise Street included Paddy Dreadnought, Dolan and Macnulty and Shanghai Davies.

Shanghaiing was a variation of crimping in which lodging-house keepers supplied their customers to ships' captains as crew, usually against their will. The name derives from the fact that Shanghai was an unpopular destination for seamen because return voyages were difficult to find. Half-asleep sailors were sometimes dragged from their beds and forcibly transplanted to ships about to sail. Ma Smyrden, a landlady of a boarding-house in Pitt Street, allegedly attempted to trick crimps into shanghaiing a corpse.[45] Paddy Houlihan operated out of Denison Street. John Da Costa, a Portuguese-American, made his name supplying crews for Yankee ships. He is celebrated in the famous sea shanty 'Heave Away Me Johnnies'.[46]

The fleecing of sailors was systematic and ruthless. In an article entitled 'Jack Ashore', Hugh Shimmin outlined the dangers facing the sailor as he entered the River Mersey: 'It is well-known that several slop-sellers and boardinghouse keepers have boat's crews waiting in the river for the purpose of boarding inward-bound vessels, and enticing the crews to the houses of their employers ashore.' Crimps, under the guise of riggers, boatmen, tailors and outfitters, would clamber aboard laden with barrels of alcohol. It is possible that some crew members were bribed to help the crimps get aboard. Once on deck, they would ply the sailors with spirits to induce them to abandon their ships in the river. The liquor was sometimes drugged. Sailors, however, were duty bound to bring the ship into the dock. To get ashore more quickly, they would offer the visiting riggers up to 10s to do the job for them.[47] Some captains were only too glad to get rid of the drunken crew, although crimps virtually took possession of the vessels. One captain of a Bombay ship docked at Liverpool declared: 'The crimps may as well take my ship. They have the fore part, and the next, I suppose, will be my cabin.' This was after 40 crimps had jumped on board at the Pier Head and began soliciting for their lodginghouses. In 1863 crimps enticed two men to jump overboard to get ashore. One of them drowned.[48] Some shipping companies condoned crimping since it meant that they were not obliged to pay the crew during their stay in the port.

The crimps would remain with the sailor until his money ran dry. On land, he would be handed over to a lodging-house keeper. In the dingy streets and back alleys of dockland Liverpool there were plenty of rough establishments with 'Seamen's Lodging-house' painted boldly on the fanlight. For an exorbitant fee, the sailor would be fed and bedded, although he would be 'lucky to escape with his life, let alone his money belt'.[49] Working on a 20 per cent commission, the lodging-house keeper would be in league with a tailor or 'slop clothier'. The sailor would be supplied with a new rig-out at a 'bargain' price, although the clothing would be up to 50 per cent cheaper if paid for by cash in the normal way. One sailor paid £10 for £4 worth of clothing. The new outfit would not last long as Shimmin pointed out: 'Jack has had one or two women "planted" on him. These harpies take him in tow. They are well instructed in their duties, and before many hours elapse Jack is soundly "drugged" and stripped of his new clothes.'[50] It was not unusual for sailors arriving with wages of £20 to £50 to be in debt a week later.

One opponent of the crimping system was Revd Edward Thring, chaplain to the Mersey Seafarers (1859–67). A first mate of the *Queen of the East* explained to Thring: 'The cargo is not safe, nor the sailors. There is not a more dreadful body of men than these crimps.' Thring therefore set about securing the co-operation of captains, mates and pilots of all the ships in the Mersey. After holding his services on board the vessels, Thring would warn crews of the temptations awaiting them in the town. He would also hand out cards with details of respectable lodging-houses. The crimps were not slow in seeking revenge on Thring. In 1862 he went aboard a vessel as it entered the Mersey. The captain had ordered that no crimps were allowed but some had already gained access to the forecastle. Thring presented the men with a stark choice: they should go to the Sailors' Home or the lodging-houses. Sensibly, they chose the Home. Thring then went ashore to arrange for a cart to take the men's belongings to the Home when the ship docked. On the cart's arrival, 'a large concourse of crimps, runners, tailors, and outfitters were assembled at the Pier Head. Many attempted to board the ship, but the police had turned them away.' The men then objected to the chaplain being allowed to board the ship and fired off a volley of abuse. When Thring and the sailors left the ship, the crimps tried to steal the sailors' boxes as they were being put on the cart. Of the 22 men who volunteered to go the Home, 17 got in safely.[51]

It was to combat the abuses of the crimps that the Sailors' Home was built. Opened in Canning Place in 1848, the refuge gave seamen inexpensive and secure accommodation, free from the clutches of the crimps. The Merchant Shipping Act of 1854 was passed in the hope of abolishing the crimping system. However, five years later the practice was still in evidence. When a captain and mate were threatened by crimps for refusing to let them board their ship, the captain sank one of their rowing boats by throwing a cannon-ball into it.[52] The Mersey Mission to Seamen, founded in 1856, campaigned vigorously for the introduction of a detachment of river police to prevent the abuses of the crimps. With the formation of the Liverpool River Police in 1865, the official porters were able to report the crimps and give evidence against them in court. They ran the risk, however, of retaliation from dockland ruffians who despised police informants.[53] In March 1870 there was said to be a revival of crimping after a reduction was made in the number of river police. Joseph Bennett, a repeat offender, was one of a gang that boarded the *San Luis* without permission. Around the same time, a river policeman spotted a crimp called Samuel Weeks approach a sailor. The officer intervened and advised the man to go to the Sailors' Home. 'If you mention the Home I will smash your _____ head,' replied Weeks. However, an 1879 report to the Watch Committee claimed that owing to the introduction of the river police, 'crimping on the Mersey is at an end'.[54] A lone crimping prosecution at the Bootle Police Court in 1896 seems an anachronism.[55]

Wrecking

Across the River Mersey, the local economy was considerably bolstered by a dramatic and sometimes barbarous maritime industry called 'wrecking'.[56] This involved plundering cargo washed ashore from shipwrecks. There was a distinction between salvaging, which was legal, and wrecking, which was illegal. Salvors rescued stranded goods in return for a share from the legitimate owners or insurers; wreckers simply grabbed the goods for themselves. Local traditions sometimes blurred the boundaries between the two activities.[57] On Merseyside, as the wreckage neared the shore, men would swim out to touch the flotsam shouting, 'That is mine.' Local custom said that this was how undisputed ownership was acquired. John Taylor Gregson, a former master mariner and agent for Lloyd's insurers, revealed that people on Wirral felt that they were entitled to the plunder. Indeed, a wreck was considered to be a 'godsend' rather than a source of crime. Lighthouse keepers sometimes made extra cash by acting as wreck spotters for those interested in local shipwrecks.[58]

The Mersey was a major wrecking area since the estuary was well-known as hazardous to shipping, with vessels occasionally coming to grief on the Burbo or Hoyle banks. Up to the middle of the nineteenth century many of the inhabitants of north Wirral were wreckers or smugglers. An old rhyme went:

> Wallasey for wreckers,
> Poulton for trees
> Liscard for honest men,
> And Seacombe for thieves.[59]

Hoylake was another village noted for wreckers. Some inhabitants pretended to be fishermen as a front for their wrecking activities. They fished in the summer merely as an amusement since the wrecks were less frequent. An old boatman, speaking of the fleets of Hoylake vessels, observed that 'not a fellow in any of those boats ever earned money enough to buy one; they are all got by wrecking [...] they make sometimes more in one day at wrecking than they could in seven years of work.' One witness, who had lived at Hoylake for some time, claimed not to have seen or tasted any fish.

People from Liverpool were also involved in rescuing salvage. Using 'speculative boats' they would sail out to stranded vessels to save what they could. Not all were legitimate. When the *Sophia* was wrecked, two or three boatloads of 'insolent wreckers from Liverpool' arrived. Gregson offered the men work as authorized salvors but they refused. They had better things to do, such as stripping the copper off the vessel's bottom. Sir William Forwood, one-time Mayor of Liverpool, recalled that wrecks off Bootle and Seaforth were also quite common. Local farmers would fence their fields with timber from the planks stranded on shore and villagers were not above plundering the cargoes.[60]

It was in Wirral, however, that most wrecking took place. In 1839 a Royal Commission investigating the need for police forces singled out the north-east corner of the peninsula as one of the most dangerous and lawless areas of the country; Cornwall was the other. It seems that wreckers were interested not only in rescuing legitimately found salvage but were also actively involved in creating shipwrecks to claim the cargo. Although there are hardly any recorded convictions for such activity, it was widely believed that on stormy nights ruthless wreckers would light a fire or false beacon to lure ships to their doom. The law stated that a ship's cargo could not be salvaged legally if members of the crew were still alive. This might have inspired wreckers to new and despicable levels of ruthlessness. Crews attempting to defend their cargoes would be overpowered. In 1778, during atrocious weather in the Mersey estuary, a French ship called the *L'Equite*, which had been captured by privateers and had a valuable cargo, hit rocks as she rounded the Perch Rock. She eventually ran ashore near New Ferry. The next day, hundreds of wreckers descended on the ship and overwhelmed the crew before removing all that they could carry. The following evening, despite the presence of four armed guards, the wreckers returned to the vessel to continue their plunder. The guards fired a warning shot before aiming directly into the mob, killing one. The angry crowd forced the guards to flee by boat, leaving the wreckers to continue with their looting.[61]

Some wreckers were grasping and heartless. When the *Earl Moira*, bound for Dublin, was wrecked off Leasowe in 1821, a Liverpool boat (thought to be one of the King's Dock rowing boats) pulled alongside but refused to help, ignoring pleas from the terrified passengers clinging to the wreck. While trunks were washed away, the rowers picked three or four cases from the water and returned to Liverpool, despite dead bodies floating alongside the vessel. Up to 60 passengers were drowned.[62] On hearing of a shipwreck the crowds would gather, not to rescue the drowning but on the lookout for loot. 'Many a half-drowned sailor,' James Stonehouse recollected, 'has had a knock on the sconce while trying to obtain a footing, that has sent him reeling back into the seething water.'[63] Survivors were robbed and dead bodies mutilated in the quest for valuables. When the *Grecian* went to pieces off the Cheshire coast in 1832, the ship's master, Captain Salisbury, was drowned. While his body lay on the shore awaiting transportation to the inquest, wreckers stripped him naked. Not content with his clothes, they hacked off one of his fingers to steal his ring. A woman from Moreton also chewed off the earlobe from a female corpse to take her earring.

Each winter the women prayed for a rich harvest of shipwrecks. In this way homes in north Wirral were able to dine on fine foods and spirits for a few weeks.[64] After a wreck had been plundered the whole neighbourhood would be in a continual state of disturbance for days as the drink flowed freely. When the *Elizabeth Buckham* was wrecked in 1866 the looters drank so much rum that at least two people died.[65] On stormy nights, crowds up to 400 strong would gather near the shore, hoping for a wreck. Smaller gangs would secrete themselves in the sand hills waiting patiently. If a ship was grounded, wreckers quickly disposed of any loot among neighbours or nearby villagers. Items were sold privately on the spot to the crowds who would flock to the scene. Some farmers would travel up to 12 miles in carts to participate in the plunder.[66] In this way the wreckers did not need to carry the contraband inland and thereby risk apprehension. Booty that was not immediately sold or taken home was hidden in the sand hills to be taken away later. In these circumstances, wreckers would even steal from each other, with sons plundering their own fathers. If anything heavy was found, such as rolls of linen, the gangs would join in and cut it up before running in different direction with the pieces. Inhabitants with local knowledge of tidal patterns and geographical features could take full advantage of the bog-ridden terrain to make their escape.[67] If the item was too bulky to carry they would inform the agent of the underwriters and make the best bargain they could for salvage. Their prices were sometimes exorbitant. They once demanded £5 for a steamer's funnel that was washed ashore. It sold for only £3 at auction.

Despite the dangers in transporting goods, some plunder found its way to

Liverpool. When the *Grecian* was wrecked, 12 cartloads of booty were later recovered from various marine stores. After the formation of the new professional police force it was felt that goods were more difficult to dispose of in Liverpool, since the town's police force included two constables stationed on the shore opposite Liverpool. The Municipal Corporations Act of 1835 gave Liverpool police jurisdiction within seven miles of Liverpool, but by the time a body of constables had travelled to the scene of a Wirral wreck the plundering would be over. They were not made welcome when they did arrive. Borough police on salvage duty had to go armed against the hostility of neighbouring villagers. Policing the wreckers had always been difficult since there was no paid constabulary force on the Wirral coast. Commissioner Dowling of the Liverpool police claimed that in Cheshire, parish constables never interfered with the wreckers. Owing to a shortage of preventive officers, there was little to stop their activities. Indeed, some customs men were married into families of the wreckers. Wrecking was a family affair. There were generations of children brought up in the profession. 'They intermarry and are nearly all related to each other,' claimed the 1839 Constabulary report. A magistrate once rushed to the beach on the occasion of a Wirral wreck, hoping to deter the looting. The crowd responded by slashing the harness of his carriage, making it difficult for him to leave. There is even the possibility that some Wirral magistrates were in league with the wreckers.[68] Although the County Police Act of 1839 enabled county magistrates to establish a rural constabulary if required, progress was slow until the Police Act of 1856 pressured the counties into organizing police forces. The foundation of county-wide policing might have helped to deter wrecking on Wirral but traces of the practice survived into the twentieth century, with the last reported incident, involving the Spanish ship *Ulloa*, occurring in December 1904.

ELEVEN

Street Robbery

Highwaymen and Footpads

Although Liverpool's maritime industries provided plenty of opportunities for local criminals, miles from the docks on the sparsely populated outskirts of town a different form of robbery thrived. By 1760 Liverpool inhabitants were beginning to leave their remote northern backwater to visit other towns. Wealthy travellers could take the stagecoach on its journey, via Prescot, to Warrington and then on to London and elsewhere. Since the police did not protect such districts, it was wise to go armed against the threat of highwaymen and footpads.[1] Working alone or in gangs, armed highwaymen would molest travellers on foot and stop coaches or horsemen on the public highway. The pack-horses of the 'carrying trade', the early nineteenth-century equivalent of the parcel delivery service, would therefore begin their journeys from Dale Street in convoys to resist the bandits that plagued the routes out of town.[2] Footpads were simply unmounted highwaymen.

In the mid-eighteenth century the actor Ned Shuter, a great favourite with Liverpool audiences, was travelling to the town in a coach when a highwayman held it up. The only other passenger in the vehicle was an elderly man who wisely pretended to be asleep, hoping to remain undisturbed. 'Your money or your life?' the highwayman barked. Shuter feigned idiocy and said that his 'uncle' wouldn't trust him with money and paid everything for him. The robber turned his attention to the elderly 'uncle', slapping him about the face to wake him before relieving him of every last penny. Shuter spent the remainder of the journey chuckling at the wheeze.[3]

At the beginning of the nineteenth century Vauxhall Road contained many lawless inhabitants and was unsafe to travel along, especially at night. An elderly resident recalled 'a family of the name of Moore that was a terror to every one'. The father was the publican of the Black Bull in Warbrick Moor, between Melling and Aintree. His two sons were blacksmiths from Maguire Street and Eldon Place. A former detective also recounted that the senior

Moore teamed up with three brothers called Grainger to commit highway robberies. Around 1805 Moore and one of his sons were either hanged at Lancaster or transported.[4]

Since their crimes carried the penalty of death, highway robbers were prepared to shoot their way out of trouble. Among those who paid the ultimate price were Tobias Toole, John Davies and William O'Brien (alias Thomas Dwyer). They were part of a gang that plagued Liverpool and neighbouring districts during the winter of 1812–13. After committing robberies in Toxteth Park and West Derby, most of them were eventually caught after they were tricked into ambushing a decoy coach driven by Robert Chambers. Inside the vehicle were seven armed policemen. During a leisurely journey from Everton to Low Hill, the coach was stopped at Mill Lane by five men armed with pistols and a blunderbuss. One screamed, 'Damn your eyes. Deliver, or we will blow your bloody brains out.' As one of the plain-clothed officers stepped out of the coach to be searched, as was the plan, the other constables attacked. 'The bloody b____rs have got fire arms. Shoot and kill them,' the robbers shouted.[5] During a fierce exchange shots were fired, leaving an officer injured and two of the robbers 'winged'. Three ran for it but were caught in Folly Lane, near the present site of St George's Hall. After a trial at Lancaster in 1813, Toole, Davies and O'Brien were hanged. Despite other members of the gang being rounded up, more highway robberies were committed soon after in Paddington, Islington and Edge Lane, demonstrating that the threat was by no means subdued.[6]

In 1818, as he walked home along Breck Lane, Robert Pendleton was robbed by cousins William and Daniel Fitzpatrick. One of the footpads pointed a pistol at Pendleton's head while the other rifled his pockets. They then fled towards Everton. Taking a shortcut, their victim overtook them in Rupert Lane where he gained the help of a passer-by called William Kelly. During a ferocious fight between the four men, the thieves drew their knives and began stabbing their captors. Undeterred, Pendleton and Kelly put up a terrific struggle and managed to hold onto the robbers. Kelly, who had been stabbed about ten times, declared, 'Damn thee villain. I have fastened on thee now, and while I have breath in my body, I'll not quit thee.' Pendleton was equally resolute: 'Damn thee, thou little know Bob Pendleton, if thee thought to rob him and get away without a tussle for't.' The thieves, one of whom was a cobbler from Circus Street, were eventually subdued and later convicted and sentenced to death. The local community raised a collection in honour of the victims' pluck.[7]

The fearsome Mulvey (or Mulvay) brothers from Naylor Street, off Vauxhall Road, terrorized travellers in the suburbs during the summer and autumn of

1830. The family, Thomas, John and Michael, aged between 30 and 50, were from Dublin and had only arrived in Liverpool in April. They were apprehended after Thomas tried to pawn a stolen watch in Tithebarn Street. Items from various other robberies were recovered from their home. Michael turned King's evidence and accused his brothers of murdering Charles Burn in West Derby Road, Tuebrook, during a botched robbery. Ninety minutes after Burn was shot dead, his cousin was robbed nearby by the same men. Although Thomas and John were acquitted of this, they were found guilty of numerous other armed robberies on the outskirts of the town. While awaiting execution at Lancaster prison, the men admitted their part in various robberies while Thomas confessed that he did indeed murder Charles Burn. The brothers were hanged holding hands, with John taking five minutes to die.[8]

By 1815 traditional highway robbery was becoming less common and by the 1830s was virtually extinct, improved policing, better roads and turnpikes all playing their part.[9] Although the label lasted well into the Victorian period, the highway robbers of the mid-century were vastly different from the romantic and gentlemanly Dick Turpin figures of legend and literature. The modern versions were more likely to be fierce muggers, operating on foot in secluded and dimly lit urban areas, out of sight of the watchmen or constables. Highway robbery was always going to be easier on the more sparsely policed outskirts of town. In January 1845 the presence in Toxteth Park of 20 to 30 so-called 'Park Rangers' caused a flurry of complaints to the police. Members of the public were knocked down and women and children out shopping were robbed of their goods. Shopkeepers were also plundered by the gang. Police arrested six well-known members, including John Brannagan, Samuel Mulholland and Daniel Myler. During the winter of 1847 there was a widespread spate of robberies. In a field near Parliament Street, a stockbroker was attacked by three men armed with a bludgeon, sword and cotton hook. A farmhouse in Kirkby was raided by a gang of five men, three of them armed with guns. Two boys were robbed near the Collegiate Institution while on the same evening a man was attacked in Elizabeth Street. A gentleman was held up at gunpoint at noon near the junction of Garston and Allerton Roads. At a meeting of the magistrates it was decided to employ an armed patrol of police on the outskirts of the town.[10] Shortly after these incidents, a man wrote to a newspaper to declare that he had lately taken to carrying a pocket pistol. He wanted to know if, when confronted by a robber and asked to 'deliver', he would be justified in shooting the scoundrel dead on the spot, even if no violence had been threatened. The newspaper replied with an emphatic 'no', adding that 'the law will require reasonable fear of personal injury'.[11]

In the crowded towns, the modus operandi of thieves changed. With the ever-present threat of patrolling constables, there was no time for civility. Traditional highway robbers at least had the advantage of being able to escape from the scene on horseback. Street robbers were forced to incapacitate their prey. Victims were often beaten into submission before being robbed rather than threatened with violence if they didn't comply with the robber's demands.

In the 1850s there was an outbreak of robberies around Chisenhale Street. Ruffians would hang about the bridge, awaiting unsuspecting emigrants travelling from the docks to their lodgings in Vauxhall Road. Victims would be robbed and thrown in the canal. Hugh Shimmin called for better street lighting to deter the robbers.[12] At the October 1852 sessions the Recorder warned, 'It is evident that some parts of the town are infested by very dangerous characters.' Not only had there been many cases of street robbery but 'pickpockets seem to abound, and we find proofs of such activity at the pier-head, the railway, the omnibus, and even in churches'.[13]

Pickpockets

While footpads patrolled the near-deserted streets at night when nobody could interfere with them, pickpockets worked the crowded streets and fairs. Picking the pockets of men was known as 'buzzing' and of women, 'tooling'. In the 1830s a Manchester thief pocketed £273 from a foreign lady as she stepped off the Manchester train at Lime Street station. The money lasted six weeks and was spent 'drinking and whoring'. The thief revealed that pickpockets used 'wires' made by dishonest wire workers. These were tools with three hooks and a spring lever. The implement was placed in the victim's pocket and once a wallet had been located the spring was activated and the contraption closed like a crab's claw, enabling the item to be lifted. Women's pockets were picked by hand. The thief would accompany the lady on her right side where the pocket was usually located. He would keep in step with her and as she raised her right leg the pocket would fall back enabling the thief to strike more easily. A colleague would come up on the victim's left side to distract her.[14] A judge blamed ladies who wore fashionable dress pockets which were easy to pick. He felt that it was foolhardy to wear such clothing in the crowded streets since it only encouraged children to steal.[15]

Many pickpockets were indeed children, stealing silk handkerchiefs and small items such as snuff boxes for others to fence. Pawnbrokers would pay as much as one shilling for a decent handkerchief.[16] In 1850, 163 child pickpockets appeared before Liverpool magistrates. One youngster claimed to have been led astray by big boys who offered him 1d or 2d for every pocket picked.[17] According to one policeman, 'the cleverest pickpocket in Liverpool', around 1848, was a 9-year-old boy called Thomas Murphy. He would travel to Glasgow, London and the rest of the country in pursuit of his profession. Not long released from a three-month stretch at Knutsford Gaol, he was caught picking ladies' pockets in the Theatre Royal and given another three months.[18] Picking pockets was certainly a young person's game, requiring adroitness and dexterity. The rough and clumsy hands of hardened adult criminals, calloused through oakum picking and shaky through drink, were less suitable for the profession.

The smooth hands of ladies, however, were ideal. A convict under sentence of transportation gave an account of the activities of gangs of female pickpockets, also called 'wires', found operating in the north-west of England in the 1840s: 'There is now in Manchester and Liverpool about 50 or 60 of these women wires, one day dressed up in their best, another day quite plain, to escape any information that may have been given.'[19] These ladies would haunt the omnibuses and shops to get close to other women. They would then place their shawls or mantles over the victim's dress pocket to conceal their hands. The stolen purse would then be handed over to one of the gang acting as a maid. Her job was to take the evidence out of the shop while her 'mistress' turned her attention to another victim. The gangs were highly organized, even attending private sales in town and country, although they never bought anything at the sale. They would also scan newspapers for details of forthcoming concerts, so that they could stand outside waiting for likely victims.

Liverpool women were also experts at another scam. A lady, accompanied by young children (themselves trainee thieves), would visit the railway station just before the train was about to leave. If she suspected that she was being watched, she would buy a ticket and enter a carriage carrying other women. She would then spend a short journey attempting to pick the pockets of her fellow passengers. If, however, she thought that the coast was clear, she would briefly enter a carriage and then suddenly declare that she was on the wrong train. In the panic and confusion, she would try to pick as many pockets as she could before she hurried out of the carriage, transferring the booty to her friends on the platform who were supposedly 'seeing her off'.[20]

A respectable lady was shopping in Victoria Market, Manchester, when she felt that her pocket was being interfered with. Aware that child thieves prowled such places, she quickly turned around only to find another respectable-looking lady with her nursemaid and baby. Remaining unsettled by the incident, she informed a policeman who went in search of the suspect. On finding the lady and her entourage, he immediately formed the opinion that she 'was not of the manor born'. Brought in for questioning, the lady, who was dripping in jewellery, was adamant that she was Mrs Bennett, of a wealthy family from St Helens. However, in another room, her maid admitted: 'Shure her misthress was Bridget Johnson from Liverpool.' Further inquiries revealed that the woman was a well-known thief who used the rail network to target easily accessible markets.[21]

In September 1868, as he was being arrested for assaulting a policeman, 15-year-old Richard Paxton warned the constable that he was one of the 'Thurlow Street swell mob'. The words seem an idle juvenile boast intended to boost the lad's criminal reputation. Members of the 'swell mob' were in fact the well-dressed and highly skilled elite among pickpockets. They were so-called because they dressed 'swell' in order to target upper-class people. In Liverpool typical haunts of the 'swell mob' were the Philharmonic Concert Hall, theatres or lectures at the Collegiate Institute. In December 1842 the swell mob visited the Queen's Theatre Tavern in Christian Street. The trick they played was said to be a new one in Liverpool. The men staged a mock fight to distract the customers. The landlady rushed to intervene, but a man called Davies took advantage of the chaos by lifting her purse. The victim's daughter witnessed the incident and alerted the police. On their arrival, the respectable-looking Davies vociferously protested his innocence and offered to go quietly to the bridewell to explain matters and call witnesses. The man's protestations duped the officer for as they got to the door he ran for it and was only arrested days later. The pickpockets were always trying new tricks. In January 1849 a Manchester member of the fraternity threw his arms around a stranger in Lime Street and declared, 'My dear Mr Smith.' His surprised new acquaintance was fortunate to realize that his coat was being unbuttoned and fingers edging towards his money.

In 1845 the swell mob was 'prowling about the town in great numbers'.[22] In April there had been a spate of robberies on the omnibuses. The following year two Manchester members were spotted around Lord Street and Dale Street working in league with two prostitutes, who were trying to entice men to follow them down dark alleys. The pickpockets were arrested, and the magistrate remarked that there were no fewer than 40 such characters in Liverpool who had travelled from other towns to commit robberies.[23] The swell mob would target particular towns and then move on when police interest intensified. In November 1843 a contingent of the London swell mob came up to Liverpool to spend the winter. In Ranelagh Street they surrounded and jostled a woman in an attempt to pick her pockets. However, the lady was wise to their tricks and called a policeman who was able to apprehend one of the men. Of all the potential victims in Liverpool the gang had picked on the wrong one. She was the wife of the governor of the Borough Gaol. A journal reported that these thieves moved freely around the country and even went abroad for rich pickings. They would

> work the Dover packets, and visit the Lakes of Killarney. They go on the Manchester Exchange, and sleep in the hotels of New York. They know the way to the Liverpool Docks, and 'wire' in the streets of Paris. They generally go the Continent in the spring, and remain there until the races and fairs are coming off in England.[24]

Lower-class pickpockets were probably more numerous and native to Liverpool, like the crowds of 'rogues' and 'vagabonds' who congregated around the Custom House every evening in June 1842. When members of the public walked past they were jostled and had their pockets picked. The rougher thieves, lacking the finesse of the elite pickpockets, often resorted to brute strength and terror. They were also more likely to operate in gangs to intimidate their victims. Although some contemporaries would argue otherwise, the art of secretly picking pockets largely gave way to more crude techniques such as 'putting the damper on', or garrotting, which involved approaching the victim from behind and strangling him while accomplices rifled his pockets.[25] Some victims were simply assaulted and robbed.

Garrotting

This brutal procedure had been used for a number of years before the press picked up on it.[26] In 1862 the country suddenly became gripped by a garrotting panic.[27] In July a national outcry was raised when the Liberal MP for Blackburn, James Pilkington, was attacked and robbed in Pall Mall, London, at one o'clock in the morning. Although garrotting wasn't exactly a new type of crime, the status of this particular victim led to a great deal of publicity, heightened by the suspicion that many of these violent offenders were ticket-of-leave men released early from prison. As press interest increased so did the number of reported incidents, even though not all cases could accurately be described as garrotting. The story seemed to feed off itself as newspapers worked themselves into such a panic that members of the public became terrified of walking the streets. Liverpool began to experience its own garrottings, the most extreme example being the death of Edwin Thomas a week after being strangled during a robbery in Great Crosshall Street in October 1864. By 1871 judge Baron Martin was referring to robbery with violence as 'the ordinary Liverpool offence'.[28] All this violence could perhaps have been averted had members of the public invested in an 'anti-Garotte', invented in 1852 by a Liverpudlian called Blissett. This was a small hardwood stick that doubled as a torch when the top was taken off and the stick struck against a hard surface. The *Liverpool Mercury* boasted: 'With such a weapon an encounter with two or three ruffians need not be feared.'[29]

The High Rip Gang

By 1875 garrotting had begun to fade from the headlines. Liverpool, in partic-ular, was by then in the grip of a new moral panic following the exploits of the Cornermen and their ferocious heirs, the High Rip Gang. Between 1884 and 1888 the gang rampaged through the north end districts, robbing and stabbing dockers, seaman and shopkeepers.[30] Brandishing knives called 'bleeders' and thick leather belts which they swung through the air, they used brute force and superior numbers to rob their lone victims in courts and back alleys around Vauxhall and Scotland Road. In 1887, at the height of the High Rip scare, the *Liverpool Mercury* printed a front-page advertisement listing the bargains to be had from a firm's bankrupt stock. Among the 'walking sticks for gentlemen', 'canes for masters' and 'switches for officers' was a selection of 'shillelaghs and bludgeons for High Rippers'.[31] The advert might have been tongue-in-cheek but the gang was no laughing matter. A Spanish sailor was murdered by the High Rip and many others badly wounded and disfigured after stabbings and brutal beatings. A group of vigilantes, called the Logwood Gang, formed to keep the High Rip under control. A series of savage battles followed with casualties on both sides.

Although street warfare involving gangs of youths was undoubtedly staged on the streets of Liverpool, there was concern at the time that much of the panic about the gangs was being constructed by the media. It was suggested that the idea of a semi-secret organization known as the High Rip had been invented by popular newspapers hoping to sell more copies. Head Constable Nott-Bower argued that press publicity about gang violence had unjustifiably whipped up public alarm, leading to undue criticism of the authorities for not doing enough to stop the outrages. Then, as now, law and order was a big election issue. In his book on street violence, crime historian Rob Sindall points out that press alarm about the High Rip built up from late August to mid-November 1886, reaching its climax in October. The scaremongering in the media might have had a lot to do with the holding of municipal elections on 1 November. It turned out that the election result exonerated both the Head Constable and the Watch Committee, for the Conservatives strengthened their hold on the council over the Liberals. Indeed, Nott-Bower was able to present figures in his annual report for 1886 to show that the number of indictable assaults for the period was, in fact, 'rather below the average'.[32]

After 1887 the High Rip was finished although the name continued to be used in Liverpool for any bunch of violent young ruffians and robbers. There was no shortage of them, particularly in the north end district, home to the descendents of the famine Irish migrants. In 1889 an inhabitant of 'brutal Bootle' revealed the horrors of the place to an investigative journalist. He warned the reporter, without wishing to frighten him, that if the locals knew what he was up to, he wouldn't get out of the place alive. The Bootle man had seen:

> men 'gone through,' that is, their pockets rifled, everything of value taken from them, and then grossly abused, kicked and belted, and all the rest of it. I've seen knives flash out and be hacked about before I even knew there was a row brewing [...] half-a-dozen or more of them would set on one man for the devilment of the thing. The fellows live by plunder, and they will go any lengths to get what they want.

If some of the terrors of the district went missing for a week or two it was to be surmised that they had been locked away in Walton or Kirkdale gaols. Women were often in league with the men, 'buncing the "lay" and the plunder alike', as the criminal jargon of the time put it. They would find victims in the sailors of the neighbourhood, enticing them into the public houses, where they would later be beaten and robbed.[33]

Thieving Prostitutes

Some women were as ruthless as the men. In 1844 Leon Faucher, a French newspaper editor, wrote that 'the prostitutes of Liverpool occupy the utmost vigilance of the police. Robbery, assaults, brawls, drunkenness, are frequent.'[34] Many prostitutes supplemented their earnings with theft. 'In Liverpool more than one-fourth of the property stolen was taken by prostitutes.'[35] In 1838 police estimated that of a total of £15,992 worth of stolen property, £4,430 was the result of prostitutes robbing their clients.[36] Over a twelve-month period, the robberies in one brothel alone involved no less a sum than £1,000.[37] Two years earlier the Head Constable had revealed the extent of the pilfering: 'The prostitutes are the greatest thieves; they plunder drunken or incautious strangers, and the nightly reports entered in this office of money thus lost varies from one to four hundred pounds [...] the other night a man lost £2,000; but there is never less than £100 thus stolen nightly.' He disclosed that the major victims were drunks, businessmen and Irish MPs on their way to London.[38] Emigrants were another worthy target.

Although the figures quoted by the authorities might seem a little overstated, what is certain is that drunken men in brothels were easy prey to the girls. A sleeping man's clothes and money were often too much of a temptation. Hugh Shimmin describes a scene from a district known as 'Little Hell':

> A tall, bony, half-drunken man is being led up to one of the lower houses in Myrtle Street by two broad-set, loose girls, with bloated faces and rough hair. They are dressed in bed-gowns, which display their brawny arms and are using what force and persuasion they are capable of to get a man along. As the women push him in the door some boys cry out across the street, 'Don't go in, master; don't go in! They are going to rob you! They are sure to rob you.'[39]

Although it wasn't in the interests of brothel owners to have crimes committed on their premises, since this would attract police attention, such pilfering was common in the more disorderly houses. Speaking of the Paradise Street and Park Lane districts, H. J. Nicholls recalls unwary strangers being 'carried off [...] by a mob of women in "Lancashire bedgowns and petticoats" to some low haunt in an off street, there to be hocused, robbed, stripped, and in many ways deposited in the street, in a state of stupor, "mit nodings on"'.[40] The men were probably sailors. An American captain recalled that it was common practice to 'skin' the sailor. Many a poor tar had to return to his ship in the morning wearing nothing but his underwear and shirt. They were the lucky ones. Some returned destitute of money and every article of clothing. One poor man was forced to run through the streets wrapped in a blanket, tied like a toga. A mob chased him through the streets hooting and pelting him with mud. While he ran, his backside was exposed.[41]

Brothel thefts were big business. There was one establishment that cost £20 a year to rent. In six months alone it was the scene of robberies worth £900. Stolen gold was quickly disposed of and banknotes easily laundered. Some shopkeepers were willing to cash high-value banknotes for girls they knew to be prostitutes, so long as they bought something for 10 per cent of the value.[42] Few victims of theft were willing to make a complaint. In February

1860 Robert Fitzsimmons had the courage to make public a visit to a disorderly house. In court, he claimed that he had been drunk when Isabella and Elizabeth Litchfield enticed him to a Gore Street brothel. Since Fitzsimmons had no money to 'satisfy the demands of the brothel keeper', the two women stripped him of his 'inexpressibles' and his coat. The man then had to sheepishly negotiate his way back to his home in Cumbermore Street. Other men in similar situations sought their own justice. Irish sailor James O'Brien vowed revenge for a robbery committed against him in Elizabeth Callahan's brothel in Spitalfields, near present-day Victoria Street. In the early hours of a June morning in 1863 O'Brien met a prostitute named Mary Ann Mathers in Lime Street and took her back to Callahan's house. When O'Brien woke up the next morning he discovered that £5 was missing from his trouser pocket. Convinced that Callahan was responsible, he bought a knife from a shop in Dale Street and returned to the house to fatally stab her.[43]

Some prostitutes were also accomplished street robbers. In the 1830s social reformer Edwin Chadwick and his missionaries interviewed several young Manchester prostitutes and learned of their tricks on the streets. One girl teamed up with two men to work the decoy trick by which a client was enticed into a deserted place before being violently robbed. Another of her tricks was 'bilking' customers. This involved working in league with a colleague in the back alleys. After agreeing the price of sex, the man would pay his fee and drop his trousers. On the signal of a cough, the accomplice, hidden nearby, would falsely shout, 'Watch!' or some other warning of an approaching policeman. The man's first reaction would be to make him himself decent and scarper without any thought of repayment for the non-event. An alternative ruse was to pick a client's pocket while his trousers were half-down before running off, leaving the victim hampered in his pursuit.

Ellen Reece, who spent two years as a prostitute on Liverpool's streets, explained that prostitutes had to be careful not to carry too much money since this would reveal their profession to any inquisitive policeman. Some corrupt officers would also steal the money. To thwart cursory searches by men, gold sovereigns were hidden intimately. Some girls were able to secrete up to 30 coins 'where decency forbids to name'. However, under orders from one shrewd Manchester police matron, prostitutes were made to jump down from a bed repeatedly until the coins dropped out. Streetwise prostitutes would swallow the sovereigns, in the same way that modern-day drug dealers dispose of wraps of heroin. Back at the lockup, the women would wait patiently for the coins to take their natural course. If nothing was forthcoming after three days, they would request a laxative.[44] On one occasion a drunken woman was put in a cell at the bridewell, among a group of prostitutes. The keeper couldn't remove her gold ring as her fingers were swollen. Needless to say, when the woman woke up the next morning her ring was missing. A search of the prostitutes failed to find the item, suggesting the likelihood that one of them had swallowed it.[45]

Child-Stripping

Another crime largely perpetrated by women was child-stripping, sometimes known as 'skinning'. This involved waylaying young children and enticing them down back alleys with promises of sweets before removing some of their clothing. The items would then be pawned. In the winter, children wearing extra layers of clothes were particularly vulnerable. The newspapers occasionally carried warnings about increases in child-stripping offences.[46] Most victims were about three years of age; old enough to play outside but too young to know what was happening to them. Sometimes older victims were targeted. In October 1857 13-year-old Mary Anne Grimes went to the docks to see some friends set sail for Ireland. After a parting drink she felt drowsy and fell asleep on some steps. Another young girl, Mary Anne Courtney, took the opportunity to steal her boots, later pledging them for 1s. Babies could also fall victim. In December 1861 Mary Slater took an 18-month-old toddler to a privy where she stripped him naked and left him screaming.

The perpetrators were usually young women but boys were occasionally convicted of the offence.[47] Adult women were not averse to the practice. In July 1849 Eliza Thompson appeared in court accused of luring children down back alleys and offering them halfpennnies to remove their boots on the pretext of trying them on her own children. She would then make off with them. In August 1869 Ann Quinn of Bevington Hill was taken into custody on suspicion of stripping a child a few days earlier. A search of her home revealed 16 hats, 20 pairs of stockings, three frocks, three pairs of boots and 20 pawn tickets relating to items of children's clothing. She was described as a 'professional child-stripper'.

Thieves on the Move

Lower-class neighbourhoods had always been particularly dangerous for well-to-do people, particularly those flaunting their wealth in the form of pocket-watches or expensive jewellery. What most alarmed the middle classes, however, was the threat of the lower orders moving out of their squalid slums looking for amusement or opportunities to thieve. In the 1830s this exodus was stimulated by two developments, the advent of rail travel and the growth of professional policing. In 1839 the First Report of the Constabulary Commissioners revealed that habitual criminals were migrating from London and other towns where an improved constabulary had replaced the old, amateurish Parish Watch.[48] This might have been mere propaganda used by those urging police reform. Yet it was likewise alleged that the formation of the new police in Liverpool drove many thieves to other towns. It was argued that generally speaking urban thieves did not work in the countryside.[49] Nevertheless, a growth of crime in south Lancashire was blamed on people from Liverpool.[50] The Lancashire Constabulary was concerned about violent robberies from farmhouses in which the culprits made their escape across the fields back to Liverpool. Although the nomadic habits of criminals were formed long before the formation of the new police, the improved constabulary might have provided an added incentive for migratory thieves. The Superintendent of Liverpool Dock Police stated that 1,000 known robbers had been driven out of town, leading to an increase in crime in the suburbs, beyond police boundaries.[51]

A 19-year-old Salford prisoner gave an account of his itinerant life of crime in the 1830s: 'Very few robberies in centre of Liverpool; all on the outskirts, out of the police districts.' He explained one of his tricks. If picking pockets in a strange town, he would be accompanied by a well-dressed colleague who would stay in the background. If caught in the act, the colleague would rush forward and offer to keep hold of the thief while the victim ran off for the police. The pair would immediately scarper. Ironically, another Manchester thief reckoned that places such as Liverpool, which boasted newly established police forces, were the best places for pickpockets since 'people there think that they are safe under the eye of the new police, and will take large sums of money in their pockets'. He felt that Liverpool was an excellent place for a Manchester criminal since he would be unknown to the police and yet still be able to exploit his victims' false sense of security.

Liverpool criminals, on their release from gaol, continued to head for Manchester or Birmingham because these places had fewer policemen. Some thieves simply sought a change of scenery or sanctuary in new pastures. An inmate of the Borough Gaol admitted stealing £35 in gold: 'I immediately cut off to Manchester with two other companions; we staid there a few weeks, and then cut off to Stockport and some other places until the money was nearly done; then we came back.'[52] As fast as Liverpool thieves flocked to Manchester, Manchester thieves flocked to Liverpool to replace them. Ellen

Reece was born in Wales but like many other criminals she travelled in search of new opportunities. In 1837, while in Salford Prison, the 24-year-old explained to the chaplain that she had previously fled Manchester's streets and set up in Liverpool when she became too well-known to the police. After two years, and a spell in prison, she returned to Manchester and was about to flee again to Liverpool when she was arrested for theft and sentenced to fourteen years' transportation: 'I should have gone this time on Monday to Liverpool, having done the robbery (of £34) on the Saturday. I might have stopped there twelve months.'[53]

Liverpool villains were often found in distant gaols, demonstrating their migratory criminal habits. An Edinburgh newspaper reported that Liverpool thieves were numerous in the city.[54] A solicitor at Welshpool explained the crime situation in the neighbourhood of Llanfyllin: 'Formerly the bold unblushing prostitute was unknown here, but now there are, at least, seven or eight who publicly prowl the streets. One of them has been following her trade in Liverpool, and had recently introduced at Llanfyllin the system of inveigling and then robbing the men.' The magistrates in Northop, Flint, spoke of 'marauders' from Liverpool and Chester visiting them. The practice of travelling to escape the attentions of the police continued throughout the nineteenth century. Basil Thomson, Walton Gaol's assistant governor, was transferred to Cardiff in 1901. His prisoners included Liverpool 'corner boys' who had taken the boat for Cardiff when Liverpool became too hot for them.[55] Upon their release from prison, after a stabbing rampage around Scotland Road, two High Rippers fled to Barry, South Wales, where they were later charged with a vicious dockland assault.[56]

The railways also offered new opportunities for criminals. Within two weeks of the opening of the Liverpool–Manchester railway in 1830 there were almost 800 passengers a day using the service.[57] Two years later, trains carried 356,000 commuters annually. By 1855 there were 473,000 visitors to the town. The Railway Act of 1844 encouraged excursionists from other areas to take advantage of cheap Sunday fares. On a single day in July 1845, 5,300 tourists arrived in Liverpool from Manchester. The following week 7,000 day-trippers caused congestion from Edge Hill station to the docks.[58] The growth of the rail network meant that the population was constantly in transit. Criminals from other areas were attracted to the challenges and obscurity of new and remote districts. Trains also enabled the rapid movement of plunder from place to place. In 1876 hourly expresses covered the 34 miles from Manchester to Liverpool in 45 minutes.[59] Goods stolen in Liverpool could easily be fenced in Manchester and vice versa.

Although trains were safer than coach and horses, and indeed helped make the old highwaymen redundant, they inspired a fear of strangers, particularly when lone women were confined in carriages with unknown men. In January 1869 Maurice (or Morris) Fitzgibbon and William Ross, 'two low-looking youths', were found guilty of using indecent and insulting language to a woman in a railway carriage travelling from Garston to Liverpool. Fellow passengers might not even look like ruffians but the potential for harm remained and indeed intensified after Britain's first railway murder took place in London in 1864. Thomas Briggs was robbed, beaten to death and thrown out of a first-class carriage.[60] This new moral panic followed on from the ticket-of-leave scandal and the garrotting outrages of 1862–63. Liverpool had its own scare. In November 1876 Aaron Ellis was travelling alone in a railway carriage between Lime Street and Chester. At Edge Hill, Thomas Holmes and his father joined him. When the train reached Runcorn, Holmes suddenly pulled out a knife and attempted to murder Ellis. Trapped in the carriage, Ellis put up a terrific struggle and had the end of his thumb bitten off before Holmes tried to commit suicide by jumping head-first out of the window of the moving train. At his trial, the court heard that the man was suffering from mental illness after the recent death of his wife. He was certified insane and detained during Her Majesty's pleasure.

By the mid-century people could travel the length and breadth of the country. John Clay spoke of the problem in 1852: 'In North Lancashire we have very few trained juvenile criminals; we have very few who commit crimes as a means of support; they come to us now from Liverpool, they come by the railway; pickpockets and so forth [...] Liverpool, Manchester and Bolton maintain a large staff of trained thieves.'[61] Likewise, pickpockets from elsewhere would flock by rail to the Liverpool race meetings.

Rail broadened the opportunities for theft and enabled thieves to develop reciprocal arrangements with other villains. In Stockport, it was reported that 'the greatest portion of the aggravated offences are committed by strangers, either from Liverpool or Manchester, who are in constant communication with the thieves of Stockport'. It seems that the Stockport thieves planned the robberies for the outsiders to put into action.[62] In Kendal, local thieves also worked in conjunction with Liverpool villains to commit robberies. Social investigator Henry Mayhew reported that London was home to burglars from Liverpool, Manchester and Birmingham. London thieves also visited other cities: 'For example, a gang of Liverpool thieves might know a house where valuable property could be conveniently reached. Their being in the neighbourhood might excite suspicion. Under these circumstances they sometimes send to thieves they are acquainted with in London, who proceed thither and plunder the house.'[63]

A further explanation for the presence of London burglars on Liverpool's streets has already been mentioned. An outbreak of burglaries in Liverpool in 1834 was attributed to a police clamp-down on the capital's housebreakers. According to a letter sent to the newspaper, the 'midnight plunderers' had been driven to the provincial towns where they could carry on their work unhindered. A type of Home Watch scheme was proposed by which residents would take turns to stay up all night guarding their properties.[64] Thirty years later the threat remained. The inhabitants of West Derby Road were warned of 'a number of well-known Birmingham thieves, London swell-mobsmen, and ticket-of-leave men, who prowl about in daylight picking pockets and robbing houses'.[65]

Liverpool, however, was not without its own gangs of burglars.

TWELVE

Burglary and Property Theft

Domestic Burglary

Liverpool's economic growth helped entrepreneurs boost their wealth through thriving business opportunities connected with shipping and its accompanying industries. Eventually the rich merchants began to move to grander houses in more affluent and isolated areas such as West Derby and Knotty Ash, free from the grime and bustle of the town centre. They were also able to fill their homes with expensive ornaments and jewellery. Some envious individuals from the backstreet slums must have looked at these grand palaces and seen their own business opportunities. In underworld parlance, these properties were simply 'cribs' to be 'cracked'.

The rich were justifiably anxious about guarding their wealth from the desperate hordes. The north end of Toxteth saw 20,000 poor people crammed together in squalor. In 1816, after the Napoleonic wars, there was an economic slump that caused further misery. In response, robbers formed themselves into gangs to commit highway robbery and burglary. The wealthier southern side of Toxteth Park formed its own private patrols to protect property. It was not uncommon for people to carry a brace of pistols when travelling alone at night. During a spate of burglaries, residents not only became vigilantes for their mutual protection but also created an early form of neighbourhood watch. Householders put large bells on the top of their houses to be rung as an alarm to alert other tenants. On hearing a bell ring, they would turn out with heavy sticks to administer swift justice to the marauders.[1]

Burglary prevention could not be left to the authorities. The community had to take its own actions to protect life and property, even after the establishment of professional policing in the 1830s. In 1849, in West Derby, a gang with blackened faces committed a series of break-ins. The thefts were blamed on the apathy of residents who had failed to offer a reward and hadn't even organized a public meeting.[2] In a similar vein, three years later a newspaper correspondent complained that despite a spate of burglaries around Allerton,

Aigburth, Seaforth and Kirkby there had been no public outcry, no reward offered, no meetings of residents to show concern and no extra police appointed to catch the culprits. It was as if people no longer cared. The writer also condemned lenient sentences for burglary together with the offers of mitigation and the 'mock mercy' shown to criminals. One burglar had been given a mere seven-month sentence. Longer spells in prison were seen as the solution.[3] In fact, as will be seen, sentences for burglary could be quite severe without providing any deterrent to hardened thieves.

The newspapers occasionally issued warnings about spates of burglaries in particular districts, such as Toxteth Park, Falkner Square and Prince's Park, all in the south end.[4] Unlike violent street robbers who struck when the opportunity arose, burglars generally had specific geographical targets and planned timetables of activity. They preferred to hit a particular district until public alarm was raised before lying low for a while to live on the proceeds of their crimes. Domestic burglary had two great seasons. In the winter, residents went to bed early leaving the house at the mercy of thieves. In the summer, the wealthy went on holiday, leaving the premises in the charge of servants who were not always so vigilant.[5] Throughout the year respectable families habitually went to church each Sunday morning. The windows of opportunity were large enough for a skilled burglar to slip in and out unnoticed.

Successful burglaries were thoroughly organized. They were rarely done on the spur of the moment. Information was needed: in built-up areas, police patrols had to be monitored; on the outskirts, getaway routes needed to be planned. Such planning often required the work of a team or gang, each member adopting a different role, for example, the look-out, somebody to carry the housebreaking tools and a network of receivers to quickly dispose of the booty. Getting into the property was the burglar's first problem. A favourite ploy was to gain inside knowledge of the building and its occupants. For the big houses this could be acquired from the servants. In 1816 an old woman was seen prowling around the property of Mr Yates in Toxteth Park, asking questions about the security arrangements and wanting to know the number of servants and dogs. Shortly after, four men wearing masks and armed with pistols invaded the house. Two stood guard outside while the others stole money and jewellery. The gang was arrested and hanged after a trial at Lancaster.[6] The punishment hardly served as a deterrent since in the same week that the men faced the gallows another burglary took place at the mill near Yates' home.

There were countless ways of entering buildings. The Head Constable's annual statistical reports each contains a breakdown of methods under the heading for burglary. The lists display the ingenuity of Liverpool's thieves. False keys, windows entered, dishonest lodgers and servants together with fake messengers calling at the property are all cited. Another popular means of gaining entry was the use of children to crawl through small spaces such as coal vaults and narrow windows. In 1839 it was reported that it was becoming 'very common' for children aged between five and six to train as burglars. The premises of a recent burglary displayed marks made by 'little feet' as they stepped from the coal vault. The newspaper warned readers to lock the vault to prevent thieves exploring the rest of the house. Ironically, the report is immediately followed by news of a new dramatic production of Charles Dickens' *Oliver Twist* showing at the Liver Theatre.[7] A famous scene shows Bill Sikes using the slightly built Oliver to break into a house. Could canny thieves have learnt a few tricks? The use of children was a risky business. In 1862 one young burglar became trapped in a house in Edge Lane and had to be noisily rescued by the rest of the gang who then fled empty-handed.[8]

In May 1888 15 prisoners, including two women and some youths, appeared in court accused of committing about 20 burglaries. The gang was headed by George Morgan. Their modus operandi was to watch residents leave the house before sending young lads around the back of the property to break windows and crawl through to open doors. The gang would then bolt the front doors to prevent the occupants re-entering. The lads were said to have been trained and terrorized by Morgan into committing the burglaries. The women were used to help pledge the goods at pawnshops. Morgan received ten years' imprisonment and left the dock screaming for mercy. The women, on being sent down for five years, also pleaded for clemency but the lads merely laughed at their two weeks in prison followed by five years in a reformatory.

Another ploy for gaining entry was to pretend to be a respectable gentleman or acquaintance of the householder. In 1840, in the Edge Hill district, there were a couple of cases where a well-dressed burglar would wait for a family to leave for Sunday mass before informing the servant that he had just met the head of household in the street and had been told to wait in the house until his return. On both occasions the strangers were sent packing but it was obviously a well-rehearsed trick and an ideal opportunity to strip a room of valuables.[9] In February 1886 there was a series of burglaries around Walton. The thieves would watch people leave the house at night before knocking at the door. If nobody answered they knew the property was empty. A trader with inside knowledge of an area and its properties was ideally placed to commit burglary. In June 1851 there was a spate of break-ins in Toxteth. It seems that Michael Hickey had a milk round in the area and targeted houses on his round.

Faced with a secure property, housebreakers had to resort to their bag of tools. A vital piece of kit was a type of brace and bit used to cut circular holes in wooden doors, big enough to insert an arm to undo bolts. In June 1850, during a three-month spree, a large gang of prolific thieves targeted the outskirts of town using the tool, which in police tests took roughly one minute to cut a large hole. To avoid suspicion, women accompanied the men carrying the equipment in a basket. Some members of the gang were eventually caught at Edge Hill railway station on a train from Manchester after attending the races at Newton. A search of the gang's hide-out in Freemason's Row uncovered pawn tickets relating to stolen items.

In May 1854, at a quarry near Old Swan, a group of boys out nesting found a cache of burglary equipment, including files, saws and a dark lantern, which was used to throw a narrow beam of light rather like a torch. This avoided lighting up the whole room, thereby attracting attention from passers-by. The tools were thought to have been hidden by a gang that had recently targeted the area. In September 1859 'notorious burglars' John Berry and Benjamin Lee were apprehended in Fox Street carrying a 'jemmy', dark lantern wrapped in paper, skeleton keys, or 'twirls', and a length of rope, used to get a better leverage on the bit and brace when boring iron safes. The reason the tools were wrapped was not simply to conceal them but keep them from clinking together in the bag, a sound certain to attract the attentions of any passing policeman.

While most burglars preferred to enter and leave an empty property with the minimum of fuss, the more crude burglars deliberately terrorized the occupants to gain compliance. They routinely carried weapons such as a cosh or lead ball attached to a short length of rope. Some armed themselves with pistols simply because some householders themselves kept firearms by their beds, particularly in isolated farmhouses. Since such properties were dispersed on the outskirts of town, making a noise was not a problem. In January 1821 there was a spate of burglaries in Sefton. At 3 a.m. three men with blackened faces broke into a house and tied the residents to their beds before warning them that if they stirred before 5 a.m. they would be murdered. In another incident, at Bickerstaffe, an old man and his female servant were disturbed during the night by the same black-faced gang trying to break in. The terrified man opened his bedroom window and offered to throw them £3 to go away but they refused the offer and after swearing vengeance continued in their noisy attempt to gain entry. They failed and the occupants managed to flee out of the back door.[10]

The outskirts were particularly vulnerable to burglars since there were so few constabulary officers on duty. Those that were on patrol were unable to call for help, unlike their inner-city colleagues. In May 1868 PC Jolly was patrolling alone in Knotty Ash when he spotted three 'rough-looking' characters outside a house. After watching them, he approached a man who appeared to be the look-out and asked him what he was doing. The man replied, 'What the _____ are you doing here? I have as much right here as you.' Before he could be arrested, the man whistled to summon his colleagues who proceeded to launch an attack on the officer. Snatching his stick, they beat him with it, fracturing his collarbone before strangling him until blood spurted from his nose and mouth. They then secured him with his own handcuffs and rifled his pockets. Unable to move, Jolly passed out.

In one sense, burgling in gangs was safer. Victims could be easily overwhelmed, different team members could adopt the necessary roles and the swag be dispersed more easily. On the other hand, the more people were involved in a raid, the less each member could share in the 'bunce' or spoils of the robbery. Also, the more people who knew about the job the greater the chance that somebody would betray the enterprise by informing the police for the reward money. Indeed, somebody could unwittingly blab to the wrong person. In 1840 the Laurel Street Gang caused havoc after committing a series of daring burglaries around Grove Street, Faulkner Street and Clarence Street. They were captured only after police received information that the gang and their booty were holed up in Laurel Street.[11]

Perhaps to keep their activities to themselves, some burglars preferred to act alone. In 1886, during a spate of housebreaking around Bootle, the district was flooded with plain-clothed officers determined the catch the culprit. One night, a sharp-eyed constable spotted a bare-footed John Toner gingerly leaving a house before retrieving his boots from a hiding place. When apprehended and searched he was found to have in his possession a quantity of money, four silver spoons, a pair of sugar tongs, a snuff box, two pencil cases, an eyeglass and penknife. When asked to account for the items, his only mitigation was that he had not touched the toast fork. Toner was a prolific but largely unsuccessful thief, having spent a total of 25 of his 42 years behind bars for various offences. He was imprisoned for a further seven years.[12]

Shop and Business Theft

Domestic properties were only one source of plunder for criminals. Stealing from shops was another popular crime. In the winter of 1822–23 a gang of shop-breakers began operating around the dockside shops. Diamonds were used to cut holes through shop windows, making it easy to pull out silks, laces and jewellery. In October 1823 a newspaper correspondent warned of the renewal of the gang's activities, following recent similar raids, and concluded that the town 'was in a worse state than London'.[13] Another technique for breaking glass was known as 'star-glazing'. Old-fashioned shop windows consisted of many small panes of glass set in a wooden frame. By pressing the point of a knife at the edge of the frame, the glass would splinter into a star-shaped pattern. A sheet of sticking plaster was then applied to the shattered glass to lift it out of the frame, leaving the goods exposed. If a group of thieves crowded around the window, passers-by would be unaware of the crime being committed. Eventually, large plate-glass sheets were used for shop windows and the technique died out, only to be replaced by the modern smash and grab raid. In February 1848 William Power was one of a gang who used a brick to break a strong plate-glass window in South Castle Street before snatching several watches. First, the gang cleverly secured the door to prevent the owner rushing out to pursue them. Power was nevertheless caught by members of the public. Since this method was noisy and liable to attract attention, a quick getaway was essential. The procedure was therefore ideally suited to the later age of the motor car.

In 1836 the Head Constable brought attention to the stripping of lead from roofs, known as 'flying the pigeon'. Marine stores eagerly bought the lead, which was worth about £20 per ton.[14] The public was warned about the actions of dishonest slaters who would call at houses offering to mend a broken slate at very low cost. Once up on the roof the gang would strip the property of lead. One businessman was delighted to get work done for next to nothing, only to discover, months later when it rained heavily, that his warehouse had sprung numerous leaks.[15]

Dockside businesses storing cash and goods were also susceptible to thieves. In 1841 a business in Waterloo Road suffered its seventh robbery in two years. For some time the area between Princes Dock and Waterloo Dock had been infested with a gang of young thieves who targeted offices and businesses.[16] During the summer and autumn of 1891 there was a run of burglaries on business premises, sometimes two each night. The gang even raided a gun shop and took revolvers to use in further raids. A policeman was shot at as he pursued the robbers but they were eventually caught.[17] Warehouses were another attraction. Father Nugent claimed that many of Liverpool's large fires were simply started as a means of covering up cotton robberies. The booty would be then taken to Oldham or Rochdale, or distributed to local dealers.[18]

Sneak Thieves

The nineteenth-century social reporter Henry Mayhew spoke of a hierarchy of thieves. Near the top were the pickpockets who relied on their manual dexterity to lift purses from victims in risky close-up situations. There were also burglars who used ingenuity, skill and cunning to gain access to locked properties. At the bottom of the scale were the sneak thieves who used 'low cunning and stealth' to snatch whatever was available or on show.[19] Such criminality took various forms. Stealing from street stalls and markets was simple and most likely carried out by children who could grab an apple and sprint away through the crowded streets. One young prisoner in the Borough Gaol stated, 'I am sure if the mayor knew how many young thieves are made in the market he would put a stop to little boys going in. I know I was ruined by going there.' Another admitted that 'meeting boys in St John's Market was the first beginning of my ruin'.[20]

Thefts from shop tills took two forms. A great deal of till theft was committed by assistants working in shops who couldn't resist taking some loose change when the shopkeeper wasn't looking. When suspicions had been raised, the culprits were usually nabbed after marked coins and notes had been placed in the till. The other form of till theft was committed by strangers who took the opportunity to snatch the entire till when the publican's or shopkeeper's back was turned. Groups of children would sometimes distract the shopkeeper to raid the till. In 1866 two youths called Robert Roberts and William Tepping appeared in court as experienced till snatchers.[21]

A valuable form of marketing was the placing of goods outside shop doors. Unfortunately, this not only attracted customers but also tempted thieves. At the May 1853 sessions the Recorder revealed that ten people had been committed for stealing goods outside Lewis's store. He also stated that in one year 218 cases were brought before the magistrates, most of them related to the practice of hanging articles outside shop doors.[22] In the suburbs linen would be left to dry in the open, sometimes on hedges or across lines. Effortlessly stolen and difficult to trace back to any particular owner, it was easy picking for travelling vagrants who could pawn the goods when they reached the town. A female accomplice was usually required to carry the goods since men looked suspicious carrying bedding. The practice was known as 'snow dropping'. Stealing from hotels and lodging-houses was another opportunist crime, often victimizing fellow paupers. In November 1853 Henry Lloyd appeared in court accused of 30 such offences. He would book a room for the night and disappear the next day laden with the belongings of fellow guests.

Fences

In the 1830s of the total amount of property stolen in Liverpool only about 10 per cent was ever recovered by the police.[23] Most was sold back on the streets and in the public houses, pawned or fenced through a network of receivers. 'There are some hundreds of receivers in Liverpool,' stated the Watch Committee in 1839.[24] With the exception of food, which was no doubt hungrily devoured, and some clothing, which would be used to replace tattered garments, goods that were stolen needed to be transformed into ready cash. The role of the professional receiver, or 'fence', was to get the items back on the market as quickly as possible. The fence lay at the living heart of the underworld. It was he or she who kept the criminal industry alive, as if by some perverse system of systole and diastole, bringing in the vital goods and then pumping them around the intricate network of back alleys and courts. An infamous receiver in the 1830s was a man known to history only as J____s A____n. An all-round criminal, he kept several brothels and practised as a 'magsman' or swindler in addition to being a fence for northern England right up to southern Scotland. He was judged to be one of the cleverest thieves in England. Although eight of his gang had already been transported, he had always escaped conviction through lack of evidence.[25]

Such men were the bane of police and judges. Stipendiary magistrate Edward Rushton told one fence that 'receivers are worse than thieves'.[26] His thinking was that if there were no receivers there would be no thieves. For this reason, J. B. Aspinall, in his role as Recorder of Liverpool, punished receivers 'not only twice but seven times as much as thieves'. He viewed fences as 'criminal capitalists'.[27] However, since they provided a vital service in the poorer communities, receivers were well respected. Head Constable Whitty felt that juries were often unwilling to convict receivers, particularly since neighbours would often come forward to supply the accused with good character references. The result was that 'the man escapes, unless he happens to be a Jew, then he is fully suspected and convicted as a matter of course'. Whitty's informant in this matter acknowledged, however, that most Jews in Liverpool were respectable.[28]

Although the Irish were not noted for their involvement in organized crime, there were some professional Irish receivers. In the 1860s one of Liverpool's most notorious fences was John McNulty, better known as 'Brockle Jack'. In May 1862 two youths called John Hughes and Thomas Connerton were arrested in Scotland Road after some silver plate had been stolen from a house in Mount Pleasant. Hughes admitted selling the goods to 'Brockle Jack'. When

McNulty's house in Sawney Pope Street was searched, police found a watch from another robbery hidden near the fireplace. A few months later, McNulty was back in court charged with possession of stolen jewellery.[29] Around this time, nearby Ben Jonson Street and Thurlow Street had become centres for the fencing of 'watches, jewellery and articles of that kind'.[30] In fact, wherever thieves congregated there were receivers. Marine store dealers have already been mentioned as ready markets for dockland loot. The Head Constable was adamant that 'brothel keepers fence all property stolen by their prostitutes'. It was believed that at least 1,000 'fancy men' lived upon the thefts and prostitution of the women, either by bullying the clients or helping dispose of stolen property.[31]

Fences often worked in the clothes trade. Second-hand clothes dealers could easily shift coats, trousers and boots. Watches and jewellery were a different prospect. Such items needed to be 'christened' by having all identifying marks obliterated and replaced with new ones. In the 1860s George Murray, a former watchmaker of Basnett Street, was a notorious christener.[32] There were numerous places that would help turn stolen goods into money. Public houses were used to shift contraband. Many street-corner premises had double entrances leading into different streets, ideal for slipping in and out unnoticed. Dishonest publicans also acted as 'bankers of thieves' by hoarding the proceeds of crime. Father Nugent revealed that women would steal small sums and leave them with the barman for safe keeping. After getting drunk, and perhaps arrested, some women would return to the public house to withdraw their deposit. The dishonest barman would insist that they spent it all on drink while inebriated.[33] Disreputable lodging-house keepers were also in a position to pass on stolen goods. With their ever-changing low-life clientele they were good places for the striking of dodgy deals. Parents were also the obvious receivers of goods stolen by their own children. One 14-year-old girl would creep up the stairs of poor people's homes to steal the bedding while the occupants were busy downstairs. The child's mother disposed of the ill-gotten gains.[34]

Perhaps the most popular means of turning stolen items into ready cash was the pawnshop. In 1855 there were 129 such establishments, taking an average of 50,000 pledges a week. The borough total for that year amounted to 557,493 pledges.[35] Along with public houses, pawnshops were vital to working-class communities. For many poverty-stricken families, pawnbrokers were the last refuge before a spell in the dreaded workhouse. Yet the 'poor man's bank' was only a short-term solution to penury. On behalf of the Anti-Monopoly Association, John Finch and his team carried out an exhaustive investigation into the economic circumstances of families living in the Vauxhall ward. By measuring the hardship and distress in the area compared to 1835, the researchers reveal the sheer desperation of the destitute in the 1840s:

> Many families I called upon had pawned and sold all they had, and were dependent on small shopkeepers, who were letting them have herrings and potatoes until they could get work; others were pledging the clothes off their backs, just as they wanted a meal. One woman had taken her apron, another all the covering they had on a bed, just before I called, in order to get something to eat.[36]

Furniture-brokers were so over-stocked that they refused to accept any more items. A man had taken the buttons off an old coat to get a few halfpence. Yet sometimes it wasn't abject poverty but an addiction to drink that drove people to pawn their belongings. Herman Melville noted that Liverpool's pawnbrokers, hidden away in the narrow alleys near the docks, were usually situated next to the spirit-vaults. He mused whether the two establishments had connecting doors, since most of the customers of the pawnshops would soon be seen next door enjoying a drink.[37]

As well as legitimately helping the poor through financial crises, pawnbrokers were also used by thieves to fence stolen property. Goods would be pledged with no intention of ever reclaiming them. It was a source of easy money. Yet owing to the regulations laid down by the Pawnbroker's Act and its various amendments, pawnbrokers had to be careful. They were the first and most obvious place the police visited in search of stolen property. Pawnbrokers were monitored and naturally feared losing their valued licences. Indeed, some directly informed the police of illegal or suspicious pledging. If respectable pawnbrokers would not touch goods that were suspect, thieves resorted to the 'dolly shops' or unlicensed backstreet pawnbrokers. These establishments would take any description of property at any hour, a service for which they charged high rates.[38] A man called Roberts kept a dolly shop in Cumberland Street, as did Thomas Kelly in Greetham Street.[39] Other outlets for ill-gotten gains were the second-hand clothing stalls at St Martin's Market in Banastre Street, more popularly known as Paddy's Market. If child-strippers and other clothing thieves were arrested carrying stolen garments they would claim that they bought them in the market.[40]

Some legitimate pawnbrokers continued to accept dubious goods without question. Surveillance of pawnbrokers was the downfall of one armed and organized gang of black-masked burglars who committed 'lawless outrages seldom equalled in the present day'. In 1852 they terrorized West Derby and the northern districts of Liverpool before moving on to commit a violent armed burglary in Didsbury, near Manchester. Police rumbled the gang after raiding a pawnshop in Scotland Road and discovering items from the robberies. It seems the gang used women to fence the loot, more of which was found in nearby pawnshops. John Cosgrove, Ellen Burke, Mary Mulholland, John Moran and his wife Mary faced trial. John Moran's death sentence was later reduced to transportation.[41]

Children also regularly used pawnshops, a state of affairs deplored by prison and court officials. Most of the goods children found on their scavenging trips and thieving expeditions ended up in the pawnshops. In June 1851 10-year-old Celia Lloyd was charged with stealing a pair of trousers from a clothes line. She was caught with a 'pawn ticket in one hand and some copper in the other'. The pawnbroker who received the child's pledge testified that she often pawned articles for her mother. He was, nonetheless, severely rebuked. Reverend Carter, the Anglican chaplain of the Borough Gaol, believed that juvenile crime would be significantly reduced if pawnshops were banned from accepting goods from children.[42] In 1863 a juvenile burglary gang, aged between 11 and 14, appeared in court. They had sold some of their booty, including cutlery, to respectable ladies who also appeared in the dock. The remainder was pledged. The magistrate spoke of the necessity of changing the law in relation to pawnbrokers. At present they could receive pledges from youngsters above 12 years of age, whereas in London it was 16 years. The magistrate wanted to extend the London Act to deter children from stealing and making easy money.[43]

To cater for their desperate clientele, pawnbrokers were situated in the roughest districts. Like shopkeepers, they needed to be on their guard against burglars and thieves. A case from March 1863 reveals the ambiguous role of the pawnbroker within the community, as both source of plunder and the means of getting rid of stolen items. On a Saturday night two youths called Thomas Brain and William Rusher burgled Joseph Healing's pawnshop in Boundary Street. Shawls and other items of clothing were taken. On the Monday morning Rusher's mother unwittingly tried to pledge two of the shawls at the very same shop. The assistant recognized them and the woman was questioned by the police, leading to the arrest of the culprits.

On a visit to Liverpool in the 1840s novelist Charles Dickens entered a pawnbroker's shop in Whitechapel. He felt that one of the major differences between Liverpool and London pawnbrokers was that 'a stout wooden barrier' divided the customers from the brokers. Dickens wondered whether this was to allow the pledger to rest his elbows or, more likely, for the protection of the broker, to prevent anybody snatching items of stock. Also, he noted that in Liverpool the owner of the shop was as likely to be a woman as a man, 'sharp eyed, quick witted and not to be done by any means'.[44]

Indeed, women played a significant role as fences. A prison report into the welfare of boys in the Borough Gaol reveals a network of female receivers frequented by juveniles in the 1840s. Unfortunately the women's names and addresses are identified only by initials, although it is sometimes possible to guess at the location by using information from elsewhere. There appear to have been several Mrs B.'s, listed as residing in Vauxhall Road, North Street, H_____ Street and a cellar in F_____ Street. They are mentioned often, one of them working in league with a Mr B. It is unlikely that the same person moved about, since two Mrs B.'s are sometimes mentioned in the same sentence. One would offer half the full value of the article and one of them was described as 'a very bad woman', who was used mostly by young thieves 'that are breaking in'. Two Mrs C.'s are mentioned, one in a cellar in North Street, another in a court off Preston Street. This time she could be the same person. She was certainly a popular receiver who generally looked after her charges. One 9-year-old stated that after offering his gang money for booty, 'she brought us a pack of cards, and she fetched us whisky and ale to drink; we slept at her house that night'. She was not always so kind. The boy knew that he was sometimes ripped off. On another occasion, Mrs C. took a pair of boots from him and despite promising him 2s, gave him nothing: 'She laughed at me.'

'I have sold clothes to P.K.', a 17-year-old explained. 'He has two or three small shops about F_____ Street. He always knew the things I sold him were stolen. When I have been some time and not called upon him to sell anything, when he saw me he would ask if I got nothing in the clothes way, or anything else.' He continued:

> I have pledged all the plate I ever stole at Ms; he knew me very well. I have pledged with him at time and time [silver] plate worth £300–£400. He always knew the same to be stolen. He never gave us more than 2s per ounce, and when he gave us the ticket he would wish us to chew it or sling it. He would say, 'You have fenced them, and you know I shall not let you have them back'.

Another user of M.'s was an 18-year-old: 'I have pledged many things for which I never got a ticket. M. knows me very well; he has told me to get out of the way when there has been any noise about anything I have pledged.' This meant police investigation. He also took items to a clothes dealer identified as Mr K. After telling him that the goods were stolen, the man replied, 'Never mind, I can send them to Ireland.' In one of the coats, the initials M.E.M. were sewn on the seam. The sharp-eyed dealer picked out the stitching while the youth watched. Another lad pledged his goods in M_____ Street (possibly Maguire Street): 'He asked me if I should ever come for them. I always said no; he then knew what to do with them.' One boy sold his stolen items to a milkman who came down Ford Street every morning. He would then send the swag directly to Wales.[45]

Contraband from elsewhere also found a ready market in Liverpool. A teenage Manchester thief listed R_____s' shop in Quay Street as a great receiver of stolen property: 'There are in Liverpool two or three [receivers] in every street about Scotland Road. Every bit of plate from here [Manchester] goes there first, and from thence to Dublin.' It would then be melted into bars. 'The Liverpool receivers are more in number, and give a better price than here; so that it will pay a man to buy plunder here to sell again in Liverpool.'[46]

The rewards of property theft and receiving in the poorer districts meant that these activities were impossible to suppress, although figures for burglary in Liverpool show a decline towards the end of the century. For the five years ending in 1889 there were 4,024 cases of burglary; for the five years ending in 1899 there were 2,027 cases. Property crime was also in decline. For the five years ending in 1889 there were 27,846 offences against property; for the five years ending in 1899 there were 17,988 offences.[47] Yet burglary continued despite heavy sentences and increased measures of security such as Chubb locks, thick metal safes and new technology. In 1882 two Liverpool burglars were caught after unknowingly tripping a remote electric bell alarm. 'It will upset their profession entirely,' boasted a journal.[48] Needless to say it didn't, and the burgling of properties continued, as did the picking of pockets and the violent mugging of strangers in the street. Indeed, these were only a small selection of methods used by the needy and the greedy to make money. Just as housebreakers travelled out of the city centre to ransack the outskirts of town, another subdivision of the underworld moved even further afield, not to steal from houses but to plunder the surrounding countryside by shooting, snaring and trapping game.

THIRTEEN

Poaching Wars

Most Victorian criminals might have been based in the city slums and rookeries but they were also migratory, travelling by necessity to wherever the spoils lay, be it a pair of silver candlesticks or a brace of pheasants. Though a seaport, Liverpool nevertheless enjoyed a close relationship with its neighbouring districts. The town was in fact surrounded by the large estates of the Earls of Derby and Sefton. Ince Blundell was also within reach of adventurous Liverpudlians. In 1880, during four days' shooting at Lord Sefton's estate in Croxteth, a party killed 6,344 head of game, including 4,832 pheasants, 197 ducks and 999 hares.[1] While this sporting carnage was taking place, families in the squalid slums a few miles away were surviving on meagre rations. At the Liverpool hide market, where the skins of the animals were dressed, the workers had a sideline slicing off slivers of meat, called 'scalps', to sell to the poor.[2]

Before 1831 only a small minority of 'qualified' gentry were allowed to shoot game. After that date game certificates were introduced that opened up the right to shoot. In practice, however, for the rest of the century game shooting remained the preserve of the landed gentry.[3] The market for game was enormous in the north-west, with 500,000 rabbits a season (from October to March) going to Liverpool.[4] This figure does not include the illegal catches of poachers who ransacked the surrounding countryside. In the 1840s Ben Jonson Street, in the heart of the Irish district, was the favourite resort of poachers from Ormskirk and Warrington selling their catches. Father Nugent revealed, 'If you wanted any game the place to go to was Ben Jonson Street.'[5]

There is evidence that Liverpool poachers travelled extensively. In 1848 a Liverpool man was caught at Rufford, having travelled a distance of twenty miles.[66] In 1891 the shooting tenant of a sizeable grouse moor in the Scottish highlands went out earlier than usual one morning and caught a large gang of Liverpool poachers in the act. It seems that they had been exploiting the area for some time by daily netting the ground and dispatching the proceeds via train to a Liverpool game dealer. After the men had been arrested, a consignment of grouse packed in boxes and heading for Liverpool was intercepted at the nearest railway station.[7] Such activity points to the work of skilled experts, but the poaching fraternity ranged from full-time professionals to unemployed and poorly paid farm workers who merely 'poached for the pot' when the need or opportunity arose. Women and children were also involved in a peripheral role. Youngsters brought up in rural communities were introduced to the practice from an early age, for example through collecting eggs. Women helped sell illicit game. To avoid suspicion and the danger of being searched by the police on their return from hunting expeditions, poachers would sometimes secrete birds and fish in ditches or old barns or hide them under stones. These would be collected later by boys and women.

Poaching was a double test of skill between, on the one hand, the poacher and nature and, on the other, the poacher and the authority of the landowner, gamekeeper and policeman. Hostilities between the sides developed into a tense and bloody campaign, particularly in Lancashire during the lean years following the end of the Napoleonic Wars.[8] Despite the severe punishments threatened by the Night Poaching Act of 1816, it remained a war fought largely in darkness, at close quarters and with guns and other weapons on both sides. Gamekeepers often came off worst. In December 1827, at 4 a.m., a group of armed poachers variously estimated at between 5 and 25 entered Lord Sefton's estate near Prescot. The keepers, aided by some watchers from the village, and armed only with bludgeons, chased the intruders towards Eccleston. Every so often the poachers stopped, turned and opened fire in the darkness. Three watchers were wounded in the exchanges, one seriously. Nevertheless, James Ashton was detained and later sentenced to death for his part in the crime.[9]

In October 1851, on Lord Derby's estate at Bickerstaffe, Liverpudlian Robert Wright was one of a gang that beat up Thomas Cropper, one of the watchers. Four years later six poachers entered the Earl of Sefton's Croxteth estate and used bludgeons and stones on the pursuing keepers. Despite severe head injuries, the keepers managed to hold onto John Moody while the others escaped.[10] In 1857, in the early hours of a Sunday morning, Lord Derby's gamekeepers took five poachers by surprise. After a desperate battle in which a keeper was severely beaten, two of the men were apprehended. One of them, Thomas Wainwright (alias Cheshire Jack) of Sutton suffered a fractured skull. At the scene of the battle, bludgeons, sticks and nets were found littered on the ground.[11] In 1864 five poachers beat up two of Lord Derby's gamekeepers near Knowsley. One was attacked so savagely that contemporary reports feared that he might die from his injuries, though the report from the subsequent Assizes suggests that he survived.[12]

What was happening in Lancashire was not unique. Such episodes were being re-enacted throughout the English countryside, with poaching fatalities periodically reported in the press. In 1845 John Bright MP revealed to the House of Commons that in the ten years between 1833 and 1843, 25 gamekeepers had been murdered in England and Wales.[13] This intense and bloody conflict, which lasted throughout the nineteenth century, has been termed 'the long affray' by one historian.[14] It was as much a battle of ideas as a war with guns and bludgeons. Poaching, along with smuggling and wrecking, are sometimes termed 'social crimes', since neither the perpetrators nor the wider community judge such actions as illegal.[15] Poor people from rural areas believed that game was nobody's property. They drew an important distinction between pheasants, hares and other wildlife and farm animals, which were classed as belonging to somebody. Since game could fly and run it was not confined to any one person's land. Who, therefore, owned the hare that ran from field to field, from one owner's property to another? Surely a wild animal was incapable of having a legal owner and was therefore the property of whoever caught it. Besides, no less than the book of Genesis (1:20–26) stated that man had dominion over the fishes of the sea, the fowl of the air and over the cattle and 'every creeping thing that creepeth upon the earth'. One newspaper asked a pertinent question: 'How do the Game Laws coincide with these words of scripture?'[16]

The government made repeated attempts to sort out the issue. Before 1831 Parliament had passed over 40 Acts designed to regulate the hunting of game.[17] In addition to lethal spring-guns and cruel mantraps, the poacher had to carefully negotiate the legal minefield of the game laws. Hares, for example, were classed as game, but rabbits were not. Between 1816 and 1862 these laws were further modernized and reformed by three statutes. The Night Poaching Act of 1816 introduced transportation for seven years for poachers caught with a net or stick with intent to take game. The Act, however, only served to intensify the animosity between poachers and gamekeepers. The severity of the sentence made poachers more determined not to be caught. To evade arrest, poaching gangs were prepared to fight or shoot their way out of trouble if they met a group of gamekeepers. Before the introduction of rural policing in Lancashire in 1839, landowners protected their property with their own private army of gamekeepers and watchers, supplemented, until 1827, by the mantraps and spring-guns already mentioned. Even after the passing of the 1839 Rural Constabulary Act, keepers and watchers, rather than policemen, remained the primary defence against the intrusion of poachers.

After the 1831 Game Reform Act all wild animals, which a working man might view as food, were legally regarded as the property of the person on whose land they were found. Trespassing on private land in pursuit of game carried a two-month prison sentence and a £2 fine. Taking deer from parks and night poaching of other animals carried a sentence of seven years' transportation or two years' hard labour. The laws might have been harsh but the means of enforcing them were weak. The rural police were sparse and ineffectual, particularly since they 'were not allowed to interfere with poachers' and could only arrest them if they were armed.[18] Superintendent Storey of St Helens spoke of an incident in which some poachers had willingly shown him the game that they had in their pockets: 'they have laughed at me, and taken the game away'.[19]

It was not until the 1862 Poaching Prevention Act that the police were officially brought in to help eradicate the practice. The Act further restricted the poacher's actions by extending the definition of 'game' and introducing rural stop-and-search powers. Officers now had the right to search on the highway for carts and individuals suspected of coming from gaming preserves. Yet the police remained handicapped. While a night-time assault on a gamekeeper would merit a prison sentence of between twelve and eighteen months, beating up a constable would result in a mere two-month spell in gaol.[20] For their part, the police were often reluctant to become involved in poaching cases since it made them even more unpopular with the public. They resented being seen as lackeys of the landed gentry.

Besides, sentences of between one and three months for day poaching were hardly a strong deterrent to determined hunters. Poaching gangs would have a whip-round to pay any fines a member might incur. Superintendent Storey had heard the boasts of men convicted of day poaching and given 40s fines: 'We can pay this penalty, but we will not pay it; I can stand on my head for a month, and care nothing about it.' The magistrate would warn the guilty to amend their ways but would refuse to take into account their previous convictions. Some of these poachers were not amateurs who worked alone by grabbing the odd hare during the daytime but hardened professionals who gained safety in numbers by operating in gangs after nightfall. Such gangs had a 'captain' or leader and adopted military-style tactics. Before a raid, weapons would be chosen and manoeuvres and rules of engagement discussed.[21] Some gangs would even swear an oath before an expedition.

The Long Company

There were numerous gangs operating throughout rural Lancashire. Superintendent Storey boasted of breaking up the Billinge Gang who once attacked a respectable man as he walked home with his wife and friend to St Helens. The men were beaten up and robbed and the woman 'ravished'. The early 1840s also saw the rise of the 45-strong Warrington Gang and the 14-strong Pepper Street Gang from Chester. Other mobs included the Hollins Green Gang, the St Helens Gang and the Haydock Gang. Thomas Guest was known as 'King of the Appleton Gang'. One of the most ruthless and powerful poaching gangs in Lancashire was the Long Company, which included a number of Liverpudlians.[22] They were so-called because of their large number and the frequency of their exploits.[23] Although considered to be 40-strong, only 27 have been identified.[24] The group is perhaps better described as a loose collective of poachers rather than a tightly knit gang, since members often operated in smaller crews of 6 to 14 members.

The gang's captain was William Cheetham. Sometimes listed as an inhabitant of Roby, and also described as a 'notorious old game poacher from Toxteth Park', Cheetham was a regular visitor to both Lord Derby's estate and the police court.[25] Although once acquitted of shooting a gamekeeper, he was imprisoned many times for trespass, poaching and assault. Storey revealed that Cheetham kept a back room in a clogger's shop where he bred pheasant chicks from stolen eggs. Ironically, he would sell the birds back to the gamekeepers, thereby perpetuating both their careers.

About 14 associates of the gang were from Liverpool and the rest from the villages of Prescot, Billinge and Eccleston. Some members were related by blood or marriage. In addition to Isaac and William Jacques there was Thomas Jacques and George Jacques from Eccleston who was brother-in-law to Henry Fillingham, a Prescot tailor. There were four sets of brothers, the Woods, Websters, Lucases and Seddons. One of the Seddons lodged with John Shaw and his son Naaman (or Nathan) at Eldon Street, off Vauxhall Road. James Hunt was a full-time poacher from Sawney Pope Street. John Roberts lived with his girlfriend in Limekiln Lane, near Scotland Road.

Roberts, aged 27, was judged to be 'one of the best shots in England'. It was said that he could kill more pheasants at night than any five poachers in Lancashire, 'his aim being more sure in the dark than in daylight'.[26] He used the alias Thomas Draper whenever he pawned the shotgun loaned to him by a Liverpool baker called Anthony McGuffey. Also known as 'Cracker Jack', Roberts had suffered a miserable childhood. As a young homeless teenager he would sleep in the summer months among the brick kilns in the north end. He lived on the proceeds of begging supplemented by potatoes stolen from the surrounding fields and roasted in the kilns. He then started making biscuits or crackers. At five feet six inches, he often carried 50 to 60lbs of crackers on his head as he tramped over a twenty-mile radius to Chester, Wigan and Warrington to sell his wares. He was unable to gain proper employment as a baker since his skills only extended to biscuit making.[27] In his mid-twenties he turned his hand to poaching.

The gang employed an array of skills and experience. In a reversal of the usual role of poacher turned gamekeeper, John Shaw had once been a keeper on both the Bold estate by the River Mersey and on Lord Derby's grounds at Knowsley. He once boasted that he could carry off 30 pheasants a night, despite the presence of gamekeepers. John Williams, a beershop keeper and game licence holder, based close to Liverpool Cattle Market, received the gang's bags after each hunt. The game would be sold on to St John's Market, revealing an entrepreneurial spirit in the Liverpool men common also to industrial workers in manufacturing regions such as the West Riding of Yorkshire. These men poached not because they were hungry and lacked money but because there was a thriving market for game for which others were willing and able to pay. These commercial poachers thrived more in a climate of economic prosperity than in a depression.[28]

Despite some of their trades and the availability of work, most of the Long Company did nothing but poach. During a government inquiry, one poacher was asked, 'Did you ever know poachers begin to poach from distress?' He replied, 'No; I think it puts them in distress.'[29] For some, the proceeds of poaching were not particularly lucrative since most of the money made went back to the beershops. Poachers had a close relationship with the beershops. Not only did the premises act as meeting places for the gangs, the freely flowing alcohol would fortify the men before their night-time raids. Storey reveals that publicans would let the poachers run up a debt knowing that it would be paid back in game. According to Storey, some poachers' wives stated that they and their children were better off when their husbands were in prison. Yet despite their considerable crimes, members of the gang often avoided gaol, sometimes through lack of evidence but mostly through the reign of terror they brought to the district.

The Long Company was judged to be 'a plague to the neighbourhood'. Farmers, in particular, refused to give evidence against the men for fear of having their premises torched or the tails hacked off their cows. Victims of robberies were so intimidated that they would also refuse to inform the police.

It was reported that travellers on the highway coming into contact with the gang freely handed over 'treats' to buy their safety.[30] Gang members were a law unto themselves, often sleeping in barns without permission. Between eight and ten men would enter the barn at 8 p.m. and sleep till 12 p.m. They would then go poaching before returning to the barn at 6 a.m. 'There was one part of the Long Company,' said Storey, 'that I do not think ever slept at home; night after night they were in the farmer's barns.'

The first reference to the Long Company appeared on 11 December 1841, after an attack on Henry Grayson, a wealthy 64-year-old farmer who was waylaid near his home at Rainford. Grayson was returning from St Helens late at night after collecting rents from his properties. He had earlier been warned by a drinking companion not to travel since members of the Long Company were about. Grayson replied, 'Oh no; I know them all; they'll not meddle with me.' His mutilated corpse was found at 5 a.m. A blunt instrument had cracked his skull and penetrated his brain. Under the force of the blow, his right eye had burst from its socket. His shoulder had also been dislocated and so many ribs broken that his sides had caved into his lungs. His trouser pocket had been cut off and his money taken. Police suspected that members of the Long Company were responsible. Thomas Meadocroft and Isaac Jacques were soon arrested, the former having blood on his knees and a bloodstained knife in his pocket. Robert and Charles Wood, William Jacques and Patrick McCadden were arrested later.[31] However, at the March Assizes the following year the suspects were acquitted through lack of evidence. The attack might have been linked to an earlier outrage in April 1841, when there had been an armed burglary at a farmhouse in Padgate near Warrington during which five hooded men fired shots and nailed in the occupants as they left.[32]

The Long Company became natural suspects for any outrages in the area. In November 1842 a farmer was travelling from Eccleston to Rainford when, not far from Grayson's house, two men jumped over a hedge and attacked him. The victim was getting the better of the fight when two others appeared and joined in. One shouted, 'Cut the bastard's throat.' The farmer was then stabbed in the neck, beaten and robbed. A little earlier the victim had seen members of the Long Company in a nearby public house. Three men called Traverse, together with one of the Jacques brothers, were apprehended in West Derby a few days later. None of them was found guilty at the following Assizes. Interestingly, Birmingham had its own gang called the Long Company. In March 1843 they were blamed for a similar attack on a cattle dealer riding home from market late at night carrying a large sum of money. The man's horse was shot at and he was beaten senseless. When he regained consciousness, he was missing £700.[33]

Superintendent Storey gave an account of a raid by a 40–50-strong gang from Liverpool on the property of Mr Hughes, a magistrate from Sherdley Hall, near St Helens. Storey believed they were connected to the Long Company. The keeper heard shots in the woods and got up to investigate. When he arrived on the scene, accompanied by a few servants, the police were also present and were able to chase off the men. Storey also recounted the time when he spotted the Lucas brothers in a hedge at 9 p.m. one winter's night. Because the men looked suspicious he gave chase and caught one of them, despite the man being armed with a bludgeon. After overpowering Lucas, he put him in handcuffs only for his brother to return. However, a gamekeeper arrived to help and the brothers were taken into custody. The party headed back to the hedge where the suspects were first spotted, when Storey saw a gun on the ground. One of the prisoners suddenly grabbed the weapon and threw it between Storey's legs where it went off. Fortunately he was uninjured. The brothers were later brought before the magistrates but discharged as the policeman was considered to have had no right to arrest them in the first place.

Despite their frequent displays of arrogance, brutality and intimidation, the Long Company found their nemesis in Superintendent Storey. To break the gang, Storey employed the services of two undercover policemen from Manchester. The officers disguised themselves as 'travelling Scotchmen' to infiltrate the gang at Holt's beershop in Eccleston. The spies succeeded in nailing the gang for a variety of offences including trespass, killing game without a licence, selling game out of season and armed night poaching. In March 1843, at Prescot Court, 14 men, including James and John Shaw and John Pendlebury, were convicted of poaching at Knowsley, Billinge and Eccleston. The prisoners were sent to Kirkdale Gaol and although some saw the sentences of two to three months as a blow to the Long Company they did little to deter the gang.[34] Indeed, a worse outrage was to be perpetrated later that year.

On 10 November members of the gang entered Lord Derby's estate in Knowsley. Early in the morning, ten of the company had already shot three pheasants when they came up against a group of keepers. The poachers, who were armed with sticks and guns, had a black dog with them. When the dog sprang to attack the head keeper, Richard Kenyon, one of his colleagues kicked the animal and it ran back to a man recognized as John Shaw, a former employee at the same estate. A keeper, remembering his ex-colleague, declared, 'Shaw, I know you very well, you don't need [to] strike a blow.' Somebody muttered, 'We will Shaw you.' Shaw allegedly shouted, 'Give it to them, shoot them, kill them.' At a distance of five yards a gun was fired at Kenyon, hitting him in the stomach. Kenyon instinctively responded by emptying both his own barrels. The keepers retreated under further gunfire, leaving the poachers to celebrate with repeated cries of 'Hurrah'. In their defence, they might have been unaware of the injuries that had been caused to Kenyon.

As one of the watchers attempted to flee, a member of the gang caught hold of him and shouted, 'Drown that devil – kill him.' Nevertheless, the watchers managed to escape. Kenyon was taken to a barn where he received medical attention, but he died three days later. After the shooting the gang split, half decamping to Eccleston and the rest to Liverpool via Knotty Ash. At 5 a.m. a policeman, a nervous carter and three women on their way to work spotted the men. One of the gang shouted reassuringly, 'We do not touch women.' Beershop keeper John Williams later accepted 20 hares, part of the proceeds of the fatal expedition.

A reward of £100 was offered for the capture of Kenyon's killers, along with a free pardon to any person involved in the crime, provided that he was not the one who fired the fatal shot. Five men were arrested, including John Shaw at his home in Eldon Street. At this point Shaw's son Naaman turned Queen's evidence to save his father and, no doubt, claim the reward money. When Thomas Jacques was arrested he immediately asked, 'Has Shaw been telling?' It was thought that Henry Fillingham had fled the country. However, three weeks later, Superintendent Storey found him hidden deep in a huge pile of straw in a loft above a stable. He had been embedded there all the time, being supplied with food by others. When Storey accidentally trod on him, Fillingham shouted for them not to stick a pitchfork into him. Nevertheless, when one of the policemen grabbed his arm he shouted, 'If you lay hold of my arm I will a run a knife into you.' Fillingham, although small in stature, was a violent man. In preparation for an earlier poaching expedition to Lord Derby's estate, accompanied by George and Thomas Jacques, he armed himself with a gun and put stones in his pocket. In Prescot he spotted a policeman approaching. In case he was stopped and questioned he reached for the gun but it was not needed. After the officer had safely passed, Fillingham remembered the stones and reflected that 'if he had not forgotten them, he would have given the policeman's bright hat a rattle'.[35]

The trial of John Roberts, Henry Fillingham, Joseph Rimmer, Thomas Jacques and James Hunt opened on Boxing Day 1843. Naaman Shaw revealed how he travelled from Liverpool to Knowsley, going from house to house and calling in on beershops along the way to muster recruits until there were ten of them with three guns. The party included the five accused and four others who remained at large. Shaw admitted to meeting his father along the way but denied that he joined them in the affray. Other witnesses provided John Shaw with an alibi. One said that he was in the Globe Tavern in Scotland Road on the night of the murder. Shaw's lodger declared that he was in bed at 2 a.m.[36]

A popular street ballad recorded the infamous events:

> Of five gallant Poachers,
>> As you shall understand,
> One night they went a Poaching,
>> Into Lord Derby's land …[37]

One of them decides to kill some game, 'Or spill some human blood'.

> John Roberts said, to Nathan Shaw,
>> What did you say to me?
> Thou said, Let's fire at Kenyon,
>> And keep each other free …

Some of the watchmen indeed claimed that it was Naaman Shaw who shouted, 'Go into them! Blast them!' immediately before the shot was fired.[38] In court, however, Shaw accused Roberts of firing the fatal shot and added that Fillingham also peppered the retreating keepers. The judge stressed to the jury that although only one poacher was charged with killing the keeper, the law viewed the men as acting in concert and so the crime of one was the crime of all. After 45 minutes, all five were found guilty of murder. The jury added a recommendation of mercy, which the judge chose to ignore. There were shrieks and shouts of 'Mercy, Mercy' from females at the back of the court as all five were sentenced to death.

Friends of the condemned men made a futile trip to Knowsley Hall to beg Lord Derby's support. His neighbour, Lord Stanley, was also unmoved. 'It was necessary an example should be made,' he said.[39] The Home Secretary later commuted the sentences of four of the men, who were then transported for life. Only John Roberts was to hang. In the condemned cell Roberts maintained that the fatal shot was fired under excitement and fear that he would be shot at. He also blamed the influence of drink. Meanwhile the rest of the gang, Thomas Tither (or Tithero), William and John Webster and Henry Robinson, remained at large. Robinson had fled and joined the army. In December 1846 he decided to hand himself in to the police and face trial. He was also sentenced to death but transported instead.[40]

In January 1844, after a breakfast of tea, bread and butter, Roberts was led to the platform outside Kirkdale Gaol to a chorus of groans and hisses from the 30,000-strong crowd, described as the 'scum and rabble' of the town. The groans were then replaced by the piercing shrieks and yells of female relatives and friends. With a bow, the illiterate Roberts gave a moving speech:

> Good people, good people all. I have made my peace with Almighty God. I hope, good people, that some of you will tell my poor old father that I am going to die happy [...] I owe no man any animosity, and I expect no man owes me any ('No! No!', cried the crowd) [...] Good people all, take this as a warning from me, and never let yourselves be entangled with the devil, nor go into bad company [...] Farewell, farewell.[41]

The bolt was drawn, the hatch dropped and Roberts fell to his doom. When the executioner steadied the rope to present the dead man's 'fat and chubby' face to the crowd, they howled in anguish, some of them showering the hangman with stones. Another ballad immortalized the affair.

> Unhappy John Roberts, the lot fell on he,
> His life for to forfeit on the gallows tree;
> It should be a warning unto all mankind,
> To see him cut off at the height of his prime.[42]

Yet Roberts' death failed to act as a warning or a deterrent and poaching continued in Lancashire and elsewhere. In April 1846 a poacher called Charles Lynn shot Lord Derby's assistant gamekeeper, John Wainwright. The keeper was enjoying a drink in the Eagle and Child tavern in Prescot when he heard gunfire outside. On going to investigate, he was blasted in the hand and leg. The ostler of the inn was able to identify the culprit who ran off only to be arrested a week later. It was thought that Lynn had a grudge against the keeper. The victim's injuries were not life threatening but the gunman was sentenced to fourteen years' transportation, a mere ballistic fluke saving him from the same fate as Roberts.

The breakup of the Long Company simply dispersed some of its members. Membership of the gangs was always fluid, with poachers moving from one team to another like modern-day footballers. When the Long Company disbanded, its captain, William Cheetham, joined the Appleton Gang which later decamped to Manchester. Only towards the end of century did the bloody and hazardous pursuit of armed night poaching become a part of history, banished by efficient policing and improvements in social conditions that helped forge changes in people's moral behaviour and economic circumstances. Besides, there were easier and less dangerous ways of making money. Poachers and burglars operated by stealth in the middle of the night but faced violent resistance from armed gamekeepers and householders. Street robbers would violently steal people's belongings in broad daylight, risking retaliation in the process. Pickpockets would steal from people unawares but had to risk getting uncomfortably close to their victims. Among the most intelligent and artful thieves were confidence tricksters and fraudsters who persuaded people to literally hand over their money. Compared to night poaching, conning gullible members of the public was quite civilized.

FOURTEEN

Scams

Nathaniel Hawthorne was no stranger to Liverpool's fraudsters. During his employment at the American Consulate, at the corner of Brunswick Street, he daily encountered the worst the town had to offer:

> The staircase and passage-way were often thronged, of a morning, with a set of beggarly and piratical-looking scoundrels (I do no wrong to our own countrymen in styling them so, for not one in twenty was a genuine American), purporting to belong to our mercantile marine, and chiefly composed of Liverpool Blackballers and the scum of every maritime nation on earth.[1]

The Liverpool dockland was the ideal place to fleece, deceive and defraud people, a swindler's paradise. The best victims were people new to the area, particularly travellers and migrants, inexperienced in the town's ruthless double-dealing practices and unable to stay around long enough to prosecute. Unwary Yorkshiremen, Manxmen and naive country bumpkins were relentlessly targeted and bamboozled. An Irish migrant warned that 'if a man had 7 senses, it would take 500 senses largely developed to counteract the sharpers of Liverpool'.[2] Sharpers were essentially swindlers who used playing cards. Another type of trickster was the 'magsman', who ran pitch and toss games using 'mags' (halfpennies). Eventually both terms were applied to any professional hustlers, particularly those who toured fairgrounds conducting gambling scams and other rip-off schemes.[3]

The scam business was extensive, involving a whole range of deceitful activities, from the simple three-card trick in a public house to more sophisticated insurance frauds. In its most basic form a scam might involve plain and simple robbery. For example, after befriending a likely victim the rogue would find out if he was travelling to America. He would then pretend that he was also sailing on the same boat and propose a celebratory meal together before embarkation. Either through drink or planted women, the dupe would then be plundered before he sailed. Other scams were a little more artful. There were deceptions that allowed the victim the chance (however slim) to win something through gambling. Other tricks offered 'valuable' goods at bargain prices. Some ruses promised the victim something valuable in return for something practically worthless. Conversely, through deft sleight of hand, some tricks involved replacing something valuable with something worthless. Unbelievably, some dodges seemed to involve simply giving money away. In their most extreme form the scams involved cold-blooded murder. Whatever the tricks, they all involved befriending, fooling and playing upon people's innocence, gullibility or greed. In contrast to garrotters who relied on their physical strength and ferocity, sharpers were intelligent, resourceful and outwardly friendly. Victims, or 'flats' as they were called, had to be identified, selected and carefully groomed before being bled dry. Whoever the victim, a close and trusting relationship was essential to any swindle.

Sharpers, Duffers and Coiners

The sharper's tools of the trade were packs of rigged playing cards, a thimble and some dried peas and a supply of fake coins. Sharpers often worked in groups, although members pretended not to know each other. Sometimes the victim would be invited for a drink where he would meet other friendly 'travellers'. A game of cards, or a demonstration of the three-card trick, would follow. This involved the punter being invited to guess the picture card from the three cards dealt faced down. Odds were offered at two to one. After the initial demonstration the picture card would be furtively removed, making it impossible to win. In any card game it was important to let the victim win the first few games to help build up his confidence and inspire him to raise his stakes. Little did he know that all the players around the table were working as a team. Knowing winks and bodily tics would act as signals to keep the crooks in contact with each other until the moment came to fleece the punter. It was not unknown for card tricksters to skin their fingertips to make them more sensitive. They could then identify playing cards by touch using a pattern of tiny pinprick holes made in the back of the cards.[4]

During the Aintree races of 1869 the tricksters were out in force. On a train back to Liverpool one group of sharpers must have thought that they were in a carriage full of greenhorns. One lit a candle and began playing the three-card trick with his colleagues who of course pretended to be strangers. After the men won a few games the sharper suggested that others in the carriage might like a chance to win. Little did he know that most of the other passengers were

Liverpool detectives returning from the races. When an officer stood up and identified himself the candle was quickly extinguished and the cards thrown out of the window.[5]

Con artists were nothing if not persistent. If one scam didn't work another was sure to follow. A farmer called William Robinson arrived in the town intending to emigrate. Walking along the dockside he met a stranger called John Thompson who suggested that they go for a drink. In the public house they were joined by two other 'strangers'. One claimed to be quite wealthy and opened a small box housing what looked like a valuable gold ring. He tried to sell it at a bargain price but Robinson declined the offer. The man then took the ring from the box and replaced it with a cinder and asked Robinson to bet any money on whether the ring was still in the box. Robinson refused to gamble. The men then went to a public house in Williamson Square where they met William Bradley and some others. Thompson offered to fight one of the men and appeared to be winning after a few rounds. Thompson then asked Robinson if he wanted to bet on the outcome. Again, Robinson refused, no doubt realizing that he was witnessing a staged bout. Playing cards were then produced and once again he refused to get involved. Perhaps drink eventually sapped Robinson's resolve for he then offered to toss a coin for a drink. Perhaps he thought that the result could not be fixed. However, the half crown that he put on the table was snatched by Thompson who proceeded to buy the company a round of drinks, much to Robinson's annoyance. Thompson then asked Robinson what money he had on him. He produced about 10s, which were then knocked from his hand. Robinson scrabbled on the floor to retrieve his coins, as Bradley attempted to pick his pockets.[6]

Another common scam involved selling something that wasn't what it seemed. Today, trading in fake goods has become a global multi-million pound industry. In the nineteenth century the deceitful trade was practised by 'duffers' selling counterfeit (duff) goods. In 1823 a newspaper correspondent warned of the activities of a 'set of fellows, dressed as sailors, who bore, cajole, and dupe the strangers, if not the natives, with pretend contraband silks, watches and mock jewellery'. Cigar boxes would also be filled with sawdust with a few cheap and nasty 'stinkeroos' laid on top.[7] Duffers dressed as seamen to fool their victims into thinking that the sham goods were smuggled. Sometimes called 'dry land sailors', they haunted the docklands, particularly near the emigrant ships. In his autobiographical novel, *Redburn*, Herman Melville wrote about gangs of boys peddling Sheffield razors at amazing prices. They turn out to be blunt and useless.[8] Perhaps the boys should have teamed up with the street hawker who sold a magic paste that allegedly sharpened razors.[9]

In Lime Street, bird lovers could buy canaries that turned out to be painted sparrows.[10]

Claiming that they were smuggled goods, Patrick Sweeney sold William McIntyre a 'satin' waistcoat and a 'camel hair' shawl. Later, when questioned in court, the duplicitous Sweeney swore that he actually claimed that the garment was 'as fine as camel hair'. In the 1850s Sweeney was part of a gang of duffers based in a public house off Dale Street, where members spent most of their time drinking and fighting. One of the gang's victims was persuaded to part with £14 in return for goods worth about 14s.[11]

The market for fake goods extended beyond the docklands. In 1845 newspapers warned farmers of a new scam. At the time, a fertilizer made of bird excrement, called 'guano', was selling for £7 to £8 per ton. With an eye to the main chance Liverpool crooks were manufacturing their own mixture and selling it cheap for £4 to £5 per ton. Like modern-day drug dealers they mixed all kinds of substances, including sand, tanner's waste and sulphate of ammonia, to produce a fake and adulterated product.[12] In another chemical-based fraud, vendors went from door to door selling a bogus and useless imitation of Greer's Patent Vermin Poison.[13] One travelling charlatan even sold ointment to be rubbed into the head to stimulate the growth of extra brain tissue. His cry was,

> Okerums-pokerum, here's your okerums-pokerum just come from Spain,
> 'twill quicken your senses and sharpen your brain!
> If you try it once, you'll try it again.[14]

It was a measure of the product's uselessness that it didn't work the first time. Another quack herbalist, of forty years' experience, was a specialist in liver and blood disorders. On his tour of the districts he would draw in the crowds with his learned patter: 'What makes you thump the missus and knock the youngsters about? Why it's your liver of course. Get your liver wrong and all's wrong.' He refused to sell bottles of his formula, preferring instead to give them away in return for sixpence, 'just for luck – not for pay'. He advised his patients not to drink the mixture all at once 'or you will grow twenty years younger in an hour and your own wife won't know you'. Interviewed by a journalist, the man admitted that trade wasn't what it used to be. Ignorant fellows had entered the profession and ruined it by duping people. Also, druggists and big shops were undercutting him with their bargains. He nevertheless revealed a holistic approach to pharmacy: 'what's good for one thing's good for another'. In fact, he merely coloured his medicine differently for the various ailments.[15]

Another form of deceit was ring dropping or 'flat catching', which involved convincing somebody that an item found in the street was more valuable than it actually was. Melville writes about a flat-catcher who prowled the docks trying to sell a 'gold' ring that he had picked out of the gutter. When Redburn refuses to buy the dodgy article he is floored by a punch in the chest.[16] Although fictional, the account is based on actual Liverpool practices. A young sailor was walking along Elliott Street when he saw a man called Edward Frost stoop to pick up a glove. Frost turned to the seaman and said, 'Well, I've picked up a prize anyhow.' It seemed that the discarded glove not only had a ring stuck in the finger but, conveniently, a receipt showing that the item was worth 14s 6d. A generous Frost promised the sailor that he could have half of the proceeds. The only problem was that he had no money on him and so asked the seaman to accompany him to a public house where he would borrow some. He was unsuccessful, however, and decided to ask the seaman if he had any money. The young man had only half a crown. Frost took it along with the seaman's address and gave him the ring as security. He promised to call around the next day to give him 7s 3d as his half of the proceeds. When the seaman got home his father said that he had been 'nicely taken in'.[17] The dodge was still going strong in 1909. H. J. Nicholls reports that a man picked up a pair of cheap spectacles from the pavement and tried to sell him them, claiming that they were silver.[18]

Another means of turning something worthless into something profitable was an early form of recycling by which rags could be exchanged for goods. The 'Toffee for Bones' men were a familiar sight as they toured the streets with their persuasive cry:

> Roll up, roll up
> Toffee for rags and bones
> Bits of brass or broken glass
> Toffee for rags and bones.[19]

However, the trade was not immune from con men. At Brownlow Hill, the men were involved in a clever scam. In exchange for some toffee they would ask young children to sneak small valuable articles out of their homes. One boy was even persuaded to give up his cap (worth 15s) for a slab of toffee.[20] Some rag-and-bone men who frequented the back alleys stole items from residents' yards. The men would strike up friendships with the servants and, by giving them pennies for rags, would encourage them to smuggle other articles from the house. The trade also gave the men the opportunity to stake out the area for future robberies.[21]

The idea of turning base metal into gold stretches back to medieval times. A related trick was to turn heavy metal into coinage. The dud coins would then be sold on to gangs of 'smashers' who would pass them on to unsuspecting shopkeepers. At its best the artifice involved high technical skills and a secret location to carry them out. In October 1863 police raided the house of a man called Marr, known as 'the father of the smashers', in Charter Street, off Vauxhall Road. Here they found crucibles for melting metal, various moulds, plaster of Paris and a galvanic battery for electro-plating the coins.

In the early 1830s thousands of pounds worth of fake 5s pieces were circulating in Liverpool and beyond, a scam said to be 'one of the most extensive ever known in this kingdom'. So convincing were the phoney coins that the Mint was amazed at the level of workmanship and the quality of metal. It was suspected that the forger had access to stolen silver plate. Following the theft of a haul of plate, police inquiries led eventually to the home of the respectable Arnett (or Harnett) family in Virgil Street. Police staked out the splendidly furnished property for some time before hitting on an excellent ploy to gain entry. Disguised as a postman a detective knocked at the door. When it opened he rushed inside followed by a colleague. The stolen plate was found, along with fake coins and the machinery for producing them. It seems that brother and sister, Isabella and Edward Arnett, used a country-wide network of agents both to steal the plate and get rid of the coins. They were convicted and transported for life. Julia's mitigation was that 'their money could do no poor man harm'.[22]

A scam related to coining was 'ringing the changes'. The more valuable fake coins, particularly gold pieces, were liable to be carefully examined by any canny shopkeeper familiar with the proverb 'all that glitters is not gold'. To overcome this, a genuine sovereign would be offered for a cheap item. The shopkeeper would examine the coin before putting it in the till. When the change was about to be given, the fraudster would then inform the shopkeeper that he had in fact the correct money and would be given back his coin. The swindler would then fumble in his pockets for the loose change only to discover to his embarrassment that he didn't have quite enough small money. He would then hand back the sovereign which had been cunningly replaced by a dud. The shopkeeper wouldn't be as observant and would accept the fake.[23]

A variation of the ploy was to change the coins of members of the public. When George Frith met Martin Higgins, 'a simple-looking' Irish lad, near the docks, he asked him if he had any money. The lad showed him two sovereigns. Frith kindly warned him about the sharpers and offered to wrap up the money in paper and twine to keep it safe. It was only later that Higgins discovered that his money had been replaced by two dud coins.[24]   Andrew Williamson, an elderly cattle dealer from Scotland, was passing through Liverpool with £71 in notes and £11 in gold when he asked a stranger for directions. The men soon struck up a friendship and went for a drink. Inside the public house they met another 'stranger' who claimed to be from the country. He said that he had come to Liverpool to collect substantial damages after suffering a railway accident. He flaunted his wealth by buying a couple of rounds of drinks before generously offering the cattle dealer two sovereigns. He asked him for his purse so that he could put them in. The man obliged and carried on drinking. It was only after the strangers had left that he realized his money was missing, the coins substituted with fakes.[25]

One scam involved giving away money. It seems too good to be true and of course it was but that didn't stop people from being duped. 'The Bouncer' was a notorious character around Scotland Road who sold pills on street corners and frequented the races to play the 'purse trick'.[26] The scam involved selling a purse containing, for example, 5s for the knockdown price of 1s. The seller would be seen dropping the coins into the purse. This unbelievable bargain would be snapped up only for the customer to later find that the cheap purse in fact contained only coppers. The skills of a conjuror and a good line in patter were essential for the success of the trick, not to mention a gullible public. In 1856 Charles Kilble appeared in court accused of performing a variation of the trick on the corner of Pembroke Place and Monument Place. His offer was a free purse containing 3s 6d for half a crown. The purse contained only pennies.[27]

Pornography

Pornography might have been available to wealthy men able to afford expensive books of erotic prints, but for the lower classes images of naked women were legally accessible only through classical paintings. For something a bit more risqué, men had to rely on illicit prints and saucy stories sold on street corners. The growth of photography and cheaper printing spawned a sizeable pornographic industry. In a nationwide purge, between 1834 and 1850, the Vice Society confiscated 385,000 obscene prints and photographs, 80,000 books and pamphlets and 28,000 sheets of obscene songs and circulars.[28] Liverpool was not immune from smut. Samuel Smith fulminated, 'The streets of this city are infested with persons who thrust indecent pamphlets into the hands of youths.'[29] Lucas Stubbs, of the Borough Magistrates Office, revealed, 'though obscene prints were suppressed by law, yet literature of a pernicious kind had

free circulation in immense quantities'.[30] A hawker arrested in London Road
had in his possession copies of a 'hideous woodcut' entitled 'A Married Man
Caught in a Trap'.[31] Hugh Shimmin felt that the sale of race cards at the Aintree
meeting was sometimes a cloak for the trade in 'filthy and obscene prints'.
Vendors with large pockets would demand high prices for the images.[32]

Certain shops also peddled porn. In 1867 a premises in Manchester Street
was raided for stocking obscene prints, pictures and drawings, including
nearly 30 photographs of the 'most indecent and disgusting character'. After
buying a few prints and requesting some more a customer was told to return
the following week for some 'blue ones'.[33] Seven years later Bernard Hopkins
was arrested in Lime Street after exhibiting erotica in a stereoscope machine.
He claimed to have bought the images from a shop in Manchester Street.[34] A
raid on a shop in Hunter Street uncovered over a thousand indecent prints.
The shop owner said that he had sold such prints for about fifteen years with
no complaints.[35] A shop in Cropper Street had 300 prints entitled 'The busy
night', featuring a drawing of a partly draped female nude accompanied by a
lewd verse. Street vendors were seen purchasing the prints in bulk and then
hawking them about town. The court case centred on whether the drawing
was in fact indecent, since more revealing images of naked women could be
found in the Walker Art Gallery and indeed the latest issue of the *Art Journal*,
which was widely on sale. The point was also made that other so-called
indecent images on sale in Liverpool were little more than photographs of
statues of classical nudes.[36] For really obscene material the aficionado had to
look to the Continent.

In 1888 three brothers were convicted of selling obscene photographs of a
'most objectionable and degrading nature'. From a house in Falkland Street,
Robert and John Murray ran an international operation selling pornographic
photos and prints, which they acquired via negatives from a dealer in Paris.
The prints were stored in another house in Shallcross Street. Some were sent
to their brother George in Glasgow to be hand-coloured. The siblings advertised the pictures for sale in sporting newspapers. When police raided the
premises they discovered a huge stash of porn and a cyclostyle machine used
to make reproductions. Letters from all round the world requesting the prints
were also found. The brothers were each sentenced to two years' imprisonment and fined.[37]

Newspaper Scams

The abolition of stamp duty on newspapers in 1855 led to cheap penny publications. The subsequent growth of the popular press allowed tricksters to reach new audiences. Newspaper advertisements were an ideal medium through which to hoodwink respectable people, particularly those unlikely to be deceived in person by the rougher sort of scam merchant. One Liverpool sharper placed an advertisement in the press revealing a scheme to 'write without pen or ink'. The secret was on offer for 15s. On paying for this piece of wizardry subscribers received a letter with the valuable information, 'Write with a pencil'.[38] Improvements in literacy also boosted the circulation of sensationalist newspapers with their titillating scandals. H. J. Nicholls recalls one Liverpool hawker who sold scurrilous and libellous printed sheets. Standing near a dark side street with convenient entries, he would shout, 'Here you have the true and interesting particulars concerning Mrs_____ and Mr _____. Only a penny.' He would fill the gaps with real or fictitious names and occurrences to suit the neighbourhood in which he was standing. After making a quick sale he would escape up the alley and start all over again somewhere else. Sometimes members of the public would give the man a shilling to spread a nasty libel about somebody. He was occasionally caught and prosecuted.[39] Councillor Robinson praised the 'excellent talents' of Liverpool's young newspaper sellers, although he admitted that some were too talented. He recalled that when he asked for the latest edition he would sometimes be sold an earlier edition. He once asked a boy what he did with the unwanted earlier editions. It seems they were sold to people getting on the omnibuses. By the time they had discovered the fiddle it would be too late. The councillor also recalled two newsboys shouting the latest news that a murderer called Stevens had been caught when in fact the man was still on the run in Paris. The false news would guarantee that the newspapers would be snapped up.[40] Other young vendors resorted to shouting out entirely fictional scoop stories.[41] The boys could hardly be blamed for their enterprise for they had the added pressure of having to sell their stock before the day ended. At least the match sellers with wares left over could go home and try again the next day. It was not usual to see young children tramping the streets until late at night. Samuel Smith revealed, 'I have often seen small boys and girls with unsold bundles of [news]papers asleep on doorsteps near midnight. When you awakened them and asked them to go home they began to cry, as they would be beaten if they returned without their stock being sold off.'[42]

Begging

Visitors to Liverpool were struck by the amount of begging on the streets. Nathaniel Hawthorne, in the 1850s, reported that 'the streets swarm with beggars by day and night'.[43] He was particularly wary of the beggars in Brunswick Street. One was described as such a 'monster' that Hawthorne would walk a mile just to avoid him. Another unfortunate man, dressed in a sailor's jacket, had no arms or legs but nevertheless turned such an unnerving gaze on passers-by that they were transfixed: 'You see him before you all at once, as if he had sprouted half-way out of the earth and would sink down and re-appear in some other place, the moment he has done with you.' At his side was a hat into which Hawthorne consistently refused to throw any coins. Yet for two or three years Hawthorne could not escape this 'truncated tyrant' who was a familiar sight around all parts of the town.[44]

Some beggars paraded sham disabilities or wretchedness to elicit sympathy. A policeman found Andrew Sullivan lying in the street trembling uncontrollably and pleading starvation. The officer took pity on him and gave him hot food and drink before sending him to a lodging-house. Shortly afterwards he found Sullivan trying the same shivering dodge.[45] In 1838 the *Liverpool Mercury* warned readers of several begging impostors loitering about town disguised as sailors and carrying fake certificates claiming to have been shipwrecked off the Irish coast.[46] Such men were known as 'shake lurks'. In *Redburn*, Melville describes the beggars who plagued the dock area waiting for sailors to walk past. The extent of human misery was quite astonishing:

> Every variety of want and suffering met the eye, and every vice showed here its victims [...] Old women, rather mummies, drying up with slow starving and age; young girls, incurably sick, who ought to have been in hospital; sturdy men, with the gallows in their eyes, and a whining lie in their mouths; young boys, hollow-eyed and decrepit; and puny mothers in the glare of the sun, formed the main feature of the scene.[47]

Some beggars used the power of art to intensify their pathos. On the dockside, another American visitor saw

> a bareheaded man drawing with colored crayons on a broad, smooth flagstone. He had represented, in a very skilful and beautiful manner, a salmon laid on a china platter, opposite a broken plate of coarse crockery; between these were some lines about a 'rich man's dish' and a 'poor man's dinner'. He was making an ornamental border about it,

and over it was written, 'Friends! I can get NO WORK; I must do this or starve.' The man's hat, with a few pence in it, stood by his side.[48]

Children were also ideal props for begging. There was one boy known as 'Little Ned' who could effortlessly put on a 'crying face' to attract the sympathy of the ladies. He was quite successful, as one envious adult beggar pointed out: 'He brings home every day more than any labouring man can earn.'[49] Borrowing children was a common ploy for beggars. Unmarried women could hire children for 3d or 4d a day; the more deformed the child, the higher the price.[50] Mary Kenny was a well-known beggar with seven or eight of her own brood, the eldest a sickly-looking 14-year-old, the youngest a 3-year-old infant. The family would sing doleful ditties, in which the children joined in the chorus. The woman was said to belong to a gang of 'jolly beggars' who haunted the streets during the day and at night drank away the proceeds. Kenny was also involved in hiring out children to other beggars. When arrested in 1855 she was carrying two young babies that were not her own. A newspaper revealed that for 6d a week 'any of the fraternity could obtain from her an unlimited number of "fatherless orfings" or "wretched cripples from their birth"'.[51] Elizabeth Shaw was charged with stealing 5-year-old John Melbourne from his home in Ford Street. She allegedly enticed the youngster by asking him to accompany her to the 'cook shop'. Shaw was found alone at two o'clock the next morning, blind drunk in the street. It was feared that she had passed on the child to a gang of beggars.[52] In November 1863 Alice Knowles stole a 2-year-old boy from his doorstep in Albion Place, Old Haymarket. After being found with the child in Great Homer Street she admitted that she wanted him for begging purposes.

Whether to give money to beggars was, and still is, a contentious moral issue. Rather than give money directly to beggars it was felt better to donate to organizations helping the poor. The Liverpool Domestic Mission Society claimed that 'the "polite heaps of walking rags" that accost us at our doors and in the street area are, for the most part, tricksters in disguise'.[53] The Mission's Francis Bishop once followed the sound of music and merriment and was led up a passage where 20 beggars of both sexes were dancing to the strains of a fiddler, their ailments temporarily forgotten. One of them had the cheek to ask Bishop for a penny admission to the ball.[54] There was once a public house not far from the Town Hall to which beggars would retire after a hard day's begging. It was nicknamed 'The Beggars' Hop'.[55] As late as 1897 it was pointed out that the begging trade was still thriving in the city, despite the fact 'that practically all beggars are rogues' who diverted much-needed charity away from the honest poor.[56]

The Church was always a good source of charity. Playing upon people's good natures was a common trick. In 1844 roaming beggars, without any authority from the Church, collected from the faithful but kept the money for themselves.[57] John Sheridan would receive charity from Catholic chapels and then get drunk on the proceeds.[58] Poor people would attend church in the hope of receiving a hand-out in recognition of their piety. Abraham Hume recalled that when he was curate at St Bartholomew's, few of the poor families could be persuaded to attend church and those who did cross the threshold 'besieged my door on Monday morning, as if by patronising the minister and sitting out a service they were entitled to a reward'. He also recalled that during his visits to his parishioners, some of those he met were 'persons who were not Protestants at all, but who thought that when a clergyman could be induced to visit them he was good for a half-a-crown at the least'.[59] Men of the cloth were seen as a soft touch. In the 1850s Hugh Stowell Brown, a Baptist minister, used the Concert Hall to give a series of Sunday afternoon lectures to the working people. He received many letters commenting upon his sermons. One businessman wrote to say that he had recently ceased trading and hoped that the minister would make a collection for him the following Sunday. After preaching about the Good Samaritan, Brown received a letter from a penniless man who wanted to travel to America. He requested the £15 fare for the steam passage, to be paid by the following Friday. The man warned the minister that if he didn't cough up with the money, he would be a bigger fraud than the priest who ignored the injured Samaritan.[60] Robert Swayne would send begging letters to prominent Liverpool Catholics pretending to be a degraded priest who had become a Protestant but now wished to return to the fold. He would request money to fund his trip to Rome to ask for a pardon. His wife called him a 'rascal'.[61] Other towns had similar problems. At a Library Association conference, held in Liverpool in 1883, a delegate revealed that the book most often stolen from Nottingham Libraries was the Clergy List. It was suggested that begging-letter writers were using it to target churchmen.[62]

Other beggars seemed intent on eliciting fear rather than sympathy. In February 1847 William Farrell went into a shop in Tithebarn Street and demanded money. He warned the shopkeeper that he would give her ten minutes before he knocked her down or smashed her windows. In January 1848 two beggars knocked at a house in Copperas Hill and asked for money. When they discovered that the master was not at home they walked into the parlour and refused to leave until they had been given 2d. They were spotted shortly afterwards entering a public house where they were arrested. During the economic crisis of February 1855 there was concern about large groups of burly men intimidating householders. Several batches of beggars, some claiming to be jobless dock labourers or unemployed carters, appeared in court charged with knocking on doors and either asking for or demanding charity. It was feared that the men were deliberately targeting houses on the un-policed outskirts of town when the owners would be at work, leaving females and servants to answer the door. A gentleman in Rodney Street once had 43 separate visits by beggars in one day.[63] It was claimed that itinerant beggars sold information to other beggars, listing their successes at the various houses.[64]

There were, of course, various charitable institutions aimed at alleviating periods of temporary economic crisis when the poor needed extra help. Liverpool had an abundance of committees and societies assisting the work of the Vestry and Board of Guardians. A Society for Bettering the Conditions of the Poor was formed as early as 1809. Many charitable societies were run by women, including the Ladies' Charity and the Ladies' Benevolent Society. It seems, however, that people sometimes milked the system by making multiple applications to the various funds. In January 1851 Mary Martin, a woman of respectable appearance, was arrested after stealing rolls of material from a shop. A search of her comfortable home in Knight Street revealed a savings book showing a £12 account, a box containing 14 sovereigns, bread vouchers and tickets from the Ladies' Charity, the District Provident Society and the Strangers' Friend Society, all in false names. Martin was also claiming parish relief. In 1863 the Central Relief Society was founded with the aim of centralizing charitable relief in the town and discouraging similar abuses of the system. Towards the end of the century the Society was said to have done away with 'the tribe of imposters, begging letter writers, and professional mendicants'.[65]

Begging-letter writers thrived after improvements in the postal system, particularly the introduction of cheap mail in the 1840s.[66] The advantage of using letters was that the recipient never had to meet the benefactor, although some preferred to hand deliver their notes to add physical corroboration of their assumed misery. Using a list of names and addresses, probably taken from a street directory, an elderly man called Morton Gadsden system- atically targeted the Dingle area with letters detailing his financial misfor- tune. Claiming to be a down-at-heel merchant, he would employ a boy to hand deliver the missives, giving him coppers when he returned successful. Gadsden appeared to be doing quite well out of the scam when, in 1863, he was arrested and sentenced to three months' imprisonment.[67]

Anne Steward was a professional begging-letter writer. On one occasion she dressed in mourning and claimed that her husband had been washed overboard at sea.[68] Thomas Russell would knock at doors and hand over a begging letter containing numerous biblical quotations, his favourite being 'Seek and ye shall find; knock and it shall be opened unto you.' The ruse certainly worked, for while the occupant was busy reading the letter Russell would make off with anything near to hand.[69] One woman made so much money from begging letters that she could afford to pay for a good education for her two girls.[70]

Fortune Telling

For poor people living precarious lives, often not knowing where their next wages were coming from or when fatal diseases would strike, being able to know what the future held was of vital importance. In the nineteenth century women came into their own as fortune-tellers. Some sat in the comfort of their own homes and had the gullible (mostly female) punters queuing at the door or else they tramped the streets offering a door-to-door service. Servant girls and young women would sit in Ann Fox's Oriel Street home until 2 a.m. waiting to have their fortunes told.[71] Various methods of looking into the future were used, including palmistry, tarot cards, teacups, crystal balls or items of jewellery belonging to the customer. The predictions given were ambiguous enough to keep people happy. When detectives called at Mary McTigue's home in Hughes Street there were eight women sitting at a table with cards spread out. Agnes Miller was told that she would have a disappointment, that she would marry a man 'between colours' and that her marriage would take place in 7 days, 7 weeks or 7 months or else on the 7th, 17th or 27th of some month or other.[72]

The seers would give advice at a rate of pay covering a certain number of weeks. The client would be eager to return for the next instalment, thus guaranteeing the psychic a steady annual income. Some fortune-tellers sold protective charms, which were simply iron discs bearing the seal of angels that ruled the air, earth, fire and water. They were snapped up by seamen who wore them on their belts. Costing between 2s and 5s, the amulets were tough enough to last a lifetime except that the charms eventually lost their magic power. Fortunately, they could be recharged (as could their wearers) for a price.[73]

Fortune telling was against the law and offenders could be prosecuted under the Vagrancy Act, particularly for extorting money. However, since it was practised indoors, arrests were difficult to make. To gain evidence the police would employ 'witnesses', usually wives or female friends, to have their fortunes told. The clairvoyants soon got wise to this trick and became very suspicious of strangers. The court report of the trial of Elizabeth Neill in 1899 recounted how Annie Glynn and Martha Brown went to a house in respectable Willoughby Street to have their fortunes told. Neill cautiously answered the door but said, 'I don't tell strangers as the police are watching me.' The women explained that they were not strangers, as Lucy Williams had sent them. That seemed to do the trick and they were invited in for a reading. The session over, Neill asked for 6d. It was reported that the police had been receiving complaints about Neill's activities for a couple of months. A policeman claimed that he often saw respectable girls visit the house, sometimes in twos and threes. A queue often formed outside with up to eight girls patiently awaiting admission. Neill was found guilty and imprisoned for one month.[74]

Fortune-tellers would also visit large houses on the pretext of selling items but mainly to tell the fortunes of the servant girls who answered the door. Jane Jones would regularly visit maids in Upper Parliament Street. Detectives hid in one house to listen to proceedings. After the cards were cut, a girl held up the Queen of Clubs and was told she would marry a black man. Upon arrest, the clairvoyant came clean. She admitted to the officer, 'If I could tell fortunes I could have told you were at the back door.' One of the servants had pawned her boots for 3s 6d to afford the reading. Sixpence was spent on the fortune and 3s on a bottle of special water to sprinkle on the doorstep to bring her a boyfriend.[75] Catherine Foster visited houses in Bedford Street under the pretence of selling jewellery but actually offering to tell fortunes. To find out if one maid's 'sweetheart' was ready to propose, she took away two of her dresses and a petticoat to be 'charmed'. She never returned.[76]

For some fortune-tellers, their psychic gifts were little more than an opportunity to practise the scam known as 'ringing the changes'. Janet Anderson went to Catherine Makin to have her fortune told. After giving a few readings, Makin sensed that she could gain more from her victim. She told Anderson that more revelations could be received by sewing two sovereigns into her stays and leaving them there for three days. Makin was handed the coins and after making a few mystic signs she secured them in the girl's stays. After three days of suspense, Anderson ripped her stays and found the coins magically transformed into a shilling and a farthing.[77] Bridget Brennan tried a similar trick on a domestic servant called Mary Jones. To boost her client's own psychic powers, she asked Jones for some salt, pepper and a golden sovereign. Brennan took the ingredients and wrapped them in a parcel. Jones was told to place the charm under her pillow to stimulate dreams of the future. She was under strict instructions not to open the parcel for a certain period of time. However, Jones' curiosity got the better of her and she unfastened the package shortly after and discovered that the sovereign was missing. Despite the slippery Sibyl's claim that the coin would eventually return, she was reported to the police and imprisoned for one month.[78]

For some women, the business of fortune telling was a little more serious. Martha Smith (alias Madame Zeila) was a palmist with premises in Bold Street. She maintained that she did not tell fortunes but only read palms. It was an important distinction. Explaining people's characters from the lines on their hands was legal but predicting the future was not.[79] Elizabeth Ann Antonio, from Lamport Street, went under the name Madame Antonio, phrenologist and clairvoyant. She examined bumps on people's heads and read the planets for 1s. Police sent two women to her house to gather information for a prosecution. Antonio explained to the magistrate that her husband was a cripple and couldn't work. She said that she paid her rates and was merely earning a living.[80]

'Merely earning a living' was the lot of so many working-class women in Liverpool. Yet some women didn't want to merely survive; they wanted to enjoy their lives, to have something to look forward to, beyond the daily grind. There is a link between the tough lives of the cotton pickers and fish hawkers and their love of a good time. After a hard week's graft the women enjoyed nothing better than to hit the town. Cabinet-maker James Hopkinson, of Mill Street, was struck by the number of Irish girls and young women who went about the streets without shoes or stockings. Yet on Sundays they would walk around in dashing red and white petticoats, often worn without a gown. The petticoat was their precious possession. After it had been displayed on the Sunday, they would take it to the pawnbroker on the Monday who gave them 2s to 3s. They would then go to the docks to buy fish, before hawking their baskets around the town. They would sell fish until Saturday evening and then redeem the petticoat, paying 3d interest upon the money which had been advanced. By the end of the year they would have paid for it over and over again.[81]

Moneylending

By the Edwardian period some Irish fish hawkers had themselves moved into the moneylending business. Known as 'fish and money' people, they would tramp the back alleys carrying their baskets of putrid fish. They would ask how the men had 'got on' down at the dock. Some desperate wives would be offered 4s in cash on the condition that they also bought 2s worth of rotten fish. The 6s debt had to be paid on the following Saturday 'or else'.[82] One notable practitioner was the mixed-race Mary Ellen Grant, known as the 'Connaught Nigger'.

One of Liverpool's most successful female moneylenders was Alice Spring of Hunter Street who operated in partnership with her son Richard, who lived in Gerard Street. Although she was not prosecuted until 1904, she had been carrying on her business for at least fifteen years. The offence of lending money was not created by Act of Parliament until 1891, which meant that Spring had been breaking the law for thirteen years. After receiving complaints about her dealings, police raided her house and found hidden under a mattress six identity certificates and six life certificates belonging to army and navy pensioners. These had been kept as pledges of security for debts. Interest was paid at 3d per shilling a week, equivalent to a rate of 1,300 per cent per annum. If money was not repaid at the end of the week, interest was added, leaving people falling into a spiral of debt. Not surprisingly, Spring owned her home, which was sumptuously furnished. Police discovered £100 in cash and a bank book showing a credit of £1,600, an incredible sum at the time. In court, the illiterate (but highly numerate) Spring claimed ignorance: 'I did not know any different,' she argued. Nevertheless, she was heavily fined.[83]

Insurance Fraud

Another source of income for women was insurance fraud, a crime not confined to commercial enterprises. One of the most horrific scams perpetrated in nineteenth-century Liverpool was a fraud that involved the murder of close relatives and friends. In those days people who could hardly afford to feed themselves and their families found it vital to save for a proper funeral. This led to the growth of so-called 'burial clubs'. Such clubs were the sad by-product of the raging disease epidemics of the Victorian age. It is no wonder that the Royal Liver Friendly Society grew from modest beginnings to become one of the most renowned Liverpool institutions. By giving a few pence per week to an agent, people could avoid the indignity of a pauper's funeral. Neighbours would pay the weekly premiums for one another if a member was short of money.

Yet the system was open to abuse. People would insure others with whom they had no family connection, without their knowledge or consent. Stand-ins would be used to formally sign any documents in the presence of the agent. Since the agents relied on the commission from new members they were not too stringent in their checks. Insurance collectors were called 'death men' by a medical officer of health. By the mid-nineteenth century it was strongly suspected that parents were neglecting and even hastening the death of their children for the sake of the money allowed by the burial clubs. In 1888 a committee formed by the Liverpool Society for the Prevention of Cruelty to Children found that a disturbingly high proportion of children 'accidently' suffocated by their parents had been insured.[84] It was feared that the high infant mortality rate in Liverpool might have been the result of the popularity of burial insurance and the temptation to shorten the life of children. On the other hand, insurance might have been popular simply because so many children were expected to die through social and environmental factors. It was this uneasy relationship between the abundance of death clubs and excessive infant mortality 'that made the Mersey region such a crucible for the whole controversy'.[85]

At the December 1853 Liverpool Assizes, following two 'burial club' murders, the grand jury called for 'a stop to the present system of money payments by burial societies [...] the system operates as a decided incentive to murder'.[86] The judge passed on the sentiments to the Home Office.[87] Ten years earlier, Betty Eccles, from Bolton, had been hanged at Kirkdale after murdering her stepson and demanding money from a 'burial club'. She was also suspected of poisoning two other children from her first husband.[88]

At its most depraved the scam involved syndicates of close friends, known as 'poisoning rings', insuring the life of an unsuspecting lodger or relative. The victim, preferably young or weak, would then be dosed with arsenic mixed in food or water. For six to eight days the poison would cause agonizing pain before death provided a merciful release. Once a doctor had signed the death certificate the funeral arrangements would be made and the insurance money divided among the investors. Poisoning cases usually involved arsenic, commonly extracted from flypapers. Despite such poisoning featuring in many Victorian murder trials, even experienced doctors were sometimes misled by the obvious symptoms, such as stomach pains and retching. In their defence, enteric disorders were commonplace during the period.

The evil was practised throughout the country but it was a Liverpool case that shocked the nation. In March 1884 sisters Margaret Higgins, aged 41, and Catherine Flanagan, aged 55, were hanged at Kirkdale Gaol for murder.[89] In 1881 Thomas Higgins took his first wife and 10-year-old daughter to lodge with the sisters at Skirving Street, off Great Homer Street. However, his wife soon died and he made the deadly mistake of marrying the recently widowed

Margaret in 1882. Within a month of the marriage his daughter Mary was dead and within a year the 36-year-old hod-carrier had also fallen ill and died. The cause of death was listed as dysentery.

Patrick Higgins, however, had his suspicions about the fate of his fit and healthy brother. He questioned the doctor who alerted the coroner who then postponed the funeral. An examination of the body revealed the presence of arsenic. It was discovered that Thomas' life had been insured by five different societies for over £108. The revelation resulted in an investigation into other sudden deaths in the Flanagan household. Three more bodies were exhumed, including Catherine's son John, an 18-year-old lodger called Maggie Jennings and Thomas Higgins' young daughter. All had died of arsenic poisoning. There were probably other victims and the sisters were unlikely to have acted alone. After her arrest Catherine named another six victims and implicated a community network of killers. Due to lack of evidence these other people were never prosecuted. Angela Brabin reveals that 'the case showed illiterate and impoverished women behaving like entrepreneurs, capable of sophisticated insurance fraud, manipulation of the medical profession and deception of the insurance companies'.[90]

The wicked deeds of Higgins and Flanagan lead us to the heart of the family unit and the shocking realization that murder was not exclusive to the rough streets and rowdy pubs. Indeed, for women and children in the lower-class districts the most dangerous place was the family home. Children were particularly vulnerable. On the path to adulthood they faced many obstacles. If they survived being aborted or arriving in the world stillborn they ran the risk of being abandoned in the street, smothered in bed by drunken parents or, as we have seen, even poisoned to claim the insurance money. If they didn't die of disease, congenital defects or malnutrition they were in danger of fatal domestic accidents after being left unsupervised. Many children were drugged with opiates to keep them quiet.[91] Some were beaten to death; others were sold on to so-called 'baby farmers' in a primitive form of adoption. Some Liverpool prostitutes even sold their male children to chimney sweeps for use as apprentices. A master sweep revealed, 'In Liverpool, where there are lots of bad women, you can get any quantity you want.'[92] As the *Liverpool Mercury* put it: 'the children of the poor grow old very early, and if they fail to take care of themselves – well, the "clubman" will pay for them'.[93]

FIFTEEN

Victorian Family Values

Infanticide

Higgins and Flanagan severely tested Victorian ideals of female decorum and maternal instinct. Sadly the sisters were not unique, merely the products of a debased and debasing social environment. The *Liverpool Review* had harsh words to say about lower-class Liverpool women: 'the steps are laden with crowds of indolent, unsexed viragoes, who, according to mood, pass coarsely humorous or pointedly insulting remarks upon the physical peculiarities of passers-by'. Like monkeys, they would sit removing the lice from each other's heads.[1] Also, 'when a Liverpool woman's tongue is loosed nobody in this world can rival her in the production of foul and bestial language. She is an oral cesspool – a philological sewer.'[2]

During a tour of the south-end slums two journalists visited a dark, narrow passage known as the 'Murderer's Court'. Two 'sluts' started shouting obscenities. One informed the men that she had given birth only three days earlier and was eager to start making another baby. She joked about the similarity of her newborn to one of the visitors and urged her mate to fetch the child as proof.[3] She at least seemed happy to extend her brood. In the days before social welfare, an extra mouth to feed could cripple a family. Yet in the nineteenth century abortion was illegal, although sometimes public sympathy lay with abortionists threatened with prosecution.[4] Chemists sold purgatives that promised to remove 'obstructions', a euphemism for unwanted foetuses. If such action failed some women ran the risk of a back-street abortion performed by local women with only the scantiest medical knowledge. Cases from the Liverpool Police Court give hints as to the prevalence of abortions, which, according to the *Liverpool Mercury* in 1869, occur 'more extensively than is generally supposed'.[5] Alice Smith took a herb called 'feverfew' to help abort her child. When this failed, she was later found dead having taken laudanum. John Brice was accused of murdering Margaret McReel by means of an instrument used for procuring abortion. She died of peritonitis aggravated by a wound to her uterus. Catherine Kearns of Ben Jonson Street accused her own daughter of visiting a herbalist's in Scotland Road for the purpose of procuring an abortion. Sarah Pollock, another herbalist from Tithebarn Street, was accused of supplying poisonous herbs to cause abortion.[6] The law against the sale of abortifacients was almost unenforceable since seemingly innocuous substances could, in large enough doses, be administered for ulterior purposes.[7] Hugh Shimmin revealed that dodgy herbalists would sometimes prescribe a harmless concoction of herbs to a pregnant woman seeking abortion. If reproached for their deception they would turn upon the woman, denounce her murderous intentions and even blackmail her by threatening exposure.[8]

William Burke Ryan, the author of a book on infanticide published in 1862, wrote that some children were undoubtedly killed immediately after birth: 'It was frequently done.'[9] Father Nugent also spoke of the 'butchery' that took place among children, largely the result of the mother's addiction to alcohol. Until he became chaplain at the Borough Gaol he was under the impression that Liverpool's prostitutes were mostly childless. He then discovered the truth. One woman had nine children, which were scattered about in various workhouses. 'It was not at all an uncommon thing,' said Nugent, 'for a woman to have had two or three children and all these children are generally "sided" within twelve months of their birth through neglect or by overlying.' When asked what he meant by 'siding', Nugent replied, 'They are got rid of.' 'Overlying' was 'accidental' suffocation of the child in bed. There were also a large number of children who were never born alive owing to the mother's intemperance.[10]

The status of stillborn children was problematic. The Home Office, as early as 1844, was aware of the practice of burying live-born corpses as if stillborn. Sometimes this was simply to save burial costs as the funerals of stillborns were cheaper.[11] It was also suspected that in some cases crimes of infanticide were being concealed by the inaccurate reporting of the causes of death. It was possible that women were killing their babies and receiving false stillbirth certificates. A survey of the number of burials of alleged stillborns in Liverpool, conducted by the Liverpool Northern Medical Society in 1868, revealed a total of 664 bodies buried in four cemeteries. Two children had been placed in a single coffin and buried as one stillborn. It was proved that one child had in fact lived for some time before death. In only one case had the veracity of the midwife's certificate been double-checked by a parish official, called the coroner's beadle, before the burial took place. Many deceitful certificates had in fact been exposed by such a measure.[12] Although largely untrained, midwives attended most births in the lower-class districts. Only the wealthy could afford doctors. The Society even sent the Home Secretary various examples of the scraps of semi-literate scribble accepted as 'certificates' by the cemeteries. It was suspicions of malpractice that partly inspired the movement from the late 1860s to have midwives qualified and registered.[13]

If a woman had a child outside marriage she risked losing her respectability. Looking after the child meant that she couldn't go to work. Owing to such pressures women sometimes attempted to deliver and dispose of their infants without detection. In November 1851 the body of a female child was found in Banastre Street. It had been born alive but then died from suffocation. On the same day the stillborn body of a male child was found in the yard of St Patrick's Chapel. The Muck Quay, a dumping ground for excrement off Vauxhall Road, was an ideal place to discard unwanted babies since people avoided it.[14] In a paper given to the National Association for the Promotion of Social Sciences in 1873, Frederick Lowndes, the Liverpool police surgeon, told of his experiences in examining the bodies of abandoned babies. Liverpool, as a seaport with a shifting seafaring population, had a more than average share of promiscuity, which led to unwanted babies and hence infanticide. It was nearly impossible to trace the perpetrators. The naked bodies were usually wrapped in rags or sacking, never in properly made clothes that would leave clues as to their identity. They were usually abandoned in badly lit and isolated parts of town, to be found by policemen and scavengers late at night or early in the morning. More rarely, children out playing during the day found the bodies hidden in fields and pits.[15] If decomposition prevented a satisfactory identification of the cause of death, a murder conviction was impossible. For this reason midwives and 'baby farmers' sometimes burned the bodies, allegedly to 'save the burial costs'.

Not all mothers got away with infanticide. In 1868 Liverpool returned 20 murder verdicts on children less than one year old.[16] Yet many other killings must have gone undetected. Even when women were brought to trial, a lesser verdict was often passed. Catherine Herbert came to Liverpool from Ireland, hoping to travel on to America. While lodging in Sherwood Street in 1849 she crept out of bed one night and gave birth. Other lodgers noticed blood on the floor and the child was later found in the privy with a cord around its neck. Since it was uncertain whether the baby was born alive or stillborn the mother was given the benefit of the doubt and imprisoned for two years for concealing the birth.[17] Bridget Cahill was a servant working for the Horne family. She had been employed for less than two weeks when she gave birth in the family home in Warren Street in September 1853. Mrs Horne uncovered the afterbirth dumped in the privy. At first Bridget denied having given birth but later she confessed to Mrs Horne, after which the body of a dead female child was found in the coal vault. Its skull had been fractured by a hammer, which was also discovered. Cahill was also found guilty only of concealment and sentenced to two years' imprisonment.[18]

For most of the nineteenth century Liverpool parish suffered the highest rate of infant mortality in England and Wales.[19] During the 1850s the death rate for children aged 0–1 averaged 283 per 1,000. In the 1860s the figure reached over 300 per 1,000. In the 1850s nearly half of all the deaths in the parish involved children under five.[20] Many babies were found dead in their parents' bed. Partly to blame was the lower-class practice of entire families huddling together in the same bed or on a straw mattress on the floor. Drink was the other factor. Drunken parents would wake up on top of their suffo-cated children. Liverpool had a high number of these overlaying cases. Hugh Shimmin revealed that 'for the year ending June 30th 1862, inquests were held on eighty-one smothered children'. Many had been suffocated by drunken parents on Saturday nights and early Sunday mornings, the peak drinking hours.[21] In a pamphlet cataloguing drink-related deaths in Liverpool in 1866, Revd John Jones listed 135 cases of infants suffocated between Saturday and Monday, all but one of the deaths occurring in the lower-class districts. Some examples are cited. At a christening a father became drunk while his wife had two glasses of whisky. In the morning their baby was dead.[22] Between 1883 and 1888 the Liverpool Society for the Prevention of Cruelty to Children (SPCC) became aware of 700 cases of overlaying.[23] It was suspected that some infants had been deliberately killed.

Indeed, there was a suspicion of a conspiracy of silence about other forms of child death. William Burke Ryan was concerned that judges and surgeons were sometimes implicated in what he viewed as perversions of justice. He cited a case heard at Liverpool Assizes in 1860, in which Ann Billington was tried for the murder of her baby: 'The girl denied her pregnancy, but on delivery she placed her child under the cellar-steps, and the surgeon found *a large gaping wound in her throat*, but he could not say that it had an "independent existence or full birth from its mother at the time the wound was inflicted".' The verdict was 'concealment of birth' and Billington received eighteen months without hard labour, a sentence whose leniency surprised Ryan.[24]

Police and some coroners also displayed a reluctance to investigate closely the sudden deaths of infants. Indeed, juries were often unwilling to convict the mother (the usual defendant). In 1862 Mary Ann Allen (alias Ellis) was charged with the manslaughter of her son, Arthur Allen. She gave birth to the boy in the West Derby workhouse but days later he was found in an entry in Cockspur Street and later died of suspected exposure. At the Assizes the mother was acquitted. The cost of autopsies and medical witnesses inhibited proper investigation into infant deaths.[25] Many 'open' verdicts were returned on babies that had been born alive but were later abandoned or possibly smothered. It is possible that the murders of infants were listed as open verdicts to help massage the crime figures.[26] In the 1860s only a few districts in the country revealed the true picture concerning suspicious child deaths. Thanks were owed to the vigilance of socially concerned coroners such as Clarke Aspinall in Liverpool who, along with the Liverpool SPCC, was said to have helped reduce the number of infant suffocations. Aspinall paid close attention to cases involving overlaying and was given credit for revealing the truth of the matter.[27]

Baby Farming

An unwanted child could be a burden but not all mothers wished to harm their offspring. In an age when formal adoption had no legal force, so-called 'baby farming' was a valid alternative for mothers who wished to part with their children. Baby farmers reared infants in exchange for money. Midwives would sometimes act as go-betweens by offering to find a home for the baby in return for a lump sum fee for its upkeep. The child might then be sold on to a baby farmer for a profit or, worse, killed. Baby farmers could also be contacted directly through advertisements in the local press. Again, some might pocket the money and allow the child to die through slow starvation or neglect. It was also feared that some children of baby farmers found their way into the hands of beggars, to be used as props. Dr William Acton, an authority on prostitution, considered that an estimate of 30,000 children nationwide in the care of baby farmers was probably under the mark.[28]

The issue of baby farming in Liverpool was highlighted by a case in 1877. Sophia Martha Todd was the 35-year-old daughter of a Glasgow civil engineer. She enjoyed a privileged upbringing and spoke five languages. This enabled her to work as a governess for noblemen in Russia and England. While teaching music in Lancaster she met a farmer called Jackson and moved to Liverpool. The couple married in St Luke's Church in Hardman Street but the relationship did not last. Now living in Prescot Street, Sophia was forced to look for some other means of earning a living. She worked as a bookkeeper in the Victoria Hotel in St John's Lane before she hit upon a novel means of making money. She placed an advert in the local newspapers: 'Wanted by a respectable married couple, a baby to adopt. A premium expected.'

While lodging in Prospect Street in the summer of 1875 Sophia took charge of an infant which suddenly disappeared. In the November she moved in with a Mrs Oldham in Springfield, taking with her a box. After two weeks she fled without paying the rent, leaving behind her box. Eventually the householder also moved, taking the box to a new address before placing an advert in the newspaper urging the owner to collect or have the box sold. Nobody replied and in March 1877 Mrs Oldham broke open the container and found the mummified remains of a child aged about four weeks. It seems that Sophia had also received a child from a Henry Thompson along with a £10 premium. She had possession of Thompson's letter when she was eventually arrested in Manchester. Sophia also had a letter from someone offering £30 per annum for the adoption of a child. That infant was sent to her from Whitehaven but was found to have gone missing. A detective found another of her charges wandering the streets of Birkenhead. He adopted the child and raised it as his own. Three other children were eventually traced. In July 1877 Todd faced trial at the Assizes. Despite arguing that the mummified baby had died of natural causes not long after she had received it, she was found guilty of murder and sentenced to death. An appeal was lodged and 2,000 people signed a petition begging for mercy. Her appeal was successful and her sentence commuted to life imprisonment.

In October 1879 John and Catherine Barnes also received life imprisonment for the manslaughter of a baby girl starved to death in their care. No strangers to the pawnshop, the pair had buried about four other children in the same year. The Tranmere baby farmers, who had also lived at numerous addresses in Liverpool, were said to have looked after about 18 children over ten years after placing advertisements in various newspapers around the country.

A very different baby farming case in Walton hit the headlines in May 1884. Whereas most baby farmers actively sought children to look after, in this tragic case it seems that nobody wanted to be left holding the baby. Mary Ann Matilda Francis gave birth to a daughter in the workhouse. After leaving the institution her husband told her he did not want the baby and so she gave it to a friend called Jane Doyle who passed it on to Mary Collins. The baby was returned to the mother who then gave it to her sister, Mrs Littler. The child was then passed on to a Mrs Kerruish who in turn gave the baby to a Mrs Astley. When Mrs Astley took charge of the infant it was already showing signs of neglect. 'The skin was off the lower part of the body', and a doctor at Stanley Hospital told Mrs Astley that it needed the care of its mother. After sixteen weeks of having been starved and neglected the baby died of consumption. There was no fat under its skin and its bowels were as thin as tissue paper. This was despite the fact that the mother had given her sister money for the child's upkeep. This money was passed on to Mrs Kerruish. However, it seems that when Mrs Kerruish in turn gave the money to Mrs Astley she kept some back for herself because she was poor. When the baby died, a total of £3 had been withheld. The jury returned a verdict of death by natural causes but censured the conduct of Mrs Littler and Mrs Kerruish.

Neglect and Cruelty

Some mothers kept their babies but were simply not up to the task of caring for them. Drink was often a factor in parental negligence. During 1899 and 1900, a study revealed that the infant death rate among alcoholic female prisoners in Walton Gaol was 55.8 per cent (including stillborns). Among the non-alcoholic inmates the rate was 23.9 per cent.[29] Samuel Smith felt that 'the people were sometimes little better than savages. The children were often maimed by their drunken parents.'[30] In July 1859 Margaret Shufflebottom's 15-month-old child died after a period of neglect. The emaciated baby had a dirty wound on the back of its head and was bruised all over its body. A neighbour once found the mother lying drunk on a landing, with the child beneath her still sucking at her breast. When the baby cried out, she hit it. In December 1866 Mary Burke, of Edgar Street, was found drunk and disorderly in Scotland Road. She was holding a 6-week-old baby by the legs and threatening to bash its brains out. She raised the child in her arms and was about to strike its head against a wall when a policeman intervened and caught the child as it fell. Burke was sent to gaol for a month.

Older children were also neglected. Sometimes this was simply because both parents worked and their offspring were left to fend for themselves, with tragic consequences. During January and February 1847, over a period of about six weeks, inquests showed that 21 children from separate Liverpool households died from burns after their clothes caught fire in domestic accidents. The youngsters, all under 12 years of age, were lifting kettles from fires, warming their hands or simply standing with their backs to the fireplaces.[31]

Other neglect was more intentional. In September 1843 William Washington and his wife were accused of keeping their two sons, aged 8 and 9, in a shocking condition. The boys were confined to the attic for nine months, their only clothing being an apron to cover the front of their bodies. Their hair was long and matted and they hadn't washed in a long time. They slept on a decayed mattress with no bedclothes. There were in fact two beds in the house but while their father was in prison for debt the mother used the family home as a brothel. A neighbour fed the boys their breakfast but they were rarely given dinner. The father said that he was reluctant to send his sons to the workhouse and blamed his own unemployment for their condition. Since no violence had been used, the magistrate decided that the boys had suffered gross negligence rather than absolute cruelty.

Deliberate cruelty was another matter, often disguised and socially accepted as parental discipline. Liverpool's Bishop Goss declared that 'there was not a nicer ornament or a more homely useful article in a house than a birch rod'.[32] Yet the beatings meted out to Victorian children often went far beyond the biblical prescription of 'spare the rod and spoil the child'. Youngsters were at the mercy of drunken and sadistic parents. A neighbour revealed that the 5-year-old daughter of Edward Evans had once been punished by being tied to a table and made to stand for ten hours on one leg with her hands bound behind her back. John and Mary Jones, from Squire Street, were accused of cruelty to 11-year-old Mary Jane Evans. The child's mother and stepfather beat her with a cane or walking stick every day, sometimes three or four times a day. A woman at whose home the family once lodged explained that when the girl was merry she was beaten because she was not quiet and when she was quiet she was beaten because she was not merry enough to amuse the other children. On one occasion the lady witnessed the girl standing naked saying her lessons while her stepfather beat her with a stick. John Clark, of Upper Frederick Street, used a strap to regularly beat his 7-year-old stepdaughter. Upon examination, her entire body was found to be a mass of discoloured weals and her eyes were blackened. Clark would send the child to search for 'chews', gobs of chewing tobacco spat out onto the pavement. Woe betide her if she returned empty-handed. Because her 10-year-old daughter couldn't find the iron, a drunken Fanny McCaig beat her with a poker across the back, arms and shoulders before smashing her head against the wall. The child fled from the house and was found slumped in a field by a passer-by. The lower part of her face was covered with congealed gore, while fresh blood still oozed from her nose. The stranger carried the child to his home only for his wife to find further marks of old beatings on her body. Hair had been torn from her head and there was evidence of her mother's bite marks on her arms. McCaig was a prostitute who had appeared in court 18 times for being drunk. She received six months' hard labour and the child was placed in the workhouse. A drunken John Mitchell argued with his partner, a woman called McLoughlin, at their home in Ben Jonson Street. He then turned on her 4-year-old son and 9-year-old daughter. Using his clogs, he kicked them unconscious and stamped on their heads before throwing them into the street where they were found by a policeman. Upon arrest, Mitchell asked, 'Are they dead?' When told they were still alive he screamed, 'I'll kick their ____ brains out.' Clumps of hair were found stuck in his clogs.[33]

Wife Beating

Child cruelty was often part of a much bigger picture of domestic violence. The private, domestic sphere remained largely out of bounds for the authorities, and consequently a great deal of such violence went unnoticed and hence unrecorded. The police needed a warrant or a very good reason to enter the family home and even then not all officers were sympathetic to the victim's plight. According to Hugh Shimmin, 'police officers think that a husband has a prescriptive right to beat his wife as often as he likes, so long as he does not actually break her limbs or knock her brains out'. Yet even this was allowed by some policemen, as illustrated by the case of Dinah Quigley who was murdered by her husband Thomas in 1868. Five constables in turn visited the address in Vernon Street while he was in the process of administering a sustained kicking. The officers had brief conversations with Thomas but only two of them bothered to look inside the house, and only then after being persuaded by a concerned neighbour. The woman lay unconscious on the blood-soaked floor. Quigley claimed that she was drunk and the constables left the house satisfied that it was a 'drunken row'. Quigley left shortly afterwards, leaving the neighbours to transport the woman to hospital where she died. She had suffered a fractured leg, seven fractured ribs and a mass of bruises over her body. Her husband's death sentence was later commuted to life imprisonment. Shimmin, meanwhile, accused the police of turning a blind eye to domestic violence.[34]

Yet whether or not the police interfered, some women continued to remain in abusive relationships. In August 1863 John Hughes, a drunkard with a history of violence, went to see a double execution at Kirkdale Gaol. Back home in his cellar in Great Homer Street he said to his wife, 'You should have been there instead of the two men.' She replied, 'Take care you are not there before me.' Later that day, Hughes promised that he would be 'hung for her yet'. The next day, after his wife refused to give him some money, he threatened 'I'll have it out of your bones.' Later that evening he kicked her and stamped on her so hard that she was left paralysed from the neck down, surviving only for three more days. For all his fascination with the gallows, on hearing that he had been sentenced to death for murder, Hughes fainted and had to be carried from the dock.

Beating women was a something of a speciality for some men. Richard O'Brien amassed over 50 spells in custody for assaults on women and the police. Known throughout the south end in the 1870s as 'Dick the Devil', O'Brien beat one woman so hard that she suffered a miscarriage. On being sentenced to six months with hard labour he turned to the judge and announced, 'That will give me appetite for my dinner.'[35]

In an age when women could not vote, early feminists such as Frances Power Cobbe and Josephine Butler fought to redress the power imbalance between women and men, not only politically and economically but also domestically. In the 1870s Cobbe began campaigning for better protection of abused wives. She spoke of the various degrees of wife beating in the different localities. London men were renowned for thrashing with their fists but this was said to be nothing compared to the kickings dished out by men in the north.[36] At the Congress of the National Association for the Promotion of Social Sciences, held in Liverpool in 1876, Serjeant Pulling exposed the amount of brutality taking place in the town. He spoke of systematic savagery and felt that the law was failing those women who lived in what he termed the 'kicking district'. He believed that the legal system discouraged complainants from reporting offences. Among other measures, he recommended the flogging of abusive husbands for their second offence.[37] Reverend Morris, chaplain of Walton Gaol and a delegate at the conference, was against the whipping of husbands since he claimed that some were undoubtedly provoked by their partners. He pointed out that sometimes the wives were at fault: 'the women of Liverpool were worse than the men'. He cited cases of sober, law-abiding husbands married to women who were regular prisoners at the gaol: 'Could they wonder that such a man coming home to a wife like that – could they wonder if he raised his hand?' As for divorce as a solution to domestic violence, Morris thought that this would only increase violent offences, 'because many a man would be only too glad to get rid of his wife'.[38] By the same token, Cobbe raises the suggestion that some women might deliberately provoke their husbands to hit them to win a separation and gain maintenance, perhaps even with the aim of taking up with a lover.[39]

Earlier in the century women had little recourse to the law. If they left violent husbands they lost their rights to any property and even their wages. Between 1839 and 1878 fathers were given custody of children over the age of 7; before 1839 husbands had absolute custody rights. No wonder women were forced to remain in violent marriages. Only slowly did the legal system grapple with the problem of domestic abuse. In 1853 Parliament responded to complaints that women and children were being inadequately protected from abusive husbands by passing the Aggravated Assault on Women and Children Act. This empowered magistrates to fine or imprison offenders for up to six months. Yet even after the legislation was passed, wives continued to drop the charges before the cases were heard or refuse to turn up at court. Women's economic dependence on men forced many to stay with violent partners. If the husband was imprisoned the wife lost the income of the breadwinner; if he was fined she was still the financial loser. What feminists wanted was not simply legal protection for women but the economic independence that would enable them to leave abusive men.

This focus on domestic violence was part of a growing judicial concern with all forms of male violence, particularly among the lower classes.[40] For some, wife beating was seen, quite wrongly, as a working-class problem, associated with squalid hovels, heavy drinking and gambling. It could be argued that the primary aim of the growing amount of legislation was the repression of male violence rather than the alleviation of female suffering. Nevertheless, the courts became an important arena where serious violence could be challenged, rebuked and punished. As the legal system began to provide more opportunities to prosecute brutal husbands, women increasingly turned to the courts for protection from male aggression. The liberating Matrimonial Clauses Act of 1878 enabled wives who had suffered from an 'aggravated assault' to be granted a separation order through the courts with maintenance and custody of children under 10 years of age. For the first time the law recognized that physical cruelty was grounds for legal separation, although women had to wait until 1937 before such cruelty became grounds for divorce. The Act was reinforced in 1895 by the Summary Jurisdiction (Married Women) Act, which allowed women to leave violent husbands before applying to the magistrates for separation and maintenance. However, women had to leave their husbands before action could begin and some had nowhere else to go other than the workhouse.[41] Forcing husbands to pay maintenance was another problem. Other deterrents to legal action included ignorance of the law, family pressures and shameful publicity. Fear of revenge and further violence were also very real factors.[42] Christopher Hughes had been living apart from his wife when he followed her to her house in Beacon Street and bit off the end of her nose.[43] One Liverpool gentleman gave another reason why some women were reluctant to prosecute violent partners: 'The women of Lancashire are *awfully fond* of bad husbands. It has become quite a truism that our women are like dogs, the more you beat them the more they love you.'[44]

All the legislation and punishments in the world could not save some faithful women from their psychopathic husbands, as in the case of James Bray. A dock labourer, Bray lived with his blind and crippled wife in a court off Harley Street. The woman had lost her sight after an earlier kicking from her husband. In December 1882 Bray came home and found his wife sitting on a stool. He grabbed her by the hair and threw her to the floor before jumping on her, breaking her leg. He said that he did not want a woman who was blind, but one with two eyes. After stripping her naked he vowed that he would 'roast her like a herring on the fire'. Bray then threw red-hot coals on her body. Seemingly willing to hang for his brutality, he promised that he would not be satisfied until he had 'got the black cap upon him for her'. He was sentenced to life imprisonment after being convicted of grievous bodily harm. 'I am as innocent as the child unborn,' claimed Bray as he left the dock.

Incest

Although the legal system slowly weakened the power that brutal husbands wielded over their partners, the dominion that parents held over their own children remained sacrosanct for much of the nineteenth century. This power sometimes went beyond physical chastisement. Another form of control took place that newspapers could only describe as 'gross', 'shocking' or 'disgusting' outrages. The sexual abuse and rape of children by their own fathers was an aspect of domestic life that never made front-page headlines but was buried away in tiny paragraphs within police court reports. Sometimes the details of the police charge are given but no follow-up story as to the verdicts and sentence. Despite the silence, incest created a great deal of middle-class moral anxiety because it called into question deeply held notions of the respectable family. In fact, there was no law on incest until 1908, despite four failed attempts at legislation from 1899. It has been pointed out that the prosecution statistics for incest are an unreliable guide to the scale of the problem.[45] Embarrassment and the ruination of the good name of the family was often at stake.

Even without hard evidence, middle-class commentators felt that over-crowding in the congested cellars and lodging-houses of the poor was shocking evidence of their immorality. Daughters shared beds with their fathers while adult brothers and sisters regularly slept together. Women's campaigner Josephine Butler stated that 'there is a mass of people, boys and girls, who begin to be unchaste and vicious from the earliest of years'. Girls were particularly vulnerable. Since families of five or six often huddled together like beasts, 'it was a common thing that their own fathers, in a fit of intoxication, had violated them'.[46] Sometimes different families shared the same sleeping quarters. After a visit to one household, Revd Johns described how 'the father, mother and children of one family sleep together in one corner; the father, mother and children of another family sleep together in another'.[47] Even worse was the presence of strangers in the bedroom. Commander Eaton, a School Board Inspector, cites the case of a female child sleeping in the same bed as her father (a widower), a girl of 16 who was a visitor, a boy of 12 or 13, plus another girl. He felt 'the result of that is, that such a girl, without having the slightest intention, or wish to become a prostitute, unless she is taken care of, becomes a prostitute'.[48] Yet it could also be argued that the lack of privacy in such crowded situations might actually have prevented inappropriate behaviour. Nevertheless, incest was committed or at least attempted. John Clare, a brothel-keeper of Hotham Street, tried to force himself on his own 13-year-old daughter as she slept. He received two years' hard labour. George Lee was found guilty of violating his own daughter, aged 15.[49]

Child Abuse

Children were also at risk from other family members, neighbours and complete strangers. An infirm man of 70 attempted to rape a 10-year-old in Toxteth Park. He was fined £5 with the alternative of two months in prison. Peter Conlon gave 10-year-old Martha Rooney a 'loathsome disease' after inviting her into his house in Freemason's Row to help him light the fire. William Wright was charged with an indecent assault on a 7-year-old. The child was considered too young to give evidence and Wright was discharged. The magistrate 'hoped the prisoner was innocent for the sake of humanity'. Thomas Reed repeatedly sexually abused his 10-year-old niece, after he was left alone with her on several occasions. A shopkeeper called Charles Dillon was imprisoned for ten years for the rape of a 12-year-old. The child had been sent to his shop on an errand. An old man called John Morris indecently assaulted a 2-year-old girl. He was fined 40s and costs. A Spanish seaman was charged with indecently assaulting an 18-month-old child.[50]

There was an old superstition that sex with a virgin cured venereal disease.[51] This led to some horrific assaults on children. In July 1848 21-year-old Thomas Looney, from Toxteth, was charged with raping his 9-year-old niece. The act was discovered after the girl became ill and was found to be suffering from a 'loathsome disease'. It was suspected that Looney committed the act to rid himself of his own infection. In October 1857 a syphilitic Amos

Greenwood raped and infected 9-year-old Mary Johnson, the daughter of a travelling showman. Greenwood joined the show and slept with the girl's family in lodgings. After moving to Wigan the girl complained of feeling unwell and revealed her ordeal. She died soon after and Greenwood was gaoled for life.

Liverpool Society for the Prevention of Cruelty to Children

In the second half of the nineteenth century attitudes towards childhood were transformed. Older concerns with sin and temptation began to give way to biological and psychological explanations of juvenile criminality. Youngsters were seen as less responsible for their actions and therefore as needing to be treated differently from adults. Instead of being punished they were to be nurtured and reformed. These changing attitudes accelerated towards the end of the century. Compulsory education physically separated children from adults, intensifying the focus upon their needs. School medical inspections highlighted the physical wellbeing of children and uncovered the disturbing extent of deprivation. Samuel Smith, in the early 1880s, reckoned that of Liverpool's 80,000 children of school age, 10,000 were inadequately clothed, housed and fed.[52] The raising of the age of sexual consent to 16 in 1885 helped sanctify childhood innocence. Other pieces of legislation, such as street-trading regulations, were aimed at rescuing children from harmful environments.

Youngsters who previously were seen as a danger to society were now being viewed as children in danger, at risk from a host of social factors, including their own families. The last two decades of the nineteenth century saw the emergence of a growing sensitivity to the plight of children suffering cruelty, abuse and neglect from their own parents. Young offenders, apprentices and working children, such as chimney sweeps, had been given statutory protection long before those in authority became interested in the treatment of children in the family home. What happened between the family's four walls had always been seen as private and none of the state's business. Nevertheless, the child's right to expect reasonable treatment from parents and guardians soon become a national issue.[53] It is to Liverpool's credit that the town was at the forefront of the campaign to give children new rights.

The movement towards child protection was largely the result of the efforts of a man called T. Frederick Agnew. He was inspired to form the country's first child protection agency after visiting a similar organization in New York in 1881. Two years later, the Liverpool Society for the Prevention of Cruelty to Children was formed to raise awareness of child cruelty and help victims of abuse. The first case involved Helen Harrecan, who had been punched in the face by her father. Her mother informed the Society and the man was prosecuted and given three months' imprisonment. The public couldn't believe the harshness of the sentence. After all, he was only chastising his own child. There was some resistance to the idea of protecting children from domestic discipline. If parents were prosecuted a second time, some magistrates accused the Society of persecuting the parents.[54] Yet the Society did not restrict itself to prosecuting cases of chastisement. The term cruelty was interpreted widely as can be judged from the cases brought to court by the SPCC in 1888. There were 26 cases of assault, 231 of excessive beating and ill treatment, 4,459 of neglect and starvation, 97 of allowing children to beg during the day, 71 of begging at night, 32 of selling at night, 36 of selling under age, 241 of exposure, 62 of sleeping out at night, 18 of living in brothels, 81 of living in dangerous surroundings, and three of criminal assault – a total of 5,357 cases.[55] The Society also opened a refuge in Islington to minister to the steady stream of starving, abused and neglected children.

A league table for the years 1895 to 1899 reveals the proportion of murders of children under one year, cruelty to children and cases of abandoning of children under two years of age relative to population. Liverpool tops the list with 103.48 per 100,000 of the population. Wolverhampton is next with 47.8. London comes low down the list with 8.94. Of the 43 smaller towns, neighbouring Bootle tops the list with 77.11.[56] Yet the figures might simply reflect the more stringent efforts of the Liverpool agencies in prosecuting cases of abuse rather than merely giving warnings. To deter child cruelty the SPCC circulated placards in the 'lower quarters of the city' informing people that a Mrs Graham had received fifteen months for the manslaughter of her child.[57] For some, the warning fell on deaf ears. Sarah Strickland, for example, described as a 'typical virago of the slums', had by 1899 clocked up 42 appearances before the magistrate. 'A great coarse creature', she was a violent drunk around the south end. Strickland was married but with no fixed abode. In February 1895 she appeared in court accused of neglecting and ill-treating her 10-month-old child. She had already had three of her children taken from her. Although permanently drunk she carried the fourth about with her from empty house to empty house. She received three months with hard labour. The SPCC revealed that over a ten-year period, as each of her children had been born, they had been forced to warn and threaten the mother as to her behaviour. The prison sentence had little effect and in September Strickland was again found drunk in Park Road. Her baby was filthy, almost naked and covered with lice. The magistrate increased the sentence to six months with hard labour.[58]

The work of the SPCC was only part of wider measures to ensure child protection. In 1889 and 1894 Parliament approved the Prevention of Cruelty to Children Acts. The legislation enabled police and magistrates to intervene in domestic circumstances where they suspected child cruelty. If necessary, they could remove a child from home. The Custody of Children Act (1891) also enabled the courts to remove at-risk children from their families. In 1895 the National Society for the Prevention of Cruelty to Children opened a branch office in Castle Street with the intention of serving those areas not covered by the Liverpool office, that is, the southern and eastern districts.

Other organizations did their bit to help children. Liverpool's Head Constable, Captain Nott-Bower, founded the Liverpool and Bootle Police Orphanage in 1895. In the same year the Police-Aided Clothing Association helped clothe 4,532 street urchins. The Shaw Street Boys Home, run as part of the Liverpool Wesleyan Mission, housed children whose mothers were incapable of looking after them. The abandoned boys were fed, clothed and eventually found employment. Even then, such children were not safe from the grasping clutches of their parents. Parents sometimes waylaid their offspring on Saturday nights as they left work with their wages. In 1896 it was reported that five lads had lost their jobs because their employers were sick and tired of drunken parents calling.[59] Instead of nurturing their children, some parents crushed them, fed off them or ruined their opportunities to advance themselves. While being interviewed in prison by a Police Court Missionary, an early form of probation officer, one young criminal asked, 'Have you seen my home? [...] Well do you wonder at my coming here again, surrounded by such influences as I have been? I have never had a chance.' Another young delinquent was asked why he looked so 'bright'. He replied that 'his mother was dead, and now he would have a chance in the world'.[60]

SIXTEEN

The Devil's Children

Juvenile delinquency was a major social problem in nineteenth-century Liver-pool. The 1839 Constabulary Report spoke of an army of young thieves, 1,200 strong, taught and manipulated by 2,000 adults.[1] The figures might have been exaggerated but others also highlighted Liverpool's unique juvenile problem. Prison inspector Captain Williams believed that more young criminals lived in Liverpool than in any other major manufacturing or commercial centre.[2] 'Juvenile crime bears an unusually dark aspect in Liverpool,' wrote John Clay in 1853. Two years later, in a letter to Lord Stanley, Clay stated that Liverpool 'stands more in need of [reformatory schools] than any place I know'.[3] *Porcu-pine* stated: 'Liverpool is overrun by these adopted children of the devil.'[4] Towards the end of the century the situation showed no signs of improving. In 1880, 1,054 juvenile offenders were arrested in Liverpool. Ten years later, 1,331 children were arrested.[5] The increase might reveal a growth of juvenile crime or it might simply illustrate a greater determination on behalf of the police to clamp down on young offenders. Nevertheless, in his 1896 report, the Chief Inspector of Reformatories maintained: 'There is no town which contains so difficult a population as that of Liverpool.'[6]

The Causes of Juvenile Crime

The causes of juvenile delinquency were much debated in Victorian Britain. A whole range of factors were thought to be involved. A private reformatory in Mason Street, Edge Hill, kept records of the boys received into its care. The various reasons for admission were listed. These included 'low Irish poverty', the bad influence of the theatre, 'felon family' and 'mother dead, father drinks' (or vice versa).[7] A lack of schooling was another cause. According to the prison inspector in 1837, 'when children from their infancy have been left to run about the streets uncontrolled, and have once acquired the taste for an idle vagabond life, there is little hope of weaning them from it to pursuits of a more restrained nature'.[8] Another prison inspector's report three years later suggested various other reasons for the large amount of youth crime, including the fickle financial circumstances of the largely maritime population, the influx of Irish, the number of destitute orphans resulting from the epidemics of fever and the temptations of so much valuable property left unguarded in the markets and docks.[9]

Lack of Employment

Father Nugent's socially conscious successor, Father Berry, blamed juvenile crime on an abundant child population lacking industrial work: 'Our criminals are bred in our streets.'[10] In Liverpool the absence of factories and mills meant that there was a dearth of employment opportunities for women and children. Yet youngsters of poverty-stricken households still had to contribute toward the family income. A street-based black economy developed in which children were given a variety of tasks, including scavenging, peddling wares, domestic chores and child-minding. Children would collect rags, pick bones or even rob drunks who had fallen unconscious in the street. Some would polish shoes or hold horses' reins while others would sing in the beershops or turn cartwheels for loose change from passers-by. Girls would help their mothers at the market. Carrying passengers' bags at the Pier Head or railway station was another popular way of earning coppers.

Ragged and barefooted urchins would also beg for food on the cobbled streets. It was feared that many graduated from begging to stealing. Samuel Smith recalls that 'one of the commonest tricks was to send out the children on snowy nights, half naked, to solicit alms'.[11] James Shaw, of the Liverpool District Provident Society, revealed that the Irish sent out their children to beg, warning them that before returning home they had to earn 6d, or as much as 18d on market day. He cites the case of a 9-year-old who was found singing in the street. He was brought to the office nearly naked. When told to go home the boy cried, explaining that he would be beaten as he had only earned 2d. After being kitted out with a new jacket and trousers he was taken home by a visitor. Rather than being grateful, his parents cursed the visitor for interfering with their family. They said that children should go out begging to maintain themselves. The poor child asked the visitor to discard his old ragged trousers as his mother would only pawn his new pair.[12]

If legitimate work was hard to come by, those with criminal records had even less chance of employment. Interviewed in the Borough Gaol, a young thief explained his circumstances:

I shall thieve directly I get out of this place. I will not starve, and I can soon get a purse or handkerchief to buy a dinner. I do not want to thieve if I can get money honestly, but how am I to get it? Will you employ me? Will anybody be fool enough to employ me? Just out of gaol, and with no character, just think of that, sir, and tell me if I must not thieve![13]

Cruel parenting forced some children into criminality. Sick and tired of ill treatment, youngsters would leave home to 'go on their own hook'. They could now earn their own money without giving it to their parents. Waterloo Road, near to the docks, was a favourite haunt for Liverpool's juvenile thieves. Those unlucky enough not to find refuge for the night would sleep on the warm flagstones outside the bakery on the corner of Canning Place. When it rained they sought the dryness of a yard near the Sailors' Home.[14] They also slept in stables, in empty barrels and under handcarts. Some huddled in shop doorways, alleyways, on basement steps or under railway arches.

Lodging-Houses

To escape the winter cold, those with money in their pockets sought a night in a penny lodging-house. Up to 12 children would share a single room.[15] Some establishments, known as 'kid's kens', catered exclusively for juvenile criminals. Not only did they provide a bed for the night, they were also good places to pass on stolen goods since proprietors often acted as fences. A common feature of these 'dosshouses' was a room with a blazing fire where residents would congregate and swop stories. Even the most innocent of children would be led astray after being regaled with tales of crime and debauchery from older villains. A prison report revealed that as the younger boys were released from the Borough Gaol they were 'received by their associates at the gate and carried off to their old haunts'. There were people in Liverpool who kept houses for the reception of these boys and girls, where they lived together without any separation with regard to age or gender.[16]

The following extract from the Liverpool Gaol Register of 1846 lists some of the worst criminal lodging-houses frequented by youngsters. One parentless 14-year-old lived with Old Granny Hunt, known as the Queen of Demons, in Preston Street. The woman's children and grandchildren were all listed as 'bad'. A 16-year-old, again with missing parents, lived mainly in the 'notorious Fitzpatrick's and Burke's houses'. One 16-year-old had the misfortune to live in Denison Street, where 'nearly every house […] is filled with black-ballers and disorderly persons'. Several children were said to live with the 'notorious Hannah Carr' in Ben Jonson Street. Carr's family and connections were all thieves.[17] A 14-year-old prisoner also revealed that he lodged with Carr who had about four beds available. Many of these establishments were run by women. Others included Mrs Fennyson's in Smithfield Street and Mrs Roberts' in Quay Street.[18]

Lack of Education

Many enlightened Victorians believed that crime could be reduced by taking children off the streets and giving them knowledge, skills, discipline and aspirations to a better life. 'Education,' wrote Father Nugent, 'is not an absolute preservative against crime, yet it must always be an incalculable advantage towards gaining an honest livelihood and making a position in the town of Liverpool.'[19] With regard to the economics of crime, Hugh Shimmin hit the nail on the head: 'There is not one of these little wretches who does not cost us ten times more in the end to punish than it would have cost us in the beginning to educate.'[20]

As early as 1833 John Finch, the founder of the Liverpool Temperance Society, called for a national system of education to remove children from their vice-ridden environments.[21] In 1827 the town council had provided two schools, in the north and south districts, but attendance was not compulsory. There were also 'ragged schools' catering for the poorest street children, particularly those too scruffy and dirty to mix with others. Admission was free and there was no uniform, unlike the church schools which provided most education. Yet conditions were so austere that they hardly encouraged attendance. In the late 1830s the mistress of a particularly filthy Liverpool dame school explained to a schools inspector that 'the children thrived best in the dirt'.[22] Inquiries in the 1840s revealed the abysmal state of school non-attendance. A Liverpool missionary spelt out the scale of the problem in the south end. In Brick Street there were 436 children under the age of 14, only 51 of them attending school. In Crosbie Street there were 484 children under 14 with only 47 attending school. The missionary pointed the finger not so much at the parents' poverty but at their indifference. Rather than pay taxes to support idleness and criminality, he thought that it would be better to provide educational opportunities to lift children out of poverty.[23] He had to wait until 1870 for the Education Act that allowed locally elected boards to create the first elementary state schools. Where there were no existing schools, board schools were created. However, elementary education did not become compulsory until 1880 and was not made free until 1891. Despite the provision of education, many children continued to miss out on schooling, preferring to gain an education on the streets. Parents would withdraw sons and daughters from school to send them begging or selling on the streets.[24] Police often found that the shoeblacks and beggars they found on the streets were not homeless orphans but youngsters earning money for their parents. By 1873 there were 26 school inspectors hunting down the truants but it was hard to keep track of them since many families frequently moved house.

Philanthropists and social reformers made their own efforts at getting children into education. Opened in 1875, the Coliseum Sunday School in Fleet Street (formerly of Paradise Street) catered for the waifs and strays who refused to attend other establishments. Just before seven o'clock on a Sunday evening up to 1,000 children from all over the city would descend on the place, no doubt enticed by the small loaf of bread awarded for attendance. Samuel Smith recalled that 'the filth and stench of the audience was indescribable. One could hardly walk through to the platform without feeling sick.'[25] Sir Donald Currie described his own attempt at practical philanthropy. Going down to the docks on a Sunday night, 'we had 400 wild young savage children to deal with. Lights were put out, forms upset, teachers rubbed against and laughed at. But they became subsequently so docile that you could lift a finger and they would say no more.'[26] Education was as much about social control as rescuing children. The Liverpool Cinderella Club provided instruction, entertainment and a hearty meal for slum children at various venues in the city. The organization, introduced in Liverpool in 1893, was one of many scattered throughout the country. Between 7 and 10 p.m., up to 500 children would cram into a large schoolroom for soup, lantern slides and songs. To keep the children captive until the very end, the slab of fruitcake was not doled out until the event had finished.[27]

If education helped tame youngsters, the development of literacy also had its negative aspects, particularly in the popularization of 'penny dreadfuls' and other sensationalist publications. Aimed at a youthful and increasingly literate audience, these books contained lurid illustrations and brutal tales of crime and adventure. Popular titles included *Sweeney Todd* and *Spring-Heeled Jack: The Terror of London*. A journalist witnessed a ragged urchin enter a shop in Scotland Road to buy a copy of *The Feast of Blood* for his mother. He returned to buy himself a biography of Jack Sheppard. The journalist was shocked that a youngster just beginning his reading career was having his mind contaminated by immoral literature.[28] In June 1846 a youth called James Mildmay was charged with attempting to shoot a policeman. When searched, he was found to be carrying two pistols and a book called *The Lives of all the Notorious Highwaymen and Robbers*. By the 1880s, after education was made compulsory, the influence of 'penny dreadfuls' became even more of a problem, leading (so it was believed) to increased juvenile crime, particularly cases of boys seeking adventure by stealing money and running away from home. In court, parents would blame the books for corrupting their children's minds.[29]

School for Thieves

In place of legitimate education, some children allegedly attended schools for thieves, familiar to many through the fictional institution run by Fagin in Charles Dickens' *Oliver Twist*. In the 1860s Liverpool was reputed to have its own thieves' commune where children learnt their trade. What one newspaper called 'The Liverpool College for the Education of Thieves' was located at the north end of Ben Jonson Street, off Scotland Road. The area was known as 'Upper Canada', although nobody knew why.[30] In addition to Hannah Carr's home, the whole neighbourhood consisted of thieves' dens, the inhabitants living mostly on plunder. Pupils enjoyed a full criminal curriculum with modules on pocket picking, burglary, garrotting, highway robbery and passing base coin. There were teachers, both male and female, called 'Professors', some of whom were experts in the art of writing begging letters. The professors, some wearing skull caps with coloured ribbon, a band or tassel, were said to attend court daily to look at the weak and strong points of cases to learn valuable lessons. The two golden rules of the academy were 'not to be caught in the act of thieving' and, if they were caught, to be sure not to leave any evidence so as to escape conviction.

The female teachers specialized in lessons in begging, thieving and the 'pious dodge', a subtle form of begging. A merchant who went daily about the Corn Exchange frequently observed a poor but clean woman accompanied by a 6-year-old child. On one occasion the child stooped to pick up a diamond pin. 'Ah baby,' the mother said, 'I knew I'd have luck today when I brought you out; this will get some comfort for your poor sick father.' The mother then offered the pin as a present to a passer-by close enough to have overheard the conversation. The present was declined but the intended recipient kindly offered a shilling or two out of sympathy. After seeing the dodge performed more than once, the man investigated the case and found that the woman was, in fact, a professor at the school.[31]

Some of the town's juvenile thieves were hardened professionals. In 1875 Arthur Wilson, a 14-year-old cutler's assistant, decided to steal his employer's takings and head for Paris. When arrested he was booted, spurred and ready to mount a pony he had hired. He had been staying at the Hotel de Rome and had taken riding lessons. Wilson was found with two revolvers, 100 cartridges and some books about highway robbers. Since his money had almost run out, it was thought that he was about to replenish his purse through robbery.[32] A year later a boy was remanded for performing 'several feats of highway robbery, although he has not yet reached the tender age of 11 years'.[33] Francis Bishop was shocked at the lack of innocence of Liverpool's streetwise children. He came face to face with juvenile deviousness when a little girl called at his door begging for help. After reciting a sad tale of family hunger and illness, the child was given food to carry home. Bishop asked the child where she lived, intending to visit her parents the next day, only later to discover that she had given him a false address.[34] Child beggars were schooled by their parents not to reveal their addresses.[35]

Dockland Temptations

Another major factor in the amount of juvenile crime in Liverpool was the treasure trove of goods lying about the docks. Cotton provided the richest source of plunder for young criminals. A report in the *Morning Chronicle* revealed the scale of the problem: 'Cotton bales lie in immense heaps on the quays where, in defiance of the utmost vigilance of the police, swarms of children prowl around during the day and night to abstract it by the handfuls and conceal it amid their rags until they can transfer it to a depraved mother or father, who watches in a dark alley or in the shed of a warehouse to receive it.'[36] The more agile boys escaped with their loot by clinging to the under-side of loaded wagons as they trundled through the dock gates. In March 1852 four girls and a boy appeared in court after being caught stealing coal from George's Dock quay. A constable saw them putting coal into their pinafores and followed them to St Nicholas' churchyard where they had already hoarded a pile of coal. Two of the girls, Maria Garvey and Ann Burke, were experienced thieves and were sentenced to seven days' imprisonment. Mudlarks also climbed aboard barges moored in the river, throwing goods overboard and picking them off the mud at low tide.

As mentioned earlier, most of the goods children acquired on their thieving and scavenging trips were fenced through a network of pawnshops and receivers. Some canny slum children, however, cut out the middleman by setting up their own 'markets' in the cellars. A convict in Preston Gaol gave the following account of the activities of street children in Liverpool's Little Ireland district:

They must bring home a certain sum or value, whether obtained by selling, begging or stealing, is immaterial. Nothing comes amiss to them; bits of iron, copper, brass, anything from the docks, warehouses, door-mats, if left exposed, and hundreds of miscellaneous articles always to be found in a sea port. These boys, some of them only 6- or 7-years of age, have their own markets in the streets above mentioned, where, in some cellars, they dispose of their 'swag,' and away out again to look for more.[37]

Born Bad

It was believed that some youngsters were simply 'born bad', their parents blamed for passing on their criminal genes. The *Liverpool Mercury* traced the development of the juvenile criminal:

The downward education of a street arab, in most cases, begins almost in infancy. He inherits the fearful craving for drink bequeathed by a besotted mother or father and, too often, has besides a natural predisposition for that form of crime which in higher walks of life is called Kleptomania, and which phrenologists account for by an abnormal development of the bump of acquisitiveness.

Inherited taints of character and an education in squalid poverty and brutal degradation commences with the first dawning of individualism. All the fates appear to be against the child becoming anything else but a criminal.[38]

Some considered law-breaking to be as much genetic as the result of social and environmental factors. From the mid-nineteenth century there was a rise in secular and scientific theories of criminal behaviour. Old religious explanations regarding moral lapses and sinful temptation were replaced by debates about biology and psychology. By the 1890s a belief in human progress was being challenged by theories of degeneracy. Evolutionary biologist Charles Darwin had proposed that over time species evolve into more sophisticated forms. However, it was also feared that some people were relapsing into lower, more animalistic forms of being. A satirical journal, for example, concluded that the 'cornerman is a unique creature – he forms a distinct link between the animal and reptile creation, combining the shuffle of a bear and the face of an ape with the craftiness of a spider and the courage of a worm'.[39] On a more serious note, the criminal classes were seen as degenerate, partly as a result of inherited characteristics passed on from generation to generation and partly owing to the stunting effects of unhealthy slum living. Darwin's half-cousin

Francis Galton coined the term 'eugenics' and wrote of the 'human refuse' that resulted from the over-breeding of sickly and inadequate individuals.[40] Others noted a cycle of immorality as the lower orders, largely Irish Catholics, perpetuated their criminal lifestyles and continued to breed similarly depraved children destined only for the prisons and reformatories.[41]

There was concern that a population explosion among the lower classes, seemingly divorced from moral, social and economic responsibilities, would overwhelm and help overthrow the law-abiding middle classes. Social historian David Taylor explains: 'Breeding prolifically, at a time when the elites in particular were limiting family size, the degenerate in society threatened to swamp respectable society, bringing physical deterioration as well as moral collapse.'[42] As if by some process of inverse Darwinism, Herbert Spencer's notion of the survival of the fittest had become, in Liverpool at least, the survival of the unfittest, the degenerate kept at a bare level of existence but thriving nevertheless by sheer force of numbers.

Nathaniel Hawthorne looked at Liverpool's young people and saw the brutalized adults of the future: 'My God, what dirty, dirty children! And the grown people are the flowers of these buds, physically and morally.' He also described the dehumanized girls from the workhouse, locked in a primitive stage of human development:

> I should not have conceived it possible that so many children could have been collected together, without a single trace of beauty, or scarcely of intelligence, in so much as one individual; such mean, coarse, vulgar features and figures, betraying an unmistakably low origin, and ignorant and brutal parents. They did not appear wicked, but only stupid, animal and soulless. It must require many generations of better life to elicit a soul in them.[43]

Speaking of male juvenile delinquents in Liverpool, the prison inspector also remarked on the children's physical similarities: 'it is impossible to fail being struck with the resemblance they bear to each other, undoubtedly the result of similar habits and pursuits; they are short, stoutly made, active in body, and acute in intellect'.[44] The difference between the 'stupid' children of the workhouse and the intellectually 'acute' youngsters in the prison system is interesting. The workhouse children were at the bottom of the social pile, often born into the system and spending their childhoods there. They were kept fed and clothed and perhaps lacked any further ambition. The prison children were more streetwise and quick-witted, with greater aspirations. Sharpness was a simple matter of survival on the streets.

Bad Parenting

Besides heredity, there were other factors involved in parental influence. Bad parenting and a lack of moral example led some children astray. Hugh Shimmin described children 'suckled in sin, cradled in crime, and catechised in blasphemy'. He felt that it was not just the poverty of the parents that drove children to crime but neglect and a lack of parental responsibility.[45] Some young thieves, such as Patrick Hart, alias Kelly, alias Nutter, alias O'Garr, were the products of notorious criminal families.[46] The string of aliases give a hint to the boy's repeated criminality throughout the 1840s. By the age of 14 Patrick had been in custody 24 times. Some youngsters were open about the effects of bad parenting. One 12-year-old inmate of the Borough Gaol admitted, 'I was first led to do bad things through the neglect of my mother. She is now in this prison.' In the words of a 9-year-old prisoner: 'I once got 9 shillings out of [a] till; my aunt made me drunk and took it from me.' The same boy stole a sovereign and gave it to his father. When asked where he got it, he admitted it was stolen. The father 'said nothing'.[47] Some parents actively encouraged their children to steal. If they were successful they were rewarded but if unsuccessful they were beaten. Children had to make a choice between the possibility of being caught by the police and the certainty of being punished at home.[48]

Elizabeth P. was an 11-year-old thief who, by 1853, could boast three spells in the lock-up and three months in the Borough Gaol. The girl, who lived in a court with her mother and stepfather, revealed her introduction to crime: 'The first time I ever took money was in Byrom Street; there was a fire in that street, and I saw a lady with three sovereigns in a purse. I went up to her and said, aye? Do you see that woman on fire? I then put my hand in her pocket and took out her money, and ran off with it.' She often handed over the proceeds of her crimes to her mother: 'she never scolded me for stealing but sometimes used to say, well Bessy how did you get on today?'[49]

The chaplain of Liverpool Gaol revealed how a 14-year-old girl, spending her seventh spell in prison, begged to be placed in the workhouse away from temptation.[50] It seemed that her mother encouraged her to steal and then drank the proceeds. She would also pledge her daughter's clothes. During an interrogation a young dockland cotton thief revealed the futility of attempting to reform some children while they remained within the family setting:

Can you read? *A little.*
Do you go to school? *Not now.*
Do you know the Ten Commandments? *Some of them.*

Do you know that one of them says 'Thou shalt not steal?' *Yes.*
Then why do you steal? *I am obliged.*
Who obliges you to steal? *My father and mother.*
Do you always steal in the docks? *There is no good chances anywhere else.*
Have you any brother or sisters? *Yes.*
Do they steal? *Yes, sometimes, and sometimes beg.*
Does your father steal? *Yes, when he gets a chance.*[51]

Extracts from the Liverpool Gaol Register of 1846 list some appalling cases of parental corruption. A 15-year-old, with two periods in custody, had written about him: 'Parents notoriously bad, their children all bad and their house an iniquitous harbour for juveniles of both sexes.' Similar shocking stories of adult contamination of children are recorded in another prison report from 1856:

> Mrs C [...] This woman excels in villainy. Her house is a second hell. Her children are now going in her track.
>
> S.B. and his wife [...] This man and his wife keep a small shop in Preston Street, where young thieves bring their plunder for sale. Their children mix with thieves, and he has been in prison for felony.
>
> E.T. [...] This woman keeps a notorious house for young thieves, who bring their plunder there. Several have been transported from her den. Her own children are thieves.[52]

Some parents sought to evade their responsibilities and hide their immoral influence by teaching their children to deny having parents if they got into trouble. It was not uncommon for children in the prison system to claim that they were orphans.[53]

Irish Children

Related to both the genetic and social factors was the racist idea that children of Irish parents were predisposed towards crime. Head Constable Whitty believed that 'the greatest portion of the juvenile thieves in Liverpool are Irish lads or of Irish parents'.[54] Father Nugent further explained: 'We were not prepared for the exodus which came from Ireland, and now we are punished by the children of those parents who came from Ireland, who have grown up in ignorance and neglect.'[55] Captain Williams also accounted for the increase in juvenile offenders in Liverpool and other large towns as being the result of the Irish influx, combined with the impact of disease. The death of Irish parents from fever meant that the children were often adopted by other families who could not adequately support them. Such children were left to get by as well as they could.[56] The Superintendent of the Liverpool Police, William Parlour, declared that 'the Irish come over with an immense number of children, without the means of providing for them; they then send them into the streets, and the next step for them is to become thieves, so that a large proportion of the juvenile thieves of Liverpool are Irish'. He added that 'there is a great deal of pilfering among the Irish; many Irish women send children out to steal, and maintain them for the purpose of thieving'.[57] An inmate of Salford Gaol gave an account of his life of crime in the 1830s. He felt that 'Manchester and Liverpool [thieves] are reckoned the most expert; they are thought to be of Irish parents, and to have most cunning.'[58] Thomas Carter, the Anglican chaplain of the Borough Gaol, described Irish boys as 'precocious' and 'generally sharp, clever lads'.[59] The gaol's schoolmaster, however, noted that his pupils were largely the sons of Catholic parents and 'very ignorant'. They were also regular visitors to the theatre.[60]

The Theatre

The nineteenth century saw a growth in explanations for juvenile criminal behaviour, from poverty to bad parenting to hereditary factors. Yet moral explanations persisted, particularly relating to the way that children were adversely affected by perverse examples from literature and theatre. The argument mutated into twentieth-century fears about the malign influence of the cinema and rock 'n' roll music, right through to present-day scares about the Internet and video games. For a pre-literate generation, watching plays was an exciting form of entertainment and a rare opportunity for laughter and a chance to escape the awful circumstances of their lives. There were strong links, however, between juvenile crime and theatre attendance. In 1841 the prison inspector noted the attraction of the theatre: 'Perhaps in no other town in the United Kingdom has the demoralising influence of low theatres and amusements upon children been so decidedly experienced as at Liverpool.' Hundreds of neglected and abandoned children haunted establishments such as the Liver in Church Street, the Sans Pareil in Great Charlotte Street and the Queen's Theatre in Paradise Street. The suppression of fairs in London was said to have led many travelling shows to become fixtures in large towns such as Liverpool. One concern was the impact of bloodthirsty plays and exhibitions. 'The Murders of Maria Martin in the Red Barn' by Corder and 'Hannah Brown' by Greenacre were typical attractions.[61]

Captain Williams examined juveniles at both the Borough Gaol and Kirkdale and concluded that 'their principal and almost universal gratification was that of attending the low theatres of the town'. He revealed that boys had frequently committed robberies for the purpose of paying their admission. A 13-year-old admitted, 'I took a handkerchief out of a man's pocket. I did not want anything but some money to go to Holloway's, where there was acting.' A 12-year-old with three convictions frequented the theatre with money acquired by stealing: 'he used to go twice a week to the theatre, sometimes to the Liver; the Sans Pareil is the one liked best [...] he never met any of the Liverpool boys, either at Lancaster Castle or Kirkdale [prisons], who he has not seen at the theatres'.[62]

In 1841 the prison inspector was so alarmed at the influence of the stage that he questioned 91 boys in the Borough Gaol to find out how familiar they were with the theatres. Many admitted to meeting bad characters there and being led astray. 'We always made our plans at or coming from the theatres', said one 15-year-old with 14 previous spells in prison. In addition to the Sans Pareil and the Liver, favourite venues included the Penny Hop in Hood Street, which catered mainly for younger boys, the Queen's and the Amphitheatre in Roe Street. Shows were also staged outside the Custom House. One lad spoke of the Penny Hop as a 'breaking-in place for boys'. Some children laid claim to hundreds of visits to the theatres. Youths spoke of theatre attendance as something akin to drug addiction: 'I got the first two or three pennies honestly,' one boy admitted. 'After that I was so much enchanted with the place, and had such a desire to go, that I stole from my mother.'[63]

Thefts were committed inside the Sans Pareil. At the end of the performance, as the crowd filed downstairs, boys on the balcony would reach through the railings to steal hats and shawls. The surge of the crowd meant that the victims had little chance of retrieving their clothing. Lads would also creep under the seats to pick and sometimes cut open the pockets of the audience. Boys would leave the theatre at so late an hour that they would be too afraid to go home. They slept in privies and lofts and this was often the beginning of them staying permanently away from home and eventually fending for themselves.

Although some lads denied that they had ever been influenced by the play, one of the most influential factors on youth crime was a dramatization of the life of Jack Sheppard, the infamous thief and gaol-breaker who was hanged in 1724. If theatre could transport young audiences to new and wonderful imaginative worlds, it could also inspire them with shocking tales of crime and wickedness. The following excerpts, taken from discussions with various young prisoners aged 9 to 18, are revealing:

I have seen Jack Sheppard performed. I think it will be the means of indu-cing boys to copy his tricks […] He was a wonderful chap. My mother has a picture of him hanging up in our house […] I had his life [the biography], but some boy took it from me; most boys have his life […] He was a clever fellow […] I have seen many boys buy his history […] If I was only as clever I should be thought one of the best of thieves […] A wonderful chap in robbing houses and breaking out of prison […] He was a capital example for those that followed the trade.

A man living in Gore Street often read the life of Jack Sheppard to gather-ings of men and boys. One lad claimed, 'I think there is none like him.' After watching Sheppard on stage picking a pocket, another boy admitted, 'It gave every one a great insight how to do it.' Another young criminal, however, dismissed Sheppard: 'I don't think anything of him; there is better men now than ever he was; if prisons were only now, as they were in his day, his tricks would look foolish.' At the Penny Hop, a performance of the play had to be abandoned as a result of frequent interruptions by the audience, who seemed to wish to take part.[64]

Such rowdy conduct became even more of a problem in the real-life public arena. On the Victorian streets young people's behaviour was increasingly contested and challenged. Street-corner gatherings were treated with growing suspicion, particularly in the 1870s and 1880s, contributing to widespread fears of unruly youths and a breakdown in law and order. Yet bad behaviour on the streets and indeed in the theatres has a long history in Liverpool.

SEVENTEEN

Gangs and Anti-Social Behaviour

Georgian Rowdies

Present-day concerns about anti-social behaviour go right back to the eighteenth century if not even earlier, to rowdy apprentices causing mayhem. Contemporary historians have left us vivid, lively and often unflattering pictures of life on the streets of late eighteenth-century Liverpool, although it must be remembered that these views belong to the educated middle classes recording their distaste for the behaviour of their social inferiors. One chronicler, in 1795, described large numbers of girls and lower-class citizens entertaining themselves in the evening in the narrow streets, much to the annoyance of peace-loving residents: 'even the squares are not exempt from this nuisance, where it is common to see boys and girls playing at ball, and other diversions, every Sunday afternoon'.[1] According to Thomas Troughton the latest craze in the 1770s was for lower-class youths to snatch nosegays from the cleavages of ladies out walking. Some unfortunate victims received 'violent blows on the breast'. Alehouse banter and the Liverpool sport of leg-pulling were very much alive: 'It was a common practice for witlings in the public houses, to make some irritable individual the object of ridicule, for the amusement of the rest of the company.' There was also the scandalous practice of impudent young men circulating handbills in which young ladies were offered for sale. Even wealthy youths were expected to get involved in brawls and other outrageous behaviour. Towards the end of the century, night-time riots involving hotheaded young men known as 'Bloods' were a regular occurrence, with innocent members of the public often targeted. Two respectable men, walking in Lord Street late one evening, were knocked down and beaten up by a gang of 'Bloods'.[2]

The returning crews of the Liverpool privateers were a brutish and anarchic bunch, responsible for many riotous incidents around the dockside district. The inns and 'slop' clothes-sellers shops in Pool Lane (now South Castle Street) would be heaving with sailors eager to squander their hard-earned prize money. Such extravagant conduct would attract the attention of prostitutes, some of whom would later betray the men to the press-gang.[3] The anti-social behaviour of the privateer crews was a cause of great concern to the authorities, particularly after a group went on the rampage and rescued some men who had been seized by the press-gang. Mayor William Pole was forced to issue a caution in 1778, warning 'armed' and 'riotous' seamen that their disgraceful conduct would not be tolerated.[4]

The town's unruliness can also be gauged by the public's appalling behaviour at the theatre. It was the custom at the Theatre Royal in Williamson Square to employ only London performers. Despite threats from disgruntled audiences, on 15 June 1778 the lessees of the theatre tried to introduce a season of little-known provincial actors. On opening night there were ominous signs of disorder. Before the play began, Mr Younger, one of the lessees, took to the stage in an attempt to calm the audience. However, they simply 'threw up their hats, hissed, kicked, stamped, bawled [...] and saluted with volleys of potatoes and broken bottles'. Younger wisely decided to make a quick exit. The audience went on to invade the stage, extinguish the lights with their hats and finally take back their money. It was reported that every wall in the town was afterwards covered with graffiti expressing contempt for the unfortunate actors.[5]

Patrons of the same theatre would also urinate into the boxes and pit. In 1795 a local newspaper reported that 'several boxes were evacuated last night in consequence of the streams which descended from above, and some of the company in the pit had their clothes soiled in the same abominable manner'.[6] A year later, the theatre's unruly clientele were again reprimanded: 'more turbulent, indecent, tasteless audiences [...] have seldom, I believe, assembled within the precincts of any theatre, amphitheatre, barn, booth or stable'.[7] In 1798 the manager of the theatre was forced to publish a notice in the newspapers, informing readers that he would prosecute any person found insulting the audience and performers by throwing bottles and missiles from the gallery. Despite the warning, incidents continued. The following year, a potentially lethal quart bottle was thrown, which fortunately missed its target. Casualties were inevitable, however, and in January 1800 Thomas Hawkes was imprisoned for hitting a lady on the head with a glass bottle thrown from the gallery. Four years later crowds besieged the theatre to see a child acting protégé known as Young Roscius. People had their clothes torn off and lost their hats and shoes in the struggle for admission.[8]

Audience behaviour in Georgian Britain was not always characterized by mindless vandalism. Sometimes the disorder was a response to perceived attacks on deeply held beliefs about justice and fairness. In September 1809, at London's Covent Garden Theatre, grievances over increases in ticket prices and the conversion of inexpensive seats into rented boxes for the wealthy led to 67 days of disorder known as the 'old-price' riots.[9] Each night the audience engaged in a series of carefully staged, almost theatrical, activities designed to disrupt the performances. Banners and placards were waved, mock battles fought in the pits and fireworks ignited. Eight months later, at the Theatre Royal, the so called 'half-price riots' took place after the management withdrew the offer of cheap tickets. In an echo of the London protests, the audience disturbed a performance by using flappers, horns and whistles before smashing all the windows in the theatre. The mob dispersed only after the Riot Act was read.[10] A handbill, reading like a declaration of war, was also distributed:

> Now sound your bugle horns my lads,
> Your catcalls whistle all,
> And boldly for your British rights,
> Like noble Briton's call.
> Ring out ye trumpets, blow horns blow,
> And soon the manager must go;
> Sound all your lungs for Britain's laws,
> For Half-price and the good old cause.[11]

The protestors were not poor people who could no longer afford admission. Among those arrested were a broker, an attorney and some clerks, who were sentenced to between two and twelve months' imprisonment. Both the Liverpool and London episodes show the British public keen to defend traditional rights and customs. Other disturbances, however, were motivated by less noble ideals. On 3 June 1810 there was small riot over the rival claims of two actors. Supporters of each went on the rampage, tearing up the gallery seats and throwing them into the pit.[12] In 1824 theatregoers were still smashing furniture and fittings over the substitution of billed performers.[13]

Growing Intolerance

Despite these outbursts of riotous indignation, in the burgeoning urban towns of the nineteenth century the 'respectable classes' became increasingly less tolerant of anti-social behaviour, particularly among the lower classes. Street gamblers, prostitutes, hawkers, gangs of youths skulking on street corners, vandalism, swearing and rough children's games were all condemned as a public nuisance. There were numerous factors that helped focus attention on these unacceptable activities. The formation of the modern police force in Liverpool in 1835 led to increased targeting of troublesome individuals who were dragged off the streets and into the criminal justice system. Yet even before the establishment of a rigorous and robust system of beat policing, members of the public were demanding the moral cleansing of the streets. In 1826 there were complaints about 'a gang of idle and disorderly young men and boys' on waste ground in Great Charlotte Street, opposite St John's Market. The gang would loiter around camp fires smoking pipes. Rather than work, they lived upon produce stolen from the market, such as eggs which they would cook over the fires. On one occasion they recklessly lit a fire under a cart which was nearly consumed by the flames. The gang's lack of employment and idleness were of as much concern as their actual behaviour.[14] In 1830 the public was alerted to the number of drunken men and women who infested Dale Street. It was difficult for pedestrians to pass them without being verbally assaulted with indecent language.[15]

The growth of popular newspapers created a forum for readers to share views and opinions. This led to columns of letters featuring complaints about every subject imaginable. A single letter would provoke a flurry of responses further highlighting pressing social problems. This was particularly the case with readers' grumbles about public nuisance. Anti-social behaviour clearly took many forms. Noise nuisance after dark, for example, was a common complaint. In 1862 Water Street, near the docks, was the scene of unbearable rowdiness, with frequent cries of 'murder' and 'police' piercing the midnight air. There were reports of disgusting language from men and women, together with regular threats and fights.[16] Daytime noise also provoked the public's anger, particularly the amount of swearing and filthy language shouted in the streets. Lewd and disgusting banter between young men and women seemed commonplace.[17]

Children were constantly criticized for lacking discipline and respect for others. Nothing was sacred. In 1870 the Sunday school at Christ Church in Hunter Street was beset by anti-social behaviour. Teachers were targeted by 'young roughs and big roughs' who would assemble outside the church shouting abuse at the clergyman. Some played marbles inside the churchyard and one of the lads even spat in the face of a teacher.[18] Mindless vandalism was another concern. One man complained of having to replace three panes of glass damaged by stone-throwing children.[19] Throwing stones at passing trains was another popular pastime for children, sometimes supplemented by placing objects on the tracks.[20]

Children's Games

Children at play were a major source of complaint, particularly when they engaged in potentially dangerous throwing and hitting games. Every evening, on the waste ground between Myrtle Street and Cambridge Street, youngsters would indulge in the physically related but morally diverse sports of cricket and stone throwing. In 1869 a lady was knocked unconscious after being hit by a ball. The noise and dust raised by the play was also said to be intolerable to the nearby residents.[21] A game called 'tip cat', or 'peggy', was considered to be far more dangerous than simple bat and ball.[22] The game was widely played and was said to be 'raging throughout the metropolis' in the 1850s.[23] A small pointed stick (called a 'cat') was laid on the floor. Using a longer stick (called a 'dog') the player would sharply tap the pointed stick so that it jumped into the air. When it reached a suitable height, the cat would be whacked with the dog, sending it as far as possible, with little concern for innocent pedestrians who happened to be in the way.[24] The game was popular in Liverpool in the 1870s and 1880s and was responsible for blinding a few members of the public, including children. A newspaper correspondent complained that it was difficult to pass through Liverpool's crowded streets without 'having our eyes knocked out by bits of wood pointed at both ends, and sent flying in all directions by a parcel of boys'.[25]

Even seemingly innocent games had the potential to bring down society. In 1832 a visitor to Liverpool complained about the lack of police and the hundreds of children that infested the streets playing whip and top and swearing at people who interrupted their game. He felt that the problem was 'peculiar to Liverpool'.[26] Another reader complained about the 30 to 40 children who constantly plagued the Exchange, playing whip and top, marbles and hide-and-seek behind the pillars.[27] Fifty years later, a reader was still protesting about boys whipping tops in the street. The gentleman had already been cut with a whip and wondered why the police didn't put a stop to the game. The letter provoked angry replies stating that the game was an 'innocent and healthy recreation' and that these sturdy young whippers 'will probably some day be showing the world how Englishmen can whip their country's enemies'. 'Boys will be boys', was the conclusion. The original complainant replied that a lady had been hit with a whip in Scotland Road and when she remonstrated with the boys she was called foul names and told to get out of the way.[28] Another reader suggested offering children alternative forms of play. He argued that the playing of games such as 'peggy' and cricket was 'one of the most hopeful signs of civilisation amongst them'. These activities at least involved co-operative play and were therefore better than selfish gambling pursuits such as pitch and toss or standing on street corners smoking.[29]

Throwing and hitting games were supplemented and eventually overtaken by kicking games, particularly as football took hold in the city. The growing popularity of street football diverted generations of children away from mischief and into sport. The game, however, proved an even greater menace, as broken windows and shattered gas lamps became the sad but inevitable by-product of matches. In 1862 Leeds Street was the scene of boisterous Sunday afternoon football games, with some matches lasting up to three hours, much to the annoyance of neighbours.[30] A Toxteth reader complained that the summer street football season was giving way to the autumn custom of 'noisy brats' throwing fireworks, squibs and crackers around the streets.[31] Once again, the letter provoked an angry reply. Someone objected to God's children being called 'brats' and warned the complainant not to be too fond of quietness for he would one day have all the peace he wanted in the grave.[32]

A running theme throughout such letters is the question, 'Where are the police?' It was felt that the beat constables needed to be more pro-active in tackling anti-social behaviour. Yet some officers probably felt that they had better things to do than break up children's games. A perceived lack of response from the police led some people to take the law into their own hands. A baker from Great Howard Street was so annoyed at lads constantly playing whip and top near his shop that when some boys dared to loiter on his cellar grid, he thrust a sharp stick through the grating, seriously damaging a young lad's genitals.[33] Eliza Peacock threw a cup of carbolic acid in the face of a 10-year-old after his ball accidentally rolled into her cellar and his pals refused her request to play elsewhere.[34] Reverend Hicks, a pastor from Bootle, had long been harassed by boys playing marbles and gambling in a field near his home. When he saw an innocent lad holding a football he went over and thrashed him with his umbrella, causing a nasty wound to his forehead.[35]

It is clear that a major cause of anti-social behaviour was a lack of recreational space. In the absence of purpose-built playgrounds where they could let off steam, children made their own play areas out of pieces of waste ground. A reader in 1858 complained that there were no suitable areas in the crowded northern districts for boys to play cricket or ball games.[36] The south-east had Wavertree Park, opened in 1856, while from 1862 east Liverpool would house Sheil Park. Eleven years later, another reader lamented the fact that Parliament Fields was now enclosed and out of bounds, leaving young people in the south end with nowhere to go.[37] Another reader complained that far from preventing people from using Parliament Fields for recreational purposes, the fencing off of the area had created an enclosed space where disorderly individuals could meet and indulge in anti-social pursuits such as Sunday dog racing, fighting, football and pitch and toss.[38] Indeed, the boards erected around the field merely created a sheltered environment for people to devise their own entertainment out of sight of the police. Around this time an intense spell of recreational provision saw the opening of Newsham Park in 1868, followed by Stanley Park in 1870 and Sefton Park two years later. At last there was plenty of open space and fresh air for people to enjoy.[39] The abundance of grass, however, failed to put an end to street games. A lack of public transport meant that a trip to the park was out of the question for many, particularly younger children who continued to play in the crowded areas nearer home.

Street Gangs

A more sinister example of anti-social behaviour than rowdy games was the practice of pushing people off the pavements. A related nuisance was 'holding the street', whereby youths on street corners would block the pavement and refuse to let pedestrians pass, forcing them to divert into the road. A group of youths would sometimes walk together along the street, making sure that approaching pedestrians had to move out of the way. Lime Street, for example, was home to 'heavy gangs of rowdy young ruffians [...] linked arm in arm, and with hats thrown backwards, and sticks in hand'. In a threatening manner, they would 'jostle and shout [...] and swear'.[40] A married couple walking along Market Street on a Sunday evening in 1866 were confronted by a gang of about 18 youths at the corner of Adelphi Street. The lads blocked their progress before stealing the lady's shawl and knocking the man's hat off his head.[41] Around the same time, residents in St Domingo Road, Everton, were being plagued by up to 30 young men, aged 16 to 25, who would assemble on the street corner 'for the express purpose of annoying and insulting the passers-by'. Their special trick was tying a length of string to a railing across the road. When pedestrians approached, the lads would sharply pull the string so that it caught the victims under the nose or knocked their hats off.[42] Stealing, crushing or knocking hats and caps from the heads of passing strangers was good fun for pranksters but often the prelude to violence, depending on the reaction of the victim. Known as 'bonneting', such behaviour was often fuelled by alcohol.

Nor were unruly gangs unique to the overcrowded and slum-stricken inner-city districts. In 1862, in West Derby village, a few miles from the town centre, about 15 youths would regularly congregate outside a beershop near the Cross every Sunday, assailing churchgoers with offensive language.[43] Anti-social behaviour in the area was highlighted again almost thirty years later. A resident complained about stone and mud throwing and called for more police around Crosby Green and Mill Lane to protect property damaged by gangs.[44] Otherwise respectable outlying districts such as Walton Breck Road were also persecuted by street-corner ruffians who would insult pedestrians and threaten violence to anyone who remonstrated with them.[45]

People were understandably wary of passing intimidating groups of youths, for fear of being spat upon, verbally abused, pelted with mud or elbowed off the pavement. The uneasiness was part of a wider concern relating to both youths and unemployed men who gathered outside the public houses. The perception of an increasingly lawless and feckless underclass, lacking a work ethic, provided a constant threat to Victorian ideas of social order, harmony and progress. *Porcupine* published a letter from an angry reader:

> Any person who is much in the streets of the north end of Liverpool must daily see numbers of men who by their very aspect and demeanour show that they belong to a class who, whilst they evidently do not starve, as evidently do not work, or, if at all, but very seldom. These men may be seen in parties of five or six loafing about the ends of streets or near the public-houses with which the neighbourhoods abound.[46]

By the 1870s these Cornermen had become a common feature of Liverpool's streets. Their rowdy behaviour and habit of monopolizing the pavement caused endless grief for the police and public alike. Most were not criminals, or even members of gangs as such, but unrelated groups of youths and young men peculiar to each neighbourhood. Nevertheless, their anti-social behaviour occupied the press for a number of years, particularly following the death of Richard Morgan in 1874 after he refused to hand over some beer money to a group of youths. The murder inflated a mere street nuisance into a potentially lethal hazard. In the words of *Porcupine*: 'The ruffians who infest the corners of our Liverpool streets [...] are ready for any deed of mischief and violence, from "pitch and toss" to manslaughter.'[47] Street-corner gangs did not even have to commit crime or cause trouble to be judged a public menace. Their sheer force of numbers and fearsome reputation simply terrified the public, even if the fear was often unwarranted. If young people were criticized for creating noise by playing rowdy and dangerous games, youths were also condemned for literally doing nothing. For some, loitering was worse than street football.

Cornermen became a 'Liverpool synonym for whatever is bone lazy, cowardly and brutal'.[48] Although most Cornermen were not aggressive, their presence on the streets was linked to an increase in violence. In 1875 it was reported that the yearly average of serious assaults in Liverpool during the previous ten years was 240. The figure for 1873 was 260 and that for 1874, the year that Morgan was killed, was 292. In sarcastic vein, a journal asked: 'Who says that the physical energies of the British people are deteriorating?'[49]

Tackling Anti-Social Behaviour

By the 1880s the existence of this seemingly wasted generation forced the middle classes to confront some urgent social problems of the Victorian age, including unstable employment, excessive drinking, patchy educational provision and a lack of suitable facilities to engage young people. A mixture of charitable concern and a fear of unruly youths led to a double-headed assault on the street-corner gangs. On the one hand, the police and judiciary were urged to get tough. Alarm about gangs resurfaced after the first High Rip murder in January 1884. Cornermen were once again headline news. At the beginning of April there was a crackdown on the street-corner menace, said to have been tolerated for years. Seventeen loiterers were dealt with in court followed closely by another batch of 21 men. At the end of the month several more groups were arrested for obstructing footpaths in the northern districts of Scotland Road and Vauxhall Road.[50] Some people still weren't satisfied. The following month, a reader congratulated the police on clearing up the Cornermen from Scotland Road before asking them to turn their attention to the 'number of big rough girls, without shoes and stockings, who parade the road nightly'.[51] Another reader wanted the crackdown extended to hawkers and children playing in the street.[52] For the public, the remedy for the Cornerman problem was always 'move them on', although nobody quite knew where to. Yet the clampdowns were sometimes counter-productive since they criminalized otherwise law-abiding citizens. In 1887 a magistrate warned over-zealous police officers to be more discriminating as to who they targeted for loitering, after four respectable young men were arrested for standing near a church in Mill Street. They were waiting for their Bible class.[53]

While some people urged tougher sanctions, philanthropists and churchmen focused on providing help and support to the Cornermen. Readers of a Christian publication called *Plain Talk* were asked to befriend the Cornermen, even invite them to the baker's shop to treat them to a loaf of bread.[54] The message was the Victorian equivalent of the 'hug-a-hoodie' attitude attributed to Conservative Party leader David Cameron in 2006.[55] Kindness might have seemed an unlikely weapon to be used against the Cornermen, yet this approach was part of a growing movement that preferred to view such groups as victims rather than miscreants. The 1873 Annual General Meeting of the Liverpool Industrial and Ragged Schools recognized that the 'young savages of the 19th century [...] are largely made what they are by circumstances over which they have no control'. Life in the squalid courts was partly to blame. Little wonder was it that they became paupers and criminals after developing 'habits of idleness, drunkenness and vice'. A speaker felt that the 'apprentices of anarchy' could be transformed through industrial education and training.[56]

While the public continued to advocate the fining, flogging and imprisonment of offenders, experts working in the criminal justice field continued looking for the causes of criminal behaviour. In the *Sunday Magazine*, another religious monthly journal, published in 1886, Revd J. W. Horsley wrote that 'the perverted taste for lollipops, caused chiefly by mothers, is a large – very large – cause of juvenile crime'. Horsley, a former chaplain of Clerkenwell Prison, believed that a craving for confectionery was worse than smoking tobacco. In light-hearted vein, a satirical magazine claimed that the recent spate of violent crime in Liverpool, probably caused by the High Rip, had been traced to a large consignment of American caramels.[57] Given current concerns over the adverse effects of additives in children's sweets, particularly their potential for causing anti-social behaviour, the Reverend gentleman might not have been far off the mark.

This early link between diet and criminality was an attempt to understand why people turned to crime rather than simply punishing them for doing so. Social environment and upbringing also became increasingly important factors in explaining criminal tendencies. For one newspaper, it was not only conditions of squalor and poverty but the lack of sunlight and the absence of trees, flowers and birdsong around the Scotland Road area that turned people bad. It was acknowledged that the boisterous energies of many slum children were being wasted in criminality and needed to be re-channelled into worthier pursuits. When 17-year-old Michael McLean became the first High Ripper to hang for murder, the comment was made that had he been educated at Eton instead of being left to the schooling of the streets, he might have achieved posthumous military glory as a hero on the battlefield.[58]

If children's games were a social problem, they were also seen as the solution to anti-social behaviour. The public school ethos of organized sports and character-building activities, promoting discipline, teamwork and physical wellbeing, became increasingly important and resulted in the development of boys' clubs. The Gordon Working Lads Institute in Kirkdale, named after the famous military leader, opened its doors in 1886, at the height of the High Rip scare. Three years later saw the foundation of the Florence Institute in Mill Street in the south end. Both establishments laid great emphasis on physical recreation as a remedy for rowdyism.[59] This link between physical fitness and moral welfare was important in reversing the decline into barbarism felt to be widespread in the slum areas. It was also related to fears over the physical deterioration of a generation of young people needed to defend the country in the future. In 1886 young members of the Cadet Corps, or Boys Brigade, of the 8th Lancashire Artillery Volunteers performed outdoor drill exercises in the south end. It was felt to be a 'means of keeping them off the streets and from becoming corner loafers'.[60] No doubt the fit new recruits could also, in future, add to the regiments of Englishmen whipping foreign enemies abroad.

Despite various philanthropic, municipal and government initiatives, including the creation of boys' clubs, the provision of playing fields and compulsory education, anti-social behaviour persisted. In 1897 a flurry of street disorder came to the attention of Mr Stewart, the stipendiary magistrate. Faced with a huge number of cases of disorderly conduct and offensive behaviour the magistrate did not hesitate to impose harsh punishments, ranging from hefty fines to imprisonment. Newspapers congratulated Stewart for taking a stand against the gangs of foul-mouthed ruffians who found it amusing to push respectable pedestrians off the pavements or brutally assault them. It was hoped that such drastic action would provide an example to other magistrates who so far had merely played around with the villains.[61]

Yet even in the face of regular police crackdowns, the street-corner gangs remained a threat to members of the public. Casual employment, the persistence of poor housing and the abundance of public houses almost guaranteed their existence well into the twentieth century where, despite further social improvements, they mutated into the 'young bucks' of the 1920s and successive youth gangs such as the Teddy Boys and skinheads, culminating in the 'hoodies' of today.

EIGHTEEN

Prostitution

During his stay in Liverpool in 1847 the American writer Ralph Waldo Emerson asked friends whether prostitution remained as 'gross' a problem as when he had first visited the town over a decade earlier, when 'no boy could grow up safe'. He was told that it was no better or worse.[1] As a major seaport, Liverpool had always attracted prostitutes. Thomas Troughton recalls the 'unrestrained licentiousness' of the town in 1773, bustling with 'common prostitutes, parading the public streets, in all the fashionable elegances of dress, or conveyed in chairs and carriages to the public amusements'.[2]

Police and prison statistics give a clue to the number of prostitutes in the nineteenth century, bearing in mind that not all of them were arrested. In 1837 the Head Constable identified 400 brothels, each housing an average of five women. There were also about 2,000 prostitutes living in lodging-houses, a total of over 4,000 women.[3] Dr William Sanger estimated that in 1839 the sailors' quarter alone supported about 2,900 prostitutes. Modern historians suspect this to be only a third of the actual number.[4] Relative to its size, Liverpool was arguably Victorian England's 'capital of prostitution'.[5]

The geography of prostitution was widespread. Women loitered about the Sailors' Home waiting for the men to be paid. Indeed, the entire waterfront district, from Lancelot's Hey through Castle Street, from Wapping to Park Lane and Paradise Street, right down to Parliament Street, was inhabited by prostitutes.[6] In 1830 a member of the public complained about the disorderly behaviour at the corner of Bold Street and Hanover Street where 'unfortunate women and their associates' would keep residents awake until the early hours.[7] The south end district of Windsor had its own 'little hell', inhabited mostly by 'unfortunates'.[8] Williamson Square was a notorious vice spot littered with gambling dens and taverns. There were 100 brothels in the neighbourhood, with one street boasting 22 such establishments.[9] Residents from the St Anne Street district complained to the Head Constable about frequent disturbances. Each night hordes of harlots from the area would trek to Williamson Square to 'ply their vocation'. Returning around midnight in the company of sailors, they would stop off at the local eating houses, causing a nuisance to their neighbours.[10]

Lime Street

To this day, however, Lime Street in the city centre is remembered as Liverpool's most infamous vice district. In Victorian times, between 11 p.m. and 1 a.m., the more wealthy prostitutes would parade up and down in their finery, while their poorer sisters would dart in and out of the public houses harassing drinkers. If soliciting in the pubs was bad, the coffee shops 'were even worse'.[11] The entire entertainment industry was devoted to the flesh trade. Following the publication of Hugh Shimmin's exposé of the town's sordid night-life in his 'Liverpool Life' series, the Society for the Suppression of Vicious Practices was founded with the aim of waging war on the offending establishments. In 1857 an inspector from the Society visited the Amphitheatre and filed a damning report: 'unrebuked acts of gross indecency were committed in the refreshment room by a notoriously depraved woman who was intoxicated'. The circle area around the pit had long been used as a promenade by prostitutes plying their trade. A train of them, headed by their madam, would file into the area at about 9 p.m. She would chat to familiar customers, broker deals and point out each girl's particular talents. After pairing off, the couples would move on to Domville's Assembly Room, otherwise known as 'the Hop', before visiting the Supper Rooms next door. They would then retire to the 'night houses' or brothels at the back of Lime Street. In the financial arrangements between prostitutes and their madams, an allowance would be made to pay for visits to such establishments. 'The Hop' was a large dancing saloon where 50 to 100 prostitutes gathered nightly, along with an equal number of men and youths. The inspector's report spared no blushes: 'Ribaldry, blasphemy, lechery, profligacy, wantonness, and waste were the order of the night; vice ran riot, abandoned wretches in the form of women, demons in the shape of men, held their orgies there.' Other establishments were equally shameless. The Parthenon was a cigar divan situated next to a public house called Reynolds Vaults in Great Charlotte Street. The upper storey was a free concert room where 'poses plastiques, tableaux vivants and the singing of coarse and obscene songs' took place. Poses plastiques were the nearest the Victorians got to a strip show. From July to September 1857, 30 to 40 prostitutes attended each night. Young men who bought a bottle of wine were allowed to mix with the performers in the dressing rooms backstage.[12]

Lime Street offered, 'old and young, French, Belgian, English […] a veritable market for the sale of flesh'. A journalist warned: 'The modest lady […] who permits herself to walk unattended through Lime Street after ten o'clock on Saturday night must not complain if she be subjected to unwelcome misapprehension.'[13] Alderman Samuel Holme once took an evening stroll along the street, an experience 'so shocking, dreadful and repulsive' that he felt quite ashamed of his own town. The street 'literally swarmed with prostitutes from end to end'. These most 'un-womanlike' women pulled at his coat and he was 'publicly solicited' as he walked along.[14] Rail passengers leaving the station were also accosted.[15] The women could not be blamed for trying their luck, for the street was the 'vortex to which hurried all the middle-class immorality of the town'.[16] Yet although the street attracted the punters, the girls also had to spread their net wide. Prostitutes were, by necessity, migratory. To escape police attention they travelled from public house to public house in search of customers, not staying long enough to attract attention. By 1893 women had moved out of the city centre to occupy outlying areas such as Walton Road, Kirkdale Road, Netherfield Road, West Derby Road, Smithdown Road and Lodge Lane.[17]

The Causes of Prostitution

In 1843, at the Music Hall, Revd Bevan gave a talk on the evils of prostitution. He listed the various causes of the trade in Liverpool, including the seduction of girls by wicked men and what he termed 'voluntary prostitution', motivated by 'unbridled lust' in the girls themselves. Depravity among young people was another factor: 'the youth of Liverpool have become notorious for their disregard of morality and law. My own eyes and ears have been assailed at midday, and in the open street, with conversations and acts among the budding childhood of the town, which have startled and agonized me.' Destitution was another reason. Women without food or lodgings were forced to sell their bodies. The vulgarity of Liverpool's public houses and music halls was considered enough to turn some girls astray. Drink was another factor guaranteed to loosen morals. Some girls were also enticed into the profession by older women who had graduated to become procuresses.[18] Father Nugent offered further reasons. He felt that orphans were particularly prone to prostitution, as were children of second marriages who were often forced into lodgings by an uncaring step-parent. These young women then had to fend for themselves.[19] Liverpool police surgeon Frederick Lowndes identified a love of fine clothes, laziness and a weakness for alcohol as three of the most common causes.[20]

Not all prostitutes were full-timers; some merely dabbled in the trade. 'Dollymops' were casual prostitutes who occasionally went with men to supplement their meagre incomes. They were described as young women 'from the bare-headed class, with hair twisted into a knot on the top of their head, and with shoulders covered with small plaid shawls'.[21] A female brothel-keeper stated that if the police paid less attention to the professional girls and devoted more time to the semi-professionals they would find richer pickings.[22]

Many prostitutes were drawn from the ranks of the Irish poor. Figures show that in 1853 almost 44 per cent of prostitutes taken into custody in Liverpool for disorderly behaviour were Irish. Furthermore, the 26 per cent who came from Liverpool probably included a fair number of Liverpool-Irish Catholics.[23] In 1865 Father Nugent pointed out that 62 per cent of prisoners in Walton Gaol were Irish Catholics, 'with a considerable proportion committed for prostitution'.[24] All this may simply prove that Irish girls were more likely to have been targeted and arrested.[25] However, a speaker at a conference organized in 1858 came to the same conclusion: 'Our prostitutes (as our criminals and paupers) are nearly all Irish.'[26] Father Nugent argued that few Irish girls came to Liverpool with the specific intention of selling their bodies. They would more usually migrate expecting to find work but end up destitute before turning to prostitution. What also happened was that young women became pregnant in Ireland and fled to Liverpool to give birth to escape family and social pressures. The pound or two given to them by their seducers would not have lasted long, forcing some to go on the game. Liverpool-Irish prostitutes were accused of corrupting and exploiting naive Irish girls who had migrated to Liverpool. These 'harpies' would befriend a girl and pretend that they came from the same part of Ireland. They would then offer her lodgings before 'plunging her into an abyss of misery, from which, alas, there is seldom any escape'.[27]

Any discussion of prostitution in Liverpool must not overlook the employment situation for women. Dr Sanger produced figures that showed that Liverpool had one prostitute for every 88 inhabitants, whereas Manchester had one for every 325 inhabitants.[28] In 1846 police reported that there were 538 brothels in Liverpool as against 200 in Manchester.[29] Leaving aside the fact that Liverpool was a seaport full of sailors, it is noteworthy that regular work for women in Liverpool was limited and for this reason the destitute were sometimes driven to sell their bodies. Liverpool employment was largely based around the docks and shipping and was restricted to men. During a visit to the West Derby workhouse, Nathaniel Hawthorne saw that lads could at least be taught a trade to guarantee some sort of future. For the girls, however, job prospects were bleaker, with many destined to lead 'shifting and precarious lives, and finally drop into the slough of evil'.[30] Liverpool had no important industry suitable for women and boasted few large factories.[31] There was some factory work in the food and tobacco, paper and sack-making industries but nothing to compare to industrialized Manchester, which had the cotton mills that at least offered women some form of employment. The *Liverpool Review* claimed that 'there are more wretched women, fewer honourable occupations for women and poorer wages in this city than in any other part of the country'. The solution? 'There must be more opportunity for single women to earn a respectable livelihood.'[32] Yet even married women in the slum districts were rarely financially stable. Owing to the low and casual wages of their husbands, women's earnings were of vital importance to the economic survival of the family. Also, while men were away at sea, women were forced to provide for their families.

It is understandable that such intermittent and profitless labour as 'slop work' was sometimes supplemented by prostitution. Father Nugent estimated that the maximum wage earned by a woman doing sewing was 10s a week, with younger sewers averaging between 2s and 4s. On the other hand, a woman who went 'to a dancing room and pick[ed] up with a sailor, or the officer of a ship' could easily earn up to £2 or £3 a week.[33] There were dangers, of course, not least the threat of a debilitating sexual disease. For the most desperate and impoverished women, prostitution offered not so much a career path as an unenviable choice between consumption and syphilis.

For some women, prostitution was an economic necessity. Immoral earnings liberated some women from lives of cheerless and grinding poverty. For others, the profession promised a life of glamour and excitement beyond the stinking courts. Successful prostitutes could eat well, afford fashionable clothes and enjoy nights out. What might be viewed as men exploiting vulnerable young women might also be seen as canny women using rich men to make easy money and a better life for themselves. It was believed that the sexual innuendos of music hall entertainment corrupted working-class girls and made them easy prey for predatory men.[34] The opposite might have been true. At the Royal Casino in Blundell Street, in 1856, Hugh Shimmin saw women 'slapping the men on the cheeks, pulling them by the whiskers, dragging them off the seats by the legs, or trying to do so, whispering and drinking with, swearing at, caressing, cajoling and kissing them'.[35] In theory at least, single prostitutes enjoyed economic independence and freedom from oppressive male authority in both the domestic and work spheres. In practice, they were often slaves to bullies and madams and were frequently mistreated by their clients. Still, for some, self-employment on the streets was arguably better than slaving away for others for fourteen hours a day in return for a pittance.

Supply and Demand

The *Liverpool Review* asked a pertinent question about the world's oldest profession: 'Does the supply create the demand or does the demand create the supply?'[36] If Liverpool had a surplus of prostitutes, it also had a voracious demand for them. By 1886 there were an estimated 40,000 to 50,000 seamen present in Liverpool at any one time.[37] They would sail home on a wave of testosterone, singing:

> And when we get to Liverpool docks,
> There we shall see the c_nt in flocks!
> One to another they will say,
> 'O, welcome Jack with his three years pay!
> For he is homeward bo-ou-ound,
> For he is homeward bound!'[38]

Prostitutes of every shade, shape and nationality scoured the streets and taverns soliciting for custom. Brothels and public houses lay indecently close to each other, the joyful roar of sea shanties drowning out the moans of more illicit pleasures. What made Liverpool unique was not simply the mass of sex-starved sailors but a piece of legislation that drove many of them into the arms of prostitutes. In 1802 a raging fire devastated the Goree warehouses, destroying a great deal of grain, sugar, coffee and cotton. So intense was the blaze that the ruins smouldered for nearly three months afterwards, leaving damage estimated at £330,000. Not long afterwards, a boat went ablaze at the docks. Although the flames were quickly extinguished, the incident alarmed both merchants and fire insurance officers who feared another disaster. The disquiet led to a provision in a subsequent Dock Act banning fires and lights on any vessel berthed at Liverpool. Other ports, such as London, allowed naked flame up to a certain hour of the evening.

The law had huge implications for Liverpool. Since sailors could no longer cook on board their vessels or safely remain in their pitch-black berths in the evening, they were practically driven ashore in search of food, warmth and comfort. Some ended up in disreputable establishments where temptations led them astray. One captain complained that his crew, in search of lodging-houses, had to pass through the most depraved districts and were constantly accosted by prostitutes. After spending all their money on alcohol and sex, some were reduced to pawning their possessions to provide funds. It was also claimed that several men who were 'sober moral captains' became ruined after a stint in Liverpool.[39] Promiscuous sailors were particularly prone to venereal infections. Frederick Lowndes quipped that some able seamen were so diseased that they should have been renamed disabled seamen.[40]

Lowndes felt that the low wages most seafarers earned discouraged them from getting married and led some young men to settle for prostitutes.[41] Father Nugent believed that up to 75 per cent of a sailor's money was spent on drink and prostitution. Some prostitutes would live with a sailor until his money ran out before moving on to another.[42] Women with more stable relationships were known as 'sailors' wives'. In return for part of the seaman's pay they would provide accommodation, companionship and sex. Father Nugent listed three types of brothels for sailors: a higher class establishment for the captains and mates, an ordinary one for the sailors and a special one for black men who would often return to the same women. Commander Eaton, the Industrial Schools inspector, revealed that 'there is a set of women in Liverpool who belong entirely to black sailors; a black sailor comes and expects a comfortable sort of home for him'.[43] Lowndes spoke specifically of Irish women going with black sailors, ship cooks and stewards in a north-end district known as 'Blackman's Alley', three long streets composed of 'black men's brothels'.[44] It was not all unseemly. Accompanying the police on a midnight tour of the town, Hugh Shimmin entered one house and witnessed a near-naked prostitute reading the Bible to a group of enthralled black men.[45]

The Dangers of Prostitution

While sailors' wives had it relatively easy, street-walking prostitutes suffered a grim and depressing existence. Reverend Isaac Holmes, chaplain of the Liverpool workhouse, claimed that prostitutes usually survived only for three to five years before meeting their maker.[46] American visitor Frederick Olmsted studied Liverpool's streetwalkers and noticed 'but a few who were not thin, meagre and pale'. He detected on their faces 'a stupid, hopeless, state-prison-for-life sort of expression [...] The very poorest women look miserably. We see bruised eyes not unfrequently, and there is evidently a good deal of hard drinking among them.'[47] A prostitute once walked up to a policeman and plunged a knife into his chest just above the heart. Fortunately he survived. On the way to the bridewell she admitted, 'I did it, I am weary of my life, I don't care if I am hung or get seven years.' She had been imprisoned 47 times.[48]

Out on the streets, prostitutes were easy prey to violent men. Ellen Burns was viciously assaulted by two seamen when she rejected their advances. The pair kicked her and slashed her across her cheek, leaving her permanently scarred.[49]

Another danger for prostitutes was police harassment. Although prostitution itself was not illegal, it was easy to find other related charges. Running brothels, living off immoral earnings and soliciting of and by prostitutes were all illegal, although the latter was often difficult to prove. The Vagrancy Act of 1824 allowed a constable to arrest a woman if he thought she was behaving in a 'riotous or indecent manner'. Under the Town Police Clauses Act of 1847 a woman could also be arrested if a policeman considered her to be obstructing passers-by as she touted for business. This law affected street hawkers as much as prostitutes and the distinction between the two trades was sometimes blurred, particularly in the eyes of ignorant policemen. In February 1864 a hawker called Catherine Flaherty was walking out of a public house in Scotland Place when a constable accused her of being a prostitute. 'Do I look like a prostitute?' asked the astonished woman. In the constable's eyes she did, for he then smacked her on the side of the head and dragged her along the street. After a further few slaps he pushed her hard against a heavy door before letting her go. He was later fined for his behaviour. As both trades were conducted on the streets, prostitutes and hawkers were frequently brought into conflict with the law. In another incident, near the Sailors' Home in November 1847, PC Kendall allegedly attacked a fruit seller called Bridget Hopkins. After chasing the woman, he was said to have knocked her down by striking her on the hips with his stick. Two years later, a man wrote to the newspaper complaining about an incident in Dale Street that he had recently witnessed. A woman was selling herrings from a basket when a policeman ordered her to move on before whacking her in the small of the back with his truncheon. The woman dropped to the ground but the officer dragged her up and proceeded to prod her in the back with his stick for a distance of 50 yards.[50]

The street-selling and streetwalking professions were indeed related, with some women dabbling in both. One newspaper correspondent claimed that orange sellers were in fact prostitutes, the fruit being a mere pretext to solicit men. The writer, who lived in Cable Street, claimed that the girls were a nuisance who took up the entire pavement and used disgusting language. When drunk, they would start fighting.[51] Like prostitutes, hawkers were a notoriously hard-swearing, hard-drinking set of women. Since some prostitutes undoubtedly hailed from the ranks of the street sellers, young and single female hawkers became the focus of intense moral concern. Reformers, politicians and churchmen were quick to make the link between women selling goods on the streets and selling their own bodies. According to Father Nugent, some young prostitutes pretended to sell 'fuzees' (matches) or newspapers while others began as basket-girls in the fruit, fish and flower trades. After becoming hardened on the streets they would begin drinking and using obscene language. Nugent knew of a large number of young women at risk: 'every girl who takes to selling newspapers in the streets is really graduating for prostitution'.[52]

To avoid arrest, savvy prostitutes would restrict their soliciting to the public houses and brothels, out of sight of the beat constables. The more desperate women, however, sought trade wherever they could and it was these poverty-stricken streetwalkers who were more likely to be arrested. The *Liverpool Review* asked what was the use of fining women who had no money. The point was made that the police never harassed the more respectable class of prostitutes. Poorer women, who arguably had a better excuse for selling themselves, were hounded to suicide, the gaol, workhouse or refuge homes, while their fur-coated colleagues from the respectable Abercromby Square area remained unmolested: 'cover vice in rags and filth, and it is hunted down: clothe it in fine linen and it is tolerated'.[53]

In addition to the ever-present threat of pregnancy, another risk was venereal disease. The Navy Report of 1867 spoke of Liverpool as a 'hot bed of syphilis'.[54] Lowndes provided figures for 1875 (which he claims are an underestimate) showing that 42 males, 28 females and 70 infants died from the disease.[55] The Liverpool Lock hospital, which opened in 1834 in Ashton Street, was specifically built to cater for victims of venereal diseases. With the exception of foreign sailors, patients were admitted freely on a voluntary basis although they were encouraged to stay until cured. The hospital treated young girls who had been raped as well as married women who had been infected by their husbands. However, a large part of the medical care was devoted to cleaning up prostitutes and educating them in the methods of personal hygiene.[56] The women would enter the hospital not simply because they were diseased but because they were *so diseased* as to be unable to continue their calling. Furthermore, within a quarter-mile radius of the hospital were scores of brothels and hundreds of prostitutes. Lowndes stated: 'For every female found in the Lock hospital and Parish Infirmary Lock wards, at least twenty might be found outside in a diseased condition.'[57] He told the story of a woman who sought medical advice for her venereal disease. A few days later she accosted the same doctor in the street and offered her services, not recognizing him. He also recalled the sad tale of 19-year-old Gertrude T_____ who had informed her brothel-keeper that she was diseased but was forced to carry on working for two months. Eventually she plucked up courage to escape and admit herself to hospital. She told the doctor that three other women in the house were also infected. Lowndes sought police help to confront the brothel owner and try to rescue the other inmates. However, they all refused help.[58]

Brothels

Women were often trapped in the clutches of brothel owners. In 1889 there were 443 such houses known to the police.[59] Establishments ranged from thief-infested bawdy-houses in the slum districts to reputable-looking properties in more upmarket streets. While some houses looked decent from the outside, through the open doors the filthy interiors could be seen: 'bits of furniture; dirty, tawdry blinds; dirty, greasy floors; and scraps of food, with a collection of ale bottles, seemed to be common to the kitchens of nearly all the houses'.[60] Some respectable-looking shops doubled as brothels. Young men would enter for a cigar only to be invited into a back room. One such 'shop' was home to six prostitutes.[61] While some prostitutes lived in shabby lodging-houses that were little more than makeshift brothels, others used 'accommodation houses'. By renting a room for a short spell they had somewhere to take their clients. For those unable or unwilling to pay such overheads, a dank wall in a dark back alley was the closest they came to comfort.

Police statistics for the period 1866 to 1882 reveal that women kept almost 90 per cent of the brothels.[62] Brothel-keeping offered lucrative opportunities for enterprising females. The more successful businesses were usually run by older women, or madams, presiding over a number of young females who would pay for their rooms out of their earnings. Sometimes known as 'dress-lodgers', the girls might be required to hand over all their money in return for being fed and decked out in fine clothes. Such girls might class themselves as dressmakers, milliners or seamstresses, although employed in no other business than prostitution.[63] Loan societies would advance money to the madams to enable them to set up their businesses: cabinet-makers would provide furniture to furnish the brothels: drapers would offer expensive wardrobes for the girls to wear and jewellers would supply necklaces. All this was supplied through hire purchase, repaid out of the proceeds of prostitution. The fine clothes would in turn be hired out to the girls at exorbitant rates that they could barely afford. In this way the girls were trapped in a cycle of debt. If they attempted to walk away from their profession they would be accused of stealing the clothes.[64] Brothels usually employed a hard man known as a 'bully' to make sure that the clients paid and that the girls did not run off with their earnings.

Not all madams were older women. In August 1857 a number of young females were charged with keeping disreputable houses in the more downmarket districts. Maria Keegan, aged 18, kept a brothel in a court in Westmoreland Street. Jane Cottrell ran another in the same street while also renting a room in Gascoigne Street, which was the scene of banjo playing, dancing and rows between the girls and black men. Dancers would after-wards adjourn to her house where further scenes of disorder would take place, including knives being drawn and bottles thrown. Mary Jarvis, a black woman, kept another brothel nearby. A neighbour complained that the street was like Sodom and Gomorrah. Some brothel operations were family affairs. Commander Eaton revealed that a woman ran a brothel while her two daugh-ters were mistresses of their own establishments. A third daughter, aged 18, was just starting out in the same business.

Josephine Butler told the tale of Mary Lomax (referred to as 'Marion' in her published accounts). Lomax was the 15-year-old daughter of a well-to-do farmer in the Midlands. After being seduced by the local squire, she was abandoned and ended up in a Liverpool brothel after being kidnapped by the infamous Fanny Wilson, alias Mrs Mandeville. Mandeville kept one of the more select upmarket establishments in Blandford Street, aided by her bully, 'Ginger Jack'. She went about 'covered in diamonds and kept between fifty and sixty girls'. The beautiful Lomax was much sought after by gentlemen clients. When her uncle came to Liverpool to seek her out, her colleagues drugged her and hid her in an empty boiler. In November 1866, aged 24, Lomax became consumptive and started coughing up blood. Her clients complained about her and she was again thrown onto the streets. In suicidal mood she entered the Brownlow Hill workhouse where she was eventually rescued by Butler. Already in the later stages of tuberculosis, she died three months later.[65]

While young prostitutes were exploited and abused, some madams did quite well out of the trade. In the 1860s a 'notorious' procuress called Jane Gallagher owned brothels in all the major towns. She kept four or five houses in Houghton Street and others in Tyrer Street. In April 1862 she appeared in court charged with keeping infamous houses. On being informed that her neighbours had complained about unseemly incidents in her house, she cheekily claimed that she would persuade the residents to sign a petition in her favour. Her son visited several complainants and offered them £20 to drop the charges. She was nevertheless found guilty and received twelve months with hard labour. In January 1866, after more complaints from neighbours, Gallagher was again charged with running a disreputable house, this time in Lord Nelson Street, near Lime Street. She appeared in the dock dressed in a fashionable, brightly coloured costume. By her side was Mary Lovesey who was charged with a similar, though unrelated, offence. When the magistrate asked whether the women were in league with each other, Gallagher cast a 'contemptuous glance at her meaner-clad companion', disgusted that anybody could think that she would mix with someone of that class.

Johanna Rosenberg, more infamously known as Madame Anna, was another high-class brothel-keeper. In the 1850s this 'portly-looking lady, elegantly attired' was based in Hotham Street, at the back of Lime Street. She always kept five or six 'very young' and 'fresh' girls, most of whom had been persuaded to enter her house under false pretences before being imprisoned. Rosenberg once invited a German girl to stay at her 'hotel' and hired another to work as a 'dressmaker'. She even sent one of her agents to the workhouse school to select a pretty-looking girl to work as a servant. As the girl was leaving the workhouse gates, her procuress was recognized and she was rescued before she could be inducted into a life of prostitution. Policemen were often called to the house, accompanied by frantic parents in search of their daughters. The wily Anna employed agents to keep a strict eye on her charges to prevent them escaping from her clutches. She was said to be good with her fists and would beat both girls and clients alike, sometimes throwing men out of her house. Madame Anna would take her girls 'on holiday' to Hamburg, where she would sell them to fellow brothel-keepers. The girls would be stranded in Germany and have to earn their fare home. Several were rescued and returned to England. A witness revealed another of her tricks: 'When Madame Anna gets new girls she walks them through the town, especially down to the Exchange, and drops her card at the feet of her usual customers, who understand the sign.' She would also take fresh victims to the Amphitheatre in Roe Street to initiate them. Rosenberg finally faced justice in December 1857. She was sentenced to what seems a quite lenient four months but afterwards fled Liverpool.[66]

Child Prostitution

Madame Anna's charges were aged about 15 or 16.[67] There was certainly a market for younger girls. A 14-year-old runaway was discovered living in another brothel in the same street, run by a German procuress called Mathilde Farise.[68] In an age of rampant venereal diseases, the practice of deflowering virgins made good sense, at least for the men. In 1837 the prison inspector pointed out that the reason there were more boys than girls in prison was probably due to the ready means of support available to girls through prostitution. Unlike the boys, they didn't need to steal.[69] Hugh Shimmin wrote of a brothel in Blandford Street that catered for old men with a taste in young girls. He claimed that in Liverpool, like-minded men were known under various amusing nicknames, as if the whole thing was a bit of a joke.[70] The landing stages at George's and Princes piers were popular meeting places for lads and girls looking to meet a 'sweetheart'. Older, respectable men would also pay a visit to leer at the young women. Shimmin recalls seeing 'one of our great public men' (he refrains from naming and shaming him) a little drunk, soliciting girls before taking 'a very young girl – a child, or little more' over the river to Seacombe.[71] A gang from Toxteth Park, known as the 'Park Rangers', included two young men said to be 'the constant associates of prostitutes of ten to twelve years of age'.[72]

Jane Doyle was a young prostitute who divided her time between Manchester and Liverpool in the early 1840s. She paints a picture of a reasonably happy childhood. Educated until the age of ten, she was sent to church by her parents but often truanted. Despite having enough to eat, she ran away with the hope of buying alcohol and clothes. Jane and a group of girls, aged 12 to 14, lived with a brothel-keeper, known as 'Old Granny', in the cellar of the George's Head in Garden Street. Jane's mother found her and rescued her. Back home, she was beaten unmercifully and locked in her bedroom without clothes. Undeterred, she escaped and returned to the streets, this time working for a Mrs Gaffery. Jane's mentor was a 15-year-old called Mary Ann Hammond. Together with another girl called Jane Shaw, Doyle was taken to Williamson Square, also known as Playhouse Square, and shown the ropes. A gentleman in his fifties was their first client. The terrified girls, who refused to be separated, were an attractive proposition, since they were both virgins. In a hired room, the man paid Shaw 10s for sex. However, upon hearing Shaw's cries of pain, Doyle had second thoughts. In an effort to put the man off, she told him that she was sexually experienced. He gave her 3s for waiting, which was easy money compared with what her friend had endured. Afterwards, an outraged Jane Shaw declared that she was giving up the game if her friend was not going to play her part.[73]

A man was about to take a 12-year-old girl into a brothel in Lord Nelson Street when a concerned neighbour warned her to stay away.[74] The brothel-keepers must have known what was going on, remaining entirely indifferent to the innocence of the children. Georgina Sergent, aged 14, thwarted an attempt by her brother-in-law, James Robinson Lancaster, to indecently assault her in the bedroom of her home in Priory Grove. Later the same day, Lancaster took the child to a brothel in Ainsworth Street on the pretext of buying her supper. On entering, Lancaster whispered some words to the female brothel-keeper. The blameless child was later called upstairs. When she entered what she thought was the dining room she found herself in a bedroom confronted by Lancaster, another man and the madam. In the nick of time, a woman who had witnessed the girl enter the property shouted up the stairs, 'Come down, you little _____.' The woman's language implies that the child was somehow a willing participant in the proceedings and reveals something about attitudes towards childhood sexuality in the rough neighbourhoods. Nevertheless, the witness took Sergent to the bridewell where her ordeal was revealed.[75] All three adults were imprisoned for twelve months.

Although the figure might have been exaggerated, in 1857 it was claimed that there were at least 200 'regular' prostitutes under 12 years of age in Liverpool.[76] Six years later the police offered a more modest figure of 21 prostitutes aged under 16 years.[77] Perhaps the practice was confined to the brothels where it was hidden and less obvious. There were certainly few prosecutions for child prostitution.[78] Until 1875, when the age of sexual consent was raised to 13, 12-year-olds could legally have sex. At the children's Cinderella Club it was perhaps more than mere prudery that kept young boys and girls seated separately. A journalist explained that this was 'a most necessary measure amongst slum children, who are aware of the physiological differences of sex at an early age, and often with horrifying results'.[79] Observers of the Liverpool slums witnessed shocking evidence of juvenile sexuality:

> There are children everywhere. Children carrying children: mothers of fifteen carrying their diminutive offspring of three and four months bolt upright, their tiny backs and chests deformed and distorted by the strain […] Children – poor little wretches! – whose faces are one mass of scrofulous sores – recording symptoms of hereditary venereal disease.[80]

Commander Eaton explained that by the 1880s brothel-keepers would not house children under the age of 14 since the police always prosecuted in such cases. Even so, he found one 6-year-old boy living in a brothel. Even after removal to an industrial school, he 'was singing most obscene songs, and swearing like a trooper'. Young prostitutes were still free to ply their trade on the streets. Eaton blamed the maze of Liverpool's back entries, long, dark, narrow passages that made ideal locations for illicit sex. He cited a case where a child kept watch at one end of an entry while a man took another child for sex. Eaton also condemned poor parenting that allowed young girls to stay out late unsupervised, since they often fell into the clutches of the Cornermen. Nevertheless, Father Nugent explained that experienced prostitutes discouraged younger girls from entering the profession. If they found girls loitering near the Sailors' Home or Central Station they would chase them. They also informed the police of any brothels housing young girls.[81]

It wasn't only girls who were at risk. When police raided the Commercial Rooms in Gloucester Street at three o'clock one morning in 1845, they not only found about 50 prostitutes and 40 men but a number of boys aged between 10 and 15 dancing with the girls.[82] Intentionally or not, Charles Dickens raises the spectre of male child prostitution in Liverpool. Around 1859 Dickens enrolled for one night only as a special constable to tour the dockland district. Accompanied by a police superintendent, he visited a room occupied by an old woman and a schoolboy. Dickens was amazed that the child was still doing his homework in the middle of the night but the woman explained that the lad had been to the theatre and was catching up on his studies. Dickens, with disturbing ambiguity, leaves the couple 'waiting for Jack'.[83]

Crackdown

The government made various attempts, both directly and indirectly, to stamp out the 'great social evil' of prostitution. The 1851 Common Lodging House Act, which allowed police to inspect premises, disrupted the activities of many prostitutes, although some women got round the legislation by claiming to be private tenants and therefore immune from interference. By the 1860s the government had begun a highly controversial crackdown on the trade. Rather than try to abolish prostitution, the authorities attempted to institutionalize and control it using the continental system of regulation. The threat of syphilis to the military inspired the Contagious Diseases Act of 1864 (extended in 1866 and 1869). The legislation, which applied only to certain garrison and seaport towns in southern England and Ireland, required suspected prostitutes to be registered and to submit to a fortnightly intimate examination. They faced nine-months' incarceration in a Lock hospital if found to be suffering from a sexually transmitted disease; if they refused to comply with the examination they could be imprisoned indefinitely. In practice, any woman loitering in the street could be assumed to be a prostitute. In 1869 efforts were made to extend the Act to northern towns, including Liverpool. In response, the Ladies' National Association, led by Josephine Butler, campaigned long and hard for the repeal of the Act. What appalled campaigners was the idea that only women were considered physically and morally responsible for spreading the disease. Also, while it was considered natural that men would want to use prostitutes, it was still considered wicked for women to supply such services. In the face of such male-centred double standards, Butler's own solution to the problem was to fight the social injustices that forced women to sell themselves in the first place. Much to her delight, the Act was eventually superseded in 1883 and finally removed from the statute books in 1886.

In the 1880s, as the Contagious Diseases Acts were waning, the government made another assault on prostitution. Rather than trying to regulate the trade, this time the authorities attempted to eradicate it entirely by closing the brothels. With the campaigning support of various religious and moral groups, temperance organizations, child-welfare workers and 'social purity' activists, the Criminal Law Amendment Act was passed in 1885. In what can be seen either as a repressive measure aimed at controlling the sexual habits of the lower classes or an attempt to raise the moral tone of the country, the age of consent for girls was raised from 13 to 16 years and all male homosexual acts were made illegal: up to that point, only the act of buggery was prohibited.[84] Ratepayers and vigilance groups were empowered to pressure the police to repress all known houses of ill repute. Yet although police powers of prosecution were also reinforced, in Liverpool few brothels were closed in the first five years after the passing of the Act. Rather than try to eradicate prostitution, the Liverpool (and London) constabularies attempted to control it by monitoring certain districts where they knew it thrived.[85]

Liverpool's Head Constable, Captain Nott-Bower, argued that taking action against the brothels would not have abolished them but simply have driven them underground where they would have remained 'unknown' to the police. Four hundred brothels were therefore localized and tolerated, a policy that had the support of the Watch Committee and the majority of the members of the city council. Police prosecuted only if a brothel opened in a previously respectable street, had children living there, was the scene of robberies or proved to be a nuisance to the neighbours, particularly if two or more of them were willing to come forward and provide evidence.[86] Landlords faced a fine of £20 for *knowingly* letting a house for immoral purposes, although the issue of consent was often difficult to prove.

The press, however, were not convinced about this lax approach. In 1888 the *Liverpool Review* revealed the scandal of corporation-owned houses being used as brothels. Howat Street, for example, was the 'most notorious hot-bed of vice in Everton', with an estimated 12 brothels springing up in the previous twelve months. A man walking down the street was propositioned seven times by seven different women from houses next door to each other. One Saturday afternoon, two young men walking home with their wages were nearly dragged into a 'bad-house'. Boys as young as 15 years of age were accosted regularly from early morning. The prostitutes were known as a 'colony'. Children playing in the street were paid halfpennies to go on errands for them. Twice a week the organ man came round and the street came alive with half-dressed, unwashed and drunken dancing girls. On Sunday the street was at its worst, being infested with loafers who would play pitch and toss and argue. The women, typical of the 'dangerous class', would engage in crude conversations or indulge in rough horseplay: 'Some of them mere girls, others old, bloated and lazy looking but all bearing sickening evidences of debauchery.' All-night rows, street brawls and drunken orgies were regular occurrences. One resident complained about a scene that occurred one Tuesday afternoon between three of the women: 'two of whom were absolutely naked […] quarrelling and fighting over a man, the language used being of the vilest description, and the whole scene revolting in the extreme. One of the women simply covered in a chemise, the other had merely a collar on and the third's wardrobe was nil.' Each night, convoys of hansom cabs would bring clients secured in the town centre; the majority of them would have been married men. It was rightly suspected that the authorities were tolerating the abuses, since the problems were contained within one area. Some constables seemed to be very friendly with the girls and one was even seen entering a property in the middle of the night.[87]

Yet while Pellew Street and Seagrave Street, near Copperas Hill, were also notorious districts, they were inhabited *solely* by prostitutes, whereas Howat Street also housed respectable residents. Thereby lay the problem. Yet for the most part, residents of the poorer districts accepted prostitution. This meant that prostitutes could often find shelter from arrest in the homes of their neighbours. A meeting of Liverpool's magistrates in 1871 revealed the difficulties faced by the police in arresting prostitutes: 'the moment any information was laid against them they would run away from one house to another, and there was really no means of catching hold of them again'.[88] Yet some respectable Howat Street tenants threatened to leave if the menace was not stopped. It was difficult to get rid of bad neighbours since some landlords tolerated their behaviour as long as the rents were paid. Even responsible owners were sometimes deceived. Shrewd prostitutes would send respectable-looking agents to arrange the terms of a tenancy only to later turn the property into a brothel.

The *Liverpool Review*'s publicity had an effect. When a journalist later visited Howat Street 24 of the houses had been cleared of their tenants, owing to the combined actions of the police and landlords. However, a little later, several tenants made attempts to re-enter the properties, declaring that they'll 'take good care nobody at all shifts them'. A fake 'gentleman' actually succeeded in securing a house for two former tenants but they were flung out again within forty-eight hours as the house had been gained by false pretences. Landlords encouraged three policemen to move into properties on a reduced rent, hoping that they would keep a respectable eye on the district.

Despite such improvements, the Liverpool authorities continued to ignore the Criminal Law Amendment Act until the end of 1890. By then the Blandford Street district had become Liverpool's capital of debauchery. The street, which runs parallel to the northern side of London Road, was renamed Kempston Street in 1894, no doubt in an attempt to erase its former notoriety. Reverend Armstrong was probably referring to the area when he complained: 'some of the streets are almost entirely composed of houses of ill-fame, some of the courts contain no other dwellings of any kind'.[89] The tightly packed courts in fact housed 235 brothels and 460 women.[90] In 1889 a wealthy man with marital problems went out and picked up a girl in Elliott Street, near Lime Street. She persuaded him that there was only one place where he could get a late drink and enticed him back to a house in Blandford Street. For three months he was held hostage to his lust in one of these 'traps for Hell'. A newspaper concluded: 'men go there and go mad. They stop in a house for a month at a stretch, drunk nearly all the time.'[91]

It was in opposition to such temptations and immorality that the Purity Crusade was founded in 1890. Reverend Armstrong explained that the movement aimed to suppress the illegal traffic in women and punish brothel-keepers who enslaved girls. He pointed out that the inmates of the brothels were virtually kept as slaves who were unable to escape the clutches of their mostly female keepers. Their earnings were confiscated and bullies watched them at work in Lime Street, ready to punish them if they did not pick up men. If by two o'clock in the morning the girls had not secured a client they were refused entry back into the house or alternatively punished on their return.[92]

The relentless campaigning of purity and temperance groups, particularly the Vigilance Association, bore fruit in November 1890 when the Liberals won the municipal election on a ticket of 'social purity'. The policy of managing rather than repressing prostitution was to change. The Watch Committee and Head Constable were instructed to use the powers of the Criminal Law Amendment Act to shut down every known brothel. This resulted in the prosecution of over 800 brothel-keepers and hundreds of women, the eviction of masses of undesirable tenants and the social sanitation of vice-infested districts.[93]

Already under intense moral surveillance from the authorities, prostitutes were further criminalized and marginalized, becoming even greater social outcasts. Although some were left homeless, others appeared to be turning a new leaf, particularly since the rescue homes began doing good business. The *Liverpool Review*, however, remained cynical, believing that the resulting success of the homes was based on the fact that prostitutes were being forced into them by the dearth of brothels. Such women did not admit themselves of their own free will and certainly showed no repentance. The shelters were simply a better alternative to the street, workhouse or prison.

Although the statistics for tackling prostitution greatly improved, the catastrophic consequence of all this upheaval was that prostitutes were scattered over a wider area. Police supervision of the trade became more difficult as women were uprooted and driven into the common lodging-houses and the maze of streets.[94] Some women might even have been evicted from the relative safety of female-dominated havens into the dark and dangerous back alleys where they came under the 'protection', or sometimes control, of male pimps and 'fancy men'.[95] A wider section of the public was directly confronted with the trade as streetwalkers migrated to respectable areas, some of the more well-off women even setting up new brothels there, much to the annoyance of their middle-class neighbours. What began as a worthy attempt to protect women from predatory males ended up further stigmatizing, criminalizing, punishing and socially isolating some of the most desperate among them.[96]

As for the anticipated improvements: 'I could detect none up to the time I left Liverpool [in 1902]', said the Head Constable. Much to his relief, no doubt, the crackdown did not last and in 1896 the council reversed its policy to return to its former system of containment. Nott-Bower would have had good reason to feel superior. In 1889 he had already explained the town's peculiar problem and revealed why government intervention would not work: 'Liverpool is a seaport with a population consisting largely of seamen, foreigners, and that floating class of young men, free from all restraints of home life, often with much money to spend, who cannot be made moral by Act of Parliament.'[97]

NINETEEN

Sport and Gambling

Animal-baiting

At the opening of the Sefton Playground and Gymnasium in 1862, Liverpool's mayor, Mr Hutchinson, boasted that a marked improvement had taken place during the present century, not only in people's recreational pursuits but also in their temperament. Bull-baiting, bear-baiting, cock-fighting and other cruel sports had disappeared, replaced by amusements having a 'rational character and a tendency to exalt and invigorate the mental faculties'.[1] The opening of the facility was part of an on-going attempt by the authorities to bring regulation, order and moral improvement to the boisterous lower classes. 'Rational recreation', as it became known, prescribed playing fields, exercise and fresh air as healthier counter-attractions to the rowdy public houses, brutal sports and gambling.

Yet the mayor was only partly correct. It was true that some baiting sports had disappeared from Liverpool's streets. In the mid-eighteenth century, to celebrate the election of the town's mayor, a chained bear was baited with large mastiffs every October at the White Cross, at the top of Chapel Street.[2] In the late eighteenth century there was also a bull-baiting arena at the top of Lord Street. All classes took part in the rowdy 'sport', betting on whose dog could hold onto the bull for the longest. Around 1783 a group of drunken sailors took an exhausted bull from the annual wake at West Derby village and dragged it into the Theatre Royal in Williamson Square. To the surprise of the ladies, it popped its head out of the centre box.[3] Bull-baiting was finally prohibited in 1835.

Yet although driven underground, other brutal blood sports were still popular throughout the nineteenth century. In 1887 the Liverpool branch of the Royal Society for the Prevention of Cruelty to Animals was still able to report that 'badger baiting had not quite vanished'.[4] Parliament Fields was a popular Sunday morning venue for dog-fighting.[5] Dog-fighting and rat-baiting could also be enjoyed in the local public houses, usually in an upstairs room.

Sunday morning events were ideal, although the time and place of the contest were closely guarded secrets until the last minute. Hugh Shimmin recalls one fight lasting three-quarters of an hour. The owners would stake as much as £10 on their animal, with additional betting taking place among the spectators. The landlord would charge admission for spectators. There were even dog-fighting clubs with subscriptions of 2d or 3d per week.[6] William Glew, a beershop-keeper from Blake Street, had a dog-fighting pit on his premises. A policeman witnessed dogs with their heads swollen and mangled and their skin torn away.[7] Ellen Langley, of Bent Street, had a room upstairs set aside for fights. A constable caught a crowd of 40 spectators and then noticed the very same people watching another dog-fight later the same day in Sawney Pope Street.[8] Dog-fighting enthusiasts were seen as particularly unsavoury characters who revelled in violent pursuits. One pugilist-cum-dog-fighter, William Doneky from Toxteth Park, once thrust a red-hot poker into his wife's eye.[9]

In November 1871 there were notices about town advertising an 'All-England Ratting Match'. Detectives paid 1s admission to attend the event at a former beershop belonging to John Evans in Circus Street. The detectives found 60 to 70 men and many terrier-type dogs. In an upstairs room was a pit covered with wire, containing seven or eight rats. A dog was placed in the pit and within a minute all the rats were dead. The procedure was repeated until the stock of rats was exhausted. Passing judgement on a sport of 'degrading and brutalising character', the magistrate was less concerned about the injury to the rats than to the damage caused 'to the morals of society' by the enjoyment of such spectacles.[10]

Most towns housed a cockpit in which birds, equipped with razor-sharp spurs on their legs, would fight to the death. Such arenas could also be used to stage dog-fights, badger-baiting or rat-killing. Cock-fighting was the first sport contested between county representatives. Such matches were called 'mains'. From 1785 Cockspur Street housed a cockpit visited by both 'low ruffians' and gentlemen. Over four days in 1790 two county families fought a mains involving 41 individual cock-fights. The winner of each match received ten guineas with two hundred guineas going to the overall winner.[11] On Shrove Tuesday, at the cockpit near Lime Kiln Lane (Lime Street), boys, with their hands tied behind their back, would chase the birds and try to capture them in their teeth for a prize.[12] In 1830 cocks owned by Lord Derby took on birds owned by John Gilliver for an incredible stake of £5,000.[13]

Cock-fighting was banned in 1849 but continued as an underground sport. In 1853, 32 people were arrested in a raid on a beershop in Burlington Street, where a 200-strong crowd had gathered to watch a cock-fight.[14] In 1875 a mains between men from Lancashire and Warwickshire took place in a room in the grandstand at Aintree racecourse. The event featured 11 individual battles for a stake of £200. There was also a large amount of betting on the results of each battle and the overall result. A police raid put a stop to the carnage but not before four of the birds had been killed and others injured. An eyewitness saw one poor bird, blinded and with blood pouring from its beak, lie on its back and seemingly stab itself with its spur, as if 'to commit suicide' and put an end to its agony.[15]

Coursing

Coursing, which involved greyhounds trying to catch hares, was a popular spectator sport capable of attracting crowds of up to 75,000 from all over the country. The premier event was the Waterloo Cup, first staged at Altcar in 1836.[16] By the 1870s the event was chaotic and dogged with reports of assaults, scams and robberies. Liverpool Cornermen provided a strong presence, along with assorted thieves, card sharpers and welshers.[17] Bet welshers were swindling bookmakers who would offer excellent odds to attract punters and then scarper from the ground without paying up. They were highly unpopular and risked a severe beating if caught. Such instant justice was used as a smokescreen by violent thieves. A dozen ruffians would surround an innocent member of the public. They would grab his watch, knock him to the ground and shout 'Hey! A Welsher!' Angry spectators would swarm upon the victim and give him another pasting. To combat the disorder, in 1882 Superintendent Jervis of the Ormskirk Division increased the number of police on duty and stationed a prison van on the course. The men combed the crowd and arrested 30 suspicious characters.[18]

Wakes and Fairs

Travelling fairs and church festivals, known as wakes, provided another link between recreation and crime. Pickpockets, rowdies and scam merchants would flock to the events to get drunk, commit thefts and dupe the public. From 1770 the Folly Fair was held at Gibson's Folly, near the present site of St George's Hall. Eventually it 'became a saturnalia of the lowest roughs in the town. Drunkenness, debauchery, and fighting, prevailed to a frightful extent.'[19] In 1818 the fair moved to the north side of London Road but lasted only a few more years. The West Derby Wakes were still held at the beginning of the nineteenth century. Originally staged to celebrate the anniversary of the dedication of the chapel of St Mary the Virgin, the wakes featured a variety of games and rural sports. Along with the Folly Fair, the wake faded as Liverpool's population grew and the event became more depraved and a threat to public order. Liverpudlians then had to travel further afield for their entertainment. The popular wakes of the Cheshire villages of Hale and Tranmere became sites of pilgrimage for the working classes. The Tranmere event in particular was the highpoint of the Liverpudlian's calendar, with up to 40,000 people crossing the Mersey on a Whit Monday. In 1856 the festival was the scene of pole-climbing along with donkey, pig and sack races. For a penny, intrigued customers could view a mermaid, which turned out to be seal trained to do tricks. Other entertainments included swing boats, shooting galleries, steam roundabouts and a peep show. There was gambling on wheels of fortune and dice, while boxing booths invited the public to take on hardened veterans such as Jackson of Toxteth Park.[20]

Prize-fighting

For the sport's critics, bare-knuckle prize-fighting was as savage and degrading as two dogs tearing each other to bits. For others, pugilism was a highly valued national sport, helping maintain the fighting spirit of Waterloo.[21] Champion fighters became regional heroes, commanding huge followings of working-class supporters. Prize-fighting was popular in Liverpool, boosted by visits from successful fighters as part of promotional tours of the growing industrial towns. In 1826 Jem Burn and White-Headed Bob (Ned Baldwin) travelled from London for a benefit at the York Hotel in Williamson Square.[22] Another Jem, the retired fighter Jem Ward, opened an inn in Liverpool as did Irish bruiser Jack Langan. Until it was overtaken by Manchester and Birmingham in the 1840s, Liverpool enjoyed a brief heyday and was lauded as 'the metropolis of milling [pugilism]'.[23] In the 1830s the town played host to the skills of such fine practitioners as the Yorkshire Snob, Robinson, the Vauxhall tinker, and world champion Deaf Burke, who was once roused from unconsciousness by a second biting off his ear.[24] World champion William Perry (the Tipton Slasher) later moved to Liverpool to train. Another world champion, Jem Mace (the Swaffham Gipsy), was a boxing instructor at the Liverpool Olympic Festival, first held in 1862. He is buried in Anfield cemetery. Fisticuff fans were kept well informed by the sporting press. While *Bell's Life in London and Sporting Chronicle* was the Bible of fight fans, the Liverpool bare-knuckle scene was also covered by an imitation publication confusingly called *Life in London* (renamed *Bethell's Life in London and Liverpool Sporting Register*), published locally

every Saturday between 1824 and 1827.[25] Fighters would place advertisements
calling out rivals and offering wagers on the result.

Since pugilism was an underground sport, promoters could not openly
advertise contests and so details of venues were circulated by word of mouth.
The fights were held at secret locations, usually early in the morning. Bootle
Marsh was a popular site. Here, in 1826, Jack Evans clobbered Tom Banks (the
Irish Gypsy). In the excitement, the ring was broken and invaded by men
armed with shillelaghs. One journalist noted: 'happy was he who escaped
without a crack on the crown'.[26] In July 1827, also at Bootle Marsh, Jack Jones
knocked out Tom Knowles after 25 furious rounds. During the fight blood
poured from Jones' ear, or as one journalist put it, he had 'claret oozing out
of his listener'.[27] Such severe injuries sometimes led to fatalities. In April 1834,
in a field near Sandhills, James Kirty beat Thomas Quine to death after 25
rounds. One hour and five minutes into the fight, a severe blow to the left side
of Quine's head left him unable to stand and he was forced to admit defeat.
Bleeding from the ear, he died the next day of a ruptured vein in the brain.[28]

Cheshire was also a popular location. Liverpool fight fans, accompanied by
an army of pickpockets, would swarm across the river in their thousands to
the sandbanks at Wallasey Pool or Fiddlers Ferry to see some blood. In October
1825, at Welch Leys near Chester, local hero Ralph Boscow fought Pat M'Gee
over 35 rounds, watched by a crowd of 5,000.[29] One fight in 1825 was due to
take place in Woodside until the authorities interfered and the crowd moved
further along to Wallasey to see John Jones take on Irishman Pat Toney. After
three hours and 25 minutes of boxing-cum-wrestling, Jones was declared the
victor. The reason the fight lasted so long was that Toney's right hand became
swollen, leaving him unable to punch.[30]

The formation of the new police in the 1830s hastened the sport's decline as
open-air fights were increasingly broken up. Fighters and spectators would be
scrambled from place to place, pursued by the police determined to prevent
disorderly scenes. The advent of railway excursions gave the sport new life
by giving both fighters and supporters the chance to escape interference.
Stations in peaceful country locations would be overrun by trainloads of
rowdy fight fans in search of the latest punch-up. Using early versions of the
football specials, Liverpudlians would flock to fights as far away as Newport
Pagnell to see the Bendigo vs. Looney championship fight. Press reports from
around the country would make reference to the notable presence of 'Liverpool roughs' in the crowd.[31] For the sport's critics, what was objectionable
was not simply the brutality of the fighters but the riotous behaviour of the
bloodthirsty spectators, some of whom 'no one would think of trusting out of

handcuffs'.[32] The sport eventually lost its upper-class patronage as it became mired in corruption and increasingly chaotic ringside scenes.

Yet mobile fight enthusiasts continued to follow their heroes throughout the land. The authorities eventually countered with the Regulation of the Railways Act (1868), which made the hiring of trains for fights illegal. It was a double blow for fans of extreme violence since the Act coincided with the abolition of public hangings.[33] Another setback to the bare-knuckle sport was the introduction of the Queensberry Rules from 1867. These helped popularize the modern form of fighting with gloves, three-minute rounds and a ten-second recovery period after a knockdown. However, the new rules were only gradually adopted and the two codes existed side by side for a number of years.

An arguably more civilized indoor version of the sport, used mainly for sparring exhibitions and benefit fights, had existed for years. In the 1820s sparring exhibitions at Houghton's Assembly Rooms in Hood Street attracted up to 300 spectators. In one bout a 'brawny son of the Emerald Isle' challenged the crowd for an opponent and was eventually matched with a smaller but more expert boxer. The Irishman laid into his opponent before the formalities of the fight had even begun. To loud cries of 'Foul', the fight was restarted with the Irishman ending up being battered for his sins. Sparring nights at the Gothic Rooms, also in Hood Street, were plagued by disorderly crowds congregating outside.[34] The Golden Lion in Dale Street also hosted sparring sessions. One competitor in 1825 was knocked senseless but 'a bucket of water soon put his knowledge-box to rights'.[35] The language of boxing journalism was quite entertaining. Hugh Shimmin gives several examples of vivid reportage, including 'he popped in his left very neatly on Sam's smeller, and opened up a fresh paint pot'.[36]

Boxing gradually came to be recognized as a skilful art rather than a brutal slogging match. In 1888 the *Liverpool Review* drew a distinction between the gloved and bare-knuckle codes, calling one 'defensive sparring' and the other 'defiant bruising'. It was clear which was the most popular, since although there were hundreds of 'boxers' in Liverpool, 'the fighting men can be counted on one hand'.[37] Establishments such as the Liverpool Gymnasium in Myrtle Street and the Liverpool Boxing Club in Pitt Street helped foster the sport's transformation from underground brawling to a more respectable physical activity. The latter club was both a fight venue and a private gym offering instruction. Printed notices on the wall displayed various mottoes that the legendary Muhammad Ali would have been proud of: 'Honey is sweet, but the bee stings' and the handy advice, 'Tis far better to give than to receive'.[38]

Yet the price of watching contests at some of the big theatres and private gentlemen's clubs was still beyond the reach of most working men. The entrance fees of about 2s meant that boxing was the preserve of the middle classes. A rougher version of the sport continued in the low dockland public houses that also catered for dog-fighting and rat-baiting. A journalist attended one such fight for £10 prize money staged at a secret venue known as 'Mulligan's crib' near Athol Street.[39] Such establishments remained magnets for members of the criminal underworld who would organize betting on the results. Although Liverpudlian George Vaughan was still partaking in bare-knuckle bouts in the 1880s, the sport continued to fade. The formation of the respectable National Sporting Club in 1891 saw the introduction of strict rules and regulations. The days of old-fashioned pugilism were finally over when John L. Sullivan used gloves to defend his world championship against James J. Corbett in 1892.[40] Grudges in the slums were still settled bare fisted 'on the cobbles' but they were hardly sport.

Nor was the 'man versus goat' contest that took place in 1891, in one of the 'Royal' streets in Kensington.[41] The bout took place after a man invited some drinking companions back to his house for a game of whist. One young man became pugnacious and after losing some money challenged the company to a fight. The host said, half-jokingly, that he had a goat in the yard, which he would back for a fiver a side. The sturdily built man took up the challenge and agreed to fight the beast by crawling on his knees with his hands clasped behind him. The spectators placed their own bets. After six rounds of being butted in the face by the goat the battered man retired soaked in blood. He was revived and sent home in a cab but was so disfigured that when his mother opened the door she didn't recognize him.

Horse racing

A less brutal animal betting sport was horse racing, although even the sport of kings was dogged by underworld activity. Chester races, on the first of May, would attract the 'legs' (betting men), thimble-riggers and 'a most vicious looking class of fellows', chiefly Irish travellers who made a living setting up fairground-style attractions.[42] In 1833 forged notes were found to be circulating through the gaming tables, apparently a new scam feared likely to be repeated on other racecourses.[43] In 1827, at the Maghull races, a crowd of 20,000 gathered. Predictably a few disturbances took place. A number of Liverpool visitors had a little too much to drink and were ready to start fighting when the police intervened. Nevertheless, the refreshments booths suffered damage with benches, flags and signposts left scattered about the field.[44] Racecourses continued to be graced by the presence of the betting underworld. At the Croxteth Hunt Club Steeplechase, held at Greenbridge in April 1881, the organizers insisted that 'no illegal betting, lists or stools' would be permitted on any part of the ground, yet the enclosure was crowded with betting men who carried on regardless. Elsewhere, the three-card-tricksters and pickpockets plied their trade, interrupted only by occasional brawls.

The law relating to gambling on horses opened up new opportunities for the criminal fringe. The Betting Houses Act of 1853 suppressed betting shops and made off-course cash betting with bookmakers illegal. The legislation was aimed at halting the growing menace of establishments in London solely devoted to betting. While still allowing the upper classes to place their bets during visits to racecourses, the Act helped create an illegal gambling industry. Secret betting clubs or 'list houses' sprang up, particularly around Williamson Square. Betting in public houses also continued. Indeed there was debate about whether the Act was intended to cover betting in pubs. In 1862 the *Racing Times* praised a Liverpool magistrate for withdrawing summonses against publicans charged with allowing betting on their premises.[45]

Organized mass betting increased as technology improved. The completion of the electric telegraph network in the 1850s made news of the racing results nationally and instantly available. A raid on the Albion Hotel in Ranelagh Street uncovered a board displaying lists of telegrams showing the latest prices of horses.[46] The new cheap mass circulation of newspapers in the 1880s further popularized gambling by including horse-racing pages complete with starting prices. The fruits of compulsory education were later seen in the increasing number of people able to read lists of runners and calculate betting odds. By the mid-1880s the bookmakers were increasingly being driven off the streets and into the clubs where they carried on their operations. The clubs were in turn raided by plain-clothed constables on 'special duty' who would place bets before nabbing the proprietors. Liverpool was not alone in the fight against 'list houses'. A raid on betting clubs in Manchester in 1885 resulted in the arrest of over 200 people and the seizure of £2,000.[47] In 1890 the Canning Club in Park Lane, the Clarendon Club in North John Street and the Rotunda Club in Great Homer Street were among many establishments raided and prosecuted for allowing betting on the premises.[48]

The irregularities relating to betting raised questions in the press. If it was legal to back a horse at a racecourse why was it illegal to place the same bet in the street or betting club? Surely the law, once passed, should cover the whole country. A Liverpool magistrate, for example, bought a racehorse and took a party of colleagues to the racecourse to bet on it. Yet back in Liverpool, members of the lower classes were being prosecuted for backing the very same horse. 'Where is the justice?' became the big question of the day.[49]

It was felt, however, that the poor were most at risk, both economically and morally. Gambling was thought to discourage thrift and hard work by promoting a 'something for nothing' mentality. For some people betting provided a harmless, exciting and relatively cheap means of entertainment coupled with dreams of prosperity. For others, speculating on horses was the beginning of their ruin. The pursuit helped the poor become poorer and was associated with other damaging elements of the criminal subculture. In the harsh words of one Liverpool moralist: 'gambling leads to other vices, namely drunkenness and murder'.[50] Hugh Shimmin also pointed out that gambling had serious consequences: 'homes neglected, wives abused, children driven to crime'.[51] Mr Raffles, the stipendiary magistrate, received a letter from a woman signing herself 'A Victim'. She begged him to put a stop to gambling since 'my husband is breaking up my home, and I have five little ones, but all his salary he backs horses with'.[52] Shimmin also cites the example of a working man who ended up in prison after borrowing his employer's money to place bets. Even judges had noticed the 'frequency of embezzlement brought about by turf practices'.[53]

Also, in the eyes of the authorities, it was the lower classes who posed more of a threat to the social order. A worrying consequence of off-course betting was the congregation of large groups of gamblers lounging about the streets, particularly outside the betting clubs as they waited for the racing results. Crowds of men and youths were a daunting sight to passing pedestrians and a challenge to patrolling constables. In the 1890s Smith Street, near Great Homer Street, occasionally suffered groups of up to 300 people, loitering 'without good and sufficient reasons'. After complaints from residents, the police made a number of arrests including that of three men for spending ten minutes reading a sporting newspaper.[54] By the 1890s respectable members of the public would also no longer tolerate street gambling, particularly the accompanying rowdiness and swearing.[55]

Street Gambling

Despite legislation, including the 1874 Betting Houses Act which further restricted street betting, gambling thrived in various forms, including card games, lotteries, wheels of fortune and dice. In the 1870s Liverpool was home to several roaming gambling gangs, largely run by ex-convicts. The 'prick the garter' gang was said to be quite successful with their hole in the board game. It seems that the various three-card-trick gangs operating around Scotland Road had fallen out of favour, since people were getting wise to their particular scam. Gambling gangs operating out of railway carriages, however, were thriving, largely owing to the absence of police on the trains and the reluctance of victims to report their losses. Most were too ashamed of being ridiculed for their gullibility. The neighbourhood of Wapping was home to the 'Billy Fairplay' gang which managed to run their street-corner swindles unmolested by the police. A 'Billy Fairplay' machine was a type of bagatelle board on which a ball was rolled down a spiral tower to find its way into numbered holes. It was believed that their leader acted as a police informant in return for tip-offs about future raids. This was despite the man apparently acting as 'Fagin' to a team of juvenile pickpockets who worked the crowds watching the gambling.[56]

Children were used as props in gambling scams. During a raid on gaming tables in Lime Street in December 1856 it was discovered that youngsters were being sent out on the streets clutching bric-a-brac that they were supposed to have won. The ruse was intended to entice other young punters. In February 1865 a girl appeared to be doing very well out of Mary Cusack's raffle in Richmond Row. After paying a penny to pull a ticket out of a bag, she was seen to win some desirable prizes, including a workbox and a 'fine large glass'. She was seen later creeping around the back of the stall to put the items back. The girl was a 'jolly' working in conjunction with the stallholder.

Young gamblers were thought to be particularly vulnerable to moral corruption. In 1832 a member of the public warned of boys playing 'pitch and toss' in Hanover Street. He felt that they were on 'the highway to the gallows'.[57] Pitch and toss involved betting on whether tossed coins landed heads or tails uppermost. The Head Constable's report for 1874 reveals that 699 people were charged with playing the game.[58] Many boys interviewed in prison cited the game as the cause of their downfall. One youth admitted, 'I first met with bad company by stopping to see boys play pitch and toss. I have often played at pitch and toss. I used generally to lose; we sometimes borrowed and lent to each other; when our money was done we used to steal more.' Another lad sank deeper into crime: 'I was first led to commit myself to evil, through meeting bad companions, playing at pitch and toss; from playing at that, I got to playing at cards in public houses, and by those means got to love drink.' St Andrews Street was listed as a great place to play the game, with one boy winning as much as £10.[59] At the canal near Dutton Street, up to 80 youths would regularly gather to play pitch and toss and other gambling games. Up to £20 would be staked on a single game. During police raids the boys would throw their winnings into the canal to destroy the evidence.[60] After complaints of the nuisance caused by the game being played on Sunday mornings in Everton, a group of youths was rounded up and prosecuted. The magistrate asked one youngster why he didn't go to church instead. He replied that he had just come from church.[61] Pitch and toss proved a nationwide problem. After new legislation was put in force to suppress street gambling, a 12-year-old player was arrested in London. In court he was asked what he had to say for himself. He replied that he was 'not aware of the new Act being passed'. The magistrate discharged him.[62]

Children were exposed to gambling from infancy. In Lord Street, in the early nineteenth century, a street cake-seller enticed the crowds with his familiar cry:

> Toss or buy! Win um and eat um!
> Loose um and look at um!
> Heads you win, tails I win,
> Tails you lose – the fairest game in town.

Young children were thus tempted to gamble their halfpenny on winning two cakes rather than buying one. If the man won the toss he would pocket the coin and the child would walk away empty-handed, sadder but wiser.[63] In 1879 no less than 300 packs of playing cards were confiscated from young Liverpool shoeblacks.[64] Youths were also attracted to the nut barrows where a handful of nuts could be won on the spin of a wheel.[65] The wheel of fortune, a primitive form of roulette, was popular. The game consisted of a board marked with squares and a revolving needle in the centre which was spun to land on a coloured square. Michael Maguire was arrested in Scotland Place for using a contraption with a spring attached to the needle that allowed him to control when it stopped revolving.[66]

'Hells'

While dockers gambled their wages on wheels of fortune in gambling stalls near the Sailors' Home, those who earned more money, such as the lumpers, would visit card-playing houses or low gaming rooms known as 'Hells'.[67] 'The Liverpool party' was a gang of itinerant hell-keepers well known as far as London. Including infamous individuals called Thorn, Godsol and Burge, they were driven out of Liverpool by the police in 1838 and decamped to Manchester, taking with them their 'faked' roulette table.[68]

Public gaming rooms were made illegal in 1846. Again, the wealthy were immune from prosecution since they were able to gamble in private clubs. The hypocrisy of the law on betting was again emphasized with the case of a 14-year-old street urchin who was found betting with cards in the street. He was taken to court, found guilty and fined 5s and costs with the option of seven days' imprisonment. Since the boy had never seen that amount of money in his life, he was sent to the cells. Here lay the inequality. There was one law for the rich and one for the poor. It was lawful for a gentleman to gamble with cards in his own garden but a crime for a poor man, who did not possess a garden, to do likewise on waste ground.[69]

While betting legislation was a laudable attempt to save the lower classes from themselves, the law was destined to fail in the same way that it failed to put a stop to prostitution. When betting was banned, it was simply driven underground. Some gaming houses were disguised as respectable hotels while hosting billiards and card games for 'sporting characters'. Many beershops had back rooms set aside where gamblers could play cards undisturbed.[70] Gambling also fell into the hands of crooks and swindlers in sordid gambling dens associated with other criminal activities such as receiving stolen goods. In 1888 a journalist gained an invitation to a secret gambling club catering for boys from 10 to 18 years of age.[71] The club was situated in a stinking unventilated cellar beneath a vile slum in the north end. A man with battered features, aged about 50, claimed to run the club to keep children off the streets and out of trouble but more likely as a means of lining his own pockets. The club boasted a membership of over 150 boys, each paying a weekly subscription of a penny. The journalist noted that the revolving pointer of one board game stopped in the banker's favour rather too often.

The police could not win. While *Porcupine* accused officers of not doing enough to prevent gambling it admitted that the spate of arrests against bookmakers running underground clubs, in defiance of the 1853 and 1874 Acts, merely motivated the bookies to take to the streets again, defying the authorities in even greater numbers in order to attract the punters.[72] Also, since street gambling operations were mobile, it was difficult for the police to catch the culprits. At the first sign of a policeman they would scarper into the maze of back alleys. In order to stage raids, uniformed men would be told to stay away from the area while plain-clothes detectives moved in.[73] The crowds would also try to rescue the operator if detained. When William Callaghan's gambling stall in Manchester Street was raided, two punters attacked the arresting officer.[74] In fact, policemen themselves were not averse to having a flutter. One off-duty officer lost 18 shillings and his job after being caught betting on a 'twirl about table' in Williamson Square.[75] Other officers were implicated in public house gaming.[76] If members of the public are to be believed, some constables turned a blind eye to street gambling, probably since arrests made them even more unpopular.[77] The law was never going to stop the practice. When a member of a Liverpool betting ring shot dead an affiliate, the other members immediately took to betting on the result of the trial, also offering odds on the killer's chance of a reprieve.[78]

Rational Recreation

It could be argued that the authorities had more success in reforming rather than repressing unsuitable popular recreations. The growing provision of morally suitable amenities, such as public parks, reading rooms, gymnasia and evening concerts, was thought to have helped wean people away from barbaric sporting spectacles and so-called 'low' entertainments. In 1887, after a visit to a new music hall in the heart of High Rip territory, a journalist could boast of vast improvements in people's leisure pursuits over the previous thirty years, despite the enduring attraction of macabre waxwork displays and the occasional rumours of cock-fighting. Indeed, a sign in a cellar window not far from St George's Hall still openly advertised 'Rats on sale: use of pits free.'[79] Other sports remained underground attractions. At Tommy the Weasle's, at the back of Banastre Street, a secret cock-fighting match took place one Sunday afternoon in 1883. Spectators were allowed into the upstairs room only if they correctly answered 'D-O-G' to the question, 'How do you spell cat?' A journalist present at the event revealed that he would rather have visited the art gallery or museum but they were of course closed on the sabbath.[80] The campaign for people's cultural and moral improvement was a long-fought battle. While museums and art galleries closed at dusk, the public houses stayed open until 11 p.m., the thirst for alcohol overriding the thirst for knowledge. After a visit to a Penny Show in Byrom Street, featuring fire-eating, feats of strength and a boxing match between a man and a woman, a journalist pointed out that the spectacle was a stone's throw from the cultural quarter of Liverpool, where the museum, library and art gallery remained closed.[81] One of the reasons given for not opening these institutions in the evening was that young people would only use them for courting. Ironically, the Picton Reading Room was built on the site of the old cockpit where birds once fought to the death, while the Walker Art Gallery overlooked the grounds of the old Folly Fair, the scene of many rough sports and entertainments.[82]

Other initiatives tapped into the public's need for popular recreation. The Hand-in-Hand Club movement, which originated in Glasgow, was brought to Liverpool in the 1870s by several eminent worthies. The clubs were created as an alternative to the public houses and offered reading rooms and various sedate amusements such as billiards, bagatelle and chess, although gambling was strictly forbidden. Tea and coffee were served instead of alcohol. Members could pay an annual or monthly subscription while non-members were charged a penny. The first club in Toxteth was followed by others in Marybone and Everton.[83]

Yet there was a positive change in working-class leisure patterns as the century progressed. Sports became increasingly governed and regulated by organizing bodies with strict rules and penalties. Reduced working hours and the provision of bank holidays gave employees time to follow worthwhile pursuits and the opportunity to escape the squalor of the slums. Hugh Shimmin, however, felt that Liverpudlians rarely went on day trips and when they did it was hardly for upright reasons: 'They work from week to week, have their Saturday night spree, their Sunday "guzzle," often have to neglect their work on Monday to overcome the Sunday's debauch.' If they did manage to reach Cheshire on a Sunday it was only in search of a drink.[84] Despite Shimmin's cynicism, family trips to the seaside became a more civilized substitute for the wild abandon and drunken orgies of the wakes and festivals. Ironically, in one of Liverpool's most notorious murder cases in 1874, Richard Morgan was murdered as he returned home from a bank holiday trip to New Ferry. His misfortune was to walk past some rough public houses where the clientele remained ignorant of any leisure pursuit except drunken violence.

By another cruel irony, Morgan was kicked across Tithebarn Street 'like a football' at a time when the game was beginning to take off in the city.[85] Four years later St Domingo Sunday FC was formed, later to become Everton Football Club. In the last quarter of the nineteenth century the new mass spectator sport of football helped divert people away from weekend drinking sprees. Workers on their Saturday afternoon holiday would rush home for a wash and brush up before attending the match. Crucially, they would leave their wages at home. This was said to have helped curb their drinking.[86] Yet even football would eventually be blighted by hooliganism as rival fans, fuelled by alcohol, aggression and a fierce sense of local pride, re-enacted some of the worst excesses of the wakes, bare-knuckle bouts and cock-fighting mains. Society's more brutal instincts have never been completely tamed. The present-day popularity of cage-fighting, as an alternative to boxing, caters for those craving a little more visual excitement, if not blood, while current scares about dangerous breeds of dogs point to the enduring attraction of underground dog-fighting.

Conclusion

Today's newspapers record the legacy of nineteenth-century social problems. Reports of knife crime, youth gangs, binge drinking, vice and anti-social behaviour all have their origins in an earlier age. The Victorians not only faced the same inner-city social problems, but faced them for the very first time. For all the benefits of social progress, we are still struggling with Victorian problems and still offering the same old solutions. It is ironic that when Liverpool City Council looked at establishing 'managed zones' for sex workers (selected districts where prostitution would be tolerated) one of the areas for consideration was Kempston Street, formerly Blandford Street, the focus of the city's brothels in the 1890s. This was the same 'red light district' permitted by Head Constable Nott-Bower and his officers.[1] It is as if we have come full circle.

Nineteenth-century distinctions about the deserving and undeserving poor have been transformed into debates about the nature of the underclass, that disreputable group consisting of the work-shy, the feckless, single mothers, uncontrollable teenagers, drug addicts and others seemingly lacking civilized values. CCTV has largely replaced the beady eyes of the beat constable but the battle for control of the streets continues. In place of Victorian officers moving on the Cornermen, we now have dispersal orders targeting unruly youths. The old slums might have been demolished but criminal districts still linger in run-down estates full of dilapidated houses, untidy gardens and barking dogs. One can imagine Abraham Hume and his team compiling a modern social survey, counting the number of ASBOs issued in each neighbourhood. 'Slum tourism' is also alive and well in television documentary programmes showing intrepid reporters venturing at night into the same crime-ridden estates to reveal strange and scary black-hooded creatures in their natural habitat. A throw-back to Victorian sensational journalism, these shocking exposés are similarly meant to shame us into acknowledging how the other half lives.

In a paper given at a conference of the National Association for the Promotion of Social Sciences in 1858, Revd Carter, the Anglican chaplain of the Borough Gaol, identified some causes of crime and offered various solutions.[2] Drunkenness was an obvious factor. Carter proposed imposing more regulation on the drink trade and reducing the number of public houses. The number of transient visitors to Liverpool, including masses of sailors, resulted in a large of pool of potential dupes, ripe for picking by the army of dockland sharpers. The presence of the destitute Irish, particularly women, was another cause of crime. Poverty and distress drove them to steal, a situation not helped by the amount of unprotected cargo stored along the docks. Existing laws were to be enforced to prohibit the exposure of goods outside shops, another great temptation to poor people. A vigilant eye was to be kept on marine store dealers and other receivers of stolen goods who further encouraged theft. The abundance of betting operations within licensed public houses was said to encourage gambling. Overcrowding in the slums helped foster vice, particularly since many families lacked religious or moral example.

Another cause of crime was 'idleness', by which Carter meant the lack of employment for young people, particularly girls. He called for more middle-class female charitable help and the use of emigration schemes to allow prostitutes a new start elsewhere. Children suffered from a lack of education. The solution was more ragged schools in the poorer districts and wider use of industrial training. For those in the criminal justice system, Carter recommended greater use of reformatories under the Youthful Offenders Act and called for improvements in the prison system. Even with 1,000 separate cells, Walton Gaol still lacked space. Shared cells meant that the separate system of prison discipline could not be fully implemented. Finally, Carter called for greater uniformity and certainty of sentences, adapted to the nature of the crime and taking into consideration the character and background of the offender's past history. It was another eleven years before the Habitual Criminals Act of 1869 required the authorities to focus upon repeat offenders and tailor sentences accordingly.

Over 150 years later, Carter's concerns are as relevant as ever. The same issues are still being raised and debated in Parliament, church pulpits, newspapers and public houses. Current alarm over the social effects of 24-hour drinking and the increased availability of alcohol in supermarkets is merely a modern version of the free-licensing controversy of the Victorian age. Recent publicity surrounding the saturation of drinking establishments in areas such as Lark Lane and Allerton Road echoes Victorian complaints about the number of beershops surrounding the Sailors' Home.[3]

Carter's condemnation of the temptations faced by poor people, in the form of exposed goods outside shops, has its modern counterpart in the alluring enticements of advertising and marketing. Sadly, the same powerful forces of consumerism still drive some people to own things that they cannot afford. Links between crime, immigration and race have continued since the destitute Irish arrived in droves and became scapegoats for a host of social ills. The racial mix in the city might have changed but resentment over housing, wages, jobs and the social burden of immigration is still voiced, often using the same arguments once directed against the Irish. Although present-day financial hardship is thankfully nowhere near as severe as the wretched squalor experienced by the Victorian destitute, the close relationship between crime and poverty remains a key factor in offending. Poverty of aspiration has perhaps replaced the worst excesses of material impoverishment. Overcrowding in poor housing is also still a reality for some. Carter's reference to a lack of religious or moral example has been transformed into the modern, more secular, search for suitable role models for young people, particularly in the light of the breakdown of the family and the absence of fathers. Unemployment and a lack of training remain important factors that can lead individuals to crime. Despite efforts to keep young people in education, a generation of NEETS (young people Not in Employment, Education, or Training) still causes concern. Although Carter's support of reformatories runs counter to current efforts to keep young people out of custody, his motives were nevertheless well-meaning. He wanted to remove youths from the bad influence of the streets and give them the skills to enable them to escape lives of poverty and crime. An army of teachers, probation officers, youth workers and social workers are today engaged in pretty much the same project.

Carter points to prison overcrowding as inhibiting the proper discipline and reformation of prisoners, an issue still being tackled with early-release schemes and non-custodial alternatives. Uniformity in sentencing and the certainty of punishment remain important talking points for the public. Letters to today's newspapers complain that the punishments no longer fit the crime and that criminals are forever laughing at the law in being offered 'soft' sentences. Readers regularly hark back to the glory years of Justice Day by urging the return of the birch.[4] The result, we are told, would be safer streets, empty gaols and a huge financial saving to the justice system. After a good flogging, surely the thugs would not come back for more. History, however, shows us that they do.

As for Liverpool, 'our wickedest city' became the European Capital of Culture in 2008. Redevelopment has transformed the dockland skyline but on the streets below there is the same old mixture of wealth and poverty. In a city founded on commerce, it is fitting that the entrepreneurial spirit is still thriving. However, it is the selling of drugs rather than the hawking of rotten fish that attracts today's underworld traders. Just as the bold privateersmen and heartless slavers once flooded the city with their wealth, today it is the drug-traffickers who keep the big money flowing. Hard-man reputations are still important, although pugilistic skill has largely been replaced by ballistic expertise, as guns become the weapons of choice for sorting out differences, however trivial. Knives also remain popular among the criminal fraternity, although their role as essential tools of the trade for dockers and seamen has long since gone. The ragged street urchins have updated their wardrobes by purchasing expensive tracksuits but have retained the same cheeky defiance and sharp tongue.

Yet all this could be said of any big city in the country. Manchester, London and Birmingham all have their problems with crime. What then makes Liverpool so special? Perhaps it is partly media hype, turning caricature into stereotype, and partly the uncomfortable fact that Liverpool does have a very real problem with a criminal minority so verbal, cocky and brazen (particularly when outside Liverpool) that they have become anti-ambassadors for the city. There is also the persistence of what the *Daily Post* once identified as the shocking intimacy of civilization and savagery, the idea that the best human achievements and the worst vices could exist side by side. Liverpool remains a town characterized by such extremes, where poverty and unemployment sit uneasily alongside great wealth and commercial opportunity. The social legacy of the city's nineteenth-century past casts a long shadow.

Notes

Preface

1 See Philip Boland, 'The Construction of Images of People and Place: Labelling Liverpool and Stereotyping Scousers', *Cities*, 25(6) (2008), pp. 355–69.
2 Kenneth Oxford, *Evidence to the Scarman Inquiry* (Liverpool, 1981), quoted in Phil Scraton, *Power, Conflict and Criminalisation* (London, 2007), pp. 27–28.
3 'Slipping on Streets Paved with Gold', *Daily Mail*, 12 July 2010.
4 *Daily Herald*, 27 July 1950.
5 *Daily Mirror*, 16 March 1947.
6 *Review of Reviews*, quoted in *DP*, 12 September 1911.
7 *LM*, 20 April 1869.
8 *BDP*, 17 August 1859.
9 *The Times*, 26 November 1877, 26 December 1874.
10 Abraham Hume, *Missions at Home: A Clergyman's Account of a Portion of the Town of Liverpool* (London, 1850), p. 16.
11 Walter Lowe Clay, *The Prison Chaplain: a Memoir of the Rev. John Clay* (Cambridge, 1861), p. 570.
12 *DP*, 4 September 1886.
13 W. C. Taylor, 'Moral Economy of Large Towns: Liverpool', *Bentley's Miscellany*, vol. 8 (1840), p. 131, quoted in J. C. Wood, *Violence and Crime in Nineteenth-Century England: the Shadow of Our Refinement* (London, 2004), p. 32.
14 Hume, *Missions at Home*, p. 19.
15 Richard Acland Armstrong, *The Deadly Shame of Liverpool: An Appeal to the Municipal Voters* (London, 1890), pp. 3–4.
16 *LM*, 9 April 1892.
17 *LM*, 17 August 1857, 'Liverpool Life', chapter XXI.
18 See, for example, the Baring Brothers scandal of 1897, when a partner in the Liverpool house of the firm was forced to resign after embezzling large sums. He wasn't even prosecuted. Gregory Anderson, *Victorian Clerks* (Manchester, 1976), pp. 35–37.
19 PP 1847–48 XXXVI, *Thirteenth Report of the Inspectors of Prisons for the Northern and Eastern District*, p. 21

'Ghastly statistics' – a Word of Warning

1 *LM*, 26 April 1850.
2 *LM*, 12 February 1850.
3 See Clive Emsley, *Crime and Society in England: 1750–1900* (Harlow, 3rd edn, 2005), chapter 2.

4 *LM*, 14 March 1894.

5 'Discrepant Criminal Statistics', *Journal of the Statistical Society*, xxxi (1868), p. 352.

6 *LM*, 12 February 1850.

7 PP 1901 LXXXIX, *Judicial Statistics, England and Wales, 1899. Part I*, p. 69.

8 PP 1860 LX, *Judicial Statistics, England and Wales, 1860. Part I*, p. 27.

9 *LM*, 26 January 1892.

10 *The Times*, 28 November 1877.

11 *The Times*, 3 December 1877.

12 *The Times*, 3 December 1877.

13 Figures from Frank Neal, 'A Criminal Profile of the Liverpool Irish', *Transactions of the Historical Society of Lancashire and Cheshire*, 140 (1990), p. 165.

14 PP 1872 (242) IX, *Report from the Select Committee on Habitual Drunkards*, p. 120, q. 2075.

15 Sir William Nott-Bower, *Fifty-Two Years as a Policeman* (London, 1926), p. 142.

16 *LM*, 22 November 1877.

1: The Black Spot on the Mersey

1 Thomas Baines, *History of the Commerce and Town of Liverpool* (1852), p. 676.

2 For the rival claims of Manchester, see Joseph O'Neill, *Crime City: Manchester's Victorian Underworld* (Wrea Green, 2008).

3 [James Stonehouse], *Recollections of Old Liverpool by a Nonagenarian* (Liverpool, 1863), p. 7.

4 J. A. Picton, *Memorials of Liverpool: Historical and Topographical, vol.1: Historical* (Liverpool, 2nd edn, 1903), pp. 191–92.

5 *Memoirs of Hugh Crow*, quoted in Gomer Williams, *History of the Liverpool Privateers and Letters of Marque with an account of the Slave Trade* [1897] (Liverpool, repr. 2004), p. 688.

6 James Aspinall, *Liverpool, a Few Years Since, by an Old Stager* (Liverpool, 1852), p. 15.

7 Stonehouse, *Recollections*, p. 10.

8 Ramsey Muir, *History of Liverpool* (London, 1907), p. 212.

9 Picton, *Memorials*, vol. I, p. 213.

10 W. R. Cockroft, 'Liverpool Police Force 1836–1902', in S. P. Bell, *Victorian Lancashire* (Newton Abbot, 1974), p. 150.

11 PP 1847–48 LIII, p. 22.

12 George Chandler, *Liverpool* (London, 1957), p. 415.

13 PP 1847 VII, *Second Report from the Select Committee of the House of Lords Appointed to Inquire into the Execution of the Criminal Law, especially Respecting Juvenile Offenders and Transportation*, p. 193, q. n1707; *LM*, 14 May 1847.

14 PP 1857–58 XXIII, *Papers Relative to Sanitary State of People of England Results of Inquiry into Proportions of Death Produced by Diseases in Different Districts in England, by E.H. Greenhow*, p. 16.

15 *The Times*, 4 May 1847.

16 *LM*, 20 February 1846; Thomas Burke, *Catholic History of Liverpool* (Liverpool, 1910), p. 82.

17 R. B. Walker, 'Religious Changes in Liverpool in the Nineteenth Century', *Journal of Ecclesiastical History*, 19(2) (1968), p. 199.

18 Frank Neal, *Black 47: Britain and the Irish Famine* (Basingstoke, 1988), p. 139.

19 *Liverpool Mail*, 6 November 1847.

20 Thomas Burke, 'The Street Trading Children of Liverpool', *Contemporary Review*, 78 (1900), p. 726.

21 Linda Grant, 'Women's Work and Trade Unionism in Liverpool, 1890–1914', *Bulletin of North West Labour History Society*, 7 (1980–81), pp. 65–83.

22 *Squalid Liverpool: by a Special Commission* (Liverpool, 1883), p. 14. Also published in *Daily Post*, 5–10 November 1883.

23 *Liverpool Mortality Sub-Committee, Report and Evidence 1865–1866*, pp. 152, 198.

24 *DP*, 5 November 1883.

25 See Martha Kanya-Forstner, 'The Politics of Survival: Irish Women in Outcast Liverpool, 1850-1890', unpublished PhD thesis, University of Liverpool, 1997, p. 96.

26 PP 1882 XIII, *Report from the Select Committee of the House of Lords on the Law Relating to the Protection of Young Girls*, p. 16, q. 104, evidence of Father Nugent.

27 *Porcupine*, 13 April 1867.

28 *Liverpool Echo*, 21 May 1887.

29 See David Taylor, *Policing the Victorian Town: the Development of the Police in Middlesbrough, c.1840–1914* (Basingstoke, 2002).

30 See David Jones, *Crime, Protest and Police in Nineteenth-Century Britain* (London, 1982), pp. 85–116

31 See O'Neill, *Crime City*.

32 Alfred Aspland, *Crime in Manchester and Police Administration* (London, 1868), p. 6.

33 Clay, *The Prison Chaplain*, pp. 517–19; Margaret Delacy, *Prison Reform in Lancashire, 1700–1850* (Manchester, 1986), p. 215.

34 John K. Walton, Martin Blinkhorn, Colin Pooley, David Tidswell and Michael J. Winstanley, 'Crime, Migration and Social Change in North-West England and the Basque Country, c.1870–1930', *British Journal of Criminology*, 39(1) (1999), p. 99.

35 *BDP*, 5 November 1890.

36 *LM*, 8 January 1866.

37 Samuel Smith, *My Life Work* (London, 1903), p. 126.

38 Hippolyte Taine, *Taine's Notes on England*, trans. with an introduction by Edward Hyams (London, 1957), p. 226.

39 *LM*, 6 February 1900.

40 *LM*, 15 February 1900.

41 *LM*, 30 November 1899.

2: Policing

1 James A. Picton, *Muncipal Archives and Records from AD 1700 to the Passing of the Municipal Reform Act, 1835* (Liverpool, 1886), p. 285.

2 Muir, *History of Liverpool*, p. 220.

3 *LM*, 29 November 1822.

4 *Williamson's Advertiser*, 2 February, 2 August 1776.

5 *LM*, 24 January 1834.

6 'A man of business' [William Rathbone], *Social Duties Considered with Reference to the Organisation of Effort in Works of Benevolence and Public Utility* (London, 1867), pp. 2–14. Charles Garrett, looking back over fifty years, makes the same point. See 'The Poor of Liverpool and What is Done for Them', *LM*, 18 September 1899.

7 *Squalid Liverpool*, p. 37.

8 Daniel Murray, *The Story of Holy Cross* (Liverpool, 1948), pp. 42–43.

9 [Thomas Troughton], *The History of Liverpool, from the Earliest Authenticated Period Down to the Present Time* (1810), p. 176.

10 Richard Brooke, *Liverpool in the Last Quarter of the Eighteenth Century* (Liverpool, 1853), pp. 266, 298–300.

11 Richard McMahon (ed.), *Crime, Law and Popular Culture in Europe* (Cullompton, 2008), p. 209.

12 Emsley, *Crime and Society in England*, p. 300.

13 George H. Pumphrey, *The Story of Liverpool's Public Services* (Liverpool, 1940), p. 175; Muir, *History of Liverpool*, p. 274.

14 Cockroft, 'Liverpool Police Force 1836–1902', p. 151.

15 *Bettell's Life in London and Liverpool Sporting Register*, vol. III, no. 139, 21 July 1827.

16 Cockroft, 'Liverpool Police Force 1836–1902', p. 151.

17 *LM*, 18 April 1895.

18 *LM*, 30 March 1821.

19 Quoted in Mike Brogden, *On the Mersey Beat: Policing Liverpool Between the Wars* (Oxford, 1991), p. 87.

20 Aspinall, *Liverpool, a Few Years Since*, pp. 104–06.

21 Aspinall, *Liverpool, a Few Years Since*, p. 106; *LM*, 4 July 1867; Pumphrey, *Story of Liverpool's Public Services*, p. 174.

22 *Liverpool Journal*, 1 August 1835.

23 W. R. Cockroft, *From Cutlasses to Computers: the Police Force in Liverpool, 1836–1989* (Market Drayton, 1991), p. 3.

24 *DP*, 19 April 1934.

25 *DP*, 7 February 1936.

26 *LM*, 18 April 1895.

27 *LM*, 10 February 1815.

28 Eric Midwinter, *Old Liverpool* (Newton Abbot, 1971), p. 62.

29 Aspinall, *Liverpool, a Few Years Since*, p. 107.

30 Cockroft, 'Liverpool Police Force 1836–1902', p. 151.

31 Picton, *Memorials*, vol. I, p. 469.

32 Aspland, *Crime in Manchester*, p. 8.

33 Figures quoted in PP 1839 XIX, *Royal Commission on Establishing an Efficient Constabulary Force in Counties of England and Wales*, p. 11.

34 Hugh Mulleneux Walmsley, *Life of Sir Joshua Walmsley by His Son* (London, 1879), pp. 80–83.

35 W. A. Miles was an investigator who worked for the Royal Commission but published a slightly different version of his findings separately. See W. A. Miles and H. Brandon (ed.), *Poverty, Mendicity and Crime, or, the Facts, Examinations, &c. Upon Which the Report Was Founded, Presented to the House of Lords* (London, 1839), pp. 57–58, 80.

36 See David Philips, *William Augustus Miles (1796–1851): Crime, Policing and Moral Entrepreneurship in England and Australia* (Melbourne, 2001).

37 *Cleave's Penny Gazette of Variety and Amusement*, 31 October 1840.

38 Walmsley, *Life of Sir Joshua Walmsley*, pp. 80–83.

39 *Liverpool Mail*, November 1836.

40 Nathaniel Hawthorne, *The English Notebooks*, ed. Randall Stewart (New York, 1962 [1941]), p. 17.

41 F. M. L. Thompson, *The Rise of Respectable Society, a Social History of Victorian Britain, 1830–90* (London, 1988), pp. 331–32.

42 *Liverpool Weekly Albion*, 30 May 1859.

43 Walton et al., 'Crime, Migration and Social Change', p. 100.

44 *LM*, 27 December 1882.

45 *LM*, 16 May 1848.

46 Anne Bryson, 'Riotous Liverpool, 1815–1860', in John Belchem (ed.), *Popular Politics, Riot and Labour: Essays in Liverpool History, 1790–1940* (Liverpool, 1992), p. 126.

47 W. J. Lowe, 'The Irish in Lancashire 1846–71: a Social History', unpublished PhD thesis, University of Dublin, 1974, pp. 227–28. Elsewhere, Lowe states that by 1870 the Irish had managed to plummet from 44 per cent of assaults on the police to 28 per cent: *The Irish in Mid-Victorian Lancashire* (New York, 1989), p. 40.

48 Barbara Weinburger, 'The Police and the Public in Mid-Nineteenth Century Warwick-

shire', in Victor Bailey (ed.), *Policing and Punishment in Nineteenth Century Britain* (London, 1981), pp. 69–71.

49 Watch Committee, Daily Board, 28 July 1849, quoted in *LM*, 7 September 1849.

50 Abstracts of Head Constable's reports in *LM*, 20 January 1858, 1 June 1857, 23 November 1865.

51 *Era*, 26 April 1890.

52 *LM*, 11 April 1899.

53 *LM*, 23 April 1852.

54 LVRO, 352 MIN/WAT, Minutes of the Watch Committee, 18 February 1854; Bryson, 'Riotous Liverpool, 1815–1860', p. 116.

55 *LM*, 26 November 1858.

56 *LM*, 24 January 1868.

57 *LM*, 30 March 1860.

58 *LM*, 30 August 1871.

59 J. E. Archer, *Violence in the North West with Special Reference to Liverpool and Manchester, 1850–1914* (Swindon, 2001), p. 12.

60 For further examples of police brutality see *LM*, 24 September 1847, 16 April 1862, 27 July 1869, 25 February 1876, 11 August 1877.

61 *LR*, 22 August 1885.

62 *LM*, 13 July 1847.

3: Prison and Punishment

1 James A. Picton, *Selections from the Municipal Archives and Records from the Thirteenth Century to the Seventeenth Century Inclusive* (Liverpool, 1883), p. 35.

2 *Williamson's Advertiser*, 11 August 1785.

3 *Notes and Queries*, 2nd series, VII (8 January 1859), p. 39.

4 Stonehouse, *Recollections*, p. 7.

5 *Gore's Advertiser*, 17 November 1825.

6 *LM*, 25 May 1927.

7 *Public Advertiser*, 3 January 1785.

8 *Whitehall Evening Post*, 1 and 12 April 1788; *Morning Chronicle and London Advertiser*, 8 April 1788.

9 Picton, *Memorials*, vol. I, p. 410.

10 *LM*, 12 April 1836.

11 *LM*, 12 May 1843.

12 *LM*, 14 September 1863.

13 *LR*, 27 September 1902.

14 See Michael Macilwee, *The Gangs of Liverpool: From the Cornermen to the High Rip: The Mobs that Terrorised a City* (Wrea Green, 2006), pp. 86–88.

15 Tod Sloan, *The Treadmill and the Rope: The History of a Liverpool Prison* (Parkgate, 1988), p. 27.

16 PP 1837–38 XXXI, *Third Report of the Inspectors Appointed Under the Provisions of the Act 5 & 6 Will. IV. c. 38. to Visit the Different Prisons of Great Britain. II. Northern and Eastern District*, p. 141.

17 National Archives. Convict Prisons: Attested List of Convicts, 1824–76. H.O.8/55 quoted in Midwinter, *Old Liverpool*, pp. 58–59 and E. C. Midwinter, *Social Administration in Lancashire: Poor Law, Public Health and Police* (Manchester, 1969), pp. 133–34.

18 Sloan, *The Treadmill and the Rope*, p. 24.

19 Barry Godfrey and Paul Lawrence, *Crime and Justice, 1750–1950* (Cullompton, 2005), p. 73.

20 Sloan, *The Treadmill and the Rope*, p. 24.

21 James Stonehouse, *Streets of Liverpool* [1869] (Liverpool, 2002), pp. 46–47. Stonehouse calls her Julia Arnett.

22 John Briggs, Christopher Harrison, Angus McInnes and David Vincent, *Crime and Punishment in England: an Introductory History* (London, 1996), p. 169.

23 Stonehouse, *Recollections*, pp. 24–25, 27.

24 *Lloyd's Evening Post*, 5 February 1770.

25 *Liverpool Vestry Books*, 9 February 1776, p. 109.

26 Benjamin Wait, *Letters from Van Diemen's Land: Written During Four Years Imprisonment* (Buffalo, 1843). Reprinted as *The Wait Letters* (Erin, Ont., 1976), p. 74.

27 Anon. [James Wallace], *A General and Descriptive History of the Ancient and Present State of the Town of Liverpool* (Liverpool, 1795), p. 178.

28 William Moss, *Georgian Liverpool: a Guide to the City in 1797*, with additional notes by David Brazendale [1797] (Lancaster, 2007), pp. 87–88.

29 See Sloan, *The Treadmill and the Rope*; J. Matthew Gallman, *Receiving Erin's Children: Philadelphia, Liverpool, and the Irish Famine, 1845–1855* (Chapel Hill, NC, 2000), p. 205.

30 Figures from Sloan, *The Treadmill and the Rope*, p. 11.

31 PP 1845 XXIV, *Tenth Report of the Inspectors Appointed Under the Provisions of the Act 5 & 6 Will. IV. c. 38, to Visit the Different Prisons of Great Britain. II. Northern and Eastern District*, p. 80.

32 William Hepworth Dixon, *The London Prisons* (London, 1850), p. 333.

33 Wait, *Letters from Van Diemen's Land*, p. 168.

34 Wait, *Letters from Van Diemen's Land*, pp. 74, 78.

35 Letter from Dr Johnston, *True Briton*, 31 July 1800; Troughton, *History of Liverpool*, p. 227.

36 PP 1837 XXXII, *Second Report of the Inspectors of Prisons of Great Britain. II. Northern and Eastern District*, p. 66.

37 PP 1839 XXII, *Fourth Report of the Inspectors Appointed Under the Provisions of the Act 5 & 6 Will. IV. c. 38. to Visit the Different Prisons of Great Britain. II. Northern and Eastern District*, p. 58.

38 PP 1837–38 XXXI, p. 122.

39 PP 1837–38 XXXI, p. 141.

40 PP 1835 XI, *Select Committee on Gaols and Houses of Correction, in England and Wales Appendix*, p. 42.

41 PP 1837–38 XXXI, p. 122.

42 PP 1843 XXV & XXVI, *Eighth Report of the Inspectors Appointed Under the Provisions of the Act 5 & 6 Will. IV. c. 38, to Visit the Different Prisons of Great Britain. II. Northern and Eastern District*, p. 2.

43 Delacy, *Prison Reform in Lancashire*, p. 202.

44 PP 1839 XIX, p. 27.

45 PP 1843 XXV & XXVI, p. 17.

46 Figures from Sloan, *The Treadmill and the Rope*, p. 15. The figures do not include prisoners executed or an unknown number of children who died within the prisons.

47 PP 1847–48 XXXVI, p. 15.

48 PP 1837 XXXII, p. 61.

49 *Kirkdale Gaol: Twelve Months Imprisonment of a Manchester Merchant* (Manchester, 1880), p. 95.

50 *Kirkdale Gaol*, p. 100.

51 *Kirkdale Gaol*, p. 101.

52 PP 1837 XXXII, p. 62.

53 PP 1839 XXII, p. 58.

54 PP 1847–48 XXXVI, p. 86.

55 *LM*, 27 July 1857.

56 Basil Thomson, *The Criminal* (London, 1925), pp. 27–28.

57 Thomson, *The Criminal*, pp. 112–13.

58 PP 1845 XXIV, p. 91.

59 *LM*, 1, 27, 29 May 1875; *John Bull*, 29 May 1875.

60 *LR*, 27 July 1889.

61 George Melly, 'On the Treatment of Adult Criminals': a Paper Read at the First Meeting of the Local Association for the Promotion of Social Science, 22 November 1860, bound in *Stray Leaves: Pamphlets, Speeches, Addresses &c. on Social and Political Questions* (Liverpool, 1856–1863), p. 9.

62 B. E. N. Lyte, 'The Development of Prisons in Liverpool' (1964), typed manuscript, LVRO, no page numbers.

63 PP 1837–38 XXXI, p. 123.

64 Thomson, *The Criminal*, p. 29.

65 W. B. Forwood, *Recollections of a Busy Life* (Liverpool, 1910), p. 158.

66 PP 1837 XXXII, p. 67.

67 *LM*, 15 May 1849.

68 PP 1847–48 XXXVI, p. 15.

69 *LM*, 12 May 1837.

70 PP 1847–48 XXXVI, p. 20.

71 PP 1837 XXXII, p. 65.

72 Geoffrey Best, *Mid Victorian Britain* (London, 1979), p. 165.

73 Quoted in Henry Smithers, *Liverpool, its Commerce, Statistics and Institutions with a History of the Cotton Trade* (Liverpool, 1825), p. 73.

74 PP 1863 IX, *Report from the Select Committee of the House of Lords, on the Present State of Discipline in Gaols and Houses of Correction*, p. ix.

75 Briggs et al., *Crime and Punishment in England*, p. 171.

76 PP 1851 XXVII, *Sixteenth Report of the Inspectors Appointed, Under the Provisions of the Act 5 & 6 Will. IV. c. 38 to Visit the Different Prisons of Great Britain. II. Northern and Eastern District*, p. 4.

77 PP 1837 XXXII, p. 66.

78 W. L. Melville Lee, *A History of Police in England* [1901] (Montclair, NJ, 1971), p. 345.

79 Charles De Motte, 'The Dark Side of the Town: Crime in Manchester and Salford, 1815–1875', unpublished PhD thesis, University of Kansas, 1977, p. 221.

80 *Bell's Life in London and Sporting Chronicle*, 14 December 1856.

81 See Jennifer Davis, 'The London Garotting Panic of 1862: A Moral Panic and the Creation of a Criminal Class in Mid-Victorian England', in *Crime and the Law: a Social History of Crime in Western Europe Since 1500*, ed. V. A. C. Gatrell, Bruce Lenman and Geoffrey Parker (London, 1980), pp. 190–213.

82 Forwood, *Recollections*, p. 158.

83 *LM*, 17 February 1875, 26 April 1876.

84 *Transactions of the National Association for the Promotion of Social Sciences, Liverpool Meeting, 1876*, ed. Charles Wager Ryalls (London, 1877), p. 358.

85 Joseph Collinson, *Facts about Flogging* (London, rev. edn, 1905), pp. 29–30.

86 *Daily Telegraph*, quoted in *Pall Mall Magazine*, 17 December 1874; *LM*, 20 August 1875.

87 See Macilwee, *The Gangs of Liverpool*, pp. 219–20.

88 Cesare Lombroso, *Criminal Man* [1876], translated with a new introduction by Mary Gibson and Nicole Hahn Rafter (Durham, NC, 2006).

89 Miles, *Poverty, Mendicity and Crime*, p. 84.

90 PP 1841 V, p. 140.

91 Emsley, *Crime and Society in England*, pp. 280–81.

92 *LM*, 18 December 1869.

93 Watch Committee for the Borough of Liverpool, *Report on the Police Establishment, and the State of Crime, with Tabular Returns* […] *1869*, p. 11.

94 *LM*, 28 September 1869.

95 Thomson, *The Criminal*, p. 26.

96 Roy Palmer (ed.), *A Touch of the Times: Songs of Social Change, 1770 to 1914* (Harmondsworth, 1974), pp. 250–52. The ballad Palmer includes is called 'Wakefield Gaol' but the same song was sung in various prisons under different names, including 'Preston Gaol' or simply 'The County Gaol'. The Kirkdale version of the street ballad (without imprint) is in W. H. N. Harding collection, Quarto Street Ballads, no. 2000, Bodleian Library.

97 Thomson, *The Criminal*, pp. 26–27.

4: Children and Women in the Justice System

1 *LR*, 21 February 1885.

2 Mary Carpenter, *Reformatory Schools* (London, 1868), p. 218.

3 PP 1839 XXII, p. 89.

4 PP 1839 XXII, p. 58.

5 Joan Rimmer, *Yesterday's Naughty Children: Training Ships, Girls' Reformatory and Farm School: a History of the Liverpool Reformatory Association Founded in 1855* (Swinton, 1986), p. 6.

6 Carpenter, *Reformatory Schools*, p. 266.

7 PP 1841 V, *Sixth Report of the Inspectors of Prisons of Great Britain II. Northern and Eastern District*, pp. 97–98.

8 *LM*, 12 October 1857, 4 November 1857.

9 *LM*, 14 April 1826.

10 Carpenter, *Reformatory Schools*, p. 265.

11 PP 1839 XXII, p. 88.

12 PP 1837 XXXII, p. 88.

13 PP 1839 XXII, p. 89.

14 PP 1837 XXXII, p. 89.

15 Miles, *Poverty, Mendicity and Crime*, pp. 81–83.

16 PP 1847 VII, pp. 191–92 q. 1696–q. 1700, quoted in Carpenter, *Reformatory Schools*, pp. 50–51.

17 Jeannie Duckworth, *Fagin's Children: Criminal Children in Victorian England* (London, 2002), pp. 135–36.

18 LVRO, 'Industrial Schools Admission and Discharge Book', 29 December 1862–14 June 1865, quoted in Terence O'Brien, 'The Education and Care of Workhouse Children in Some Lancashire Poor Law Unions, 1834–1930', unpublished MEd thesis, University of Manchester, 1975, p. 209.

19 Burke, *Catholic History of Liverpool*, pp. 173–74.

20 Rimmer, *Yesterday's Naughty Children*, p. 65.

21 Godfrey and Lawrence, *Crime and Justice, 1750–1950*, p. 136.

22 *LM*, 21 April 1863.

23 PP 1852–53 XXIII, *Report from the Select Committee on Criminal and Destitute Children*, p. 116, q. 1348, p. 124, q. 1429, q. 1430.

24 PP 1845 XXIV, p. 84.

25 Rimmer, *Yesterday's Naughty Children*, pp. 26–30.

26 Rimmer, *Yesterday's Naughty Children*, p. 42.

27 Rimmer, *Yesterday's Naughty Children*, pp. 37–38.

28 PP 1837 XXXII, p. 88.

29 Patricia Runaghan, *Father Nugent's Liverpool, 1849–1905* (Birkenhead, 2003), p. 37.

30 LM, 12 October 1885.

31 Godfrey and Lawrence, *Crime and Justice, 1750–1950*, p. 128.

32 LM, 26 October 1847.

33 *Englishwoman's Review*, 1 October 1874.

34 Mary Carpenter, *Our Convicts* (London, 1864), vol. II, p. 242.

35 Liverpool Council Proceedings, Prison Ministers Reports, 1865–66, p. 581.

36 PP 1897 XXXV.1, *Royal Commission on Liquor Licensing Laws*, p. 43, q. 12263, evidence of T. E. Sampson.

37 John Davies, 'Father James Nugent, Prison Chaplain', *North West Catholic History*, XXII (1995), p. 19.

38 PP 1901 LXXXIX, p. 74.

39 Stonehouse, *Recollections*, p. 50.

40 John Howard, *State of the Prisons of England and Wales* (Warrington, 1794), p. 437.

41 Brooke, *Liverpool in the Eighteenth Century*, p. 354; Smithers, *Liverpool*, p. 72; Stonehouse, *Recollections*, p. 50.

42 PP 1837–38 XXXI, p. 126.

43 PP 1845 XXIV, p. 81.

44 PP 1841 V, p. 117.

45 Frederick W. Lowndes, *The Extension of the Contagious Diseases Act in Liverpool and other Seaports Practically Considered* (Liverpool, 1876), p. 81.

46 Frederick W. Lowndes, *Prostitution and Syphilis in Liverpool; and The Working of the Contagious Diseases Acts in Aldershot, Chatham, Plymouth and Devonport* (London, 1876), p. 12.

47 *The Times*, 17 February 1843; LM, 10 March 1843.

48 LM, 20 and 27 November 1849.

49 Jane Jordan, *Josephine Butler* (London, 2001), p. 67.

50 LM, 3 March 1865.

51 Glen Petrie, *A Singular Iniquity: the Campaigns of Josephine Butler* (London, 1971), pp. 51–52.

52 PP 1843 XXV & XXVI, p. 2.

53 PP 1884 XLII, *Seventh Report of the Commissioners of Prisons*, p. 66.

54 Thomson, *The Criminal*, pp. 24, 31–33.

55 PP 1837 XXXII, p. 67.

56 PP 1877 XI, p. 21, q. 8207.

57 Carpenter, *Our Convicts*, vol. II, p. 244.

58 LM, 16 January 1885.

59 PP 1844 XXIX, *Ninth Report of the Inspectors Appointed under the Provisions of the act 5 & 6 Will. IV. c. 38, to Visit the Different Prisons of Great Britain. II. Northern and Eastern District*, p. 137.

60 LM, 24 April 1867.

61 LM, 17 November 1891.

62 LC, 29 July 1905.

63 See Lucia Zedner, *Women, Crime and Custody in Victorian England* (Oxford, 1991), pp. 259–63.

64 LR, 28 February 1891.

65 Burke, *Catholic History of Liverpool*, p. 152.

66 Sometimes referred to as the 'Magdalen Asylum' or 'Institution', the Female Penitentiary should not be mistaken for the Magdalen Institution, a Church of England refuge founded in 1855 for the same purpose.

67 LVRO, Liverpool Female Penitentiary Annual Reports, 1855–1877.

68 LR, 4 March 1893.

69 LR, 31 August 1889.

70 LR, 12 December 1891.

5: 'The Scum of Ireland'

1 Figures from Neal, 'A Criminal Profile of the Liverpool Irish', p. 167 and PP 1836 (40) XXXIV, *Royal Commission on the Condition of the Poorer Classes in Ireland, Appendix G, The State of Irish Poor in Great Britain*, p. vii.
2 See Terry Coleman, *The Railway Navvies: a History of the Men Who Made the Railways* (London, 1965).
3 *LM*, 10 February 1827.
4 PP 1846 XIII, *Select Committee on Railway Labourers*, p. 193.
5 PP 1846 XIII, pp. 194–97.
6 For examples see *LM*, 3 July 1846, 4 December 1846.
7 PP 1839 XIX, p. 156.
8 PP 1836 XXXI, p. 20.
9 *LM*, 11 January 1848.
10 *LM*, 8 August 1840.
11 PP 1846 XIII, p. 63.
12 Letter from Peter M'Donough, *LM*, 8 November 1839.
13 Neal, 'A Criminal Profile of the Liverpool Irish', p. 166.
14 Nott-Bower, *Fifty-Two Years as a Policeman*, pp. 147–48.
15 *Porcupine*, 8 August 1874.
16 Neal, 'A Criminal Profile of the Liverpool Irish', p. 166.
17 Neal, 'A Criminal Profile of the Liverpool Irish', p. 167.
18 PP 1870 VIII, *Report from the Select Committee on Prisons and Prison Ministers Acts*, p. 149.
19 *Liverpool Domestic Mission Society Annual Report, 1847* (Liverpool, 1847).
20 PP 1847–48 LIII, *Reports and Communications on Vagrancy*, p. 2; *LM*, 15 May 1849.
21 PP 1847–48 LIII, p. 15.
22 PP 1847 LIV, *Destitute Irish (Liverpool). Copies Of, Or Extracts From, Any Correspondence Addressed to the Secretary of State for the Home Department, Relative to the Recent Immigration of Destitute Irish into Liverpool*, p. 8.
23 PP 1849 LI, *Captain Denham's Report on Passenger Accommodation in Steamers between Ireland and Liverpool*, p. 6.
24 PP 1849 XLVII, *Letter to Secretary of State for Home Dept., by Stipendiary Magistrate of Liverpool, April 1849, Respecting Influx of Irish Poor*, p. 2; *LM*, 15 May 1849.
25 PP 1847 XXVIII, *Thirteenth Annual Report of the Poor Law Commissioners, with appendices*, p. 6. See Lowe, *The Irish in Mid-Victorian Lancashire*, p. 25.
26 *LM*, 25 December 1846, 22 January 1847.
27 *Liverpool Weekly Albion*, 10 May 1847.
28 *LM*, 20 July 1847.
29 PP 1836 (40) XXXIV, p. 15.
30 *Liverpool Chronicle*, 15 May 1847.
31 *LC*, 21 February 1855.
32 *LM*, 16 July 1847.
33 Frederick Law Olmsted, *Walks and Talks of an American Farmer in England* (Columbus, OH, new edn, 1859), p. 4.
34 PP 1836 (40) XXXIV, pp. 10, 14–15.
35 *Liverpool Mail*, 6 November 1847.
36 *LC*, 14 February 1855.
37 *Liverpool Mail*, 5 February 1847.
38 PP 1847 LIV, p. 13.
39 *LM*, 11 May 1847.

40 Clay, *The Prison Chaplain*, pp. 517–19.

41 PP 1847 VII, p. 194, q. 1713.

42 PP 1847–48 XXXVI, p. 13.

43 Figures from W. J. Lowe, quoted in Roger Swift and Sheridan Gilley (eds), *The Irish in Britain, 1815–1939* (London, 1989), p. 26.

44 See Neal, 'A Criminal Profile of the Liverpool Irish'; Roger Swift, 'Heroes or Villains? The Irish, Crime and Disorder in Victorian England', *Albion*, 29 (1997), pp. 339–421; Gallman, *Receiving Erin's Children*, pp. 187–91.

45 F. G. D'Aeth, 'Liverpool', in Helen Bosanquet (ed.), *Social Conditions in Provincial Towns* (London, 1912; New York, repr. 1985), p. 38.

46 PP 1836 (40) XXXIV, p. 20.

47 Nott-Bower, *Fifty-Two Years as a Policeman*, pp. 147–48.

48 PP 1836 (40) XXXIV, p. 10.

49 PP 1836 (40) XXXIV, p. xxi.

50 PP 1836 (40) XXXIV, pp. 19–22.

51 Frank Neal, *Sectarian Violence: the Liverpool Experience, 1819–1914: an Aspect of Anglo Irish Experience* (Liverpool, repr. 2003 [1988]), p. 111.

52 PP 1836 (40) XXXIV, p. 20.

53 PP 1851 XXVII, pp. 14–15.

54 *Liverpool Herald*, 17 November 1855.

55 Neal, 'A Criminal Profile of the Liverpool Irish', p. 114.

56 PP 1836 (40) XXXIV, p. 27.

57 For examples, see *LM*, 18 June 1847 and 12 March 1885.

58 *LM*, 2 May 1900.

59 Richard Hobson, *What Hath God Wrought: An Autobiography* (Liverpool, 1903), p. 49.

60 John Denvir, *The Irish in Britain: From the Earliest Times to the Fall and Death of Parnell* (London, 1892), p. 435.

61 Clay, *The Prison Chaplain*, p. 569.

62 *Liverpool Mail*, 24 February 1855.

6: Protest, Riot and Disorder

1 Carpenter, *Our Convicts*, vol. II, pp. 351–52.

2 R. M. Jones, 'The Liverpool Bread Riots, 1855', *Bulletin of the North West Labour History Society*, 6 (1979–80), p. 39.

3 Nicholas Rogers, *The Press-Gang: Naval Impressment and its Opponents in Georgian Britain* (London, 2007), p. 8.

4 Aspinall, *Liverpool, a Few Years Since*, pp. 7–11.

5 J. R. Hutchinson, *The Press-Gang, Afloat and Ashore* (London, 1913), p. 56.

6 Aspinall, *Liverpool, a Few Years Since*, pp. 7–11; Michael O'Mahoney, *Ways and Byways of Liverpool* (Liverpool, 1931), p. 122.

7 Williams, *History of the Liverpool Privateers*, p. 85.

8 Williams, *History of the Liverpool Privateers*, pp. 157–59; *London Evening-Post*, 31 July 1759.

9 Williams, *History of the Liverpool Privateers*, p. 85.

10 Stonehouse, *Recollections*, p. 57.

11 George Chandler, *William Roscoe of Liverpool* (London, 1953), p. 59.

12 Picton, *Memorials*, vol. I, p. 601.

13 Aspinall, *Liverpool, a Few Years Since*, pp. 7–11.

14 PRO Northern Ireland, T 3541/5/3 ff. 140–1, quoted in Rogers, *Press-Gang*, p. 74.

15 Williams, *History of the Liverpool Privateers*, p. 194.

16 TNA, Adm 1/1788 (John Fortescue), 19 February 1762, quoted in Rogers, *Press-Gang*, pp. 73–74.

17 *Williamson's Advertiser*, 22 November 1776; *Daily Advertiser*, 25 November 1776.

18 *British Chronicle or Pugh's Hereford Journal*, 30 March 1780.

19 Williams, *History of the Liverpool Privateers*, p. 319.

20 TNA, Adm 1/1787 (Fortescue), 6 September 1761, TNA, Adm 1/1788 (Fortescue), 18 April 1762; TNA, Adm 1/1618 (Smith Child), 27 October, 16 November 1793; all quoted in Rogers, *Press-Gang*, pp. 64, 67, 65, 42.

21 Rogers, *Press-Gang*, p. 73.

22 See R. B. Rose, 'A Liverpool Sailors' Strike in the Eighteenth Century', *Transactions of the Lancashire and Cheshire Antiquary Society*, 68 (1958), pp. 85–92.

23 *Billing Advertiser*, 28 June and 2 August 1819; *Newcastle Courant*, 3 July 1819.

24 P. J. Waller, *Democracy and Sectarianism: A Political and Social History of Liverpool, 1868–1939* (Liverpool, 1981), p. 10.

25 Picton, *Memorials*, vol. I, p. 180.

26 Bryson, 'Riotous Liverpool, 1815–1860', p. 105.

27 Waller, *Democracy and Sectarianism*, p. 11.

28 Denvir, *The Irish in Britain*, p. 130.

29 PRO CO904.7.77–92, statement of John Kelly, 6 December 1839.

30 PP 1835 XV, *Second report from the Select Committee Appointed to Inquire into the Nature, Character, Extent and Tendency of Orange Lodges, Associations or Societies in Ireland*, p. 40.

31 See Lisa Rosner, *The Anatomy Murders: Being the True and Spectacular History of Edinburgh's Notorious Burke and Hare and the Man Who Abetted Them in Their Most Heinous Crimes* (Philadelphia, PA, 2010).

32 Thomas Herbert Bickerton, *Medical History of Liverpool from the Earliest Days to the Year 1920* (London, 1936), pp. 80–86.

33 *LM*, 6 and 13 June 1823.

34 *The Times*, 2 November 1827.

35 Bickerton, *Medical History of Liverpool*, pp. 80–81.

36 See Michael Durey, *The Return of the Plague: British Society and the Cholera, 1831–2* (Dublin, 1979).

37 *LM*, 1 June 1832.

38 *LC*, 6 June 1832.

39 See *LM*, 1, 8, 22 June 1832; Christine Anne Bryson, 'Riot and its Control in Liverpool, 1815–1860', unpublished MPhil thesis, Open University, 1989, p. 59.

40 Burke, *Catholic History of Liverpool*, p. 67; *LM*, 18 June 1841.

41 LVRO, Liverpool Watch Committee Minutes, vol. 2, 3 July 1841.

42 Neal, *Sectarian Violence*, p. 58.

43 See Kevin Moore, '"This Whig and Tory Ridden Town": Popular Politics in Liverpool in the Chartist Era' and John Belchem, 'Liverpool in the Year of Revolution: The Political and Associational Culture of the Irish Immigrant Community in 1848', both in Belchem (ed.), *Popular Politics, Riot and Labour*, pp. 38–67, 68–97; Louis R. Bisceglia, 'The Threat of Violence: Irish Confederates and Chartists in Liverpool in 1848', *Irish Sword*, 14 (1981), pp. 207–15.

44 Belchem, 'Liverpool in the Year of Revolution', p. 90.

45 John Saville, *1848: British State and the Chartist Movement* (Cambridge, 1987), p. 150.

46 *LM*, 11 April 1848.

47 *The Times*, 13 December 1848.

48 *LM*, 1 August 1848.

49 Neal, *Sectarian Violence*, p. 120.

50 Urban Young, *Life of Father Ignatius Spencer* (London, 1933), p. 178.
51 *Liverpool Journal*, 25 April 1857.
52 James Hopkinson, *Memoirs of a Victorian Cabinet Maker* (London, 1968), p. 99.
53 Watch Committee for the Borough of Liverpool, *Report on the Police Establishment* […] *1874*.
54 PP 1851 XXVII, pp. 14–15.
55 *Liverpool Mail*, 24 February 1855.
56 *The Times*, 20 February 1855.
57 *Liverpool Weekly Albion*, 19 February 1855.
58 E. P. Thompson, 'The Moral Economy of the English Crowd in the Eighteenth Century', *Past and Present*, 50 (1971), pp. 76–136.
59 *Liverpool Weekly Albion*, 22 February 1855.
60 *The Times*, 20 February 1855.
61 *LC*, 21 February 1855.
62 *Liverpool Mail*, 24 February 1855.
63 *LM*, 19 January 1867.
64 Lowe, *The Irish in Mid-Victorian Lancashire*, p. 40.
65 See Neal, *Sectarian Violence*, chapter VII.
66 *Liverpool Domestic Mission Society Annual Report, 1852*, p. 45.
67 John Belchem, 'Introduction: The Peculiarities of Liverpool', in Belchem (ed.), *Popular Politics, Riot and Labour*, pp. 17–18.

7: The Lowest Circle of Hell

1 PP 1836 (40) XXXIV, p. 27.
2 *DP*, 6 November 1865.
3 Hume, *Missions at Home*, p. 18.
4 PP 1844 XVII.1, *First Report of the Commissioners for Inquiring into the State of Large Towns and Populous Districts*, p. 28.
5 G. K. Behlmer, *Child Abuse and Moral Reform in England, 1870–1908* (Stanford, CA, 1982), p. 49.
6 John Burnett, *A Social History of Housing, 1815–1985* (London, 2nd edn, 1986), p. 21.
7 PP 1840 XI, *Report from the Select Committee on the Health of Towns*, p. 149.
8 PP 1840 XI, p. viii.
9 PP 1840 XI, p. viii.
10 PP 1845 XVIII.1, *Reports from Commissioners: 1845, vol. 5, State of Large Towns and Populous Districts*, p. 17.
11 Midwinter, *Old Liverpool*, p. 97.
12 LVRO, Health Committee Minute Books, 17 June 1847.
13 *LM*, 4 January 1839.
14 Egerton Smith, *Some Account of the Liverpool Night Asylum for the Houseless Poor* […] (Liverpool, 1832), p. 7.
15 PP 1847-48 LIII, p. 39.
16 Lionel Rose, *Rogues and Vagabonds: Vagrant Underworld in Britain, 1815–1985* (London, 1988), p. 90.
17 *LM*, 6 May 1842.
18 PP 1851 XIX1, *Report from the Select Committee on Passenger's Act*, p. 303, q. 2879, evidence of George Stephen.
19 Melly, 'Juvenile Crime and Reformatory Schools', 1857, bound in *Stray Leaves*, p. 3.
20 *LM*, 15 December 1856, 'Liverpool Life', second series, no. VI.

21 *DP*, 10 November 1883.

22 PP 1845 XVIII.1, p. 25.

23 Kanya-Forstner, 'The Politics of Survival', p. 175.

24 *LM*, 17 May 1853.

25 J. J. Tobias, *Crime and Industrial Society* (London, 1967), p. 166.

26 Hawthorne, *The English Notebooks*, pp. 17–18.

27 Taine, *Taine's Notes on England*, p. 226.

28 PP 1844 XVII.1, p. 29.

29 PP 1836 (40) XXXIV, p. 20.

30 PP 1836 (40) XXXIV, p. 27.

31 *The Sunday at Home*, part 16, February 1896, p. 251.

32 Nott-Bower, *Fifty-Two Years a Policeman*, pp. 147–48.

33 *Squalid Liverpool*, p. 50.

34 *LM*, 21 August 1888; *LR*, 27 July 1889.

35 W. T. McGowan, *Sanitary Legislation with Illustrations From Experience* (Liverpool, 1859).

36 *The Sunday at Home*, p. 250.

37 *LM*, 24 November 1865.

38 Mortality Sub-Committee, *Report of Evidence 1866* (Liverpool, 1866) p. 197; *DP*, 10 November 1883; LVRO, 352 MIN/WAT Minutes of the Watch Committee, 21/4, 25 May 1841, p. 515.

39 *DP*, 20 September 1886.

40 *LR*, 2 September 1899.

41 *LR*, 1 July 1899. For a similar drain story see Clive Emsley, *Hard Men: The English and Violence Since 1750* (London, 2005), p. 135.

42 *LR*, 9 September 1899.

43 'The Mysteries of the Courts', chapter V, *Porcupine*, 13 December 1862.

44 Hobson, *What Hath God Wrought*, p. 49.

45 Quoted in *LM*, 11 January 1848.

46 Abraham Hume, *The Conditions of Liverpool* (1888), pp. 28, 25–26. For an analysis of Hume's findings see J. J. Tobias, 'A Statistical Study of a Nineteenth Century Criminal Area', *British Journal of Criminology*, 14(3) (1974), pp. 221–35.

47 Hume, *Missions at Home*, p. 15.

48 Abraham Hume, *Misrepresentation of the Established Church: A Reply and Correction* (Liverpool, 1884), pp. 18–19.

49 Taylor, 'Moral Economy of Large Towns', p. 136.

50 *LM*, 5 September 1845.

51 *LM*, 27 July 1857, 'Liverpool Life,' chapter XVIII.

52 *Squalid Liverpool*, p. 77.

53 *LM*, 9 March 1871.

54 PP 1847 LIV, p. 11.

55 Iain C. Taylor, 'Black Spot on the Mersey: A Study of Environment and Society in Eighteenth and Nineteenth Century Liverpool', unpublished PhD thesis, University of Liverpool, 1976, vol. I, p. 179.

56 PP 1844 XVII.1, p. 28.

57 Medical Officer's report for 1847, quoted in Burke, *Catholic History of Liverpool*, p. 84.

58 W. H. Duncan, *Report to the Health Committee of the Borough of Liverpool, on the Health of the Town During the Years 1847–48–49–50, and on Other Matters Within his Department* (1851), p. 17, LVRO; Taylor, 'Black Spot on the Mersey', vol. I, p. 210; Neal, *Black 47*, p. 139.

59 PP 1877 XI, *Select Committee of House of Lords for Inquiring into Prevalence of Habits of Intemperance, and Effects of Recent Legislation: Third Report*, pp. 22–23.

60 *Liverpool Journal*, 13 July 1844.

61 PP 1841 V, p. 126.

62 *LM*, 12 January 1855.

63 W. S. Caine (ed.), *Hugh Stowell Brown: His Autobiography, His Commonplace Book and Extracts From His Sermons and Addresses: A Memorial Volume* (London, 2nd edn, 1887), pp. 209–10.

64 *Full Report on the Commission of Inquiry Into the Subject of the Unemployed in the City of Liverpool* (1894), pp. 101–02.

65 *LM*, 18 September 1899.

66 W. H. Duncan, *On the Physical Causes of the High Rate of Mortality in Liverpool* (Liverpool, 1843), p. 56.

67 Arthur B. Forwood, *The Dwellings of the Industrial Classes in the Diocese of Liverpool and How to Improve Them* (1883), pp. 10–11.

68 *Liverpool Domestic Mission Annual Report, 1834/4* (Liverpool, 1835), p. 12, quoted in Taylor, 'Black Spot on the Mersey', vol. I, p. 160.

69 *Liverpool Herald*, 17 November 1855.

70 Pamphlet in PP 1884–85, report 14, quoted in Waller, *Democracy and Sectarianism*, p. 82.

71 *LM*, 28 October 1836.

72 *LM*, 7 December 1838.

73 PP 1842 XXVII, *Local Reports on the Sanitary Condition of the Labouring Population of England, in Consequence of an Inquiry Directed to be made by the Poor Law Commissioners*, p. 292.

74 Hume, *Missions at Home*, p. 19.

75 Samuel Smith, 'Social Reform', *Nineteenth Century*, May 1883, pp. 897–98.

76 *The Times*, 11 January 1875.

77 *Squalid Liverpool*, p. 77.

78 Smith, 'Social Reform', p. 900.

79 Burke, *Catholic History of Liverpool*, pp. 85, 90, 169, 37.

80 *LM*, 3 July 1847.

81 Smith, 'Social Reform'.

82 *DP*, 6 November 1865.

83 After a brutal case, tried at the Liverpool Assizes, Justice Mellor exclaimed: 'if there are missionaries wanted to the heathen, there are heathens in England who require them quite as much'. *LM*, 16 December 1874.

84 Quoted in Nicholas Murray, *So Spirited a Town: Visions and Versions of Liverpool* (Liverpool, 2007), p. 20.

85 Between November 1862 and March 1863, *Porcupine* conducted a seventeen-week survey of Liverpool's slum districts, entitled 'The Mysteries of the Courts'. In 1865 the *DP* followed this up with a five-part series entitled 'The Real Condition of the Liverpool Poor', 31 October, 6, 9, 15, 23 November 1865.

86 See Judith R. Walkowitz, *Prostitution and Victorian Society: Women, Class and the State* (Cambridge, 1980), p. 251.

87 *LM*, 18 October 1876, 'The State of Crime in Liverpool', report of the National Association for the Promotion of Social Sciences conference, 1876.

88 PP 1839 XXII, p. 89.

89 *LR*, 1 July 1899.

8: The Demon Drink

1 *LR*, 16 September 1899.
2 *LR*, 9 September 1891.
3 Walter Clay, Prison Chaplain's report for 1848–49, in Delacy, *Prison Reform in Lancashire*, p. 215.
4 *The Times*, 26 December 1874.
5 *Prison Ministers Reports, 1866–67, Liverpool Council Proceedings*, p. 640.
6 *Englishwoman's Review*, 1 October 1874.
7 'The State of Crime in Liverpool', report from *NAPSS Conference 1876*, quoted in *LM*, 18 October 1876.
8 PP 1877 XI, pp. 21–22.
9 William Hoyle, *Crime in England and Wales in the Nineteenth Century: An Historical and Critical Retrospect* (London, 1876), pp. 107, 110.
10 *First Report Public Houses*, leaflet bound in Nathaniel Smyth, *Maps Showing Licensed Premises*, LVRO, 657.94 SMY (includes various leaflets, maps and publications bound together).
11 PP 1851 XXVII, p. 2.
12 Hoyle, *Crime in England and Wales*, p. 111.
13 *LM*, 22 November 1895.
14 *Porcupine*, 15 April 1880.
15 Mortality Sub-Committee, *Report of Evidence 1866*, pp. 200–01; *Porcupine*, 22 September 1866.
16 PP 1898 XXXVI.1, *Royal Commission on Liquor Licensing Laws. Third Report of the Royal Commission on Liquor Licensing Laws*, p. 3.
17 Hopkinson, *Memoirs of a Victorian Cabinet Maker*, p. 107.
18 *LR*, 19 August 1899.
19 *LR*, 28 February 1885.
20 *LM*, 13 July 1847.
21 *LR*, June 20, 1891.
22 Thomson, *The Criminal*, p. 27.
23 PP 1877 XI, pp. 21–22.
24 *The Times*, 26 November 1877.
25 Taine, *Notes on England*, p. 226.
26 *Punch*, quoted in *LM*, 2 April 1852.
27 Nathaniel Hawthorne, *Our Old Home* (London, 1863), p. 233.
28 *LM*, 15 August 1834.
29 Terry Cook, *The Pubs of Scotland Road* (Liverpool, 1999), p. 11.
30 PP 1898 XXXVI.1, p. 15.
31 PP 1839 XIX, p. 216.
32 John Jones, *The Slain in Liverpool During 1864 by Drink* (Liverpool, 1864) p. 61. Reprinted in *LM*, 23 February 1865.
33 *LM*, 7 April 1871.
34 Robert Henry Lundie, *The Dark Side of Liverpool* (Liverpool, 1880), p. 3. Reprinted in *LM*, 3 November 1880.
35 PP 1877 XI, p. 186.
36 Hopkinson, *Memoirs of a Victorian Cabinet Maker*, p. 107.
37 Lundie, *Dark Side of Liverpool*, p. 2.
38 Hawthorne, *The English Notebooks*, pp. 13, 17.
39 *LM*, 31 March 1866.
40 *LM*, 25 November 1853.

41 Prison Chaplain's report quoted in *LM*, 19 October 1869. See also Mortality Sub-Committee, *Report of Evidence 1866*, p. 201.

42 *Porcupine*, 7 September 1861.

43 *LM*, 17 November 1856.

44 Watch Committee for the Borough of Liverpool, *Report on the Police Establishment* [...] *1869*.

45 PP 1898 XXXVI.1, p. 1.

46 Neil Collins, *Politics and Elections in Nineteenth Century Liverpool* (Aldershot, 1994), p. 162.

47 *LM*, 19 May 1871.

48 Watch Committee for the Borough of Liverpool, *Report on the Police Establishment* [...] *1869* and *Report on the Police Establishment* [...] *1870*. Each apprehension did not mean a separate person. The same old faces would be arrested again and again.

49 Leaflet no. 2, produced by the Liverpool Permissive Bill Association, bound with Smyth, *Maps Showing Licensed Premises.*

50 Jones, *The Slain in Liverpool by Drink.*

51 Watch Committee for the Borough of Liverpool, *Report on the Police Establishment* [...] *1873*.

52 *Liverpool Daily Courier*, 4 November 1872.

53 *The Times*, 13 September 1875; Waller, *Democracy and Sectarianism*, p. 23.

54 *LR*, 16 September 1899.

55 Hawthorne, *Our Old Home*, p. 233.

56 Mortality Sub-Committee, *Report of Evidence, 1866*, p. 202; PP 1877 XI, p. 186.

57 Harriet M. Johnson, *Children and Public-Houses* (Nottingham, 3rd edn, 1897), p. 6.

58 Alan Brack, *All They Need is Love* (Neston, 1983), p. 25.

59 *The Times*, 26 November 1877; Waller, *Democracy and Sectarianism*, p. 24.

60 Smith, *My Life Work*, p. 127.

61 Johnson, *Children and Public-Houses*, p. 10.

62 Miles, *Poverty, Mendicity and Crime*, p. 79.

63 PP 1837 XXXII, p. 87.

64 PP 1851 XXVII, p. 2.

65 *LM*, 15 January 1850.

66 MC, 2 September 1850, 'The Amusements and Literature of the People', Letter XVI.

67 PP 1852–53 XXIII, p. 109. q. 1265.

68 Watch Committee for the Borough of Liverpool, *Report on the Police Establishment* [...] *1876*.

69 Johnson, *Children and Public-Houses*, p. 6; *LM*, 9 November 1892.

70 Smyth, *Maps Showing Licensed Premises*, no page reference.

71 Waller, *Democracy and Sectarianism*, p. 95.

72 PP 1877 XI, p. 22.

73 Armstrong, *The Deadly Shame of Liverpool*, pp. 7, 15.

74 Smith, *My Life Work*, p. 126.

75 *Transactions of the NAPSS*, 1876, p. 372.

76 [Hugh Shimmin], *Liverpool Life: its Pleasures, Practices, and Pastimes* (Liverpool, 1856–57), 1st series, pp. 83, 44, 28, 9; 2nd series, p. 55. Articles reprinted in *LM*.

77 PP 1877 XI, p. 29, q. 8276, evidence of Father Nugent.

78 *Porcupine*, 5 January 1875.

79 *Sea Liverpool: Maritime History of a Great Port* (Liverpool, 2005), pp. 43–44.

80 Smith, *My Life Work*, p. 107.

81 Forwood, *Recollections of a Busy Life*, p. 159.

82 *LR*, 21 October 1899.

83 Lilian Lewis Shiman, *Crusade Against Drink in Victorian England* (Basingstoke, 1988), p. 195; *LM*, 16 January 1895.

84 Indeed, it wasn't only drink-related offences that decreased. Most crime (with the exception of burglary) also levelled off towards the end of the century. See V. A. C. Gatrell, 'The Decline of Theft and Violence in Victorian and Edwardian England', in V. A. C. Gatrell, Bruce Lenman and Geoffrey Parker (eds.), *Crime and the Law: a Social History of Crime in Western Europe Since 1500* (London: Europa, 1980), pp. 238–337.

85 PP 1898 XXXVI.1, pp. 1–2.

86 *LM*, 6 March 1897.

87 PP 1898 XXXVI.1, p. 2.

88 PP 1898 XXXVI.1, p. 3.

9: Violence

1 *DP*, 5 November 1883.

2 Hugh Shimmin, *Liverpool Sketches, Chiefly Reprinted from Porcupine* (London, 1862), p. 122.

3 *Porcupine*, 22 May 1875.

4 *LR*, 8 July 1899.

5 *Penny Illustrated*, 19 September 1874.

6 See Henry Mayhew, *London Labour and the London Poor, 1861–62* (New York, 1968), vol. II, p. 338. After the murder of Richard Morgan in Tithebarn Street, the press immediately seized on the culprits' Irishness. See *Daily Courier, Evening Express*, 5 August 1874.

7 *Liverpool Times*, 11 March 1834.

8 Example from *Clonmel Chronicle*, 18 July 1888, quoted in Carolyn Conley, 'The Agreeable Recreation of Fighting', *Journal of Social History*, 33(1) (1999), p. 60; See also Andrew Davies, *Gangs of Manchester: the Story of the Scuttlers: Britain's First Youth Cult* (Wrea Green, 2008), pp. 46–47.

9 *Gore's General Advertiser*, 26 January 1826.

10 *LM*, 7 March 1834; *Gore's General Advertiser*, 6 March 1834.

11 'Lines on the Death of Acting-Inspector Ross on 6 July 1838', *LM*, 6 July 1838. See also LVRO 352 MIN/WAT Minutes of the Watch Committee, 21/3, p. 82.

12 *LC*, 24 April 1839.

13 *LM*, 14 October 1851.

14 *Liverpool Mail, Liverpool Journal*, 13 July 1844.

15 *The Times*, 16 December 1847.

16 *LC*, 26 May 1852.

17 *LM*, 7 September 1852.

18 *Liverpool Weekly Albion*, 27 March 1854.

19 W. Steuart Trench, *Realities of Irish Life* (London, 5th edn, 1870), pp. 82–86. See also John Belchem, *Merseypride: Essays in Liverpool Exceptionalism* (Liverpool, 2nd edn, 2006), p. 92.

20 *LM*, 10 May 1853.

21 *Liverpool Journal*, 17 April 1858.

22 *LC*, 12 June 1858.

23 *LM*, 10 August 1864.

24 *LM*, 7 September 1847

25 *LM*, 1 September 1874.

26 Quoted in *LM*, 28 September 1832.

27 *LM*, 13 August 1852.

28 *LM*, 9 December 1853; *Liverpool Times*, quoted in *Bell's Life in London and Sporting Chronicle*, 27 November 1853.

29 *LM*, 4 November, 9 December 1853.

30 *LM*, 25 August 1856, 'Liverpool Life', no. IX.

31 *LM*, 1 August 1896.

32 Watch Committee for the Borough of Liverpool, *Report on the Police Establishment* [...] *1858* quoted in *LM*, 26 November 1858.

33 *LM*, 11 August 1860.

34 *LM*, 30 December 1861.

35 Watch Committee for the Borough of Liverpool, *Report on the Police Establishment* [...] *1863*.

36 *LM*, 29 May 1862.

37 *LM*, 15 July 1862.

38 *LM*, 2 November 1877.

39 Picton, *Memorials of Liverpool*, vol. II, pp. 136–37, 372–73; *LR*, 28 June 1890, 'The Last Duel in Liverpool'.

40 *Porcupine*, 4 July 1874.

41 *Bethell's Life*, no. 42, 10 September 1825.

42 See John E. Archer, '"Men Behaving Badly?": Masculinity and the Uses of Violence, 1850–1900', in Shani D'Cruze (ed.), *Everyday Violence in Britain, 1850–1950: Gender and Class* (Harlow, 2000), pp. 42–43.

43 *LM*, 12 August 1825.

44 *LM*, 10 August 1857, 'Liverpool Life', no. XX.

45 *LM*, 9 January 1849.

46 *LM*, 9 May 1859, 16 May 1864.

47 *LM*, 18 October 1876, 'The State of Crime in Liverpool', report from NAPSS Conference, 1876.

48 Herman Melville, *Redburn* [1849] (Harmondsworth, 1986), p. 277.

49 *Daily Courier*, 23 and 30 January 1850.

50 *LM*, 24 May 1853.

51 *LM*, 1 May 1875.

52 *LM*, 30 March 1832.

53 *Liverpool Journal*, 22 November 1834.

54 *Liverpool Journal*, 7 February 1835; *LC*, 20 May 1835.

55 *LM*, 26 October 1847.

56 John E. Archer quoted in Stephen Wade, *Foul Deeds and Suspicious Deaths in Liverpool* (Barnsley, 2006), p. 37.

57 Hawthorne, *Our Old Home*, p. 238.

58 Hawthorne, *The English Notebooks*, p. 36.

59 PP 1836 (40) XXXIV, p. 20.

60 *Liverpool Weekly Albion*, 3 January 1848.

61 Smith, *My Life Work*, p. 126.

62 *LM*, 11 September 1878.

63 *LM*, 2 January 1857, 30 September 1862, 11 and 18 March 1879.

64 *LM*, 11 March 1879, 18 May 1863, 25 September 1878, 22 September 1896.

65 *LM*, 11 November 1853, 14 November 1896, 26 April 1868, 20 March 1849.

66 *LM*, 8 January 1863.

67 *LM*, 20 February 1856, 5 October 1868, 20 July 1865, 3 May 1871, 3 January 1873.

68 Tobias, *Crime and Industrial Society*, pp. 122–25.

69 Gatrell, 'The Decline of Theft and Violence in Victorian and Edwardian England', pp. 238–337.

70 David Wood, 'Community Violence', in John Benson (ed.), *The Working Class in England,*

1875–1914 (London: Croom Helm, 1985), p. 166.

71 *LM*, 9 January 1857.

72 Figures quoted from *LM*, 1 November 1860, 26 November 1863, 16 November 1864, 17 November 1886, 14 November 1888.

73 *BDP*, 19 October 1891.

74 Figures from *LM*, 17 November 1891, 10 November 1892.

75 *BDP*, 7 November 1892.

76 *LM*, 6 February 1900.

77 Waller, *Democracy and Sectarianism*, p. 108.

78 John E. Archer, 'The Violence We Have Lost: Body Counts, Historians and Interpersonal Violence in England', *Memoria y Civilizacion*, 2 (1999), p. 186.

79 *Saturday Review*, 18 July 1891.

80 *Saturday Review*, 18 July 1891.

81 See Howard Taylor, 'Rationing Crime: the Political Economy of Criminal Statistics Since the 1880s', *Economic History Review*, LI(3) (1998), pp. 569–90.

82 Archer, 'The Violence We Have Lost', p. 184; John E. Archer, 'Mysterious and Suspicious Deaths: Missing Homicides in North-West England (1850–1900)', *Crime, History and Societies*, 12(1) (2008), pp. 45–63.

83 Melville, *Redburn*, p. 251.

10: Maritime Crime

1 Melville, *Redburn*, p. 192.

2 *LM*, 29 January 1841.

3 Watch Committee report, 2 March 1836, quoted in Miles, *Poverty, Mendicity and Crime*, p. 80.

4 Unless otherwise stated the material for the section on dock crime is taken from *MC*, 27 May 1850, 'Letter II: Labour and the Poor'.

5 Maritime Archives and Library, National Museums Liverpool, MDHB/MISC/12, Customs Officer to the Dock Committee, 18 July 1814, quoted in William J. Ashworth, *Customs and Excise: Trade, Population and Consumption in England, 1640–1845* (Oxford, 2003), p. 305.

6 Maritime Archives and Library, National Museums Liverpool, MDHB/MISC/12, 'Minutes of Evidence Taken by a Sub-Committee of the Dock Committee, as to the Expediency of Uniting the Dock Police with the Town Police', 21 November 1836, quoted in Ashworth, *Customs and Excise*, p. 306.

7 *LM*, 19 December 1854.

8 Isaac Holmes, *Thieves, Beggars and Prostitutes* (Liverpool, 1853), p. 14.

9 See 'Police Intelligence', *LM*, 12 March 1852, for a variety of examples of female and juvenile dock theft.

10 *LM*, 17 May 1853.

11 *LM*, 19 August 1857, 7 December 1863, 11 October 1864, 3 February, 18 March, 6 May, 6 June 1865.

12 Miles, *Poverty, Mendicity and Crime*, pp. 58–59.

13 PP 1839 XIX, p. 49.

14 E. Cuthbert Woods, 'Smuggling in Wirral', *Historic Society Transactions*, 79 (1927), pp. 125–31; *LM*, 23 June 1854.

15 *LM*, 3 December 1855.

16 *LM*, 6 September 1850.

17 *LM*, 29 January 1850.

18 *LM*, 5 February 1850.

19 *LM*, 7 August 1868.

20 Unless otherwise stated the information on runners and 'man-catchers' is taken from *MC*, 15 July 1850, 'Letter IX: Emigrants and Man Catchers'.

21 Quoted in Gallman, *Receiving Erin's Children*, p. 2.

22 For many of the following abuses see chapter 5, 'Liverpool and the Last of England', in Terry Coleman, *Passage to America: a History of Emigrants from Great Britain and Ireland to America in the Mid-Nineteenth Century* (London, 1972).

23 Colonial Office Papers, 384/84, 4584 Emigration, 22 May 1849, quoted in Oliver MacDonagh, *A Pattern of Government Growth 1800–60: the Passenger Acts and their Enforcement* (London, 1961), pp. 219–20.

24 Robert Scally, 'Liverpool Ships and Irish Emigrants in the Age of Sail', *Journal of Social History*, 17(1) (1983), pp. 17–18.

25 Lieutenant Low, 'An Exposition of Frauds upon Emigrants', Colonial Office Papers, 384/32, 5972, Emigration, quoted in Robert Scally, *The End of Hidden Ireland: Rebellion, Famine and Emigration* (Oxford, 1995), p. 201.

26 PP 1854 XIII.1, *First Report from the Select Committee on Emigrant Ships*, p. 92, qq. 1590–91, evidence of S. Redmond.

27 *LM*, 10 May 1850; PP 1851 XIX1, p. 216, q. 2099, evidence of Lieut. Prior; *LM*, 5 May 1871.

28 LVRO, Revd John Welsh, in *The Port and Docks of Birkenhead. Minutes of Evidence and Proceedings on the Liverpool and Birkenhead Dock Bills in Sessions of 1844 to 1852* [of House of Commons] by Thomas Webster (London, 1873). See Coleman, *Passage to America*, p. 75.

29 PP 1851 XIX1, p. 409, q. 3735, evidence of F. Sabel, p. 300, q. 2867, evidence of G. Stephen.

30 PP 1854 XIII.1, p. 92, qq. 1594–95, evidence of S. Redmond; *LM*, 10 May 1850.

31 *LM*, 18 July 1848.

32 *MC*, 8 July 1850.

33 Scally, 'Liverpool Ships and Irish Emigrants in the Age of Sail', p. 18.

34 PP 1854 XIII.1, p. 92, q. 1594, evidence of S. Redmond.

35 *The Nation*, 23 May 1846.

36 PP 1854 XIII.1, p. 91, q. 1582, p. 93, q. 1609, evidence of S. Redmond.

37 Thomas Carter, 'On the Crime of Liverpool', *Transactions of the NAPSS*, 1858, edited by George W. Hastings (London, 1859), p. 353.

38 PP 1851 XIX1, p. 408, q. 3732, evidence of F. Sabel.

39 PP 1851 XIX1, p. 436, q. 3944, evidence of F. Marshall.

40 MacDonagh, *A Pattern of Government Growth*, p. 314.

41 *Sunday at Home*, part 18, April 1896, p. 377.

42 *LM*, 27 September 1850.

43 *MC*, 3 June 1850, 'Labour and the Poor', Letter III.

44 Melville, *Redburn*, p. 202.

45 Howard Channon, *Portrait of Liverpool* (London, 1970), p. 90.

46 W. R. Cockroft, *The Albert Dock and Liverpool's Historic Waterfront* (Market Drayton, 1992), p. 70.

47 *Porcupine*, 31 May 1862; Carter, 'On the Crime of Liverpool', pp. 351–32.

48 A. R. B. Robinson, *Chaplain of the Mersey, 1859–67* (1987), pp. 17–22.

49 *Evening Express*, 14 May 1954.

50 *Porcupine*, 31 May 1862; Carter, 'On the Crime of Liverpool', p. 352.

51 Robinson, *Chaplain of the Mersey*, pp. 16–21.

52 *LM*, 24 September 1859.

53 Cockroft, *The Albert Dock*, pp. 68–69.

54 *LM*, 3 March 1879.

55 *LM*, 12 September 1896.

56 Unless otherwise stated the material for the section on wrecking is taken from PP 1839 XIX, pp. 56–60.

57 Douglas Hay, *Albion's Fatal Tree: Crime and Society in Eighteenth-Century England* (London, 1972), p. 172.

58 Stonehouse, *Recollections*, p. 60.

59 Woods, 'Smuggling in Wirral', p. 134.

60 Forwood, *Recollections of a Busy Life*, p. 8.

61 Williams, *History of the Liverpool Privateers*, pp. 232–33.

62 Picton, *Memorials*, vol. I, pp. 378–79; LM, 10 August 1821; Hilda Gamlin blames Wallasey boats. See *Twixt Mersey and Dee* (Liverpool, 1897), p. 133.

63 Stonehouse, *Recollections*, p. 61.

64 Stonehouse, *Recollections*, p. 60.

65 Gavin Chappell, *Wirral Smugglers, Wreckers and Pirates* (Birkenhead, 2009), p. 132.

66 Miles, *Poverty, Mendicity and Crime*, p. 75.

67 Stonehouse, *Recollections*, p. 60.

68 Chappell, *Wirral Smugglers*, pp. 97–115.

11: Street Robbery

1 Stonehouse, *Streets of Liverpool*, p. 215.

2 Stonehouse, *Recollections*, pp. 119–20.

3 R. J. Broadbent, *Annals of the Liverpool Stage: From the Earliest Period to the Present Time* (Liverpool, 1908), p. 30.

4 Stonehouse, *Streets of Liverpool*, p. 31; Richard Jervis, *Chronicles of a Victorian Detective* [1907] (Runcorn, 1995), pp. 68–69.

5 *The Trial of Tobias Toole, John Davies and William O'Brien (alias Thomas Dwyer) for Robbing Robert Chambers* […] (Lancaster, n.d.), pp. 7, 11.

6 *Derby Mercury*, 26 November 1812; Stonehouse, *Recollections*, pp. 223–24.

7 Stonehouse, *Recollections*, p. 214.

8 Stonehouse, *Recollections*, p. 31; LM, 15 and 22 October 1830, 8 April 1831.

9 Tobias, *Crime and Industrial Society*, p. 189.

10 LM, 31 December 1847.

11 LM, 7 January 1848.

12 LM, 10 August 1857.

13 LM, 26 October 1852.

14 PP 1839 XIX, p. 29.

15 LM, 17 May 1853.

16 Miles, *Poverty, Mendicity and Crime*, p. 59.

17 PP 1841 V, p. 126.

18 LM, 14 July 1848.

19 Carpenter, *Our Convicts*, vol. I, p. 68.

20 Holmes, *Thieves, Beggars and Prostitutes*, p. 13.

21 *Lady's Newspaper*, 21 July 1849.

22 LM, 5 August 1845.

23 LM, 21 August 1846.

24 *Cornhill Magazine*, vi (November 1862), p. 650.

25 In 1862 the *Cornhill Magazine* argued that the 'violence and cruelty' of thieves had diminished during the previous fifteen or twenty years. 'The modern thief depends upon his skill': *Cornhill Magazine*, vi (November 1862), pp. 646–47. However, there is a garrotting case in the LM, 2 January 1857.

26 Isaac Holmes, in the early 1850s, describes garrotting, *Thieves, Beggars and Prostitutes*, p. 14.

27 Davis, 'The London Garotting Panic of 1862', pp. 190–213.

28 *LM*, 21 September 1871.

29 *LM*, 13 February 1852.

30 Macilwee, *The Gangs of Liverpool*.

31 *LM*, 10 March 1887.

32 Rob Sindall, *Street Violence in the Nineteenth Century: Media Panic or Real Danger?* (Leicester, 1990), p. 67.

33 *LR*, 27 July 1889.

34 Leon Faucher, *Manchester in 1844: Its Present Conditions and Future Prospects* (Manchester, 1844, repr. London, 1969), p. 41.

35 *Journal of the Statistical Society*, II (April 1839), p. 182.

36 Neal, 'A Criminal Profile of the Irish', p. 177.

37 PP 1839 XIX, p. 12.

38 Miles, *Poverty, Mendicity and Crime*, pp. 57–58.

39 *Porcupine*, 13 December 1862.

40 H. J. Nicholls, *Sixty Years Random Reminiscences of Old Liverpool and its Departed Trades and Customs* (Liverpool, 1909), pp. 5–6.

41 *MC*, 3 June 1850, 'Labour and the Poor', Letter III.

42 Miles, *Poverty, Mendicity and Crime*, p. 58.

43 *Liverpool Mail*, 27 June 1863; *Liverpool Daily Courier*, 23 June 1863.

44 University College London, Papers of Edwin Chadwick, Depositions Box 129, quoted in Tobias, *Crime and Industrial Society*, pp. 94–95.

45 *LM*, 22 January 1847.

46 *LM*, 1 July 1842, 8 October 1850, 30 May 1851, 16 March 1893.

47 *LM*, 22 November 1850, 16 March 1852.

48 Unless otherwise stated the information on the migratory habits of thieves is taken from PP 1839 XIX.

49 Miles, *Poverty, Mendicity and Crime*, pp. 59–60.

50 Public Record Office, HO 73/5 pt 2, *Returns to Constabulary Commission 1839, reply from Kirkdale*.

51 PP 1839 XIX, p. 16.

52 PP 1841 V, p. 129.

53 Papers of Edwin Chadwick, quoted in Tobias, *Crime and Industrial Society*, pp. 69–70, 112; J. J. Tobias, *Nineteenth Century Crime: Prevention and Punishment* (Newton Abbot, 1972), pp. 58–63.

54 Miles, *Poverty, Mendicity and Crime*, p. 60.

55 Thomson, *The Criminal*, p. 153.

56 *Western Mail*, 16 October 1894; *Women's Signal*, 16 March 1899. The two were later acquitted due to conflicting evidence.

57 *Bell's Life in London and Sporting Chronicle*, 30 October 1830.

58 Cockroft, 'Liverpool Police Force 1836–1902', pp. 160–61.

59 John R. Kellett, *Railways and Victorian Cities* (London, 1979), p. 194.

60 *The Times*, 11 July 1864.

61 PP 1852-53 XXIII, p. 194. See also Clay, *The Prison Chaplain*, p. 522.

62 Miles, *Poverty, Mendicity and Crime*, p. 65.

63 Henry Mayhew, *London's Underworld: Being Selections from 'Those That Will Not Work' the Fourth Volume of 'London Labour and the London Poor'*, ed. Peter Quennell (London, 1950), p. 270.

64 *LM*, 24 January 1834.

65 *LM*, 26 September 1865.

12: Burglary and Property Theft

1 Stonehouse, *Recollections*, p. 247.
2 *LM*, 21 December 1849.
3 *LM*, 26 March 1852.
4 *LM*, 22 September 1873, 20 September 1879, 2 November 1886.
5 *Liverpool Weekly Albion*, 18 July 1903.
6 Stonehouse, *Recollections*, p. 247; *LM*, 23 August 1816.
7 *LM*, 15 February 1839.
8 *LM*, 14 March 1862.
9 *LM*, 11 December 1840.
10 *LM*, 26 January 1821.
11 *LM*, 4 December 1840.
12 *LM*, 22, 29 October, 10 November 1886.
13 *LM*, 17 October 1823.
14 Miles, *Poverty, Mendicity and Crime*, p. 59.
15 *Porcupine*, 24 August 1878.
16 *LM*, 29 January 1841.
17 *LM*, 10 October 1891.
18 PP 1877 XI, p. 27, q. 8256, evidence of Father Nugent.
19 Mayhew, *London's Underworld*, p. 136.
20 PP 1841 V, p. 132.
21 *LM*, 9 March 1866.
22 *LM*, 17 May 1853.
23 *Journal of the Statistical Society*, II (April 1839), p. 182.
24 PP 1839 XIX, p. 215, Appendix 7.
25 Miles, *Poverty, Mendicity and Crime*, p. 58.
26 *LM*, 26 June 1849.
27 Walter Lewin, *Clarke Aspinall: A Biography* (London, 1893), p. 157.
28 Miles, *Poverty, Mendicity and Crime*, p. 59.
29 *LM*, 12 May, 22 November 1862.
30 Mortality Sub-Committee, *Report of Evidence 1866*, p. 197.
31 Miles, *Poverty, Mendicity and Crime*, pp. 57–59.
32 *LM*, 5 March 1863.
33 Mortality Sub-Committee, *Report of Evidence 1866*, p. 201.
34 *LM*, 2 April 1852.
35 Taylor, 'Black Spot on the Mersey', vol. I, p. 94.
36 John Finch (ed.), *Statistics of Vauxhall Ward, Liverpool: the Condition of the Working Class in Liverpool in 1842* (Liverpool, 1986, facsimile reprint of 1842 edn), p. 50.
37 Melville, *Redburn*, p. 270.
38 LVRO, *Head Constable's Reports to the Watch Committee*, 11 April 1859.
39 *LM*, 13 July 1858, 26 May 1859.
40 *LM*, 14 June 1845, 1 April 1864, 15 April 1871.
41 *LM*, 5 October, 14 December 1852; *MC*, 15 December 1852.
42 PP 1852–53 XXIII, p. 110, q. 1271, evidence of T. Carter.
43 *LM*, 29 October 1863.
44 C. C. Bowes, *The Associations of Charles Dickens with Liverpool* (Liverpool, 1905), pp. 12–13.
45 PP 1841 V, pp. 124–32.
46 PP 1839 XIX, p. 29.
47 *LM*, 6 February 1900.
48 *Fun*, 14 June 1882.

13: Poaching Wars

1 *Preston Chronicle*, 18 December 1880.
2 *Porcupine*, 19 February 1870.
3 See P. B. Munsche, *Gentlemen and Poachers: The English Game Laws, 1671–1831* (Cambridge, 1981).
4 PP 1873 XIII, *Select Committee on the Game Laws*, p. 67, q. 1809, evidence of Mr Muirhead.
5 Mortality Sub-Committee, *Report of Evidence 1866*, p. 197.
6 *Lloyd's Weekly London Newspaper*, 27 February 1848.
7 *County Gentlemen: Sporting Gazette, Agricultural Journal and Man About Town*, 14 November 1891.
8 John E. Archer, 'Poaching Gangs and Violence: the Urban–Rural Divide in Nineteenth-Century Lancashire', *British Journal of Criminology*, 39(1) (1999), p. 28.
9 *Saturday Advertiser*, quoted in *John Bull*, 31 December 1827; *The Times*, 18 March 1828.
10 *John Bull*, 20 October 1855; *Caledonian Mercury*, 17 October 1855.
11 *Preston Chronicle*, 17 January 1857.
12 *Preston Chronicle*, 10 September 1864.
13 *The Times*, 28 February 1845.
14 See Harry Hopkins, *The Long Affray: the Poaching Wars in Britain* (London, 1985).
15 See John Rule 'Social Crime in the Rural South in the Eighteenth and Nineteenth Centuries', *Southern History*, 1 (1979), pp. 135–53, reprinted in John Rule and Roger Wells, *Crime, Protest and Popular Politics in Southern England, 1740–1850* (Rio Grande, OH, 1997).
16 *Weekly Dispatch*, quoted in *Northern Star and Leeds General Advertiser*, 13 January 1844.
17 John E. Archer, 'Poachers Abroad', in G. E. Mingay (ed.), *The Unquiet Countryside* (London, 1989), p. 53.
18 PP 1846 Parts 1 and 2, *Select Committee on the Game Laws*, p. 346, q. 6425, evidence of A.B.
19 PP 1846 Parts 1 and 2, p. 373, q. 6961, evidence of W. Storey. The following references to Storey are taken from the same report, pp. 367–89.
20 See Archer, 'Men Behaving Badly?', p. 50.
21 PP 1846 Parts 1 and 2, p. 346, q. 6420, p. 347, qq. 6448–49, evidence of A.B.
22 PP 1846 Parts 1 and 2, pp. 363–65.
23 *Preston Chronicle*, 11 December 1841.
24 Archer, 'Poaching Gangs and Violence', p. 35.
25 LM, 10 August 1855, 30 September 1863, 12 April 1865.
26 *Preston Chronicle*, 13 January 1844.
27 LM, 12 January 1844.
28 See Hopkins, *The Long Affray*, p. 203.
29 PP 1846 Parts 1 and 2, p. 343, q. 6315, evidence of A.B.
30 LM, 2 December 1842; *Preston Chronicle*, 1 April 1843.
31 *Bell's Life in London and Sporting Chronicle*, 2 December 1841; *Preston Chronicle*, 11 December 1841; PP 1846 Parts 1 and 2, p. 370, q. 6970, evidence of W. Storey.
32 *Preston Chronicle*, 3 April 1841.
33 *Hull Packet and East Riding Times*, 24 March 1843.
34 LM, 24 March 1843; *Preston Chronicle*, 1 April 1843.
35 *Liverpool Times*, quoted in *Preston Chronicle*, 1 April 1843.
36 *Preston Chronicle*, 18 November 1843.
37 'The Fate of the Liverpool Poachers', street ballad printed by T. Pearson, Manchester, 1861–72. See the Bodleian Library *Allegro* archive, Firth collection, c. 19, p. 56; stanza quoted in Hopkins, *The Long Affray*, p. 207.
38 Hopkins, *The Long Affray*, pp. 207–08.
39 *Preston Chronicle*, 13 January 1844.

40 *Bell's Life in London and Sporting Chronicle*, 13 December 1846.
41 *Glasgow Herald*, 26 January 1844; *Northern Star and Leeds General Advertiser*, 27 January 1844.
42 'Lines on the Execution of Roberts the Poacher', Bodleian Library *Allegro* archive. See Harkness in the W.H.N. Harding collection, B 20, p. 198.

14: Scams

1 Hawthorne, *Our Old Home*, pp. 5–6.
2 Thomas Reilly, private letter to Kelly, 19 June 1848, National Library of Ireland, Mss. 10, 511 (2).
3 Kellow Chesney, *The Victorian Underworld* (Harmondsworth, 1972), pp. 269–70.
4 Donald Thomas, *The Victorian Underworld* (London, 1998), p. 43.
5 *LM*, 8 March 1869.
6 *LM*, 7 June 1853.
7 *LM*, 17 October 1823; see also 13 February 1848, 2 August 1853.
8 Melville, *Redburn*, p. 270.
9 Nicholls, *Sixty Years Random Reminiscences*, p. 15.
10 *LM*, 30 September 1865.
11 *LM*, 13 January 1854.
12 *LM*, 4 April 1845.
13 *LM*, 27 January 1858.
14 *Liverpool Citizen*, 14 March 1888.
15 *Liverpool Citizen*, 21 November 1888.
16 Melville, *Redburn*, p. 269.
17 *LM*, 31 January 1862.
18 Nicholls, *Sixty Years Random Reminiscences*, p. 16.
19 *Liverpool Citizen*, 7 March 1888.
20 *LM*, 15 May 1835.
21 *LM*, 11 May 1852.
22 *Preston Chronicle*, 4 September 1836; *LM*, 31 March 1837; Stonehouse, *Streets of Liverpool*, pp. 46–47.
23 Mayhew, *London Labour and the London Poor*, vol. IV, p. 295.
24 *LM*, 9 February 1849.
25 *LM*, 25 May 1864.
26 *Squalid Liverpool*, p. 88.
27 *LM*, 5 December 1866.
28 Edward J. Bristow, *Vice and Vigilance: Purity Movements in Britain Since 1700* (Dublin, 1977), p. 49.
29 *LM*, 30 July 1888.
30 *Transactions of the NAPSS, Liverpool Meeting, 1876*, p. 373.
31 *LM*, 20 April 1875.
32 Hugh Shimmin, 'The Aintree Carnival', originally published in *Liverpool Life*, quoted in John K. Walton and Alastair Wilcox (eds), *Low Life and Moral Improvement in Mid-Victorian England: Liverpool Through the Journalism of Hugh Shimmin* (Leicester, 1991), p. 76.
33 *LM*, 7 November 1867.
34 *LM*, 17 August 1874.
35 *LM*, 24 November 1862.
36 *LM*, 27 August 1886.
37 *LM*, 10 August 1888.
38 *Boys of England and Jack Harkaway's Journal of Travel, Fun and Instruction*, 30 March 1894.

39 Nicholls, *Sixty Years Random Reminiscences*, p. 13.

40 *LM*, 3 January 1867.

41 *LM*, 17 August 1866.

42 Smith, *My Life Work*, p. 108.

43 James O'Donald Mays, *Mr Hawthorne Goes to England* (Burley, 1983), p. 58.

44 Hawthorne, *The English Notebooks*, p. 43; Hawthorne, *Our Old Home*, p. 243.

45 *LM*, 22 January 1847.

46 *LM*, 14 December 1838.

47 Melville, *Redburn*, pp. 261, 259–60.

48 Olmsted, *Walks and Talks of an American Farmer in England*, p. 47.

49 *Liverpool Domestic Mission Annual Report, 1851*, p. 44.

50 Holmes, *Thieves, Beggars and Prostitutes*, p. 25.

51 *LC*, 14 February 1855.

52 *Liverpool Journal*, 25 April 1857.

53 *Liverpool Domestic Mission Society Annual Report, 1851*; *LM*, 13 April 1852.

54 Anne Holt, *A Ministry to the Poor, Being the History of the Liverpool Domestic Mission Society, 1836–1936* (Liverpool, 1936), p. 55.

55 *LM*, 4 February 1831.

56 *LWM*, 13 March 1897.

57 Burke, *Catholic History of Liverpool*, p. 82.

58 *DP*, 28 March 1862.

59 Hume, *Misrepresentation of the Established Church*, p. 17.

60 Caine, *Hugh Stowell Brown*, p. 89.

61 *LM*, 9 August 1844.

62 *LM*, 14 September 1883.

63 *LM*, 4 February 1831.

64 Holmes, *Thieves, Beggars and Prostitutes*, p. 22.

65 *LM*, 22 November 1880.

66 See Chesney, *The Victorian Underworld*, pp. 246–47.

67 *LM*, 14 January 1863.

68 *LM*, 3 January 1851.

69 *LM*, 26 May 1897.

70 *LM*, 18 September 1899.

71 *LM*, 3 April 1878.

72 *LM*, 16 June 1893.

73 *LM*, 6 April 1857, 'Liverpool life', chapter III.

74 *LWM*, 29 April 1899.

75 *LM*, 20 December 1877.

76 *LM*, 19 October 1857.

77 *LM*, 23 April 1847.

78 *LM*, 26 July 1844.

79 *LM*, 22 January 1897.

80 *LM*, 18 November 1875.

81 Hopkinson, *Memoirs of a Victorian Cabinet Maker*, pp. 98–99.

82 Pat O'Mara, *The Autobiography of a Liverpool Irish Slummy* (London, 1934), pp. 66–67. See also Belchem, *Merseypride*, pp. 134–35.

83 *LWM*, 13 August 1904.

84 Liverpool Society for the Prevention of Cruelty to Children, Executive Committe Minutes, 20 February 1888.

85 Lionel Rose, *Massacre of the Innocents: Infanticide in Britain, 1800–1939* (London, 1986), p. 150.

86 The grand jury was a panel of local worthies given the task of deciding whether or not an indictment was 'a true bill' and therefore a case to proceed to trial. They sometimes offered a statement on the state of law and order in the town.

87 *LM*, 9 December 1853.

88 William Burke Ryan, *Infanticide: its Law, Prevalence and History* (London, 1862), p. 23.

89 Angela Brabin, *The Black Widows of Liverpool: A Chilling Account of Cold-Blooded Murder in Liverpool* (Lancaster, 2003).

90 Angela Brabin, 'The Black Widows of Liverpool', *History Today*, 52(10) (October 2002), p. 46.

91 *LM*, 20 January 1885.

92 PP 1863 XVIII.1, *Children's Employment Commission (1862). First Report of the Commissioners*, p. lxxxviii, q. 624, evidence of Francis Peacock.

93 *LM*, 31 October 1897.

15: Victorian Family Values

1 *LR*, 8 July 1899.

2 *LR*, 16 September 1899.

3 *LR*, 9 September 1899.

4 Rose, *Massacre of the Innocents*, p. 86.

5 *LM*, 20 October 1869.

6 *LM*, 25 October 1856, 15 July 1857, 5 April 1858, 29 January 1870.

7 Rose, *Massacre of the Innocents*, p. 88; For the legal subtleties see Justice Denman's address to the grand jury, *LM*, 20 April 1880.

8 *LM*, 6 April 1857, 'Liverpool Life', no. III.

9 Ryan, *Infanticide*, p. 65.

10 *Report of the Mortality Committee, 1866*, quoted in *Porcupine*, 22 September 1866.

11 See Rose, *Massacre of the Innocents*, p. 127; see also PP 1871, VII, *Report from the Select Committee on Protection of Infant Life*, p. 173, q. 3760.

12 PRO H.O. 45/8044 (old series), Liverpool Northern Medical Society to Home Secretary, June 1869, quoted in Rose, *Massacre of the Innocents*, p. 131; *LM*, 20 October 1869.

13 See Rose, *Massacre of the Innocents*, pp. 85, 131.

14 *LM*, 23 June 1854, 'Coroner's Inquests'.

15 *NAPSS Journal and Sessional papers 1873, Infanticide in Liverpool*.

16 Rose, *Massacre of the Innocents*, pp. 69–69.

17 *LM*, 27 March 1849.

18 *LM*, 6, 9 December 1853.

19 Peter Doyle, *Mitres & Missions in Lancashire: the Roman Catholic Diocese of Liverpool, 1850–2000* (Liverpool, 2005), p. 195.

20 John K. Walton and Alastair Wilcox, 'Introduction', in Walton and Wilcox (eds.), *Low Life and Moral Improvement in Mid-Victorian England*, pp. 13–14.

21 See Shimmin, 'Smothering Children', in Walton and Wilcox (eds.), *Low Life and Moral Improvement in Mid-Victorian England*, pp. 134–45.

22 Jones, *The Slain in Liverpool During 1866 by Drink*, p. 8, reprinted in *LM*, 4 February 1867.

23 Brack, *All They Need Is Love*, p. 34.

24 See Ryan, *Infanticide*, pp. 64–65.

25 Emsley, *Hard Men*, p. 72.

26 Archer, 'The Violence We Have Lost', pp. 182–83.

27 Rose, *Massacre of the Innocents*, p. 68.

28 William Acton, *Prostitution, Considered in its Moral, Social and Sanitary Aspects* (2nd rev. edn, 1870), p. 278.

29 Figures in Rose, *Massacre of the Innocents*, p. 13.
30 Smith, *My Life Work*, p. 126.
31 *LM*, 1, 15, 22, 29 January, 5, 12, 19 February 1847.
32 *John Bull*, 29 July 1871.
33 *LM*, 26 April 1858, 1 April 1864, 4 August 1864, 9 June 1867, 21 February 1867.
34 *Porcupine*, 4 January 1868; *LM*, 24 March 1868.
35 *LM*, 22 July 1869, 9 May 1871, 11 January, 3 March 1873.
36 Frances Power Cobbe, 'Wife-Torture in England', *Contemporary Review*, 32 (1878), p. 59.
37 Serjeant Pulling, 'Why Legislation is Necessary for the Repression of Crimes of Violence', in *Transactions of the National Association for the Promotion of Social Sciences, Liverpool Meeting, 1876*, pp. 345–49.
38 *Transactions of the National Association for the Promotion of Social Sciences, Liverpool Meeting, 1876*, p. 358.
39 Cobbe, 'Wife-Torture', p. 86.
40 See Martin Wiener, *Men of Blood: Violence, Manliness and Criminal Justice in Victorian England* (Cambridge, 2004).
41 Emsley, *Hard Men*, p. 66; see also Anna Clark, 'Domesticity and the Problem of Wifebeating in Nineteenth-Century Britain: Working-Class Culture, Law and Politics', and Catherine Euler, '"The Irons of Their Fetters Have Eaten into Their Souls": Nineteenth-Century Feminist Strategies to Get our Bodies onto the Political Agenda', in Shani D'Cruze (ed.), *Everyday Violence in Britain, 1850–1950: Gender and Class* (Harlow, 2000), pp. 27–44, 198–212.
42 Wood, 'Community Violence', p. 187.
43 *LM*, 2 February 1869.
44 Quoted by Cobbe, 'Wife-Torture', p. 64.
45 Emsley, *Hard Men*, p. 170.
46 PP 1871 XIX.1, *Report of Royal Commission upon the Administration and Operation of the Contagious Diseases Acts*, p. 439, q. 12,879, evidence of Mrs J. Butler.
47 *Liverpool Domestic Mission Society Annual Report, 1847*.
48 PP 1882 XIII, p. 26, q. 211, evidence of Commander Eaton.
49 *LM*, 14 August 1847, 16 November 1883.
50 *LM*, 2 August 1839, 5 February 1847, 26 October 1866, 20 August, 15 December 1863, 28 August 1866, 19 September 1874.
51 Frederick W. Lowndes, *Prostitution and Venereal Diseases in Liverpool* (London, 1886), p. 43.
52 Smith, 'Social Reform', pp. 896–912.
53 See Behlmer, *Child Abuse*, p. 12.
54 Brack, *All they Need is Love*, p. 22.
55 *LR*, 14 October 1899.
56 PP 1901 LXXXIX, p. 45.
57 Behlmer, *Child Abuse*, p. 69.
58 *LM*, 1 February 1895; *LR*, 12 August 1899.
59 *Sunday at Home*, part 17, March 1896, p. 312.
60 *LM*, 18 September 1899.

16: The Devil's Children

1 PP 1839 XIX, p. 11.

2 PP 1841 V, p. 123.

3 Clay, *The Prison Chaplain*, pp. 456, 569.

4 *Porcupine*, 22 September 1866.

5 Head Constable's annual reports, 1880 and 1890, quoted in *LM*, 24 November 1880, 12 November 1890.

6 Quoted in John Belchem, *Irish, Catholic and Scouse: The History of the Liverpool Irish* (Liverpool, 2007), p. 87.

7 George Melly, 'Second Report of the Mason Street Reformatory School for Juvenile Male Delinquents', 1857. Bound in *Stray Leaves*, p. 10.

8 PP 1837–38 XXXI, p. 7.

9 PP 1841 V, p. 123.

10 *The Sunday at Home*, part 17, March 1896, p. 310.

11 Smith, *My Life Work*, p. 108; Holmes, *Thieves, Beggars and Prostitutes*, pp. 30–31.

12 PP 1836 (40) XXXIV, p. 15.

13 Miles, *Poverty, Mendicity and Crime*, p. 83.

14 *LM*, 13 December 1856, Liverpool Life, second series, no. V.

15 Holmes, *Thieves, Beggars and Prostitutes*, p. 16.

16 PP 1837–38 XXXI, p. 141.

17 'Reports of a House to House Visit Made to the Parents of the Boys Named in this List, Who Were in Walton Gaol, February 4, 1856', quoted in Carpenter, *Our Convicts*, vol. I, pp. 70–72.

18 PP 1845 XXIV, p. 84.

19 Watch Committee for the Borough of Liverpool, *Report on the Police Establishment* [...] *1864*; quoted in Burke, *Catholic History of Liverpool*, p. 90.

20 *Porcupine*, 22 September 1866.

21 *LM*, 4 January 1833.

22 PP 1845 XVIII.1, p. 30.

23 Carpenter, *Reformatory Schools*, p. 206.

24 Finch, *Statistics of Vauxhall Ward*, p. 54.

25 Smith, *My Life Work*, pp. 106–07.

26 Donald Currie, 'Sir Donald Currie at the Jubilee Reunion of the Young Men's Society', quoted in *Canning Street Presbyterian Church, 1846–96* (Liverpool, 1896), p. 55.

27 *LR*, 15 July 1899.

28 *LM*, 4 June 1847.

29 See Macilwee, *The Gangs of Liverpool*, pp. 118–21.

30 *LR*, 8 April 1899, 'Squalor and Sin at the Church's Door'.

31 *LM*, 20 September 1866.

32 *John Bull*, 27 November 1875.

33 *John Bull*, 2 December 1876.

34 *Liverpool Domestic Mission Annual Report, 1848* (Liverpool, 1848), p. 9.

35 Holmes, *Thieves, Beggars and Prostitutes*, p. 31.

36 *MC*, 27 May 1850.

37 28th report of Revd J. Clay, quoted in Mary Carpenter, *Juvenile Delinquents* (London, 1853), pp. 31–32; also quoted in *LM*, 24 February 1852.

38 *LM*, 25 December 1879, quoted in Rimmer, *Yesterday's Naughty Children*, p. 5.

39 *Fun*, 23 April 1884.

40 See Barry S. Godfrey, Paul Lawrence and Chris A. Williams, *History & Crime* (London, 2008), pp. 91, 174–75.
41 *Porcupine*, 9 January 1875.
42 David Taylor, *Crime, Policing and Punishment in England, 1750–1914* (Basingstoke, 1998), p. 51.
43 Hawthorne, *The English Notebooks*, pp. 17, 13.
44 PP 1837 XXXII, p. 86.
45 *LM*, 13 December 1856. 'Liverpool Life', second series, VI.
46 PP 1852–53 XXIII, pp. 448–49.
47 PP 1841 V, p. 127.
48 Miles, *Poverty, Mendicity and Crime*, p. 82.
49 H. S. Joseph, *Memoirs of Convicted Prisoners; Accompanied by Remarks of the Causes and Prevention of Crime* (London, 1853), pp. 45–46.
50 PP 1845 XXIV, p. 83.
51 MC, 27 May 1850.
52 'Reports of a House to House Visit Made to the Parents of the Boys Named in this List, Who Were in Walton Gaol, Feb. 4, 1856' and 'Reports Made of Notorious Harbours for Juveniles of Both Sexes', in Carpenter, *Our Convicts*, vol. I, pp. 69–70.
53 PP 1852–53 XXIII, p. 122. q. 1408.
54 Miles, *Poverty, Mendicity and Crime*, p. 82.
55 PP 1877 XI, p. 32.
56 PP 1841 V, p. 123.
57 PP 1836 (40) XXXIV, pp. 19–20.
58 PP 1839 XIX, p. 18.
59 PP 1852n53 XXIII, p. 126. q. 1449.
60 PP 1839 XXII, p. 89.
61 PP 1841 V, pp. 123, 133.
62 PP 1837 XXXII, pp. 87–88.
63 PP 1841 V, p. 132.
64 PP 1841 V, pp. 124–33.

17: Gangs and Anti-Social Behaviour

1 Wallace, *A General and Descriptive History*, p. 272.
2 Troughton, *The History of Liverpool*, pp. 151, 192.
3 Williams, *History of the Liverpool Privateers*, pp. 237, 323.
4 Troughton, *History of Liverpool*, pp. 162–63.
5 *Memoirs of Mrs Inchbald*, vol. I, pp. 91–93, 15 June 1778, quoted in Broadbent, *Annals of the Liverpool Stage*, pp. 71–72.
6 Quoted in Midwinter, *Old Liverpool*, p. 27.
7 *The Monthly Mirror*, quoted in Midwinter, *Old Liverpool*, p. 27.
8 Troughton, *History of Liverpool*, pp. 202, 243.
9 See Marc Baer, *Theatre and Disorder in Late Georgian London* (Oxford, 1992).
10 Broadbent, *Annals of the Liverpool Stage*, pp. 123–24.
11 *The Times*, 31 May 1810.
12 Picton, *Memorials*, vol. I, pp. 380–81.
13 *LM*, 17 December 1824.
14 *LM*, 22 September 1826.
15 *LM*, 12 March 1830.

16 *LM*, 30 April 1862.
17 *LM*, 12 April 1884.
18 *LM*, 1 February 1870.
19 *LM*, 6 October 1864.
20 *LM*, 30 March 1875, 30 July 1883.
21 *LM*, 14 June 1869.
22 *LM*, 4 July 1867.
23 *The Times*, 16 April 1853.
24 Brian Sutton-Smith, *The Folkgames of Children* (Austin, TX, 1972), pp. 156–57.
25 *LM*, 12 May 1871, 12 May 1879, 7 March 1883, 24 May 1884.
26 Cited in *LM*, 5 August 1896.
27 *LM*, 17 February 1837.
28 *LM*, 19, 20, 25 February 1884.
29 *LM*, 18 June 1869.
30 *LM*, 24 September 1862.
31 *LM*, 1 September 1896.
32 *LM*, 3 September 1896.
33 *LM*, 4 April 1862.
34 *LM*, 10 August 1866.
35 *LM*, 5 October 1887.
36 *LM*, 22 October 1858.
37 *LM*, 18 June 1869.
38 *LM*, 30 April 1874.
39 Ray Physick, *Played in Liverpool: Charting the Heritage of a City at Play* (Manchester, 2007), chapters 5 and 6.
40 *Liverpool Critic*, vol. II, no. 36, 27 January 1877, p. 59, 'Liverpool by Gaslight: Lime Street on a Saturday Night'.
41 *LM*, 27 February 1866.
42 *LM*, 6 August 1866.
43 *LM*, 26 November 1862.
44 *LM*, 24 November 1890.
45 *LM*, 22 January 1875.
46 *Porcupine*, 9 January 1875.
47 *Porcupine*, 19 December 1874.
48 *LM*, 30 April 1884.
49 Figures from *Liverpool Albion*, quoted in *Melbourne Punch*, 15 April 1875.
50 *LM*, 3, 30 April 1884.
51 *LM*, 28 May 1884.
52 *LM*, 31 May 1884.
53 *LM*, 22 November 1887.
54 *Plain Talk*, March 1875, p. 6.
55 *Daily Mail*, 2 November 2006.
56 *LM*, 8 April 1873.
57 *Funny Folks*, 3 July 1886.
58 *DP*, 4 September 1886.
59 Physick, *Played in Liverpool*, chapter 16.
60 *LM*, 17 November 1886.
61 *LM*, 16 March 1897.

18: Prostitution

1 Ralph Waldo Emerson, *The Journals and Miscellaneous Notebooks of Ralph Waldo Emerson* (Cambridge, MA, 1847–48), vol. X, pp. 333, 550–51.

2 Troughton, *The History of Liverpool*, p. 151.

3 Miles, *Poverty, Mendicity and Crime*, p. 58. The 1839 Constabulary Report states that there were 520 brothels, each housing four prostitutes, plus 136 lodging-housing containing many more (PP 1839 XIX, p. 9).

4 William W. Sanger, *The History of Prostitution: its Extent, Causes and Effects throughout the World* (New York, 1913), pp. 340–41; see Jones, *Crime, Protest and Police in Nineteenth-Century Britain*, p. 25.

5 Philip Howell, David Beckingham and Francesca Moore, 'Managed Zones for Sex Workers in Liverpool: Contemporary Proposals, Victorian Parallels', *Transactions of the Institute of British Geographers*, new series, 33(2) (2008), p. 235.

6 Cockroft, *From Cutlasses to Computers*, p. 18.

7 *LM*, 12 March 1830.

8 Hobson, *What Hath God Wrought*, p. 113.

9 PP 1839 XIX, p. 216.

10 LVRO, Reports of the Head Constable to the Watch Committee, 21 May 1877.

11 *LR*, 11 March 1893; *LM*, 27 November 1857.

12 Society for the Suppression of Vicious Practices, Report of the Annual Meeting, Liverpool, 1858, p. 5, reprinted in *LM*, 28 May 1858; *Liverpool Critic*, vol. II, no. 38, 10 February 1877, p. 86, 'Liverpool by Gaslight: Lime Street'.

13 *Liverpool Critic*, vol. II, no. 36, 27 January 1877, p. 59, 'Liverpool by Gaslight: Lime Street on a Saturday Night'.

14 *LM*, 8 March 1859.

15 *LM*, 17 November 1858.

16 *Liverpool Critic*, vol. II, no. 38, 10 February 1877, p. 86.

17 *LR*, 28 January 1893.

18 W. Bevan, *Prostitution in the Borough of Liverpool* (Liverpool, 1843).

19 Unless otherwise stated, Father Nugent's comments are from PP 1882 XIII, pp. 14–23.

20 Lowndes, *Prostitution and Venereal Diseases in Liverpool*, p. 26.

21 *LR*, 28 February 1885.

22 *LR*, 28 January 1893.

23 See Neal, 'A Criminal Profile of the Liverpool Irish', pp. 177–78. The figures are taken from PP 1854 (396) XVII.1, *Report from the Select Committee on Poor Removal*, minutes of evidence, A. Campbell, qq. 4993–4995.

24 Quoted in Neal, 'A Criminal Profile of the Liverpool Irish', p. 178.

25 Lowe, *The Irish in Mid-Victorian Lancashire*, pp. 102–03.

26 *Transactions of the NAPSS, 1858*, p. 367.

27 *Catholic Institute Magazine*, Vol. III, 2, 1857, p. 54, 'The Outcasts of Society'.

28 Sanger, *The History of Prostitution*, p. 342.

29 *LM*, 7 August 1846.

30 Hawthorne, *Our Old Home*, p. 255.

31 Amy Harrison, *Women's Industries in Liverpool* (Liverpool, 1904), p. 13.

32 *LR*, 26 May 1888, 9 June 1888.

33 PP 1882 XIII, pp. 15–16, q. 102, evidence of Father Nugent.

34 Peter Bailey, *Leisure and Class in Victorian England: Rational Recreation and the Contest for Control, 1830–1885* (London, 1978), pp. 167–68.

35 *LM*, 21 July 1856, 'Liverpool Life', no. V.

36 *LR*, 9 June 1888.

37 Lowndes, *Prostitution and Venereal Diseases in Liverpool*, p. 2. Figures vary according to source and decade. Neal states about 30,000 sailors ashore at any one time ('A Criminal Profile of the Liverpool Irish', p. 177), while in 1881 Father Nugent reckoned there were 114,000 sailors paid off in Liverpool (PP 1882 XIII q. 94).

38 Adapted from Chesney, *Victorian Underworld*, p. 378.

39 *MC*, 3 June 1850, 'Labour and the Poor, Letter III'.

40 Lowndes, *Prostitution and Syphilis in Liverpool*, p. 14.

41 Lowndes, *The Extension of the Contagious Diseases Act in Liverpool*, p. 81.

42 PP 1877 XI, p. 22.

43 Eaton's comments in this chapter are from PP 1882 XIII, pp. 23–30.

44 Lowndes, *Prostitution and Syphilis in Liverpool*, p. 8; *Prostitution and Venereal Diseases in Liverpool*, p. 4; *The Extension of the Contagious Diseases Act in Liverpool*, p. 81.

45 *LM*, 10 August 1857, 'Liverpool Life', no. XX.

46 Holmes, *Thieves, Beggars and Prostitutes*, p. 34.

47 Olmsted, *Walks and Talks of an American Farmer in England*, pp. 37–38.

48 Father Nugent, Social Science Congress, 1877, quoted in Lowndes, *Prostitution and Venereal Diseases in Liverpool*, p. 20.

49 *Liverpool Daily Courier*, 23 June 1863.

50 *LM*, 24 July 1849.

51 *LM*, 3 February 1862.

52 PP 1882 XIII, p. 15 qq. 98–99, p. 17, qq. 112–13, evidence of Father Nugent.

53 *LR*, 21 February 1891, 11 March 1893.

54 Quoted in Danielle Pettit, 'Attitudes to Venereal Contagion in Victorian Liverpool', in *Wives and Whores in Victorian Liverpool: Varieties in Attitude Towards Medical Care for Women: Papers Delivered at a Meeting of the Liverpool Medical History Society, 4 April 1998*, ed. J. M. Bone and Christine Hillam (Liverpool, 1999), p. 62.

55 Lowndes, *Prostitution and Venereal Diseases in Liverpool*, p. 49. Others believed that syphilis was not a serious threat to Liverpool. J. Birkbeck Nevins, a consulting surgeon to the Liverpool Eye and Ear Infirmary, argued that the same figure showed that only one adult in nearly 8,000 died annually. Although not a venerealogist, Nevins provided statistical support to Josephine Butler in her opposition to the Contagious Diseases Act of 1864. See *The Medical Enquirer*, 15 June 1876.

56 Lowndes, *Prostitution and Venereal Diseases in Liverpool*, p. 43.

57 Frederick W. Lowndes, 'The Liverpool Lock Hospital and the Prevalence and Severity of Constitutional Syphilis in Liverpool', *British Medical Journal*, 15 May 1880, p. 727.

58 Lowndes, *Prostitution and Venereal Diseases in Liverpool*, pp. 8, 16.

59 Nott-Bower, *Fifty-Two Years a Policeman*, pp. 139–46; *Vigilance Record*, October 1892, p. 141.

60 *LR*, 21 July 1888.

61 *LM*, 8 June 1847.

62 LVRO, Annual Police Returns, Liverpool Council Proceedings, 1868–1882.

63 Lowndes, *Prostitution and Venereal Diseases in Liverpool*, p. 15; Chesney, *Victorian Underworld*, p. 407.

64 *LM*, 28 May 1858.

65 Jordan, *Josephine Butler*, pp. 70–73; *LM*, 11 January 1869.

66 *LM*, 16 December 1857; for continental trade in prostitutes, see Chesney, *Victorian Underworld*, pp. 407–14.

67 *John Bull*, 29 March 1856. The letter in the report omits Rosenberg's name but is undoubtedly about her.

68 *LM*, 25 July 1862.

69 PP 1837 XXXII, p. 86.
70 *Porcupine*, 1 July 1871.
71 *Porcupine*, 1 July 1871, 15 December 1860.
72 *LM*, 17 January 1845.
73 University College London, Papers of Edwin Chadwick, Depositions Box 129, quoted in Thomas, *Victorian Underworld*, pp. 87–88.
74 *LM*, 7 February 1863.
75 *LM*, 28 August 1885.
76 *Report on Female Prostitution* (Edinburgh, 1857), quoted in Frances Finnegan, *Poverty and Prostitutes: a Study of Victorian Prostitutes in York* (Cambridge, 1979), p. 81.
77 Watch Committee for the Borough of Liverpool, *Report on the Police Establishment* […] 1863.
78 See Dorothy M. Kitchingman, 'A Study of the Effects of the Criminal Law Amendment Act 1865 on Prostitution in Liverpool, 1885–1895', unpublished MA dissertation, Open University, 2001, p. 29.
79 *LR*, 15 July 1899.
80 *LR*, 8 July 1899.
81 PP 1882 XIII, q. 139.
82 *LM*, 25 April 1845.
83 Charles Dickens, 'Poor Mercantile Jack', in *The Uncommercial Traveller and Reprinted Pieces etc.* (London, 1958), p. 56.
84 See Walkowitz, *Prostitution and Victorian Society*, pp. 246–52.
85 Paula Bartley, *Prostitution: Prevention and Reform in England, 1860–1914* (London, 2000), p. 167.
86 Nott-Bower, *Fifty-Two Years a Policeman*, pp. 139–46; *Vigilance Record*, October 1892, p. 72.
87 *LR*, 21, 28 July, 11, 18 August, 1 September 1888; see also *Porcupine*, 24 June 1871, 'A Cabman on the Social Evil'.
88 LVRO, Magistrates' Court Records, Justices Sessions, Gaol and House of Correction, 26 January 1871.
89 Armstrong, *The Deadly Shame of Liverpool*, p. 11.
90 LVRO, Head Constable's Special Report Book, 1890–92, 2 September 1890. For a discussion of the figures see Howell et al., 'Managed Zones for Sex Workers in Liverpool', pp. 242–44.
91 *Liverpool Citizen*, 18 September 1889.
92 *LM*, 4 June 1892.
93 Head Constables Report, 1891, quoted in *LM*, 30 October 1891.
94 *LR*, 12 December 1891.
95 Kitchingman, 'A Study of the Effects of the Criminal Law Amendment Act', pp. 54–55.
96 See Walkowitz, *Prostitution and Victorian Society*, pp. 192–213.
97 Nott-Bower, *Fifty-Two Years a Policeman*, pp. 145, 142.

19: Sport and Gambling

1 *LM*, 12 March 1862.
2 Troughton, *History of Liverpool*, p. 93.
3 Brooke, *Liverpool in the Last Quarter of the Eighteenth Century*, p. 267; Muir dates this episode to 1775: *History of Liverpool*, p. 283.
4 *LM*, 16 April 1887.
5 *LM*, 17 September 1869, 'Proposed Re-opening of Parliament Fields'.
6 *LM*, 8 September 1856, 'Liverpool Life', no. XII.

7 *LM*, 14 March 1854.

8 *LM*, 23 January 1846.

9 *LM*, 18 October 1860.

10 *LM*, 2 December 1871.

11 Stonehouse, *Recollections*, p. 200; John Harland and T. T. Wilkinson, *Lancashire Legends: Traditions, Pageants, Sports etc.* (Wakefield, 1973), p. 144.

12 Brooke, *Liverpool in the Last Quarter of the Eighteenth Century*, p. 266.

13 Physick, *Played in Liverpool*, p. 10.

14 *LM*, 4 February 1853.

15 *LM*, 20 April 1875.

16 Physick, *Played in Liverpool*, p. 19.

17 *LM*, 26 February 1877.

18 Jervis, *Chronicles of a Victorian Detective*, pp. 52–54.

19 Picton, *Memorials*, vol. II, p. 303.

20 *LM*, 14 May 1856.

21 Bailey, *Leisure and Class in Victorian England*, p. 36.

22 *Bethell's Life*, vol. II, no. 83, 24 June 1826.

23 Denis Brailsford, *Bareknuckles: a Social History of Prize-Fighting* (Cambridge, 1988), p. 119.

24 William Donaldson, *Brewer's Rogues, Villains, Eccentrics: an A–Z of Roguish Britons Through the Ages* (London, 2002), p. 610.

25 *Bethell's Life*. LVRO has no. 5, 25 December 1824 to no.153, 27 October 1827 (incomplete run).

26 *Bethell's Life*, vol. II, no. 94, 9 September 1826.

27 *Bethell's Life*, vol. III, no. 138, 7 July 1827.

28 *LM*, 4 April 1834.

29 Ray Physick, *Liverpool's Boxing Venues* (Liverpool, 2008), p. 16.

30 *Bethell's Life*, no. 25, 14 May 1825.

31 *Bell's Life in London and Sporting Chronicle*, 21 September 1845, 20 June 1847, 19 January 1859.

32 *LM*, 14 December 1863.

33 Brailsford, *Bareknuckles*, p. 155.

34 *LM*, 19 June 1829.

35 *Bethell's Life*, no. 21, 16 April 1825.

36 *LM*, 25 August 1856, 'Liverpool Life', no. IX.

37 *LR*, 29 September 1888.

38 *LR*, 1 August 1891, 'A Night at the Boxing Club'.

39 *Liverpool Citizen*, 2 May 1888.

40 Brailsford, *Bareknuckles*, pp. 158–60.

41 *LR*, 7 March 1891.

42 Miles, *Poverty, Mendicity and Crime*, p. 72.

43 *Liverpool Albion* quoted in *Satirist, and the Censor of the Time*, 26 May 1833.

44 *LM*, 27 July 1827.

45 *Racing Times*, 1 December 1862.

46 *LM*, 3 May 1860.

47 *Manchester Evening News*, 20–21 May 1885.

48 *LM*, 18 April 1890.

49 *LR*, 3 September 1892.

50 *LM*, 23 May 1861.

51 *LM*, 5 January 1857, 'Liverpool Life', second series no. VII.

52 *LM*, 24 February 1874.

53 *LM*, 1 December 1856, 'Liverpool Life', second series, no. IV. See also 18 October 1876, 'The State of Crime in Liverpool'.

54 *LM*, 8 October 1895.

55 *LM*, 28 April 1890, 26 May 1897.

56 *Porcupine*, 26 April 1879.

57 *LM*, 30 March 1832.

58 Watch Committee for the Borough of Liverpool, *Report on the Police Establishment* […] *1874*.

59 PP 1841 V, pp. 128, 129, 133.

60 *LM*, 22 June 1858.

61 *LM*, 22 March 1865.

62 *LM*, 7 October 1868.

63 *Bethell's Life*, vol. III, no. 128, 5 May 1827; *Liverpool Citizen*, 14 March 1888.

64 *Funny Folks*, 22 March 1879.

65 *LM*, 24 February 1843.

66 *LM*, 25 May 1862.

67 Cockroft, *The Albert Dock*, pp. 48–49.

68 *Satirist, and the Censor of the Time*, 9 September 1838.

69 *LWM*, 10 October 1896.

70 *LM*, 20 December 1856.

71 *Liverpool Citizen*, 25 July 1888.

72 *Porcupine*, 10, 31 March 1877.

73 *LWM*, 30 March 1889.

74 *LM*, 14 May 1847.

75 *LM*, 18 November 1862.

76 *LM*, 7 December 1882.

77 *LM*, 28 April 1890.

78 *LM*, 20 August 1875.

79 *LM*, 3 October 1887, 'Saturday Night Resorts'.

80 *Liverpool Citizen*, 14 March 1883, 'Sunday Strolls into Strange Places'.

81 *LM*, 31 October 1897.

82 *LM*, 6 September 1857.

83 *LM*, 13, 14 March 1873, 27 July 1875.

84 Hugh Shimmin, 'Recreations', originally published in *Town Life*, reprinted in Walton and Wilcox (eds.), *Low Life and Moral Improvement*, p. 180.

85 *LM*, 16 September 1874.

86 PP 1898 XXXVI.1, p. 2, qq. 26,310–26,311, evidence of Captain J. W. N. Bower.

Conclusion

1 Howell et al., 'Managed Zones for Sex Workers in Liverpool'.

2 Carter, 'On the Crime of Liverpool', pp. 354–61.

3 *Liverpool Echo*, 8 September 2009, 'Allerton Road and Lark Lane Bar Consultation Plan Approved by Liverpool Council'.

4 *Liverpool Echo*, 3, 15 November 2008. See letters pages.

Bibliography

1. Manuscript sources

Bodleian Library, Oxford

Allegro archive. Firth collection, c.19, p. 56
Allegro archive. Harkness in the W. H. N. Harding collection, B 20, p. 198
W. H. N. Harding collection, Quarto Street Ballads, no. 2000

Liverpool Record Office

352 MIN/WAT, Minutes of the Watch Committee, 81 vols.
Duncan, W. H., *Report to the Health Committee of the Borough of Liverpool, on the Health of the Town During the Years 1847–48–49–50, and on Other Matters Within his Department*, 1851
Head Constable's Special Report Book, 1890–92
Health Committee Minute Books, 17 June 1847
Industrial Schools Admission and Discharge Book, 1862–1865
Liverpool Council Proceedings
Liverpool Female Penitentiary Annual Reports, 1855–1877
Liverpool Society for the Prevention of Cruelty to Children, Executive Committe Minutes
Liverpool Vestry Books
Lyte, B. E. N., 'The Development of Prisons in Liverpool' (1964). Typed MS
Magistrates' Court Records, Justices Sessions, Gaol and House of Correction
The Port and Docks of Birkenhead. Minutes of Evidence and Proceedings on the Liverpool and Birkenhead Dock Bills in Sessions of 1844 to 1852 [of House of Commons] by Thomas Webster (London, 1873)
Smyth, Nathaniel, *Maps Showing Licensed Premises*, 657.94 SMY (includes various leaflets, maps and publications bound together)
Watch Committee for the Borough of Liverpool, *Report on the Police Establishment, and the State of Crime, with Tabular Returns* […] (various years)

National Archives, Kew

Adm 1/1618 (Smith Child), 27 October, 16 November 1793
Adm 1/1787 (John Fortescue), 6 September 1761
Adm 1/1788 (John Fortescue), 19 February 1762
Adm 1/1788 (John Fortescue), 18 April 1762
Colonial Office Papers, 384/84, 4584, Emigration, 22 May 1849
Colonial Office Papers, 384/32, 5972, Low, Lieutenant, 'An Exposition of Frauds upon Emigrants'
C.O.904.7.77-92, statement of John Kelly, 6 December 1839
H.O.8/55, Convict Prisons: Attested List of Convicts, 1824–76
H.O. 45/8044 (old series), Liverpool Northern Medical Society to Home Secretary, June 1869
HO 73/5 pt 2, Returns to Constabulary Commission 1839, reply from Kirkdale

Maritime Archives & Library, National Museums Liverpool

MDHB/MISC/12, 'Minutes of Evidence Taken by a Sub-Committee of the Dock Committee, as to the Expediency of Uniting the Dock Police with the Town Police', 21 November 1836
MDHB/MISC/12, Customs Officer to the Dock Committee, 18 July 1814

National Library of Ireland, Dublin

Thomas Reilly, private letter to Kelly, 19 June 1848, Mss. 10, 511 (2)

University College London

Papers of Edwin Chadwick, Depositions Box 129

2. Newspapers and periodical publications

Bell's Life in London and Sporting Chronicle
Bentley's Miscellany
Bethell's Life in London and Liverpool Sporting Register
Billing Advertiser
Birmingham Daily Post
Boys of England and Jack Harkaway's Journal of Travel, Fun and Instruction
British Chronicle or Pugh's Hereford Journal
British Medical Journal
Caledonian Mercury
Catholic Institute Magazine
Cleave's Penny Gazette of Variety and Amusement
Clonmel Chronicle
Contemporary Review

Cornhill Magazine
County Gentlemen: Sporting Gazette, Agricultural Journal and Man About Town
Daily Advertiser
Daily Herald
Daily Mail
Daily Mirror
Daily Post
Daily Telegraph
Derby Mercury
Englishwoman's Review
Era
Evening Express
Fun
Funny Folks
Glasgow Herald
Gore's Advertiser (Gore's General Advertiser)
Hull Packet and East Riding Times
John Bull
Journal of the Statistical Society
Lady's Newspaper
Liverpool Chronicle
Liverpool Citizen
Liverpool Courier
Liverpool Critic
Liverpool Daily Albion
Liverpool Echo
Liverpool Herald
Liverpool Journal
Liverpool Mail
Liverpool Mercury
Liverpool Times
Liverpool Weekly Albion
Liverpool Weekly Mercury
Lloyd's Evening Post
Lloyd's Weekly London Newspaper
Medical Enquirer
Melbourne Punch
Monthly Mirror
Morning Chronicle
Morning Chronicle and London Advertiser
Nation
Newcastle Courant

Nineteenth Century
Northern Star and Leeds General Advertiser
Notes and Queries
Pall Mall Magazine
Penny Illustrated
Plain Talk
Porcupine
Preston Chronicle
Public Advertiser
Racing Times
Review of Reviews
Satirist, and the Censor of the Time
Saturday Review
Sunday at Home
Sunday Magazine
The Times
True Briton
Vigilance Record
Weekly Dispatch
Western Mail
Whitehall Evening Post
Williamson's Advertiser
Women's Signal

3. Parliamentary papers

PP 1835 XI, *Select Committee on Gaols and Houses of Correction, in England and Wales Appendix*

PP 1835 (475) XV, *Second Report from the Select Committee Appointed to Inquire into the Nature, Character, Extent and Tendency of Orange Lodges, Associations or Societies in Ireland*

PP 1836 (40) XXXIV, *Royal Commission on the Condition of the Poorer Classes in Ireland, Appendix G, The State of Irish Poor in Great Britain*

PP 1837 (89) XXXII, *Second Report of the Inspectors of Prisons of Great Britain. II. Northern and Eastern District*

PP 1837–38 (134) XXXI, *Third Report of the Inspectors Appointed Under the Provisions of the Act 5 & 6 Will. IV. c. 38. to Visit the Different Prisons of Great Britain. II. Northern and Eastern District*

PP 1839 (169) XIX, *Royal Commission on Establishing an Efficient Constabulary Force in Counties of England and Wales*

PP 1839 (199) XXII, *Fourth Report of the Inspectors Appointed Under the Provisions of the Act 5 & 6 Will. IV. c. 38. to Visit the Different Prisons of Great Britain. II. Northern and Eastern District*

PP 1840 (384) XI, *Report from the Select Committee on the Health of Towns*

PP 1841 (339) V, *Sixth Report of the Inspectors of Prisons of Great Britain II. Northern and Eastern District*

PP 1843 (517) XXV & XXVI, *Eighth Report of the Inspectors Appointed Under the Provisions of the Act 5 & 6 Will. IV. c. 38, to Visit the Different Prisons of Great Britain. II. Northern and Eastern District*

PP 1844 (572) XVII.1, *First Report of the Commissioners for Inquiring into the State of Large Towns and Populous Districts*

PP 1844 (595) XXIX, *Ninth Report of the Inspectors Appointed under the Provisions of the act 5 & 6 Will. IV. c. 38, to visit the different prisons of Great Britain. II. Northern and Eastern District*

PP 1845 (602) XVIII.1, *Reports from Commissioners: 1845, vol. 5, State of Large Towns and Populous Districts*

PP 1845 (675) XXIV, *Tenth Report of the Inspectors Appointed Under the Provisions of the Act 5 & 6 Will. IV. c. 38, to Visit the Different Prisons of Great Britain. II. Northern and Eastern District*

PP 1846 (463) IX, Parts 1 and 2, *Select Committee on the Game Laws*

PP 1846 (530) XIII, *Select Committee on Railway Labourers*

PP 1847 (193) LIV, *Destitute Irish (Liverpool). Copies of, or Extracts from, any Correspondence Addressed to the Secretary of State for the Home Department, Relative to the Recent Immigration of Destitute Irish into Liverpool*

PP 1847 (534) VII, *Second Report from the Select Committee of the House of Lords Appointed to Inquire into the Execution of the Criminal Law, Especially Respecting Juvenile Offenders and Transportation*

PP 1847–48 (987) LIII, *Reports and Communications on Vagrancy*

PP 1847–48 (997) XXXVI, *Thirteenth Report of the Inspectors of Prisons of Great Britain II. Northern and Eastern District*

PP 1849 (266) XLVII, *Letter to Secretary of State for Home Dept., by Stipendiary Magistrate of Liverpool, April 1849, Respecting Influx of Irish Poor*

PP 1849 (339) LI, *Captain Denham's Report on Passenger Accommodation in Steamers between Ireland and Liverpool*

PP 1851 (632) XIX1, *Report from the Select Committee on Passenger's Act*

PP 1851 (1355) XXVII, *Sixteenth Report of the Inspectors Appointed, Under the Provisions of the Act 5 & 6 Will. IV. c. 38 to Visit the Different Prisons of Great Britain. II. Northern and Eastern District*

PP 1852–53 (515) XXIII, *Report from the Select Committee on Criminal and Destitute Children*

PP 1854 (163) XIII.1, *First Report from the Select Committee on Emigrant Ships*

PP 1854 (396) XVII.1, *Report from the Select Committee on Poor Removal*

PP 1857–58 (2415) XXIII, *Papers Relative to Sanitary State of People of England Results of Inquiry into Proportions of Death Produced by Diseases in Different Districts in England, by E.H. Greenhow*

PP 1860 LX, *Judicial Statistics, England and Wales, 1860. Part I*

PP 1863 (499) IX.1, *Report from the Select Committee of the House of Lords, on the Present State of Discipline in Gaols and Houses of Correction*

PP 1863 (3170) XVIII.1, *Children's Employment Commission (1862). First Report of the Commissioners*

PP 1870 (259) VIII, *Report from the Select Committee on Prisons and Prison Ministers Acts*

PP 1871 (372) VII, *Report from the Select Committee on Protection of Infant Life*

PP 1871 (408) XIX.1, *Report of Royal Commission upon the Administration and Operation of the Contagious Diseases Acts*

PP 1872 (242) IX, *Report from the Select Committee on Habitual Drunkards*

PP 1873 (285) XIII, *Select Committee on the Game Laws*

PP 1877 (418) XI, *Select Committee of House of Lords for Inquiring into Prevalence of Habits of Intemperance, and Effects of Recent Legislation: Third Report*

PP 1882 (344) XIII, *Report from the Select Committee of the House of Lords on the Law Relating to the Protection of Young Girls*

PP 1884 (4180) XLII, *Seventh Report of the Commissioners of Prisons*

PP 1897 (c8523) XXXV.1, *Royal Commission on Liquor Licensing Laws. Second Report of the Royal Commission on Liquor Licensing Laws*

PP 1898 (8693-94) XXXVI.1, *Royal Commission on Liquor Licensing Laws. Third Report of the Royal Commission on Liquor Licensing Laws*

PP 1901 LXXXIX, *Judicial Statistics, England and Wales, 1899. Part I*

4. Unpublished theses

Bryson, Christine Anne, 'Riot and its Control in Liverpool, 1815–1860', MPhil thesis, Open University, 1989

De Motte, Charles, 'The Dark Side of the Town: Crime in Manchester and Salford, 1815–1875', PhD thesis, University of Kansas, 1977

Kanya-Forstner, Martha, 'The Politics of Survival: Irish Women in Outcast Liverpool, 1850–1890', PhD thesis, University of Liverpool, 1997

Kitchingman, Dorothy M., 'A Study of the Effects of the Criminal Law Amendment Act 1865 on Prostitution in Liverpool, 1885–1895', MA dissertation, Open University, 2001

Lowe, W. J., 'The Irish in Lancashire 1846–71: a Social History', PhD thesis, University of Dublin, 1974

O'Brien, Terence, 'The Education and Care of Workhouse Children in Some Lancashire Poor Law Unions, 1834–1930', MEd thesis, University of Manchester, 1975

Taylor, Iain C., 'Black Spot on the Mersey: A Study of Environment and Society in Eighteenth and Nineteenth Century Liverpool', PhD thesis, University of Liverpool, 1976, 2 vols.

5. Contemporary books, pamphlets etc.

Acton, William, *Prostitution, Considered in its Moral, Social and Sanitary Aspects* (2nd rev. edn, 1870)

Armstrong, Richard Acland, *The Deadly Shame of Liverpool: An Appeal to the Municipal Voters* (London: George Philip and Son, 1890)

Aspinall, James, *Liverpool, a Few Years Since, by an Old Stager* (Liverpool, 1852)

Aspland, Alfred, *Crime in Manchester and Police Administration* (London: Longman's Green, 1868)

Baines, Thomas, *History of the Commerce and Town of Liverpool* (1852)

Bevan, W., *Prostitution in the Borough of Liverpool* (Liverpool, 1843)

Bosanquet, Helen (ed.), *Social Conditions in Provincial Towns* (London: Macmillan, 1912; New York: Garland, repr. 1985)

Bowes, C. C., *The Associations of Charles Dickens with Liverpool* (Liverpool: Lyceum Press, 1905)

Broadbent, R. J., *Annals of the Liverpool Stage: From the Earliest Period to the Present Time* (Liverpool: Edward Howell, 1908)

Brooke, Richard, *Liverpool in the Last Quarter of the Eighteenth Century* (Liverpool: Mawdsley, 1853)

Burke, Thomas, *Catholic History of Liverpool* (Liverpool: Tinling, 1910)

—, 'The Street Trading Children of Liverpool', *Contemporary Review*, 78 (1900), pp. 720–26

Caine, W. S. (ed.), *Hugh Stowell Brown: His Autobiography, His Commonplace Book and Extracts From His Sermons and Addresses: A Memorial Volume* (London: Routledge, 2nd edn, 1887)

Carpenter, Mary, *Juvenile Delinquents* (London, 1853)

—, *Our Convicts*, 2 vols. (London, 1864)

—, *Reformatory Schools* (London, 1868)

Carter, Thomas, 'On the Crime of Liverpool', in *Transactions of the National Association for the Promotion of Social Sciences, 1858*, ed. George W. Hastings (London, 1859), pp. 354–61

Clay, Walter Lowe, *The Prison Chaplain: a Memoir of the Rev. John Clay* (Cambridge: Macmillan, 1861)

Cobbe, Frances Power, 'Wife-Torture in England', *Contemporary Review*, 32 (1878), pp. 55–87

Collinson, Joseph, *Facts about Flogging* (London: A.C. Fifield, rev. edn, 1905)

Currie, Donald, *Canning Street Presbyterian Church, 1846–96* (Liverpool: Read & Co., 1896)

D'Aeth, F. G., 'Liverpool', in Helen Bosanquet (ed.), *Social Conditions in Provincial Towns* (London, 1912; New York, repr. 1985), pp?/

Denvir, John, *The Irish in Britain: From the Earliest Times to the Fall and Death of Parnell* (London: Kegan Paul, 1892)

Dickens, Charles, *The Uncommercial Traveller and Reprinted Pieces etc.* (London: Oxford University Press, 1958)

'Discrepant Criminal Statistics', *Journal of the Statistical Society*, xxxi (1868), pp. 349–53

Dixon, William Hepworth, *The London Prisons* (London: Murray, 1850)

Duncan, W. H., *On the Physical Causes of the High Rate of Mortality in Liverpool* (Liverpool: Liverpool, Literary & Philosophical Society, 1843)

Emerson, Ralph Waldo, *The Journals and Miscellaneous Notebooks of Ralph Waldo Emerson*, 15 vols. (Cambridge, MA: Belknap Press of Harvard University Press, 1847–48)

Faucher, Leon, *Manchester in 1844: Its Present Conditions and Future Prospects* (Manchester: Abel Heywood, 1844; London: Cass & Co., repr. 1969)

Finch, John (comp. and ed.), *Statistics of Vauxhall Ward, Liverpool: the Condition of the Working Class in Liverpool in 1842* (Liverpool: Toulouse Press, 1986, facsimile reprint of 1842 edn)

Forwood, Arthur B., *The Dwellings of the Industrial Classes in the Diocese of Liverpool and How to Improve Them* (1883)

Forwood, W. B., *Recollections of a Busy Life* (Liverpool: Henry Young, 1910)

Full Report on the Commission of Inquiry Into the Subject of the Unemployed in the City of Liverpool (1894)

Gamlin, Hilda, *Twixt Mersey and Dee* (Liverpool: Marples & Co., 1897)

Harrison, Amy, *Women's Industries in Liverpool* (Liverpool: Liverpool University Press, 1904)

Hawthorne, Nathaniel, *The English Notebooks*, ed. Randall Stewart (New York: Russell & Russell, 1962 [1941])

—, *Our Old Home* (London: Walter Scott Ltd, 1863)

Hobson, Richard, *What Hath God Wrought: An Autobiography* (Liverpool: J. A. Thompson, 1903)

Holmes, Isaac, *Thieves, Beggars and Prostitutes* (essays reprinted from *LC*) (Liverpool: Deighton & Laughton, 1853)

Holt, Anne, *A Ministry to the Poor, Being the History of the Liverpool Domestic Mission Society, 1836–1936* (Liverpool, Henry Young & Sons, 1936)

Hopkinson, James, *Memoirs of a Victorian Cabinet Maker* (London: Routledge & Kegan Paul, 1968)

Howard, John, *State of the Prisons of England and Wales* (Warrington: Eyres, 1794)

Hoyle, William, *Crime in England and Wales in the Nineteenth Century: an Historical and Critical Retrospect* (London, 1876)

Hume, Abraham, *The Conditions of Liverpool* (1888)

—, *Misrepresentation of the Established Church: A Reply and Correction* (Liverpool, 1884)

—, *Missions at Home, A Clergyman's Account of a Portion of the Town of Liverpool* (London, 1850)

Jervis, Richard, *Chronicles of a Victorian Detective* (Runcorn: P&D Riley, 1995) [first published as *Lancashire's Crime and Criminals*, 1907]

Johnson, Harriet M., *Children and Public-Houses* (Nottingham: W.H. Greenwood, 3rd edn, 1897)

Jones, John, *The Slain in Liverpool During 1864 by Drink*, (Liverpool, 1864)

Joseph, H. S., *Memoirs of Convicted Prisoners; Accompanied by Remarks of the Causes and Prevention of Crime* (London: Wertheim & Co., 1853)

Kirkdale Gaol: Twelve Months Imprisonment of a Manchester Merchant (Manchester, 1880)

Lee, W. L. Melville, *A History of Police in England* (Montclair, NJ: Patterson Smith, 1971 [1901])

Lewin, Walter, *Clarke Aspinall: A Biography* (London: Edward W. Allen, 1893)

Liverpool Domestic Mission Society Annual Reports (Liverpool: Thomas Baines, 1834, 1847, 1848, 1851, 1852)

Lombroso, Cesare, *Criminal Man*, trans. Mary Gibson and Nicole Hahn Rafter (Durham, NC: Duke University Press, 2006 [1876]).

Lowndes, Frederick W., *The Extension of the Contagious Diseases Act in Liverpool and other Seaports Practically Considered* (Liverpool: Adam Holden, 1876)

—, 'The Liverpool Lock Hospital and the Prevalence and Severity of Constitutional Syphilis in Liverpool', *British Medical Journal*, 15 May 1880, pp. 727–29

—, *Prostitution and Syphilis in Liverpool; and The Working of the Contagious Diseases Acts in Aldershot, Chatham, Plymouth and Devonport* (London: Churchill, 1876)

—, *Prostitution and Venereal Diseases in Liverpool* (London: Churchill, 1886)

Lundie, Robert Henry, *The Dark Side of Liverpool* (1880)

McGowan, W. T., *Sanitary Legislation with Illustrations From Experience* (Liverpool: Harris & Co., 1859)

Mayhew, Henry, *London Labour and the London Poor* (New York: Charles Griffin, 1968 [1861–62])

—, *London's Underworld: Being Selections from 'Those That Will Not Work' the Fourth Volume of 'London Labour and the London Poor'*, ed. Peter Quennell (London: Spring Books, 1950)

Mays, James O'Donald, *Mr Hawthorne Goes to England* (Burley: New Forest Leaves, 1983)

Melly, George, *Stray Leaves: Pamphlets, Speeches, Addresses &c. on Social and Political Questions* (Liverpool: Benson & Holmes, 1856–1863)

Melville, Herman, *Redburn* (Harmondsworth: Penguin, 1986 [1849])

Miles, W. A., *Poverty, Mendicity and Crime, or, the Facts, Examinations, &c. Upon Which the Report Was Founded, Presented to the House of Lords*, ed. H. Brandon (London: Shaw & Sons, 1839)

Mortality Sub-Committee, *Report of Evidence 1866* (Liverpool, 1866)

Moss, William, *Georgian Liverpool: a Guide to the City in 1797*, with additional notes by David Brazendale (Lancaster: Palatine Books, 2007 [1797])

National Association for the Promotion of Social Sciences Journal and Sessional papers 1873

Nicholls, H. J., *Sixty Years Random Reminiscences of Old Liverpool and its Departed Trades and Customs* (Liverpool: Tinling, 1909)

Nott-Bower, Sir William, *Fifty-Two Years as a Policeman* (London: Edward Arnold, 1926)

O'Mahoney, Michael, *Ways and Byways of Liverpool* (Liverpool: Liverpool Daily Post, 1931)

O'Mara, Pat, *The Autobiography of a Liverpool Irish Slummy* (London: Martin Hopkinson, 1934)

Olmsted, Frederick Law, *Walks and Talks of an American Farmer in England* (Columbus, OH: J. A. Riley, new edn, 1859)

Picton, James A., *Memorials of Liverpool: Historical and Topographical*, 2 vols. (Liverpool: G. G. Walmsley, 2nd edn, 1903)

—, *Selections from the Municipal Archives and Records from the Thirteenth Century to the Seventeenth Century Inclusive* (Liverpool: G. G. Walmsley, 1883)

—, *Muncipal Archives and Records from AD 1700 to the Passing of the Municipal Reform Act, 1835* (Liverpool: G. G. Walmsley, 1886)

[Rathbone, William], 'A Man of Business', *Social Duties Considered with Reference to the Organisation of Effort in Works of Benevolence and Public Utility* (London, 1867)

Rathbone, William, *Local Taxation and Poor Law Administration in Great Cities* (Liverpool, 1869)

Ryan, William Burke, *Infanticide: its Law, Prevalence and History* (London: Churchill, 1862)

Sanger, William W., *The History of Prostitution: its Extent, Causes and Effects throughout the World* (New York: Medica Publishing, 1913)

Shimmin, Hugh, *Liverpool Life: its Pleasures, Practices, and Pastimes*, 2nd series (Liverpool: Egerton Smith, 1856–57)

—, *Liverpool Sketches, Chiefly Reprinted from the Porcupine* (London, 1862)

—, *Town Life* (London: William Tweedie, 1858)

Smith, Egerton, *Some Account of the Liverpool Night Asylum for the Houseless Poor* [...] (Liverpool: Egerton Smith, 1832)

Smith, Samuel, *My Life Work* (London: Hodder & Stoughton, 1903)

—, 'Social Reform', *Nineteenth Century*, May 1883, pp. 896–912

Smithers, Henry, *Liverpool, its Commerce, Statistics and Institutions with a History of the Cotton Trade* (Liverpool, 1825)

Squalid Liverpool: by a Special Commission (Liverpool, 1883)

[Stonehouse, James], *Recollections of Old Liverpool by a Nonagenarian* (Liverpool: J. F. Hughes, 1863)

Stonehouse, James, *Streets of Liverpool* (Liverpool, 2002 [1869])

Taine, Hippolyte, *Taine's Notes on England*, trans. Edward Hyams (London: Thames & Hudson, 1957)

Taylor, W. C., 'Moral Economy of Large Towns: Liverpool', *Bentley's Miscellany*, vol. 8 (1840), pp. 131–36

Thomson, Basil, *The Criminal* (London: Hodder & Stoughton, 1925)

Trench, W. S., *Realities of Irish Life* (London: Longman's Green, 5th edn, 1870)

—, *Report on the Health of Liverpool* (Liverpool, 1866)

The Trial of Tobias Toole, John Davies and William O'Brien (alias Thomas Dwyer) for Robbing Robert Chambers … At Lancaster Assizes, on Saturday, March 27, 1813 (Lancaster, n.d.)

[Troughton, Thomas], *The History of Liverpool, from the Earliest Authenticated Period Down to the Present Time* (1810)

Wait, Benjamin, *Letters from Van Diemen's Land: Written During Four Years Imprisonment* (Buffalo, 1843) [reprinted as *The Wait Letters*, Erin, Ont.: Porcepic, 1976]

[Wallace, James], *A General and Descriptive History of the Ancient and Present State of the Town of Liverpool* (Liverpool, 1795)

Walmsley, Hugh Mulleneux, *Life of Sir Joshua Walmsley by His Son* (London, 1879)

Williams, Gomer, *History of the Liverpool Privateers and Letters of Marque with an account of the Slave Trade* (London: Heinemann, 1897; Liverpool: Liverpool University Press, repr. 2004)

Young, Urban, *Life of Father Ignatius Spencer* (London: Burns, Oates & Washbourne, 1933)

6. Secondary sources

Anderson, Gregory, *Victorian Clerks* (Manchester: Manchester University Press, 1976)

Archer, John E., '"Men Behaving Badly?": Masculinity and the Uses of Violence, 1850–1900', in Shani D'Cruze (ed.), *Everyday Violence in Britain, 1850–1950: Gender and Class* (Harlow, 2000), pp. 41–54

—, 'Mysterious and Suspicious Deaths: Missing Homicides in North-West England (1850–1900)', *Crime, History and Societies*, 12(1) (2008), pp. 45–63

—, 'Poachers Abroad', in G. E. Mingay (ed.), *The Unquiet Countryside* (London, 1989), pp. 52–64

—, 'Poaching Gangs and Violence: the Urban–Rural Divide in Nineteenth-Century Lancashire', *British Journal of Criminology*, 39(1) (1999), pp. 25–38

—, *Violence in the North West with Special Reference to Liverpool and Manchester, 1850–1914* (Swindon: Economic and Social Research Council, 2001)

—, 'The Violence We Have Lost: Body Counts, Historians and Interpersonal Violence in England', *Memoria y Civilizacion*, 2, (1999), pp. 171–90

Ashworth, William J., *Customs and Excise: Trade, Population and Consumption in England, 1640–1845* (Oxford: Oxford University Press, 2003)

Baer, Marc, *Theatre and Disorder in Late Georgian London* (Oxford: Clarendon Press, 1992)

Bailey, Peter, *Leisure and Class in Victorian England: Rational Recreation and the Contest for Control, 1830–1885* (London: Routledge & Kegan Paul, 1978)

Bailey, Victor (ed.), *Policing and Punishment in Nineteenth Century Britain* (London: Croom Helm, 1981)

Bartley, Paula, *Prostitution: Prevention and Reform in England, 1860–1914* (London: Routledge & Kegan Paul, 2000)

Behlmer, G. K., *Child Abuse and Moral Reform in England, 1870–1908* (Stanford, CA: Stanford University Press, 1982)

Belchem, John, *Irish, Catholic and Scouse: the History of the Liverpool Irish* (Liverpool: Liverpool University Press, 2007)

—, 'Liverpool in the Year of Revolution: The Political and Associational Culture of the Irish Immigrant Community in 1848', in John Belchem (ed.), *Popular Politics, Riot and Labour: Essays in Liverpool History, 1790–1940* (Liverpool: Liverpool University Press, 1992), pp. 68–97

—, *Merseypride: Essays in Liverpool Exceptionalism* (Liverpool: Liverpool University Press, 2nd edn, 2006)

— (ed.), *Popular Politics, Riot and Labour: Essays in Liverpool History, 1790–1940* (Liverpool: Liverpool University Press, 1992)

Bell, S. P., *Victorian Lancashire* (Newton Abbot: David & Charles, 1974)

Benson, John (ed.), *The Working Class in England, 1875–1914* (London: Croom Helm, 1985)

Best, Geoffrey, *Mid-Victorian Britain* (London: Fontana, 1979)

Bickerton, Thomas Herbert, *Medical History of Liverpool from the Earliest Days to the Year 1920* (London: John Murray, 1936)

Bisceglia, Louis, R., 'The Threat of Violence: Irish Confederates and Chartists in Liverpool in 1848', *Irish Sword*, 14 (1981), pp. 207–15

Boland, Philip, 'The Construction of Images of People and Place: Labelling Liverpool and Stereotyping Scousers', *Cities*, 25(6) (2008), pp. 355–69

Bone, J. M., and Hillam, Christine (eds.), *Wives and Whores in Victorian Liverpool: Varieties in Attitude Towards Medical Care for Women: Papers Delivered at a Meeting of the Liverpool Medical History Society, 4 April 1998* (Liverpool, 1999)

Brabin, Angela, 'The Black Widows of Liverpool', *History Today*, 52(10) (2002), pp. 40–46

—, *The Black Widows of Liverpool: A Chilling Account of Cold-Blooded Murder in Liverpool* (Lancaster: Palatine Books, 2003)

Brack, Alan, *All They Need is Love* (Neston: Gallery Press, 1983)

Brailsford, Denis, *Bareknuckles: a Social History of Prize-Fighting* (Cambridge: Lutterworth Press, 1988)

Briggs, John, Harrison, Christopher, McInnes, Angus, and Vincent, David, *Crime and Punishment in England: an Introductory History* (London: UCL Press, 1996)

Bristow, Edward, J., *Vice and Vigilance: Purity Movements in Britain Since 1700* (Dublin: Gill and Macmillan, 1977)

Brogden, Mike, *On the Mersey Beat: Policing Liverpool Between the Wars* (Oxford: Oxford University Press, 1991)

Bryson, Anne, 'Riotous Liverpool, 1815–1860', in John Belchem (ed.), *Popular Politics, Riot and Labour: Essays in Liverpool History, 1790–1940* (Liverpool, 1992), pp. 98–134

Burnett, John, *A Social History of Housing, 1815–1985* (London: Methuen, 2nd edn, 1986)

Chandler, George, *Liverpool* (London: Batsford, 1957)

—, *William Roscoe of Liverpool* (London: Batsford, 1953)

Channon, Howard, *Portrait of Liverpool* (London: Hale, 1970)

Chappell, Gavin, *Wirral Smugglers, Wreckers and Pirates* (Birkenhead: Countyvise, 2009)

Chesney, Kellow, *The Victorian Underworld* (Harmondsworth: Pelican, 1972)

Clark, Anna, 'Domesticity and the Problem of Wifebeating in Nineteenth-Century Britain: Working-Class Culture, Law and Politics', in Shani D'Cruze (ed.), *Everyday Violence in Britain, 1850–1950: Gender and Class* (Harlow: Pearson Education, 2000), pp. 27–44

Cockroft, W. R., *The Albert Dock and Liverpool's Historic Waterfront* (Market Drayton: S.B. Publications, 1992)

—, *From Cutlasses to Computers: the Police Force in Liverpool, 1836–1989* (Market Drayton: S.B. Publications, 1991)

—, 'Liverpool Police Force 1836–1902', in S. P. Bell, *Victorian Lancashire* (Newton Abbot: David & Charles, 1974), pp. 150–68

Coleman, Terry, *Passage to America: a History of Emigrants from Great Britain and Ireland to America in the Mid-Nineteenth Century* (London: Hutchinson, 1972)

—, *The Railway Navvies: a History of the Men Who Made the Railways* (Harmondsworth: Penguin, 1965)

Collins, Neil, *Politics and Elections in Nineteenth Century Liverpool* (Aldershot: Scolar Press, 1994)

Conley, Carolyn, 'The Agreeable Recreation of Fighting', *Journal of Social History*, 33(1) (1999), pp. 55–72

Cook, Terry, *The Pubs of Scotland Road* (Liverpool: Bluecoat Press, 1999)

D'Cruze, Shani (ed.), *Everyday Violence in Britain, 1850–1950: Gender and Class* (Harlow: Pearson Education, 2000)

Davies, Andrew, *Gangs of Manchester: the Story of the Scuttlers: Britain's First Youth Cult* (Wrea Green: Milo Press, 2008)

Davies, John, 'Father James Nugent, Prison Chaplain', *North West Catholic History*, XXII, (1995), pp. 15–24

Davis, Jennifer, 'The London Garotting Panic of 1862: A Moral Panic and the Creation of a Criminal Class in Mid-Victorian England', in *Crime and the Law: a Social History of Crime in Western Europe Since 1500*, ed. V. A. C. Gatrell, Bruce Lenman and Geoffrey Parker (London, 1980), pp. 190–213

Delacy, Margaret, *Prison Reform in Lancashire, 1700–1850* (Manchester: Manchester University Press, 1986)

Donaldson, William, *Brewer's Rogues, Villains, Eccentrics: an A–Z of Roguish Britons Through the Ages* (London: Cassell, 2002)

Doyle, Peter, *Mitres & Missions in Lancashire: the Roman Catholic Diocese of Liverpool, 1850–2000* (Liverpool: Bluecoat Press, 2005)

Duckworth, Jeannie, *Fagin's Children: Criminal Children in Victorian England* (London: Hambledon and London, 2002)

Durey, Michael, *The Return of the Plague: British Society and the Cholera, 1831–2* (Dublin: Gill and Macmillan, 1979)

Emsley, Clive, *Crime and Society in England: 1750–1900* (Harlow: Longman, 3rd edn, 2005)

—, *Hard Men: The English and Violence Since 1750* (London: Hambledon and London, 2005)

Euler, Catherine, '"The Irons of Their Fetters Have Eaten into Their Souls": Nineteenth-Century Feminist Strategies to Get our Bodies onto the Political Agenda', in Shani D'Cruze (ed.), *Everyday Violence in Britain, 1850–1950: Gender and Class* (Harlow: Pearson Education, 2000), pp. 198–212

Finnegan, Frances, *Poverty and Prostitutes: a Study of Victorian Prostitutes in York* (Cambridge: Cambridge University Press, 1979)

Gallman, J. Matthew, *Receiving Erin's Children: Philadelphia, Liverpool, and the Irish Famine, 1845–1855* (Chapel Hill, NC: North Carolina University Press, 2000)

Gatrell, V. A. C., 'The Decline of Theft and Violence in Victorian and Edwardian England', in V. A. C. Gatrell, Bruce Lenman and Geoffrey Parker (eds.), *Crime and the Law: a Social History of Crime in Western Europe Since 1500* (London: Europa, 1980), pp. 238–337

Gatrell, V. A. C., Lenman, Bruce, and Parker, Geoffrey (eds.), *Crime and the Law: a Social History of Crime in Western Europe Since 1500* (London: Europa, 1980)

Godfrey, Barry, and Lawrence, Paul, *Crime and Justice, 1750–1950* (Cullompton: Willan, 2005)

Godfrey, Barry, Lawrence, Paul, and Williams, Chris, *History & Crime* (London: Sage, 2008)

Grant, Linda, 'Women's Work and Trade Unionism in Liverpool, 1890–1914', *Bulletin of North West Labour History Society*, 7 (1980–81), pp. 65–83

Harland, John, and Wilkinson, T. T, *Lancashire Legends: Traditions, Pageants, Sports etc.* (Wakefield: E.P. Publishing, 1973)

Hay, Douglas, *Albion's Fatal Tree: Crime and Society in Eighteenth-Century England* (London: Allen Lane, 1972)

Hopkins, Harry, *The Long Affray: the Poaching Wars in Britain* (London: Secker & Warburg, 1985)

Howell, Philip, Beckingham, David, and Moore, Francesca, 'Managed Zones for Sex Workers in Liverpool: Contemporary Proposals, Victorian Parallels', *Transactions of the Institute of British Geographers*, new series, 33(2) (2008), pp. 233–50

Hutchinson, J. R., *The Press-Gang, Afloat and Ashore* (London: Eveleigh Nash, 1913)

Jones, David, *Crime, Protest and Police in Nineteenth-Century Britain* (London: Routledge & Kegan Paul, 1982)

Jones, R. M., 'The Liverpool Bread Riots, 1855', *Bulletin of the North West Labour History Society*, 6 (1979–80), pp. 33–42

Jordan, Jane, *Josephine Butler* (London: John Murray, 2001)

Kellett, John R., *Railways and Victorian Cities* (London: Routledge & Kegan Paul, 1979)

Lowe, William J., *The Irish in Mid-Victorian Lancashire* (New York: Peter Lang, 1989)

—, 'Lancashire Fenianism, 1864–71', *Transactions of the Historical Society of Lancashire and Cheshire*, 126 (1977), pp. 156–85.

MacDonagh, Oliver, *A Pattern of Government Growth 1800–60: the Passenger Acts and their Enforcement* (London: Macgibbon and Kee, 1961)

Macilwee, Michael, *The Gangs of Liverpool: From the Cornermen to the High Rip: The Mobs that Terrorised a City* (Wrea Green: Milo Press, 2006)

McMahon, Richard (ed.), *Crime, Law and Popular Culture in Europe* (Cullompton: Willan, 2008)

Malcolm, Tim, *Anti-Booze Crusaders in Victorian Liverpool* (Birkenhead: Countyvise, 2005)

Midwinter, Eric, *Old Liverpool* (Newton Abbot: David & Charles, 1971)

—, *Social Administration in Lancashire: Poor Law, Public Health and Police* (Manchester: Manchester University Press, 1969)

Mingay, G. E. (ed.), *The Unquiet Countryside* (London: Routledge & Kegan Paul, 1989)

Moore, Kevin, '"This Whig and Tory Ridden Town": Popular Politics in Liverpool in the Chartist Era', in John Belchem (ed.), *Popular Politics, Riot and Labour: Essays in Liverpool History, 1790–1940* (Liverpool: Liverpool University Press, 1992), pp. 38–67

Munsche, P. B., *Gentlemen and Poachers: The English Game Laws, 1671–1831* (Cambridge: Cambridge University Press, 1981)

Muir, Ramsey, *History of Liverpool* (London: University Press of London, 1907)

Murray, Daniel, *The Story of Holy Cross* (Liverpool, 1948)

Murray, Nicholas, *So Spirited a Town: Visions and Versions of Liverpool* (Liverpool: Liverpool University Press, 2007)

Neal, Frank, *Black 47: Britain and the Irish Famine* (Basingstoke: Macmillan, 1988)

—, 'A Criminal Profile of the Liverpool Irish', *Transactions of the Historical Society of Lancashire and Cheshire*, 140 (1990), pp. 161–99

—, *Sectarian Violence: the Liverpool Experience, 1819–1914: an Aspect of Anglo Irish Experience* (Liverpool: Newsham Press, 2003 [1988])

O'Neill, Joseph, *Crime City: Manchester's Victorian Underworld* (Wrea Green: Milo Press, 2008)

Palmer, Roy (ed.), *A Touch of the Times: Songs of Social Change, 1770 to 1914* (Harmondsworth: Penguin Education, 1974)

Petrie, Glen, *A Singular Iniquity: the Campaigns of Josephine Butler* (London: Macmillan, 1971)

Pettit, Danielle, 'Attitudes to Venereal Contagion in Victorian Liverpool', in *Wives and Whores in Victorian Liverpool: Varieties in Attitude Towards Medical Care for Women: Papers Delivered at a Meeting of the Liverpool Medical History Society, 4 April 1998*, ed. J. M. Bone and Christine Hillam (Liverpool, 1999), pp. 51–63

Philips, David, *William Augustus Miles (1796–1851): Crime, Policing and Moral Entre-preneurship in England and Australia* (Melbourne: University of Melbourne, 2001)

Physick, Ray, *Liverpool's Boxing Venues* (Liverpool: Trinity Press, 2008)

—, *Played in Liverpool: Charting the Heritage of a City at Play* (Manchester: English Heritage, 2007)

Pumphrey, George H., *The Story of Liverpool's Public Services* (Liverpool: University of Liverpool, 1940)

Rimmer, Joan, *Yesterday's Naughty Children: Training Ships, Girls' Reformatory and Farm School: a History of the Liverpool Reformatory Association Founded in 1855* (Swinton: Neil Richardson, 1986)

Robinson, A. R. B., *Chaplain of the Mersey, 1859–67* (A.R.B. Robinson, 1987)

Rogers, Nicholas, *The Press-Gang: Naval Impressment and its Opponents in Georgian Britain* (London: Continuum, 2007)

Rose, Lionel, *Massacre of the Innocents: Infanticide in Britain, 1800–1939* (London: Routledge & Kegan Paul, 1986)

—, *Rogues and Vagabonds: Vagrant Underworld in Britain, 1815–1985* (London: Routledge & Kegan Paul, 1988)

Rose, R. B., 'A Liverpool Sailors' Strike in the Eighteenth Century', *Transactions of the Lancashire and Cheshire Antiquary Society*, 68 (1958), pp. 85–92

Rosner, Lisa, *The Anatomy Murders: Being the True and Spectacular History of Edinburgh's Notorious Burke and Hare and the Man Who Abetted Them in Their Most Heinous Crimes* (Philadelphia, PA: University of Pennsylvania Press, 2010)

Rule, John, 'Social Crime in the Rural South in the Eighteenth and Nineteenth Centuries', *Southern History*, 1 (1979), pp. 135–53

Rule, John, and Wells, Roger, *Crime, Protest and Popular Politics in Southern England, 1740–1850* (Rio Grande, OH: Hambledon Press, 1997)

Runaghan, Patricia, *Father Nugent's Liverpool, 1849–1905* (Birkenhead: Countyvise, 2003)

Saville, John, *1848: British State and the Chartist Movement* (Cambridge: Cambridge University Press, 1987)

Scally, Robert James, *The End of Hidden Ireland: Rebellion, Famine and Emigration* (Oxford: Oxford University Press, 1995)

—, 'Liverpool Ships and Irish Emigrants in the Age of Sail', *Journal of Social History*, 17(1) (1983), pp. 5–30

Scraton, Phil, *Power, Conflict and Criminalisation* (London: Routledge, 2007)

Sea Liverpool: Maritime History of a Great Port (Liverpool: Liverpool City Council, 2005)

Shiman, Lilian Lewis, *Crusade Against Drink in Victorian England* (Basingstoke: Macmillan, 1988)

Sindall, Rob, *Street Violence in the Nineteenth Century: Media Panic or Real Danger?* (Leicester: Leicester University Press, 1990)

Sloan, Tod, *The Treadmill and the Rope: The History of a Liverpool Prison* (Parkgate: Gallery Press, 1988)

Storch, Robert D., 'The Plague of Blue Locusts: Police Reform and Popular Resistance in Northern England, 1840–57', *International Review of Social History*, 20 (1975), pp. 61–89

Sutton-Smith, Brian, *The Folkgames of Children* (Austin, TX: University of Texas Press, 1972)

Swift, Roger, 'Heroes or Villains? The Irish, Crime and Disorder in Victorian England' *Albion*, 29 (1997), pp. 399–421

Swift, Roger, and Gilley, Sheridan (eds.), *The Irish in Britain, 1815–1939* (London: Pinter Publishers, 1989)

Taylor, David, *Crime, Policing and Punishment in England, 1750–1914* (Basingstoke: Macmillan, 1998)

—, *Policing the Victorian Town: the Development of the Police in Middlesbrough, c.1840–1914* (Basingstoke: Palgrave Macmillan, 2002)

Taylor, Howard, 'Rationing Crime: the Political Economy of Criminal Statistics Since the 1880s', *Economic History Review*, LI(3) (1998), pp. 569–90

Thomas, Donald, *The Victorian Underworld* (London: John Murray, 1998)

Thompson, E. P., 'The Moral Economy of the English Crowd in the Eighteenth Century', *Past and Present*, 50 (1971), pp. 76–136

Thompson, F. M. L., *The Rise of Respectable Society, a Social History of Victorian Britain, 1830–90* (London: Fontana, 1988)

Tobias, J. J., *Crime and Industrial Society* (London: Batsford, 1967)

—, *Nineteenth Century Crime: Prevention and Punishment* (Newton Abbot: David & Charles, 1972)

—, 'A Statistical Study of a Nineteenth Century Criminal Area', *British Journal of Criminology*, 14(3) (1974), pp. 221–35

Wade, Stephen, *Foul Deeds and Suspicious Deaths in Liverpool* (Barnsley: Wharncliffe, 2006)

Walker, R. B., 'Religious Changes in Liverpool in the Nineteenth Century', *Journal of Ecclesiastical History*, 19(2) (1968), pp. 195–211

Walkowitz, Judith R., *Prostitution and Victorian Society: Women, Class and the State* (Cambridge: Cambridge University Press, 1980)

Waller, P. J., *Democracy and Sectarianism: A Political and Social History of Liverpool, 1868–1939* (Liverpool: Liverpool University Press, 1981)

Walton, John K., Blinkhorn, Martin, Pooley, Colin, Tidswell, David, and Winstanley, Michael J., 'Crime, Migration and Social Change in North-West England and the Basque Country, c.1870–1930', *British Journal of Criminology*, 39(1) (1999), pp. 90–112

Walton, John K., and Wilcox, Alastair (eds.), *Low Life and Moral Improvement in Mid-Victorian England: Liverpool Through the Journalism of Hugh Shimmin* (Leicester: Leicester University Press, 1991)

Weinburger, Barbara, 'The Police and the Public in Mid-Nineteenth Century Warwickshire', in Victor Bailey (ed.), *Policing and Punishment in Nineteenth Century*

Britain (London: Croom Helm, 1981), pp. 65–93

Wiener, Martin, *Men of Blood: Violence, Manliness and Criminal Justice in Victorian England* (Cambridge: Cambridge University Press, 2004)

Wood, David, 'Community Violence', in John Benson (ed.), *The Working Class in England, 1875–1914* (London: Croom Helm, 1985), pp. 165–205

Wood, J. C., *Violence and Crime in Nineteenth-Century England: the Shadow of Our Refinement* (London: Routledge & Kegan Paul, 2004)

Woods, E. Cuthbert, 'Smuggling in Wirral', *Historic Society Transactions*, 79 (1927), pp. 125–31

Zedner, Lucia, *Women, Crime and Custody in Victorian England* (Oxford: Oxford University Press, 1991)

Index